PATTON'S AIR FORCE

Forging a Legendary Air-Ground Team

David N. Spires

Smithsonian Institution Press
Washington and London

By special arrangement with the U.S. Air Force, this publication is being offered for sale by the Smithsonian Institution Press, Washington, D.C. 20560-0950.

Library of Congress Cataloging-in-Publication Data
Spires, David N.
   [Air power for Patton's Army]
   Patton's Air Force : forging a legendary air-ground team / David N. Spires.
      p. cm.
   Originally published: Air power for Patton's Army. Washington, D.C. : Air Force History and Museums Program, 2002.
   Includes bibliographical references and index.
   ISBN 1-58834-087-2 (alk. paper)
   1. World War, 1939–1945—Aerial operations, American.   2. United States Army Air Forces. Tactical Air Command, 19th—History.   3. Close air support—History—20th century.   4. United States. Army. Army, 3rd—History.   I. Title.
   D790.S65   2002b
   940.54'4973—dc21   2002021789

British Cataloging-in-Publication Data available

Manufactured in China, not at government expense
09 08 07 06 05 04 03 02   5 4 3 2 1

In Memory of
Colonel John F. "Fred" Shiner, USAF
(1942–1995)

Foreword

This insightful work by David N. Spires holds many lessons in tactical air-ground operations. Despite peacetime rivalries in the drafting of service doctrine, in World War II the immense pressures of wartime drove army and air commanders to cooperate in the effective prosecution of battlefield operations. In northwest Europe during the war, the combination of the U.S. Third Army commanded by Lt. Gen. George S. Patton and the XIX Tactical Air Command led by Brig. Gen. Otto P. Weyland proved to be the most effective allied air-ground team of World War II.

The great success of Patton's drive across France, ultimately crossing the Rhine, and then racing across southern Germany, owed a great deal to Weyland's airmen of the XIX Tactical Air Command. This deft cooperation paved the way for allied victory in Western Europe and today remains a classic example of air-ground effectiveness. It forever highlighted the importance of air-ground commanders working closely together on the battlefield.

The Air Force is indebted to David N. Spires for chronicling this landmark story of air-ground cooperation.

RICHARD P. HALLION
Air Force Historian

Editor's Note

One of the striking features of this story is the broad sweep taken by Third Army and XIX Tactical Air Command across France. It demanded a large number of maps be used to show places and activities in ways that words could not. However, to the greatest extent possible this work relies on maps prepared by contemporaneous creators, and thus has a number of maps reproduced from original histories of the period. Moreover, those which came from other sources largely were taken from the *West Point Atlas of American Wars*, a pair of volumes produced for the use of classes at the U.S. Military Academy at West Point, New York. That volume has maps in larger format and with more explanation, so readers who wish to study the maps in greater detail are referred to that source, listed with each map.

Preface

Patton's Air Force is a case study of one air-ground team's experience with the theory and practice of tactical air power employed during the climactic World War II campaigns against the forces of Nazi Germany. By the summer of 1944, the Allies had four fighter-bomber tactical air commands supporting designated field armies in northwest Europe, and in the fall they added a fifth (making four American and one British). Of these, the U.S. Third Army commanded by Lt. Gen. George S. Patton and the XIX Tactical Air Command (TAC) led by Brig. Gen. Otto P. Weyland deserve special attention as perhaps the most spectacular air-ground team of the Second World War on the Allied side.

From the time Third Army became operational on August 1, 1944, until the guns fell silent on May 8, 1945, Patton's troops covered more ground, took more enemy prisoners, and suffered more casualties than any other Allied army in northwest Europe. General Weyland's XIX TAC was there every step of the way: in the high summer *blitzkrieg* across France to the Siegfried Line, in the battle of attrition and positional warfare in Lorraine reminiscent of World War I's western front, in the emergency drive to rescue American troops trapped at Bastogne and help clear the Ardennes of Germans in the Battle of the Bulge, and finally, in crossing the Rhine and charging across southern Germany to the Czech and Austrian borders. There, Third Army forces linked up with Soviet military units converging on the fabled German Redoubt area from the east.

This study does not suggest that Weyland's XIX TAC proved superior to other tactical air commands in the European theater or that Weyland emerged as the only effective air leader. Indeed, numerous laurels were garnered by Weyland's colleagues and their respective TACs: Maj. Gen. Elwood R. Quesada's IX TAC that supported the First Army, Brig. Gen. Richard Nugent's XXIX TAC that supported the Ninth Army, and Brig. Gen. Gordon P. Saville's XII TAC that supported the Seventh Army *and* the French First Army. Moreover, during Ninth Air Force's eight-month buildup prior to Overlord (the invasion of France in June 1944), IX TAC, under an innovative General Quesada, played the central role in preparing for air operations at Normandy and on the continent. General Weyland remained in the background until Patton's forces entered combat on August 1, 1944. Because the XIX TAC entered combat later, it could and did use to good advantage the valuable experience of the IX TAC.

Traditional army and air force antagonisms and unsound tactical air doctrine are frequently cited as the major impediments to smooth air-ground relations and effective combat operations. Much of that contention was apparent in Washington, D.C., even during World War II, where, facing the demands of a worldwide conflict, headquarters' staffs all too frequently focused on problems of intraservice and interservice competition at all levels. For military leaders and staffs in Washington, service politics often took precedence and preferred doctrine often served to buttress disagreement. With their respective service priorities and in their role as advocates, these officers viewed matters of doctrine more rigidly than did their counterparts in the field. For them, unalloyed service doctrine prescribed the right conduct of air-ground relations; deviations could hardly be tolerated.

In the turbulent postwar period, Army Air Forces (AAF) leaders moved swiftly and purposefully to create an independent Air Force. In the late 1940s many U.S. Army officers, with some justification, worried that the new U.S. Air Force's absolute control of tactical airplanes and equipment, its doctrinal assertions, and its overwhelming focus on strategic priorities in the emergent Cold War meant that the army would receive less rather than more tactical air support for ground combat operations. In the charged atmosphere of that day, critics often found fault with the air-ground relationship forged during the Second World War and returned to doctrinal citation and interpretation when supporting one position or another in air-ground disagreements or other controversy. Had the various partisans reflected instead on the cooperative, wartime air-ground record of those "comrades in arms" in the XIX TAC-Third Army in Europe, they would have found their worst fears refuted, as indeed they would find similar fears refuted today. When genuflecting before the altars of doctrine in peacetime, it seems the absolute importance of pairing military leaders of goodwill in wartime who respect, trust, and rely on their service counterparts as comrades in arms is easily forgotten.

In preparing this study, I received help from many quarters. Above all I wish to thank Dennis Showalter and Daniel Mortensen for their unflagging support and enthusiasm for the project. Dennis read the entire manuscript and, as always, offered insightful comments and unstinting encouragement. Dan generously shared his wealth of knowledge on tactical aviation in general and Operation Torch, in particular. It was he who first called my attention to the cooperative, rather than confrontational, nature of air-ground relations. I remain in his debt.

Individuals at two major military archives also deserve special thanks. My friend Elliott V. Converse III, a former commander of the Air Force Historical Research Agency at Maxwell Air Force Base, went far beyond the call of duty to support my research efforts. As a result, I benefited from the knowledge and helpfulness of the agency's outstanding group of archivists and historians: Richard E. Morse, Robert M. Johnson, James H. Kitchens, Timothy D. Johnson, Archangelo DiFante, Marvin Fisher, Sarah Rawlins, and SSgt. Edward Gaines. They made special arrangements to accommodate my every request for information on the XIX TAC and related tactical aviation subjects. Joseph Caver in the Research Division had copied from Weyland's XIX TAC scrapbook many of the pictures that appear in this volume. I am grateful to John Slonaker, archivist at the USA Military History Institute, Carlisle Barracks, who introduced me to a wealth of information on the Army and Army Air Forces, beginning with Third Army's magnificent *After Action Report* of its 1944–45 campaign. Mr. Slonaker also went out of his way to help with long-distance requests.

I also wish to express my appreciation to the people in Norlin Library's Inter-Library Loan Department at the University of Colorado. They enjoyed nothing better than to pursue my requests for obscure military reference material. Their success record was outstanding and I am grateful. Several others assisted on specific areas of the work. Jerold E. Brown of the Army's Combat Studies Institute at Fort Leavenworth supplied me with important material on the Lorraine Campaign and shared his understanding of the Army's special long-term interest in it. David MacIsaac willingly tracked down Gen. James Ferguson's television interview and provided useful information on the Battle of the Bulge. My friend Bang Nguyen assisted enormously with the maps and charts.

Special thanks are owed several former participants in World War II tactical air campaigns in Europe, and I will always be grateful for the privilege of sharing their recollections and insights. They are Lt. Gen. John J. Burns, 371st Fighter Group P-47 pilot; Maj. Gen. Robert L. Delashaw, Commander, 405th Fighter Group; Brig. Gen. Russell A. Berg, Commander, 10th Photo Reconnaissance Group; Gen. James Ferguson, XIX TAC Combat Operations Officer; and Gen. Robert M. Lee, Ninth AF Deputy Commander for Operations.

I am especially indebted to Cargill Hall, the person responsible for contract histories at the Air Force History and Museums Program, who carefully edited the final manuscript and helped make the story more readable, understandable, and convincing. Others who read and contributed most helpful suggestions are: Perry D. Jamieson, Eduard Mark, David R. Mets, Daniel R. Mortensen, John Schlight, Richard K. Smith, David Tretler, and Herman S. Wolk. Any errors of fact or interpretation that remain, of course, are my own.

At the end of this project I am more than ever convinced that the tale of Generals Weyland and Patton, of the XIX TAC teamed with the U.S. Third Army in World War II, deserves to be told. These men's achievements continue to inspire and instruct, and I am pleased to spread the word.

David N. Spires
Boulder, Colorado

Contents

Contents

Charts

Maps

Contents

Photographs

Contents

Patton's Air Force

Chapter One

The Doctrinal Setting

The U.S. Third Army–XIX Tactical Air Command air-ground combat team is better understood in light of the doctrinal developments that preceded its joint operations in 1944 and 1945. Well before World War II, many army air leaders came to view close air support of army ground forces as a second- or third-order priority. After World War I the Air Service Tactical School, the Army Air Service's focal point for doctrinal development and education, stressed pursuit (or fighter) aviation and air superiority as the air arm's primary mission. Air superiority at that time meant primarily controlling the air to prevent enemy reconnaissance. At least among airmen from the early 1920s, tactical air doctrine stressed winning air superiority as the number one effort in air operations. Next in importance was interdiction, or isolation of the battlefield by bombing lines of supply and communications behind them. Finally, attacking enemy forces at the front, in the immediate combat zone, ranked last in priority. Airmen considered this "close air support" mission, performed primarily by attack aviation, to be the most dangerous and least efficient use of air resources.[1] Even in this early period, the air arm preferred aerial support operations to attack targets outside the "zone of contact."[2]

Evolution of Early Tactical Air Doctrine

By the mid-1930s, leaders of the renamed Army Air Corps increasingly focused their attention on strategic bombardment, which had a doctrine all its own, as the best use of the country's emerging air arm. Certainly among senior airmen at that time, tactical air operations ran a poor second to strategic bombardment as the proper role for the Army Air Corps. But this preference for strategic bombardment was not entirely responsible for the decline in attention paid to pursuit and attack aviation. Scarce resources and technical limitations contributed to tactical air power's decline in fortune. Pursuit prototypes, for example, competed with bombers for resources, and Air Corps leaders hesitated to fund them when they often could not agree among themselves or with their Army counterparts on the desired performance characteristics and engine types. At the same time, the aircraft industry preferred the more expensive bombers for obvious economic reasons, and also because that particular Army-funded development offered technological benefits for commercial aviation.[3]

1

In attack aviation, the Spanish Civil War demonstrated the high risks of relying on traditional tactics of low-level approach with the restricted maneuverability at that altitude, in the face of improving antiaircraft defenses. Attack aircraft thus had to be given whatever advantages of speed, maneuverability, and protective armor that technology allowed, and they also had to be mounted with sufficiently large fuel tanks to ensure an extended range with a useful bomb load. For single-engine aircraft, this challenge proved insurmountable in the late 1930s. Under the circumstances, civilian and military leaders considered the twin-engine light bomber the best available answer. In the spring of 1939, Army Air Corps chief, Maj. Gen. Henry H. (Hap) Arnold selected the Douglas A–20 Havoc for production. The fastest and most advanced of the available light bombers, it was clearly a major improvement over previous tactical aircraft. Nevertheless, it was neither capable of nor intended for precise, close-in support of friendly troops in the immediate battle zone. The A–20 fell between two schools: airmen criticized its light bomb load while Army officials considered it too large and ineffective for close air support of ground operations. The Army also disagreed with the Air Corps over enlisting pursuit aircraft in a ground support role. According to Air Corps tactical doctrine, pursuit aircraft should not provide close air support except in emergencies. As a result, before 1941 Army Air Corps fighters such as the Bell P–39 Airacobra and the Curtiss P–40 Warhawk, though suited to the close air support role, were seldom equipped or flown with bomb racks.[4]

After 1935, desires for an independent air force, doctrinal preferences, and financial limitations reinforced the airmen's focus on the strategic bombardment mission. Increasingly, Air Corps leaders relied on bombers rather than fighters in their planning for Western Hemisphere defense. Turned against an enemy's vital industries, they saw strategic bombing as a potential war-winning strategy. Above all, such a strategy promised a role for an Air Corps independent of direct Army control. For many airmen, a strategic mission represented the key to realizing a separate air force. The Boeing four-engine B–17 heavy bomber that first flew in 1935 appeared capable of performing effective strategic bombardment. Furthermore, in 1935, when the U.S. Army contributed to the revision of Training Regulation 440, *Employment of the Air Forces of the Army*, it gave strategic bombardment a priority equal to that of ground support. In an earlier 1926 regulation, strategic bombardment was authorized only if it conformed to the "broad plan of operations of the military forces." If the primary mission of the Army's air arm remained the support of ground forces, by 1935 the growing influence of the Army Air Corps and the need for a consolidated air strike force resulted in the establishment of General Headquarters (GHQ) Air Force, the first combat air force and a precursor of the numbered air forces of World War II. Although Air Corps leaders might emphasize strategic bombardment, they also upheld conventional Army doctrine, asserting that "air forces further the mission of the territorial or tactical commander to which they are assigned or attached." Taken as a whole, the revised 1935 regulation represented a compromise on the question of operational independence for the air arm: although the air commander remained subordinate to the field commander, the changes clearly demonstrated the Air Corps' growing influence and the Army leadership's willingness to compromise.[5]

German *blitzkrieg* victories at the beginning of World War II rekindled military interest in tactical aviation, especially air-ground operations. On April 15, 1940, the U.S. Army issued Field Manual (FM) 1–5, *Employment of the Aviation of the Army*. Written by a board that Army Air Corps General Arnold chaired, it reflected the German air achievement in Poland and represented a greater compromise on air doctrine than did the 1935 Army training regulation. The field manual, however, reaffirmed traditional Air Corps principles in a number of ways. For example, it asserted that tactical air represented a theaterwide weapon that must be controlled centrally for maximum effectiveness, that the enemy's rear rather than the "zone of contact" was the best area for tactical operations, and that those targets ground forces could bracket with artillery should not be assigned to the air arm.[6] To some unhappy Army critics, the new manual still clearly reflected the Air Corps' desire to control its own air war largely independent of Army direction.

On the other hand, the 1940 Field Manual did not establish Air Corps-desired mission priorities for tactical air employment, but it did authorize decentralized air resources controlled by ground commanders in emergencies. Although the importance of air superiority received ample attention, the manual did not advocate it as *the* mission to be accomplished first. Rather, assessments of the particular combat situation would determine aerial mission priorities. Among other important intraservice issues it ignored, the manual did not address organizational arrangements and procedures for joint air-ground operations.[7] Field Manual 1–5 attempted to strike a balance between the Air Corps' position of centralized control of tactical air forces by an airman and the ground forces' desire to control aircraft in particular combat situations. Given this compromise approach to air support operations, much would depend on the role of the theater commander and the ability of the parties to cooperate and make the arrangements effective.

The common theme that emerges from these prewar doctrinal publications is one of compromise and cooperation as the most important attributes for successful air-ground operations. This theme reappeared in the manual issued following the air-ground maneuvers conducted in Louisiana and North Carolina in 1941 that tested the German system of close air support. In these exercises, newly formed air support commands operated with specific ground elements, but a shortage of aircraft, unrealistic training requirements, inexperience, and divergent air and ground outlooks on close air support led both

General Arnold and Lt. Gen. Lesley J. McNair, Commanding General of the Army Ground Forces, to declare the joint training unsatisfactory. Although the air and ground leaders exhibited patience and a willingness to cooperate, that spirit did not always filter down to the lower echelons of command. As a result, despite greater attention paid to close air support in all quarters, the state of air-ground training in the U.S. Army by the spring of 1942 was cause for genuine concern.[8] In response to these shortcomings and the country's entry as a combatant in World War II, the War Department published FM 31–35, *Aviation in Support of Ground Forces*, on April 9, 1942. This field manual stressed organizational and procedural arrangements for the air support command. Here, as in previous publications, there was much to satisfy the most ardent air power proponents in the newly designated Army Air Forces (AAF). The air support command functioned as the controlling agency for air employment and the central point for air request approval **(Chart 1)**. Later, in Northwest Europe, Air Support Command would be renamed the Tactical Air Command (TAC) in deference to air leaders in Washington and would support specified field armies. Centralized control of air power would be maintained by collocating air and ground headquarters and assigning air support parties to ground echelons down to the division level. The field manual called for ground units to initiate requests for aerial support through their air support parties, which sent them to the air support command. If approved, the latter's command post issued attack orders to airdromes and to aircraft.[9]

Field Manual 31–35 of 1942, like FM 1–5 (1940), acknowledged the importance of air superiority and isolation of the battlefield. It also declared that air resources represented a valuable, but scarce commodity. Accordingly, it deemed as inefficient the use of aircraft in the air cover role in which, when they were based nearby or circling overhead, they remained on call by the supported unit. The 1942 manual nonetheless stressed the importance of close air support operations "when it is not practicable to employ other means of attack upon the desired objective in the time available, or when the added firepower and moral effect of air attacks are essential to insure the timely success of the ground force operations."[10] Despite opposition expressed later by key air leaders, this rationale for close air support would govern the actions of General Weyland and other tactical air commanders in Northwest Europe. On the central question of establishing priorities for missions or targets, however, the manual remained silent, and this would cause difficulty.

In the final analysis, would the ground or air commanders control scarce air resources? The manual's authors attempted to reach a compromise on this fundamental issue. The 1942 Field Manual declared that "designation of an aviation unit for support of a subordinate ground unit does not imply subordination of that aviation unit to the supported ground unit, nor does it remove the combat aviation unit from the control of the air support commander." Attaching air units directly to ground formations was judged an excep-

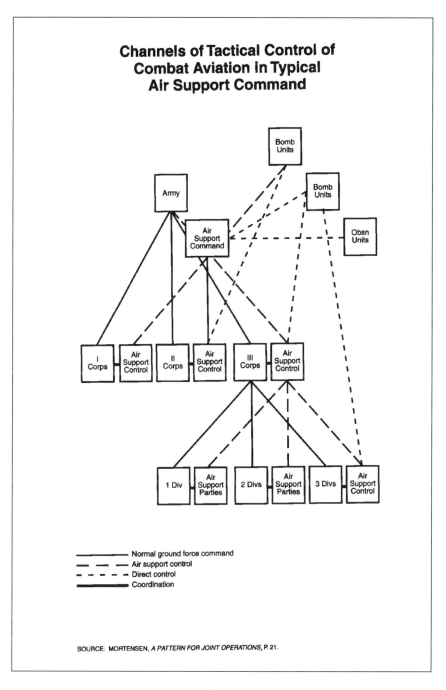

Channels of Tactical Control of Combat Aviation in Typical Air Support Command

SOURCE: MORTENSEN, *A PATTERN FOR JOINT OPERATIONS*, P. 21.

**Chart 1
Channels of Tactical Control of Combat Aviation in
Typical Air Support Command**

tion, "resorted to only when circumstances are such that the air support commander cannot effectively control the combat aviation assigned to the air support command."[11] Yet "the most important target at a particular time," FM 31–35 added, "will usually be that target which constitutes the most serious threat to the operations of the supported ground force. The final decision as to priority of targets rests with the commander of the supported unit."[12] In principle, therefore, air units could be parceled out to subordinate ground commanders, who were authorized to select targets and direct employment. Despite the central position accorded the commander of an air support command and explicit recognition that air assets normally were centralized at theater level, aviation units still could be allocated or attached to subordinate ground units.

Field Manual 31–35 of 1942, like its predecessors, attempted to achieve a balance between the extreme air and ground positions. This manual, however, underscored the importance of close cooperation among air and ground commanders:

> The basis of effective air support of ground forces is teamwork. The air and ground units in such operations in fact form a combat team. Each member of the team must have the technical skill and training to enable it to perform its part in the operation and a willingness to cooperate thoroughly.[13]

To its credit, the manual discussed in detail the command organization and air-ground techniques to be used across a broad spectrum of subjects, and airmen and ground officers involved in tactical air operations would adopt this manual as their how-to guide throughout the war. Though some have criticized it, they often seem to forget that it was AAF officers who drafted and issued FM 31–35; it was not forced on a reluctant air arm by antagonistic ground officers who failed to appreciate the uses of air power.

In the spring of 1942 time was needed to achieve the desired cooperation and to train air and ground personnel at all levels in the command and employment of air-ground operations. When the field manual appeared in April, however, Operation Torch, the Allied invasion of North Africa, was a scant six months away. How could the participants master the complexities of the most challenging of joint operations in so short a period? Despite what might appear as an irreconcilable conflict between air and ground perspectives of the day, the joint action called for by the manual proved to be less a problem than the limited time available to absorb its precepts and to solve practical problems at the field level. There was not enough time.

Doctrine in Practice: Operation Torch

Operation Torch became the desert crucible in which the Allies tested tactical air doctrine in combat. This initial Allied ground offensive of the Second World War also exposed the many weaknesses of an American nation unprepared for large-scale air and ground combat operations.[14] Although air-ground command arrangements for the invasion largely conformed to the 1942 FM 31–35, Allied headquarters completed a memorandum the month before the invasion that sought to clarify further air-ground command and control procedures. If anything, it served to enhance the role of the ground commander and, in the eyes of the air commanders, increase the chance that air power might be misused. Only after failure in the field would Lt. Gen. Dwight D. Eisenhower, Supreme Commander of Allied forces in northwest Africa, turn to the British example of teamwork displayed in the northeast African desert. There, Air Vice Marshal Sir Arthur Coningham and Lt. Gen. Sir Bernard "Monty" L. Montgomery, Commander of the British Eighth Army, operated an effective air-ground system based on equality of forces, joint planning, good communications, and a Royal Air Force (RAF) in command and control of its limited forces in the joint air-ground plan.[15]

In command of the invasion, General Eisenhower controlled all military resources in northwest Africa. If he thought of air forces in terms of theater interests, he chose not to designate a theater air commander, and British and American invasion forces remained loosely integrated. United States air forces were further decentralized to support the separate task forces during the invasion. Twelfth Air Force had its components parceled out to the three task forces, whose commanders had direct operational control of the air forces assigned to them as authorized by FM 31–35 **(Map 1)**. Similarly, the planners assigned British Eastern Air Command to support operations of the Eastern Task Force. Once the initial landings succeeded, plans called for an Allied task force to push eastward toward Tunisia, with supporting American air forces. Later, U.S. ground forces would be consolidated into U.S. Fifth Army, which would function as a planning and training headquarters, with XII Air Support Command attached to provide close air support to Fifth Army ground forces as required.[16]

Although the November 8, 1942, landings in French Algeria on the northwest African coast of the Mediterranean Sea succeeded easily, combat inexperience, logistics shortages, and the inability to establish all-weather airfields close to the battle zone during the race eastward toward Tunisia, combined to prevent defeat of the Axis forces. Effective close air support failed in the face of poor communications, an absence of radar, and the prevailing tendency of ground forces commanders to call for and rely on defensive air cover, and of airmen willing to give it. By December 1942, the Allied ground offensive proved unable to penetrate hastily formed German defensive lines west of

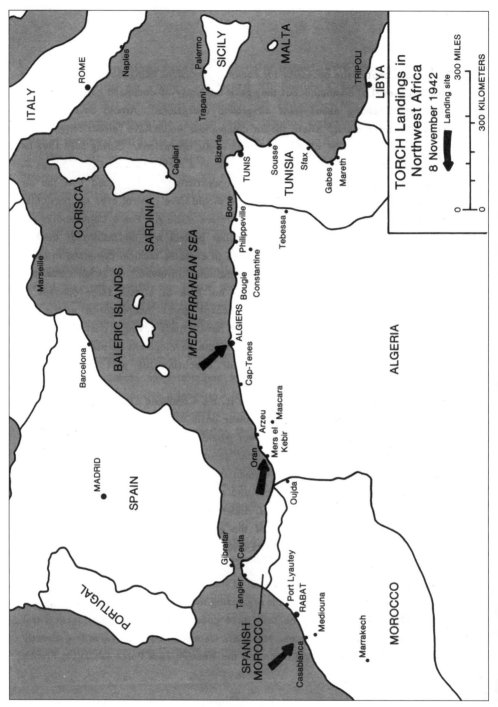

Map 1
Torch Landings in Northwest Africa: November 8, 1942

Reprinted from: Daniel R. Mortensen, *A Pattern for Joint Operations: World War II Close Air Support, North Africa*, (Washington, D.C.: Center for Military History, 1987), p 54.

Tunis. With the onset of winter, Eisenhower halted the offensive. Reviewing recent events, he criticized insufficient air support. With air forces larger than the enemy's, the Allies proved unable even to wrest local air superiority from the Germans and Italians. Clearly, it was time to regroup and reassess.[17]

In early January 1943, General Eisenhower centralized control of his tactical air forces in northwest Africa by creating the Allied Air Force. Commanded by Lt. Gen. Carl Spaatz, it was composed of the U.S. Twelfth Air Force and the British Eastern Air Command. Spaatz chose as his deputy Brig. Gen. Laurence S. Kuter who had been serving as the air operations officer on Eisenhower's staff. Kuter would prove to be a staunch proponent for adopting the British air-ground system, one that centralized control of aircraft under one airman reporting to the lead ground commander. Eisenhower sought in the reorganization to end piecemeal, decentralized air action largely along national lines. Yet, the vast distances, poor communications, and commanders who preferred operating along national rather than functional lines ensured that coordinating and centralizing the direction of close air support operations with ground forces would remain a problem. Even so, creation of the Allied Air Force served as an important move toward eventual centralized control of all air forces in the Mediterranean theater.[18]

Adversaries of the war in North Africa, Gen. Bernard Montgomery, Commander, British Eighth Army...

During the second Allied offensive in northwest Africa in January 1943, XII Air Support Command deployed from French Morocco on Africa's Atlantic coast to support II Corps in central Tunisia. Despite the best-laid plans of the XII's commander, Brig. Gen. Howard A. Craig, the airmen could muster little support when the Germans counterattacked II Corps in force on January 18. Among the many operational problems cited, air force officials stressed the misuse of air assets by the corps commander, Maj. Gen. Lloyd R. Fredendall. Army officers, however, judged enemy air superiority to be the most alarming. The Allies simply did not have sufficient aircraft to achieve local air superiority everywhere.[19]

At this juncture Eisenhower acted to achieve greater centralization of the air support effort by assigning General Kuter to command the newly created Allied Air Support Command in the Allied Air Force. Kuter collocated his headquarters at Constantine, Algeria, with that of Lt. Gen. K. A. N. Anderson, the British army commander of all Allied forces in northwest Africa involved in the Tunisian offensive. Kuter immediately set about controlling all Allied air support of ground operations. Yet, a few days later, when the Germans counterattacked in central Tunisia on January 30, 1943, Allied tactical air support broke down. Ground commanders repeatedly insisted on defensive air umbrellas that divided and dissipated the strength of the tactical air forces. Either many more aircraft had to be made available—most unlikely at that time—or the process of allocating aircraft had to be improved. Eisenhower and other key leaders in the theater did not believe the air doctrine to be at fault. They believed that doctrine was misapplied on the battlefield.[20]

The Battle of Kasserine Pass in mid-February 1943, highlighted the shortcomings of tactical air support of ground forces. Enemy troops over-

... and Field Marshal Erwin Rommel, Commander, Afrika Corps.

**Brig. Gen. Laurence S. Kuter
was deputy to General Spaatz
and assumed command
of the newly created
Allied Air Support Command in
the Allied Air Force.**

ran Allied bases, communications broke down, bad weather restricted close air support activity, and unexpected friendly fire often proved more lethal to Allied airmen than did hostile German flak.[21] Of the many critics of air support during the land battle, British Air Vice Marshal Coningham, who assumed command of the Allied Air Support Command from Kuter during the course of the engagement, was perhaps the most influential and outspoken—as subsequent events at Gafsa made plain. Coningham immediately reorganized tactical air forces on the basis of the British Western Desert system of centralized resources, established mission priorities designed to conserve scarce forces, and placed senior airmen in control of *all* air elements.[22]

The colorful if volatile American tactician Maj. Gen. George S. Patton commanded II Corps near Gafsa during the battle for Tunisia in early 1943. On April 1, unopposed German aircraft bombed and strafed his command post killing three men including his aide-de-camp. Patton vented his anger against Allied tactical air forces in an April Fool's Day situation report, which, for emphasis, he transmitted under his own name. That brought an equally sharp retort from Coningham, now commander of Northwest African Tactical Air Force (NATAF), who bluntly questioned Patton's understanding of air power and the bravery of his troops. Intervention by senior officers and a personal meeting between the two soothed frayed tempers, but did not prevent further friction in air-ground operations.[23]

Patton's displeasure with air support in North Africa emphatically underscored the differing air and ground perspectives of tactical air operations in 1942–1943. Patton's complaints typified those of a field commander facing unopposed air attack without air support of his own. The solution for the ground commander most often fixed on securing direct control of the aircraft that could provide continuous air cover over his lines. (Unchallenged air attack against ground forces could hardly be explained away by airmen offering assurances that the supporting air force contributed best when attacking the enemy elsewhere. To front line troops, what remained unseen did not appear effective.) In response, Coningham could argue that the army misused tactical air power by parceling out aircraft to individual army units for combat air patrol missions to serve as a local air umbrella. That prevented the tactical air force from taking advantage of its flexibility and ability to concentrate forces to achieve air superiority. Even though Allied fighter-bombers might not be seen frequently by the foot soldier, Coningham believed them to be more effective in most cases when used primarily to attack the enemy's air forces in a counterair role and to perform interdiction operations to isolate the battle-field, rather than when committed in direct support of troops under fire.[24]

The air support changes that Coningham introduced reflected a larger reorganization of all Allied air and ground forces in the Mediterranean theater approved earlier at the Casablanca summit conference in late January 1943, and subsequently implemented throughout northwest Africa on February 18. General Eisenhower became the Mediterranean theater commander and controlled all Allied forces (**Chart 2**). For the first time, he operated with a genuine unified command set up along functional lines. British Air Chief Marshal, Sir Arthur Tedder, assumed command of all Allied air units in the Mediterranean. The Northwest African Air Forces (NAAF), led by General Spaatz, replaced the Allied Air Force, becoming the most important of Tedder's three regional air forces. It, in turn, consisted of three functional commands, with NATAF responsible for all tactical air support of ground forces in the region. Appropriately, Air Vice Marshal Coningham was named its commander.[25]

The new organizational arrangement also formally recognized distinct aerial priorities, with air superiority and interdiction preceding those of close air support. Air officers approved targets based on need and suitability, and air and ground officers performed planning functions jointly. Coningham issued a pamphlet which he circulated to reach the widest possible audience. Based on a short talk by British field commander General Montgomery (which, incidentally, Coningham authored), it praised the British Western Desert system of air-ground cooperation. That system, Montgomery asserted, succeeded by virtue of the coequality of the land and air forces and the spirit of cooperation.[26]

Despite the attack on Patton's headquarters by German aircraft in early April 1943, no one could doubt that air support improved after the reorganization. The organizational changes combined with good flying weather, more

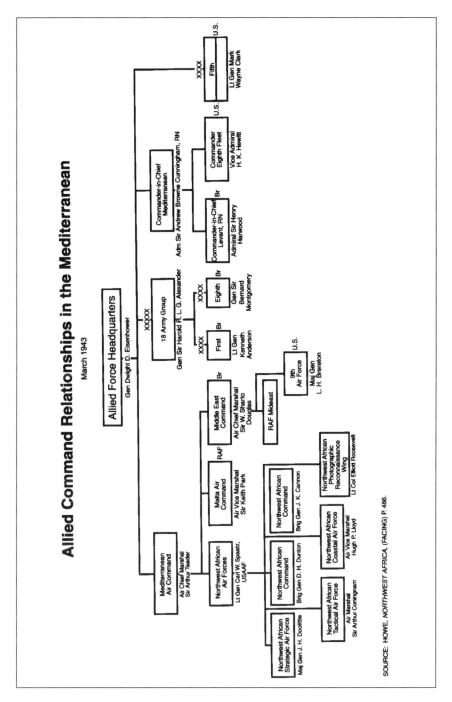

Allied Command Relationships in the Mediterranean

March 1943

Allied Force Headquarters
Gen Dwight D. Eisenhower

XXXXX
18 Army Group
Gen Sir Harold R. L. G. Alexander

XXXX Br
Eighth
Gen Sir Bernard Montgomery

XXXX Br
First
Lt Gen Kenneth Anderson

Commander-in-Chief Mediterranean
Adm Sir Andrew Browne Cunningham, RN

Br
Commander-in-Chief Levant, RN
Admiral Sir Henry Harwood

U.S.
Commander Eighth Fleet
Vice Admiral H. K. Hewitt

XXXX U.S.
Fifth
Lt Gen Mark Wayne Clark

Mediterranean Air Command
Air Chief Marshal Sir Arthur Tedder

Northwest African Air Forces
Lt Gen Carl W. Spaatz, USAAF

RAF
Malta Air Command
Air Vice Marshal Sir Keith Park

Br
Middle East Command
Air Chief Marshal Sir W. Sholto Douglas

RAF Mideast

U.S.
9th Air Force
Maj Gen L. H. Brereton

Northwest African Command
Brig Gen D. H. Dunton

Northwest African Command
Brig Gen J. K. Cannon

Northwest African Strategic Air Force
Maj Gen J. H. Doolittle

Northwest African Tactical Air Force
Air Marshal Sir Arthur Coningham

Northwest African Coastal Air Force
Air Vice Marshal Hugh P. Lloyd

Northwest African Photographic Reconnaissance Wing
Lt Col Elliott Roosevelt

SOURCE: HOWE, *NORTHWEST AFRICA*, (FACING) P. 486.

Chart 2
Allied Command Relationships in the Mediterranean, March 1943

13

support people, and many more aircraft improved Allied military performance. Air planning became more integrated as Montgomery's Eighth British Army, advancing westward from Egypt, forced retreating German troops back into Tunisia where General Anderson's forces, moving eastward from Algeria, sought to close the pincers. In this offensive, theater interests received top priority in decision-making. The successful attack in mid-March 1943, against the German-held Mareth Line, located along a 22-mile stretch of central Tunisia running from the sea to the Matmata Hills, and the ultimate defeat of German forces in May, highlighted the new flexibility and concentration of tactical air forces that, selectively, made local air superiority possible.

Some intractable problems nonetheless remained. Coningham, for example, never quite solved the air-ground request system to the satisfaction of ground commanders. Although centralized, the process functioned too slowly, especially for "on call" or "immediate" missions.[27] Poor communications equipment also could not transmit and satisfactorily receive over long distances. The solution would come later in Italy and Northwest Europe when pilots and ground controllers acquired improved radio communications equipment and the Allies had far more aircraft available for support. Strained relations among some commanders in North Africa also forced General Spaatz to spend most of the spring in 1943 keeping peace between air and ground officers and educating both sides on the need for cooperation. Nevertheless, communication problems and local enemy air attacks continued to prevent the Allies from achieving complete air supremacy until near the end of the campaign. Even then, success primarily came when Allied forces overran German airfields in Tunisia.[28]

Tactical Air Doctrine Refined

As military operations in North Africa drew near a close in the spring of 1943, tactical air doctrine became an increasingly important issue for airmen like General Kuter and others in Washington, D.C. Should FM 31–35 of 1942 be retained or, if revised, should it reflect the system now operating in North Africa? Additionally, could such a revision be done by air and ground officers in the spirit of cooperation and compromise that had characterized earlier doctrinal statements? Some officers were convinced that it was too late for compromise, and only wholesale acceptance of the new theater tactical air doctrine would do. In a scathing review of early failures in North Africa, written as he left his five-month combat tour for an air staff assignment in May 1943, Kuter described for AAF commander General Arnold what he judged to be specific misuses of tactical air power.[29] The air umbrella topped his list; he and other air force leaders judged this to be the core of the air-ground problem in North Africa. For them, it represented a wasteful and inefficient use of limited air forces that made the attainment of air superiority impossible. Yet, not all ground commanders embraced the air umbrella concept. General Eisenhower, for one, firmly believed that ground forces should not expect permanent, defensive air cover. Not only were theater resources insufficient for such a task, he believed troops dependent on air cover were unlikely to exhibit the aggressiveness fostered by the combat of arms. Other Army officers, however, were much less inclined to forego the air umbrella idea.[30]

General Kuter also argued forcefully for American adoption of the British close air support system, contrasting the mistakes made between November 1942–February 1943, with the successes achieved after the post-Casablanca reorganization. Among the lessons cited, he called attention to concentrated forces employed against specific objectives, a composite theater force, and equality with the Army in decisions of air employment. By the spring of 1943, these lessons had become a familiar refrain in higher AAF circles. At the same time, Kuter acknowledged that the air forces required better communications with ground forces, and he criticized the AAF for shortages of communication equipment, deficient radar, and an inability to provide early warning of aircraft attack, or provide a reliable fighter control system. He saw the ultimate solution in an independent air force, where decisions on air operations would be made by airmen. Until that happened, air forces had to be made "coordinate"—coequal—with the ground forces to achieve successful air-ground operations.[31]

Gens. Lewis H. Brereton, Carl A. Spaatz, and Dwight D. Eisenhower (left to right) critique tactical air doctrine.

Patton's Air Force

Generals Marshall, Arnold, and others in the War Department had previously been impressed with General Montgomery's pamphlet, written by Coningham, *Some Notes on High Command in War*, and with reports from other key participants in North Africa such as Generals Spaatz, Brereton, and Quesada. Kuter's critique helped prompt a revision of tactical air doctrine. Marshall assigned the task of revising American air-ground doctrine to the War Department General Staff's operations division and a special board of air and ground officers.[32] The resultant FM 100–20, *Command and Employment of Air Power*, issued July 21, 1943, epitomized AAF headquarters' interpretation of experiences in North Africa and the influence of Coningham's RAF system. Army chief of staff George Marshall, who initiated the project, approved the final document.

This field manual specifically addressed mission priorities and command arrangements. Like FM 31–35 of 1942, the new manual gave the preponderant role in the employment of aircraft to airmen, subject to the theater commander's final authority. In addition, it directed that air forces be centralized and not parceled out to specific ground commands, and that close air support missions be limited because of their difficulty, high casualty rate, and relative inefficiency.[33] New provisions reflected AAF thinking and influence in the War Department. In a dramatic opening section, FM 100–20 employed capital letters to proclaim and emphasize the equality of air power in joint warfare: "LAND POWER AND AIR POWER ARE CO-EQUAL AND INTERDEPENDENT

Gens. George C. Marshall and Henry H. "Hap" Arnold were impressed with the tactical air doctrine refined in North Africa under the British.

British Air Vice Marshal Sir Arthur Coningham (left), designer of close air support in North Africa, shares experiences in the African desert with Brig. Gen. Auby C. Strickland (center) and Lt. Gen. Frank M. Andrews.

FORCES; NEITHER IS AN AUXILIARY OF THE OTHER. THE INHERENT FLEXIBILITY OF AIR POWER IS ITS GREATEST ASSET...CONTROL OF AVAILABLE AIR POWER MUST BE CENTRALIZED AND COMMAND MUST BE EXERCISED THROUGH THE AIR FORCE COMMANDER IF THIS INHERENT FLEXIBILITY AND ABILITY TO DELIVER A DECISIVE BLOW ARE TO BE FULLY EXPLOITED."[34]

Field Manual 100–20 set an unequivocal hierarchy of aerial missions. "The gaining of air superiority is the first requirement for the success of any major land operation."[35] The manual specifically addressed, as a first prerequisite for air superiority, obtaining improved communications equipment for an effective fighter offense and, for defense, a reliable early warning radar network. In listing appropriate targets for the air superiority mission, it eliminated provisions for an air umbrella because it was "prohibitively expensive and could be provided only over a small area for a brief period of time."[36]

Next to air superiority, interdiction—aerial attack on enemy lines of communication and supply behind the front line—designed to achieve isolation of the battlefield received second priority. Close air support—attacking

17

enemy forces near or on the front line—ranked third. In justifying a last place for close air support, air power proponents normally cite only two sentences from the relevant paragraph: "In the zone of contact, missions against hostile units are most difficult to control, are most expensive, and are, in general, least effective....Only at critical times are contact zone missions profitable."[37] Criticism of the close air support mission as wasteful, of course, was hardly new. Indeed, airmen had made it a major doctrinal point throughout the interwar period. The authors, however, clearly took pains to explain the difficulties of extensive close air support while stressing the importance of cooperation and coordination in attaining common goals. Even so, Army Ground Forces did not share the AAF's enthusiasm for the 1943 manual. In its view, the new doctrinal publication envisioned an air force less inclined than ever to support army operations. Army leaders complained, and legitimately so, that FM 100–20 had been issued *without* the concurrence of the Army Ground Forces. Obviously publication of the new manual would not improve air-ground relations overnight.

In a brief 14 pages, FM 100–20 (1943) attempted to end the imprecision and ambiguity in air-ground doctrine that characterized earlier attempts to create an effective air-ground relationship. From the AAF perspective, it emphatically stated the co-equality of aerial missions in joint operations, clarified lines of command and control, and established aerial mission priorities on which ground commanders could reflect. Yet, in practice FM 31–35 (1942) remained the key air-ground manual because it prescribed precise organization and procedures for specific combat situations, although that manual's cumbersome air-ground communications system and procedures remained problem areas.[38] Future air-ground teams, relying on trial and error and a cooperative spirit, would still have to devise arrangements that suited their peculiar theater circumstances and took advantage of better equipment in larger quantities. The regular army, it seems clear, never completely accepted FM 100–20; the manual remained largely a philosophical rather than a practical treatise. Indeed, FM 31–35 would be the manual later revised to incorporate wartime experiences.[39]

However gratifying it might be to airmen, in practice the new doctrine did little to influence future operations in a formal sense. Although FM 100–20 (1943) gave airmen greater independence and more say in the disposition and employment of air assets, General Weyland and other air commanders in the field still reported to Army officers of higher rank whom they were committed to support tactically. If these pragmatic airmen generally followed the 1943 precepts of FM 100–20, they never allowed theory to stand in the way of mission accomplishment. As a result, they would take liberties with command arrangements and mission priorities never envisioned by air advocates such as General Kuter and others like him on the air staff in Washington, D.C.

Despite legitimate areas of concern in air-ground relationships, Allied officers in North Africa during World War II for the most part cooperated earnestly and tried sincerely to solve the thorny issues of command and control and of air-power mission priorities. The severe criticism of published doctrine used during Operation Torch is largely undeserved.[40] This combat effort, the first Allied combined and joint operation of the war, suffered most from inexperienced and inadequate forces operating with an air-ground doctrine yet to be tested in combat. The problems and frustrations encountered in the North African and Sicilian Campaigns did promote important improvements in command and control of air-ground operations. By the time of the Normandy buildup in early 1944, many air and ground officers had tested doctrine under combat conditions, worked out problems, and created bonds of friendship and trust that they brought with them to the campaigns in Northwest Europe. When confronting a common enemy, reality tempered the application of formal doctrine in the field, and cooperation tended to override intraservice and interservice rivalries.

Chapter Two

Preparing for Joint Operations

As Allied preparations for the invasion of the continent began in earnest, Generals Patton and Weyland appeared in the United Kingdom within a week of each other. Patton arrived by air at Prestwick, Scotland, *incognito* on January 26, 1944, following a painful five-month exile in Sicily. The so-called slapping incidents, in which he lost his temper and struck two hospitalized soldiers suffering from combat fatigue, left him sidelined while others received choice European command assignments: Lt. Gen. Mark Clark assumed command of the U.S. Fifth Army in Italy, and Lt. Gen. Omar Bradley, Patton's former subordinate in North Africa and Sicily, became commander of all American troops during the buildup in the United Kingdom. Immediately on arrival, Patton journeyed to London where General Eisenhower, Supreme Commander, Allied Expeditionary Forces, informed him that he would lead the U.S. Third Army, which would enter the conflict only after Bradley's U.S. First Army had ensured success in the initial landing on the coast of France. At that time, Bradley would turn over command of the First Army to Lt. Gen. Courtney H. Hodges and assume command of an army group, with both Patton and Hodges reporting to him. By all accounts, Patton was grateful for the opportunity.[1]

Lt. Gen. Clark, soon to take command of the Fifth Army in Italy, confers with Lt. Gen. Patton in Sicily.

Lt. Gen. Omar N. Bradley, commander of all American troops for the Normandy invasion.

At the beginning of February 1944 Patton personally welcomed the advance party of Third Army Headquarters personnel at Peover Hall in Knutsford, near Chester, in Cheshire. The main body of his army would not arrive until late March, and Third Army units would continue to disembark until D-Day on June 6, by which time 275 separate Third Army camps dotted the northern English countryside. For the next five months Patton faced the challenge of molding his inexperienced headquarters and subordinate units into the capable fighting force he demanded. Meanwhile, General Eisenhower directed him to remain *incognito*, misidentified as the commander of a mythical U.S. Army group in southern England preparing to land in France at Calais. In this covert operation known as Fortitude, Allied leaders took advantage of the Germans' known apprehension about Patton's next appearance, successfully deceiving them into believing that Calais was the appointed landing site for Operation Overlord.[2]

Largely unknown outside the AAF, General Weyland looked forward to his first combat assignment. While Patton busied himself establishing headquarters at Peover Hall, Weyland arrived without fanfare on January 29, 1944, after leading his 84th Fighter Wing of P–47 fighter-bombers on a four-week trans-Atlantic flight that staged from North Carolina southward across the Caribbean through Brazil and French West Africa, then north from Africa across the Bay of Biscay to Keevil and nearby airfields in the vicinity of Salisbury in southern England. Weyland immediately was reassigned as deputy to General Quesada, commander of the IX Fighter Command. With headquarters at Uxbridge, 16 miles northwest of London, IX Fighter Command would prepare and train American fighter contingents for the invasion. The reassignment orders also named Weyland commander of a IX Fighter Command subordinate organization, the XIX Air Support Command—redesignated XIX Tactical Air Command (TAC) in April 1944—one of several tactical operational commands earmarked for service in support of field armies in France. Like Patton and with two jobs to manage, Weyland began almost from scratch to assemble and shape a largely inexperienced group of American aviators and support personnel into an effective fighting force.[3]

The Generals Paired

Despite arriving within a week of each other, the two commanders probably did not meet personally until much later. Given their disparate personalities and backgrounds, at first glance this selection of officers as combat partners could hardly seem to be a likely combination. Though both hailed from California and had married women of prominent families, each exhibited vast differences in temperament, outlook, and experience.

Born in the affluent Pasadena suburb of San Marino in 1885, George S. Patton, Jr., grew up on a palm tree-covered estate that abuts what is today the Huntington Library and Gardens. His family, rooted in Virginia aristocracy, was

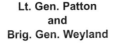

**Lt. Gen. Patton
and
Brig. Gen. Weyland**

steeped in a tradition of military service. Patton's father and grandfather gradu-
ated from the Virginia Military Institute (VMI); the latter died under arms for the
Confederate States of America during the Civil War. After attending the
Classical School for Boys in nearby Pasadena, California, where he developed a
lifelong interest in military history and the deeds of great men, Patton spent a
year at VMI before entering West Point in 1904. There, despite a poor first year's
performance in mathematics, he distinguished himself in military science and
athletics, and stood 46th in the 1909 graduating class of 103. Throughout his life,
Patton suffered from dyslexia, which his biographer, Martin Blumenson, con-
siders important to an understanding of his complex personality. If the dyslexia
provoked inner turmoil and a sense of insecurity, it likely helps explain his well-
known outbursts of profanity and arrogant behavior. Unquestionably, he drove
himself to surmount that particular affliction and become a great military leader.[4]

Indeed, by the early 1920s Patton had made a name for himself in the
United States Army. After graduating from West Point, he entered the cavalry
and achieved prominence for his superb horsemanship, swordsmanship, and as
a U.S. pentathlon athlete in the 1912 Olympics. Serving briefly as an aide to
Chief of Staff Gen. Leonard Wood, in 1916 he joined Gen. John Pershing's well-
publicized "expedition" into Mexico in search of Pancho Villa. While there,
Patton gained notoriety by wounding one of Villa's generals in a dramatic pistol
fight, "man-to-man." When America entered World War I in 1917, Patton left
for France as commander of the American Expeditionary Force's Headquarters
Troop. More important to his future career, however, General Pershing placed
him in charge of organizing an American tank corps. Leading this First Tank
Brigade in the battles of St. Mihiel and the Meuse-Argonne in 1918, his mechanized force helped propel the American assaults before German machine gun
fire left him wounded and out of action. In a field hospital he accepted the
Distinguished Service Cross, the Purple Heart, and promotion to colonel.

During the interwar period, Patton held important posts in the cavalry and
tank corps and along the way attended both the Army's Command and General
Staff School, the Army War College, and served as the G–2 operations chief in
Hawaii. His drive and leadership skills brought him to the attention of a future
chief of staff, Gen. George C. Marshall. As the U.S. Army's foremost authority
on tanks and mechanized warfare at the outset of World War II, Patton was the
logical choice to organize the U.S. Armored Force at Ft. Benning, Georgia. As
commander of the 2d Armored Division he participated in the Tennessee and the
Carolina maneuvers, and served as an umpire in the Louisiana war games. He
was also a private pilot and thus predisposed to view air favorably. In 1942 he
assumed command of the First Armored Corps and organized the Desert
Training Center at Indio, California, in preparation for Operation Torch, the
invasion of North Africa.

In the invasion of North Africa in November 1942, Patton commanded
the Western Task Force, which landed at Casablanca in French Morocco. Then,

in March 1943, he led the U.S. II Corps following the Kasserine Pass battle. Later, he assumed command of Seventh Army for the invasion of Sicily in July 1943, where he achieved recognition by besting British General Montgomery's forces in a race for Palermo and his subsequently undesired notoriety in the slapping incidents. George Patton combined temperamental outburst and tactless public conduct with a mastery of mechanized *blitzkrieg* warfare and, under fire, leadership by example. At least the latter attribute moved General Eisenhower to call him the best driver of troops in combat on the Allied side, while it caused the German High Command to fear him in the field above all Allied army commanders.[5]

O. P. Weyland, 17 years Patton's junior, was born in 1903, 100 miles east of Los Angeles in blue-collar Riverside the second son of an English mother and a German immigrant father, who was a musician turned itinerant farmer. In 1919, after attending a number of public schools in southern California and in Corpus Christi, Texas, he enrolled at Texas A&M University, graduating with a degree in Mechanical Engineering in 1923 as a member of the Reserve Officers Training Corps (ROTC). After graduation, and before deciding on an aviation career, he entered the United States Army Air Service as a reservist and went to work for Western Electric in Chicago, Illinois. The engineering profession, as Weyland recalled later, offered little excitement in a cold climate, and he was bitten by the flying bug while serving reserve weekends at Chanute Field. In 1924, he exchanged reserve status for a regular Army commission and began flight training at Kelly Field, Texas. Weyland impressed his contemporaries as quiet, competent, and altogether without a flair for the dramatic.

General Patton with troops of the 3d Infantry Division awaiting evacuation from Sicily by air.

25

After completing flight training in 1925, Weyland joined the 12th Observation (Reconnaissance) Squadron at Fort Sam Houston where he first acquired his knowledge of, and appreciation for, tactical air requirements in support of army ground forces. He went on to command the 4th Observation Squadron at Luke Field, Hawaii, an assignment he chose over a more prestigious post in the Philippines because it offered tactical work with a full-strength army division. In the mid-1930s he returned to Kelly Field as an instructor pilot and chief of the observation section. His early career involved more than operational flying assignments; he attended the Air Corps Tactical School at Maxwell Field, Alabama, in 1937 where his field experience with the ground forces helped him graduate as number one in his class. Two years later, in 1939, he completed the Army's Command and General Staff School course at Ft. Leavenworth, Kansas.

During the first years of World War II, Weyland served with the renamed Army Air Forces primarily in Washington, D.C. There, he was assistant to the chief of the National Guard Bureau's Aviation Division before receiving assignment to AAF headquarters, first as Deputy Director for Air Support and then as Chief of the Allocations and Programs Division in the office of the Assistant Chief of the Air Staff. The latter assignment placed him at the center of the aviation buildup, which included work on AAF air inspector Maj. Gen. Follett Bradley's plan for building up the forces needed in the cross-channel invasion. This brought him into frequent contact with the AAF commander, General Arnold.

Between Washington assignments, Weyland commanded the 16th Pursuit Group in Panama, which flew P–40s, and in 1941 he became chief of staff of the Caribbean Air Force (later redesignated Sixth Air Force). Weyland's

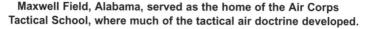
Maxwell Field, Alabama, served as the home of the Air Corps Tactical School, where much of the tactical air doctrine developed.

commander, Gen. Frank Andrews, judged this air force to be "tied to no island commanders but available for a concentrated blow for the defense of the Canal."[6] Here, Weyland helped army leaders understand the benefits of centralizing limited air resources in support of ground forces scattered over a large geographic area. With that background and experience and promoted to brigadier general in late 1943, he assumed command of the 84th Fighter Wing. On January 1, 1944, he flew with it to England and a new assignment.

Shortly after arriving in England, the U.S. Army notified General Weyland that he and the XIX TAC would be paired with the Third Army and its famous commander, General Patton. Privately, Weyland harbored doubts about this assignment with the fiery army commander—an understandable reaction given Patton's public criticism of Allied air support in North Africa. Long afterward, Weyland recalled that he had no idea why he and his organization were paired with Patton and his Third Army, though he admitted: "nobody was just real anxious to do it [join Patton]. Nobody was *really envious* of me, let's put it that way."[7] Doubtless at that moment in time, Patton's air subordinate could anticipate confrontations if he were to avoid being bulldozed on major air employment decisions. Despite his quiet demeanor, however, Weyland could be entirely forceful when the occasion demanded. General Ferguson, his operations officer in World War II, perhaps described him best as "soft-spoken but a firm and very capable fellow."[8]

Whatever Patton's feelings might have been on learning that his air commander lacked any combat experience, Weyland brought to the partnership a military background in tactical operations that would prove excellent preparation for the air-ground mission that both would face. Though without combat experience, he had spent his entire career in tactical aviation and he understood air-ground requirements better than most did in the AAF. He also brought to the XIX TAC extensive experience in fighter operational units, a thorough knowledge of tactical air operations, and a willingness to cooperate in fixing air-ground objectives. Moreover, his subdued, more taciturn personality complemented Patton's flamboyancy. If Patton dramatically referred to their association as "love at first sight," the two commanders apparently understood one another and got along well from the very beginning.[9] Certainly, by war's end, Patton emphatically would describe Weyland as "the best damn general in the Air Corps."[10]

Even before Patton and Weyland began assembling and training the troops of their new commands for combat in France, however, Allied leaders had to organize the multinational air and ground forces that would be required in that enterprise to function in concert.

Organizing Allied Assault Forces for Joint Operations

Plans for a cross-channel invasion of France received renewed impetus when Allied leaders met at Casablanca, French Morocco, back in January 1943.[11] At that time in North Africa, Allied forces were firmly established and had begun to close on German and Italian forces in Tunisia from the east and west. In Russia, Soviet forces had halted the Germans' eastward onslaught at Stalingrad. In the Southwest Pacific, Americans had seized the initiative at Guadalcanal and seemed to have checked Japanese expansion. The Allies now had reason to believe that the tide of war at last had turned in their favor. To ensure the success of an assault on Fortress Europe, the Allies at Casablanca decided to stress operations against the German submarine menace, intensify pressure on German resources and morale through the so-called Combined Bomber Offensive originating in the United Kingdom, and clear the Mediterranean Sea by invading the island of Sicily.

Following the Casablanca Conference, the Combined Chiefs of Staff undertook a detailed study of cross-channel invasion requirements based on the tragic landing made at Dieppe, France, by British and Canadian forces in August 1942. A successful assault, the study concluded, required a massive landing of forces at a beachhead that offered access to a key port with a good road network leading into the French interior and within range of Allied fighter aircraft in England. For that beachhead, planners chose the Normandy coast

President Roosevelt and Prime Minister Churchill at Casablanca.

between Cherbourg and Caen. In March 1943 they submitted their analysis to British Lt. Gen. Frederick E. Morgan. His appointment as Chief of Staff to the (as yet unnamed) Supreme Allied Commander (COSSAC) charged him to plan for an invasion as early as possible in 1944. Allied leaders at the Trident Conference in Washington, D.C., in May 1943 set that date for May 1, 1944, and confirmed it in November at the Teheran Conference in Iran. In late January 1944 however, shortly after General Eisenhower's arrival in London to assume the duties of Supreme Commander, he and British General Montgomery, the designated ground forces commander for the invasion, decided to expand the COSSAC's initial plan in Operation Overlord. They opted for an assault force strengthened, from an original three to five army divisions and a landing-frontage expanded from an original 25 to 40 miles. To procure the needed equipment for Overlord—especially landing craft—Eisenhower postponed an Allied landing on the Mediterranean coast of southern France by one month.

Providing for the necessary tactical air support for the invasion, Allied leaders moved the Ninth Air Force from Egypt to England. On the continent, the Ninth would pair with the 12th Army Group in the American contribution to the air-ground campaign in Northwest Europe. More significantly for tactical air developments, however, the Ninth's subordinate tactical air commands would work directly with armies in the field.[12] Commander of Eighth Air Force's VIII ASC, Brig. Gen. Robert C. Candee, offered a proposal for the specific organization of the Ninth Tactical Air Force (TAF) in England to include a bomber command, a fighter command with two air support divisions, an air service command, and for the first time, an air defense command and an engineer command. The Air Support Divisions, later renamed Air Support Commands, then Tactical Air Commands, would support designated field armies on the continent. Candee's proposal reflected the findings of a seminal Eighth Air Force observers' report, *Air Operations in Support of Ground Forces in North West Africa (March 15–April 5, 1943).*[13]

Colonel Philip Cole prepared the air operations observers report in the spring of 1943. Cole, with a small team of Eighth Air Force officers, visited and assessed the air-ground operations of 18 separate North African theater units. Their report considered especially the experience of the RAF's Western Desert Force and the U.S. XII ASC—redesignated XII TAC in April 1944—which had collocated its headquarters near General Patton's II Corps advance headquarters. The 42-page report focused on tactical air organization, control, and operations. The team found that FM 31–35 (1942) provided the organizational guidelines (the division of headquarters into rear and advance elements, in particular) which allowed the air commander's staff to keep up with and remain collocated with the army in mobile operations. Air-ground teamwork also received high marks for "close and continuous" liaison among the air headquarters and the supported ground units. The observers described the critical importance of "air support parties" assigned to army units, and of the army counterpart liaison officers stationed at each air field. The air commander, in keeping with FM 31–35, retained responsibility for directing aerial units that flew against targets requested by the ground forces.[14]

Indeed, the Cole team's report became the blueprint for organizing, commanding, and controlling tactical air operations in Northwest Europe. To control air resources, the team recommended that the air organization with tactical units assigned to support ground forces "be organized as an Air Force headquarters."[15] To ensure that proper control could be exercised, this tactical air headquarters at any one time should be allocated no more than two wings of six fighter groups. The team recommended an increase of 100 percent (from 8 to 16) in the number of air support parties assigned directly to the Air Support commander in addition to a battalion of Aviation Engineers. Successful air-ground military operations in North Africa had required additional air support parties in the field and the ambitious airfield construction program contemplated for mobile military operations on the continent warranted engineers assigned to each field air command. The report also urged that these "principles of Air Support organization and control evolved by the Western Desert Force RAF and modified to suit American organization and procedure, as represented by XII TAC, be accepted as the current model for the organization of such units."[16] Ninth Air Force would adopt all of these recommendations for the campaign in Northwest Europe.[17]

A few months after Cole submitted his report, American and British leaders met at the Quadrant Conference in Quebec, Canada, in August 1943, and confirmed the cross-channel invasion, now codenamed Overlord, for the spring of 1944. The Allied leaders also called for a massive air offensive, termed Pointblank, designed to destroy German air forces prior to the landings, and creation of an Anglo-American tactical air force to be known as the Allied Expeditionary Air Force (AEAF). The U.S. component of this command, Ninth Air Force, thus would be largely independent of and separate from the Eighth Air Force and other strategic air forces.[18] The Ninth Air Force, which moved from Egypt to England on October 16, 1943, under the command of Maj. Gen. Lewis H. Brereton (**Chart 3**), initially consisted of a small headquarters contingent from the Ninth and elements of the Eighth Air Force's VIII ASC, including Colonel Cole. A vast influx of new, largely inexperienced personnel as yet untested by combat accounted for the bulk of this tactical air force, which over the next seven and a half months grew to more than 170,000 officers and enlisted.

The Ninth Air Force, however, depended on the Eighth for basic support. Administrative matters remained centralized under the Eighth Air Force, which dominated the AAF in the United Kingdom and, after January 1, 1944, its successor, the United States Strategic Air Forces (USSTAF) in Europe. Supply officers in Weyland's XIX TAC repeatedly complained that logistic bottlenecks could have been prevented had they been able to establish an inde-

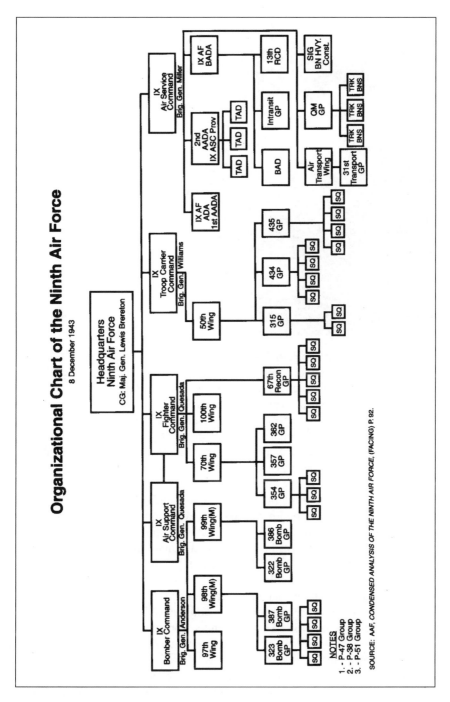

Chart 3
Organizational Chart of the Ninth Air Force, December 8, 1943

Maj. Gen. Lewis H. Brereton

pendent administrative channel directly to AAF supply agencies stateside. As for operational matters, the Ninth like its British counterpart the Second TAF, looked to the Anglo-American AEAF for direction. Here, the issue of command prerogatives appeared much less clear.

Two weeks after the Ninth Air Force arrived in England, on November 1, 1943, the Allies activated the AEAF under the leadership of Air Chief Marshal Sir Trafford Leigh-Mallory, the most controversial air commander on the Allied side. Leigh-Mallory reportedly was possessed of a difficult personality. Yet, personality clashes normally reflect issues of larger importance. In this case, from the time of his appointment, Leigh-Mallory and the AEAF became the focus of a complex tug-of-war over command authority involving not only American tactical air forces but all U.S. and British strategic forces as well. Recent studies have been more sympathetic to this British officer in view of the challenges he faced.[19] Simply put, Leigh-Mallory believed that he should have the authority to plan and direct all Allied strategic and tactical air forces in support of the invasion, rather than simply to coordinate plans and operations of the AAF's Ninth Air Force and the RAF's Second TAF.

General Spaatz, USSTAF commander, for one, thought otherwise and opposed the use of strategic air forces against tactical targets in Normandy. Heavy bombers, he declared, should be employed against strategic targets in Germany. Moreover, as General Brereton's diaries make clear, American airmen resisted placing U.S. tactical air forces under a British officer.[20] These issues festered throughout the winter of 1943-1944 as Leigh-Mallory, General Eisenhower, and the strategic bomber leaders argued over the use and control of heavy bombers. Eventually, Eisenhower received the authority he needed to use the strategic bombers in support of Overlord objectives. But in tactical matters, the AEAF's authority was more clearly drawn. According to the Joint Operations Plan for the invasion, Ninth Air Force would "execute air operations in the U.S. sector as directed by AEAF" and together with Second TAF, would support ground forces "in coordination with AEAF."[21] As it turned out, the various tactical agencies cooperated reasonably and efficiently after the invasion.

Jurisdictional disputes among the top commanders, however, seldom affected leaders at lower echelons who, like General Weyland, had excellent relations with their fellow airmen and army counterparts. In any case, Weyland and his colleagues had challenges enough to face in building up their forces, training for the invasion, fighting enemy air forces in Operation Pointblank, and participating in the attacks against German rocket and buzz bomb launching sites on the continent.

Manning and Equipping the Assault Forces

General Weyland's XIX TAC, headquartered at Aldermaston Court, near Reading in Berkshire, in February 1944 consisted of 30 officers and 77 enlisted men—but it counted no pilots or aircraft. The XIX TAC was a subordinate element of the IX Fighter Command led by General Quesada, recently arrived from the Middle East with the original Ninth Air Force contingent. The Ninth Air Force was a tactical air force, and its IX Fighter Command controlled the

Air Marshal Leigh-Mallory presides at a squadron briefing.

fighter and fighter-bombers employed in the close air-support role. Both air-men, in effect, wore more than one command hat. Quesada commanded the IX Fighter Command with its two subordinate air support commands, the IX and XIX TACs, and commanded the IX TAC, while Weyland served as his deputy commander at IX Fighter Command headquarters at Uxbridge and as commander of the XIX TAC.

General Quesada directed the equipping and training of both air support commands. Quesada's IX TAC received priority over Weyland's XIX TAC for personnel and equipment during the buildup in England. The former support command, augmented by fighter groups later destined for Weyland's command, would be the first to deploy to airfields in France in support of the lodgement and breakout. Weyland's XIX TAC would become operational on the continent, along with the Third Army, *after* the breakout. Initially, air leaders planned to inactivate IX Fighter Command once the two tactical air commands, as they were redesignated in April, had grown to full combat strength. The fighter command proved too valuable as an operational coordinating agency, however, and did not inactivate until the last fighter-bomber group deployed to the continent in late July 1944.[22]

Generals Weyland and Quesada also contrasted with respect to personality, leadership style, and the experience each brought to the European theater.[23] Unlike Weyland, Pete Quesada, to use his own words, had an impulsive personality. A hands-on leader, he enjoyed flying combat missions with younger pilots (he was 40 years old in 1944). His assignments included duty as an aide to key Air Corps and political figures and as chief of the Air Corps' foreign liaison section. He had attended courses at the Air Corps Tactical School and the Army's Command and General Staff School when, as commander of XII Fighter Command, he left North Africa for England, he brought to his new Ninth Air Force post tactical operations experience, an appreciation for technical innovation, and tremendous energy and drive. Responsible for directing all tactical air training and operations for fighter-bomber groups in the United Kingdom, he would lead IX TAC in operations supporting the First Army, commanded initially by General Bradley in Normandy and, after the breakout, by General Hodges. The First Army would operate on the Third Army's left flank in the drive across France.

If Quesada had arrived in England several months before Patton, and if his combat experience made him the best choice to direct training in England and tactical air operations in Normandy, army and air force leaders might have deliberately avoided putting these two headstrong personalities on the same air-ground team. By pairing Weyland and Quesada, these complementary personalities were able to contribute to teamwork at IX Fighter Command. Both brought to their commands extensive tactical experience, a willingness to innovate, a commitment to air-ground objectives, and the drive to make the cooperative effort successful.

As for Weyland's XIX TAC's staff structure, administratively it represented a normal air support command organization including a chief of staff, deputy chief of staff, and four assistant chiefs of staff to head the main branches, that is, personnel (A–1), intelligence (A–2), operations (A–3), and supply (A–4). After a number of personnel changes in the spring of 1944 Weyland (the ROTC graduate from Texas A&M), assembled a team that remained mostly together throughout the entire campaign. His chief of staff, Col. Roger J. Browne (West Point, class of 1929), and his deputy chief of staff, Col. James F. Thompson, Jr. (West Point, class of 1932), brought to their posts extensive prewar experience as pursuit and observation (reconnaissance) pilots. The other officer most directly involved in flying operations, Operations Chief Col. James Ferguson, rose rapidly after entering the Air Corps in 1936 from a civilian school and, like General Weyland, had received a regular Army commission. He arrived in England as commander of the 405th Fighter Group. In the forthcoming campaign, Colonel Browne would command the XIX TAC's rear headquarters while Colonel Ferguson would direct activities from the command's advance headquarters, and Colonel Thompson would form a small X-Ray (small, mobile command post) detachment to keep pace with General Patton's rapidly moving command post echelon during the dash through France. The remaining support branch chiefs consisted of Maj. Robert C. Byers (A–1), Lt. Col. Charles H. Hallett (A–2), and Lt. Col. Howard F. Foltz (A–4), all of whom belonged to the Air Corps rather than the regular Army.[24]

Among the many important attached units supporting the XIX TAC, the communications and engineer troops proved indispensable. The command's operations turned on effective communications and two battalions of Signal Corps personnel under the command of Col. Glenn C. Coleman (West Point, class of 1938) constructed and operated equipment for routine command communications as well as the radios and vehicles used for the air support nets. Over the course of the campaign, Colonel Coleman's troops developed four communications networks. The command net linked the command with the wings and groups as well as adjacent units; the control net centered on the Tactical Control Center, linking it with the command's radars, radio intelligence unit, and ground observers; the liaison net tied the command to its tactical air parties at the Army's corps, divisions, and combat commands; and finally, the air-ground net included aircraft, ground stations at airfields, and tactical air parties that moved with the army. The four networks relied on five types of communication. Air-ground communications used VHF radio while point-to-point communications employed land-line telephone and teletype, FM radio telephone and teletype, HF radio, and both ground and air couriers.[25]

The engineers comprised the second major support group. Based on a recommendation from Colonel Cole's Eighth Air Force Observers Report, Ninth Air Force's Engineer Command assigned brigades consisting of self-contained aviation battalions of 27 officers and 760 enlisted men directly to the

Major General Quesada

tactical air commands. Fortunately for the XIX TAC, Col. Rudolf E. Smyser, Jr., commanded the 2d Aviation Engineer Brigade. A West Point graduate (class of 1928), Smyser had been a driving force in developing aviation battalions in the prewar Air Corps and had served for two years as Eighth Air Force's Engineer Chief. During that time he had visited the North African theater and gained first-hand knowledge of engineering construction requirements for mobile warfare conditions. In the coming offensive, elements of his battalions would construct or refurbish a total of 43 airstrips using six different types of surfacing material.[26]

In the spring of 1944, while Ninth Air Force's engineer and signals officers labored to form operational units for the tactical air commands, General Weyland wrestled with major command problems of his own. Beginning in February 1944, Weyland faced four simultaneous challenges: first, building XIX TAC with the required personnel and equipment; second, properly training all members of the command; third, conducting flying operations in support of Eighth Air Force bombers; and, finally, participating in air-ground training with General Patton's Third Army. Because Quesada's command received priority for personnel and equipment, the XIX TAC remained a small force until the spring of 1944. By the end of March, it still totaled only 3,223 personnel in contrast with IX TAC's 27,093. The command's personnel problems extended beyond insufficient numbers to fill the authorized billets. Technical specialists remained in short supply, and in some cases, the table of organization did not include essential functions. One of the most glaring omissions involved air liaison officers to work with the army. Recommendations like those of Colonel Cole's North African Campaign analysis and Patton's lessons learned report on the Sicily operation seem to have escaped the attention of planners at AAF headquarters in Washington, D.C. Air Staff officials failed to foresee the need for airmen in air support parties who would work together with army operations officers down to division level. To meet that need, the tactical air command had to assign them from existing authorizations, which intensified the overall shortage of personnel in Weyland's command.[27]

Within two months, by the end of May 1944, General Weyland's manning situation improved considerably. On the eve of D-Day, XIX TAC had grown from 3,232 to 11,965 officers and enlisted men—though it was not yet half the size of General Quesada's IX TAC. The major increase in personnel occurred when the XIX TAC received its first operational flying units in April 1944.

During the Second World War, in contrast to later practice, it was the fighter group rather than the wing that served as the primary flying organization.

100 Fighter Wing				303 Fighter Wing		
354 FG	358 FG	362 FG	363 FG	36 FG	373 FG	406 FG
(P–51)	(P–47)	(P–47)	(P–51)	(P–47)	(P–47)	(P–47)

Then, wings served a coordination and communications function linking the fighter groups with the headquarters and its associated tactical control center. During the campaign in France, the command found the wings to be an unnecessary administrative echelon and recommended their elimination in future operations. Normally, each fighter group consisted of three squadrons for a total of approximately 200 officers, 800 enlisted, and 75 aircraft.[28]

The rugged, well-armored P–47 Thunderbolt
proved to be an ideal fighter-bomber.

The 100th Fighter Wing joined Weyland's command in late March 1944 and became operational on April 15. Its groups already had been in the European theater for as long as four months under IX TAC control for training and operations. The 354th Fighter Group, in fact, had been the first operational fighter group in Ninth Air Force and proudly called itself the Pioneer Mustang Group. Units of the 303d Wing, however, joined the command directly from the States and needed two to three weeks to become operational. Even after both wings achieved operational status in early May 1944 they continued to be assigned to IX Fighter Command and IX TAC for flying operations, rather than to the XIX TAC.

The XIX TAC had the distinction of being the only tactical air command in the theater that flew P–51 aircraft. Both the P–51 Mustang and P–47 Thunderbolt, or Jug, had been designed initially as high-altitude fighters. The P–51's six .50-caliber machine guns, superior maneuverability, and extended range when equipped with drop-tanks made it the ideal aircraft for long-range escort and fighter sweeps. Because Ninth Air Force visualized the need for at least a modest P–51 capability to counter the *Luftwaffe* threat, it retained two groups, the 354th and 363d Fighter Groups. Although both belonged to Weyland's command, the great flexibility of tactical air power made them readily available, as required, to assist the operations of other Ninth Air Force tactical air commands. The P–51 proved less capable as a fighter-bomber. Its liquid-cooled, in-line engine made it more vulnerable to antiaircraft flak and even small arms fire at low altitudes, and during steep dives it tended to develop stability problems. The well-armored P–47, on the other hand, proved to be an ideal fighter-bomber. Its ruggedness, turbo-supercharged air-cooled radial engine, ample bomb-carrying capability, ease of operation and maintenance, and lower vulnerability to flak damage readily offset its high fuel consumption and restricted forward visibility. Above all, the Thunderbolt's eight .50-caliber machine guns gave it outstanding firepower for strafing—the most important of the fighter-bomber air support roles.[29]

The original Ninth Air Force plan called for 1,500 tactical aircraft, enough to equip each group with 75 planes. The plan provided for an additional 10 aircraft in reserve locally and a further 15 in depot reserve. Planners predicted a 30 percent attrition-replacement rate for the campaign. However, normally two months elapsed before a group received its full complement of 75 aircraft. Even then, the new planes usually arrived without their full quota of associated equipment or requested modifications, which meant that achieving operational capability might be delayed as long as six weeks.[30]

At XIX TAC headquarters, the officers resented their preinvasion *stepchild* status and liked to blame Eighth Air Force's administrative control of Ninth Air Force logistics for many of their problems. They believed supply officers in the strategic forces failed to appreciate the special needs of a tactical force and did not submit their requirements for modifications promptly to the appropriate organizations stateside. Even so, given the four-month period from the time Weyland assumed command until D-Day, one marvels that, despite the speed and the scale in the buildup of forces, the bureaucratic snafus encountered in so enormous an effort never became insurmountable.

Training Underway

To prepare for cross-channel operations, XIX TAC personnel participated in individual and group training programs from the time they arrived in England until they moved to the far shore. Flexibility and mobility became instant watchwords. Beginning in December 1943 Ninth Air Force–wide ground training stressed mobile command post communications exercises. Aircraft warning and control units had no time to take part, however, which severely limited the scope and realism of this training. The results seldom pleased evaluators. As one noted in early 1944, "the most that can be said for this exercise is that enough mistakes were made to warrant the doubling of efforts for further Command Post Exercises."[31] In fact, the command post exercises continued until the spring, when XIX TAC could issue standard operating procedures for mobile, combined operations.

Ninth Air Force aircrews participated in an especially rigorous flight training program, General Weyland's second command challenge. Ground orientation training for new pilots emphasized airdrome procedures, communications, and minor aircraft maintenance and refueling exercises designed to prepare aircrews for the austere airstrip conditions expected in highly mobile combat operations on the continent.[32] Flight training stressed close-air bombing techniques. When new groups began arriving at the end of 1943, General Quesada immediately focused this program on dive-bombing, skip-bombing, and low-level attack training. Despite their stateside preparation, new pilots required many additional hours to master dive-bombing techniques in the P–47. Moreover, their skills deteriorated because flying operations in early 1944 called for them to provide bomber escort rather than to perform low-level interdiction missions. Characteristically, Quesada wasted no time in attacking the problem on several levels. He selected two experienced officers from the North African Campaign and sent them to operational groups and to RAF Millfield, which specialized in training flight leaders in low-level attack procedures. As newly arrived P–47 pilot Lt. John J. Burns recalled, shortly after arriving in England in March 1944 he checked-out in his airplane and then spent late March and April at "Clobber College" at Atcham, practicing dive-bombing techniques when not flying operational missions. Quesada also established a research project at Salisbury Range where a team of pilots and civilian specialists determined the best bombing techniques for reducing particular targets.[33]

Operational flying became Weyland's third major challenge during the preparation phase. Although groups from his 100th Fighter Wing had been flying against the enemy since late 1943, until February 1944 only P–51s flew bomber escort and photo and weather reconnaissance missions. On February 3, 52 P–47s joined 71 P–51s in support of VIII Bomber Command aircraft attacking special targets, the high-threat buzz bomb sites in northern France and Belgium. Together with fighter sweeps, escort missions predominated with few exceptions until late March, when the Allies could claim air superiority in the skies over Europe.[34]

The main Allied effort to wrest control of the skies from the *Luftwaffe* began in earnest on February 19, 1944, with a six-day assault popularly known as Big Week. During this period, RAF Bomber Command and the U.S. Eighth and Fifteenth Air Forces flew more than 4,000 sorties against 23 airframe and three aero-engine factories in Germany. Supported now by sufficient numbers of the long-range P–51 Mustang fighter, the bombers could put all of Germany at risk, and together with the fighters, they dealt the *Luftwaffe* air defenses a severe blow. By March, Allied pilots found that *Luftwaffe* fighters often failed to challenge them and analysts estimated that the *Luftwaffe*'s western front fighter force of 1,410 in early January 1944 had been reduced by more than 500 planes as a result of Big Week and the subsequent air attacks against targets in France and Germany.[35]

With air superiority over France largely assured, air leaders in March 1944 increasingly sent P–47s over specific areas on the continent to dive-bomb and strafe interdiction targets of opportunity. Dive-bombing missions that month for the first time outnumbered bomber escort missions by 45 to 38. The number of high-altitude fighter sweeps, nonetheless, remained high for both tactical air commands because they provided good practice in orientation flying for newly arrived pilots. Fighter-bomber aircrews seemed overjoyed to be flying fewer escort missions for heavy bombers now that Eighth Air Force fighters were on hand in sufficient numbers. Their enthusiasm was quickly tempered by the danger and challenges of low-altitude interdiction missions. In a perceptive observation, a veteran airman observed: "Our pilots are learning what we learned in Africa—that air support work is a lot of hard work without the glory and the huge claims of destroying enemy aircraft that are obtained in escorting the heavy bombers into Germany." Yet, high-altitude escort and fighter sweep assignments were the most characteristic fighter missions, the ones most likely to produce the traditional dogfight. With air superiority, however, high-altitude encounter missions that produced dogfights became increasingly rare.[36]

When the so-called Transportation Plan to isolate the Normandy battlefield began, May 1944 became the busiest flying month prior to D-Day. In one of the most contentious decisions of the spring, General Eisenhower overruled the commanders of both the RAF and U.S. strategic bomber forces and diverted them from an exclusive bombing of the German homeland to attacks against transportation facilities in France. Of the five key target groups—coastal batteries, radar stations, marshaling yards, airfields, and bridges—aircraft of the two tactical air commands concentrated their efforts against the latter three. Attacks on railroad and highway bridges in northern France became crucial in preventing a timely German reinforcement of Normandy defenses. By D-Day, the Allied air assault on 12 railroad and 14 highway bridges over the Seine River delayed significantly all crossings below Paris.[37]

Well before D-Day, the Allies planned and directed all tactical air operations from Uxbridge, near London. In early February 1944, the AEAF and its two tactical commands, the Ninth Air Force and Second TAF, established their advance headquarters in Hillingdon House, Uxbridge, where a short time later IX Fighter Command's advance headquarters joined them. At Hillingdon House, the commands operated side by side with the RAF's 11 Group in a combined control center that directed all Allied fighter operations. Later, the British 21st Army Group and U.S. First Army personnel arrived at the center to coordinate the air-ground request system for the invasion. The combined control center later would direct air support operations on D-Day.[38]

In March 1944, General Weyland's command began controlling its own aircraft operations, thereby relieving IX TAC of operational responsibility. Early that month Weyland sent 10 officers and 14 enlisted signal corps controllers to the RAF's Biggen Hill sector control center for training. In late March, his command began moving flying units of both wings to advanced landing grounds (ALGs) in southeast Kent (**Map 2**). Deployed in full view opposite the Pas de Calais region of France, XIX TAC units comprised an important element of Operation Fortitude, the grand deception that convinced the Germans that the Allied invasion would come from "Army Group Patton," directed against Calais.[39]

The ALGs in Kent were designed to resemble those planned for the continent. They proved to be excellent sites for mobility training and for operating under rather stark conditions, but they lacked adequate housing, sufficient water supplies, and road networks able to support operations under combat field conditions. Even though the objective called for operating only with essential support, the airstrips still needed basic operating equipment and supplies. General Weyland spent a good part of his time in April and May 1944 working to obtain sufficient fuel supplies, to upgrade the road networks, and to improve overall operations at the ALGs. This would prove good practice for conditions he shortly would encounter in France.[40] By the end of May, XIX TAC had 2,000 men under canvas at each airstrip. Preparing the ALGs and conducting operational flying, however, made joint field training with Third Army more unlikely as D-Day approached. Even so, air-ground training progressed considerably over the late winter and spring of 1944.

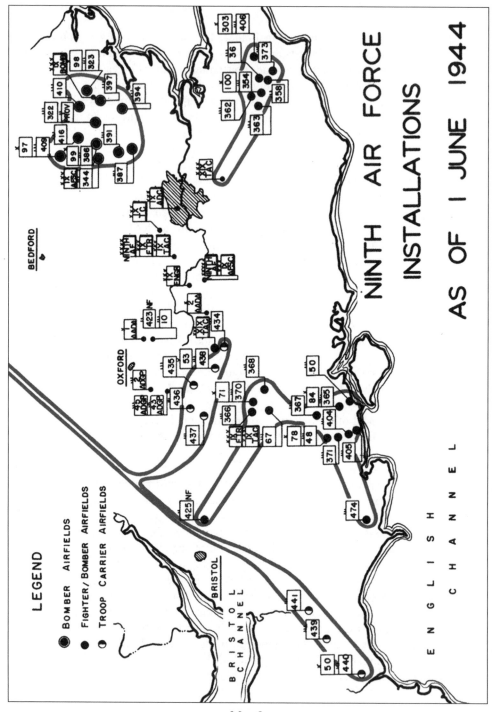

Map 2
Ninth Air Force Installations: June 1, 1944

SOURCE: Rpt, AAF Evaluation Board, ETO, "Effectiveness of Third Phase Tactical Air Operations," p. 47, AFHRA.

The Issue of Joint Training

Joint training among air and ground elements, another major part of the training program, represented a fourth challenge for General Weyland. Because the Ninth Air Force had moved to England for the express purpose of conducting joint operations with field armies, training in air-ground organization and procedure was a priority. Although the planners stressed joint training from the start, Ninth Air Force officials seldom seemed to move from theoretical and organizational instruction to actual air-ground exercises in the field. A recent study attributes this condition to recalcitrant airmen who expressed traditional hostility toward ground support requirements: "the prewar attitude that close air support of ground forces was not a priority air mission still prevailed among flyers at all levels."[41] This conclusion overlooks entirely the real impediments to joint training and the wide degree of cooperation among air and ground leaders that existed in the last few months before Overlord. To be sure, Generals Arnold and Spaatz and other leading airmen remained sensitive to any perceived threats to air force control of air resources. After the North African experience General Follett Bradley, as well as Generals Arnold, Kuter, and others, believed the term *air support* was used too freely, implied a subservient role, and should be changed. That specific term did not appear in FM 100–20, Arnold advised his fellow airmen. The 1943 field manual prescribed "coequal operations," whereby "one force does not support the other in the sense the word was used in the past." He recommended substituting the phrase "in cooperation with" in place of "air support."[42] Such sentiments already had produced a notable change in terminology when, in April 1944 AAF headquarters redesignated all air support commands as tactical air commands. Indeed, all postwar XIX TAC publications on operations in Northwest Europe would refer only as to its aerial action being "in cooperation with" Third Army.[43] This emphasis on coequality and air prerogatives characterized the view in Washington that produced FM 100–20 at the close of the North African Campaign in 1943, and it would reemerge near the war's end. Army Air Forces leaders took their stand not on the practical lessons learned on the field of combat, but on doctrine as it was expressed in FM 100–20.

Fortunately for Overlord, airmen in the field paid scant attention to pronouncements that reflected doctrinal concerns in Washington, D.C. Indeed, General Quesada's IX TAC historian, writing in April 1944 on behalf of IX and XIX TACs, seemed to express the sentiment in England. Delays in beginning air support training did not occur as a result of "traditional hostility" toward the ground support mission, he observed, but rather resulted from the emphasis in early 1944 on escorting heavy bombers.[44] This escort experience reinforced air force doctrine that properly stressed gaining air superiority as the first priority. Following the successes of Big Week, and as planners adopt-

**Lt. Gen. "Hap" Arnold,
commander of
U.S. Army Air Forces,
on his way to visit the
Ninth Air Force in the
Middle East following the
Casablanca Conference.**

ed the Transportation Plan in April, Ninth Air Force fighter-bomber pilots found themselves flying interdiction missions—an airman's second priority according to doctrine—almost exclusively until the D-Day invasion. Consequently, precious little time could be spared for close air support joint training. Actual close air support operations would have to await ground combat on the continent. In short, theater requirements dictated specific air operations in preparation for the assault on France, and those requirements converged with the air leaders' doctrinal preferences. Together, they explain the failure to conduct extensive air-ground training much more completely than do simpleminded explanations that rely on a traditional hostility of airmen toward the close air support mission.

If the Overlord buildup, training program, and operational commitments precluded a sustained joint field training effort, at least the airmen could seize the opportunity to spread their understanding of air-ground responsibilities. They did so by providing lectures on joint operations, sending personnel on field trips to the combat zone in Italy, assigning air and ground liaison personnel to designated units, and when feasible, conducting small-scale air-ground activities. Tactical airmen implemented all of these measures cooperatively without reference to the formal doctrinal pronouncements of FM 100–20.[45]

As for the forces of Weyland and Patton, the special challenge to cooperative efforts in England resulted from their relatively late arrival in the theater and the lengthy period required for both organizations to become operational. Third Army officers spent most of their time supervising the buildup and conducting essential orientation training for their personnel. Weyland's command, in the meantime, received its first fighter-bomber groups and began meeting a full operational flying commitment. Under these circumstances, in the time available, Third Army and XIX TAC officers could hardly be expected to conduct effective joint field training.

Both XIX TAC and Third Army officers realized the importance of acquiring airfields in France as rapidly as possible and they jointly identified potential sites. The Army intelligence officers based their analyses on reconnaissance photography obtained by the Ninth Air Force at Third Army's request beginning in March 1944. In another move designed to enhance cooperation and to provide realistic training for ground elements, on April 11 XIX TAC assumed responsibility from Ninth Air Force's Director of Reconnaissance for meeting all Third Army requirements.[46] In early May, Third Army assigned its first group of ground liaison officers to XIX TAC units. By the middle of the month, the army operations officer could affirm that those plans requiring air force support had been discussed with XIX TAC, with "many such conferences...held before plans were considered final."[47] Referring to joint air-ground efforts in England in early 1944, another air operations officer affirmed:

> Little was known at that time about the actual close Air-Ground Cooperation that we were later to experience. It was up to the Air-Ground Cooperation Officers themselves to work out ideas, try different methods, argue with one another, and finally arrive at a uniform method of operation.... When the time came for the actual invasion, the Air-Ground Officers who found themselves fifth wheels originally with the ground forces were by then an integral part of the unit upon which the Commanding General relied for maximum help.[48]

This officer's enthusiasm over the progress achieved by the liaison officers on D-Day was not entirely warranted, particularly since most had no joint field practice or combat experience in North Africa on which to rely.

As for Weyland and Patton, they appear to have spent relatively little time together before May 1944, the month before D-Day. Weyland, who knew of Patton's unhappy experience with air support in North Africa and believed that he "came up to England with a rather low opinion...of air power," acted to develop good professional and personal rapport with the army commander. He visited all of Third Army's corps and division headquarters, where he discussed the role of tactical air power and the lessons learned in the North African and Italian campaigns. In the latter part of May, Weyland and his intelligence and operations chiefs visited Third Army headquarters to review plans for their movement to France and projected joint operations in August.[49]

Patton's Air Force

Weyland made a special effort to acquaint Patton directly with tactical air capabilities and the details of flight planning and scheduling. According to Weyland, his air base orientation program impressed Patton; moreover, his visit set the stage for effective XIX TAC–Third Army training in April and May and made possible the true partnership that emerged in the summer.

Patton did not visit XIX TAC bases until late in May 1944, and his correspondence refers only to a visit on May 27–28 to observe 354th Fighter Group P–51s return from an escort mission and to hear P–47 pilots of the 362d Fighter Group plan an interdiction mission against a bridge at Rouen. The airmen impressed Patton with the thoroughness of their flight planning and take-off precision. To oblige General Weyland, Patton spoke to officers and enlisted men about the importance of teamwork, later observing how these activities "added greatly to the entente between the ground and air forces."[50] It must be added, however, that Patton already possessed a solid understanding and realistic appreciation of air power. He learned to fly in the early 1920s at Mitchel Field on Long Island during interludes in one of the polo seasons and he often flew a private plane during the interwar period. In the spring of 1941, Patton wrote to an airman friend: "I am personally getting so air-minded that I own an aeroplane." Late that summer he flew his own light airplane as the senior umpire in the Louisiana maneuvers of IV Corps. Thereafter, he experimented with the use of light planes in a variety of combat missions, which doubtless contributed to the Army ground forces adopting and employing them extensively in liaison and medical evacuation roles.[51]

In a larger sense, Patton certainly understood that air support had become critical to an Army that emphasized mobility over firepower. Indeed, with the rapid expansion of the air arm beginning in 1941, War Department planners made a conscious decision to provide the army primarily with light and medium artillery and to rely on tactical aviation for additional heavy artillery support. Significantly in North Africa, Patton went from the outburst at Gafsa for the support he needed, to praises in Tunisia for the tactical air support he received, knowing full well the role of this support for mechanized warfare.

Patton's after-action report on the Sicily campaign revealed a perceptive student of tactical aviation's capabilities and limitations.[52] During amphibious operations, for example, he advocated limited use of an air umbrella—and only *if* the "mastery of the air permits" air forces to maintain it to thwart counterattacks. His solution called for aircraft circling 10 minutes of every hour over sensitive areas at the front, with a secondary bombing mission assigned to them afterward. If these aircraft possessed radio communication with the air support unit on the ground, "any counterattack can be met from the air."[53] This novel approach to the controversial issue of a permanent, orbiting air umbrella would be followed in principle in the Normandy invasion *and* in practice by Weyland's XIX TAC in its support of Patton's rapid drive across France.

Patton readily accepted the proposition that controlling enemy activities in the air was "solely a function of the air," while interdiction or bombing ahead of the ground forces required teamwork for success through target selection from the ground side and a bomb line chosen in conjunction with air officers, one that was easily identifiable from the air. Patton's assessment of close air support deserves special mention for its realism. One should not "count on a very great effect" from air support, he said, until air units had trained extensively with ground forces. The airman's "primary mission was…attacking targets which are adversely affecting the progress of the ground troops [when] called for by the ground." Patton did not advocate control of the air forces by the ground commander, nor did he have any sympathy for ground officers and their troops who expected too much from the air arm. It would be "illusory" to expect fighter-bombers to destroy roads and railways, Patton conceded, because direct hits seldom occurred and, in any case, such targets required constant attention to keep them inoperable.[54]

Relying on his experience in Operations Torch and Husky, to improve air-ground support, Patton recommended extensive joint planning that would include the assignment of well-trained air staff officers to all division and higher G–3 operations sections, more extensive training for radio operators in air-support parties, and joint exercise training among air-support parties and pilots in units earmarked for combat.[55] Thus, in England, Weyland could arrive at a basic understanding with Patton about control over air operations with far less difficulty than he at first might have supposed. "I had full control of the air," Weyland, with some satisfaction declared later, "The decisions were mine as to how I would allocate the air effort."[56]

Considering the team, one might expect Patton to have ridden roughshod over his subordinate and junior air commander whose mission, after all, was to support his Third Army in the field. That did not occur, and Patton's response to Weyland's orientation program helps explain much about his air-mindedness. Patton expressed great interest in what he saw, complimented the airmen accordingly, and spoke about the importance of air-ground teamwork for future operations. If Patton possessed no direct command authority over Weyland and the XIX TAC, he praised them and appealed to their sense of mission. Patton nonetheless was a lieutenant general and Weyland a brigadier general in the same service, and a deferential, if not command, relationship always characterized their association. Beyond this, Patton realized that he had in Weyland an air commander who believed that ground forces deserved all the assistance his command could provide, an air commander who, if he had resources available, was willing to overlook convention and doctrinal precepts to provide that assistance whenever it was needed. Weyland always believed that Patton remained faithful to their original agreement, that the air commander would retain full control of the air forces, even if at times some Third Army staff officers did not. Because of the basic understanding and rapport between the two commanders, the contentious issue of command and control of tactical aviation never became serious.[57] General Patton took pleasure in supporting the airmen and referred to the XIX TAC–Third Army association as the most outstanding example of air-ground cooperation in his combat experience. Others with more claim to objectivity would echo his sentiments.

Whatever the initial success and future promise of XIX TAC–Third Army cooperative efforts in the late spring of 1944, joint training on the whole continued to worry Allied leaders. In early May, as D-Day approached, General Montgomery, who commanded the invasion land forces, expressed his dismay in a letter to Patton—his Sicilian nemesis—and most likely in identical copies to other ground force commanders as well. He decried the apparent separation between the armies and their supporting tactical air forces in England. To link them into "one fighting machine," the two sides needed to go beyond paying lip service to the principle of cooperation and establish the actual procedures and methods necessary for success. Recalling the unity achieved in North Africa, he counseled Patton to consider establishing air and ground headquarters side-by-side, integrating air and ground personnel at all organizational levels, and never move his army without consulting his air headquarters. Indeed, Montgomery observed, an army should take no action before first asking: "How will this affect the air?" Every pilot supporting ground forces likewise had to realize his only function was to aid the army in winning the land battle. This meant "coming right down and participating in the land battle by shooting up ground targets." Air commanders were currently working hard on this aspect of the problem, Montgomery averred, and he urged Patton to give the matter his personal attention because much needed to be done and little time remained available.[58]

General Patton replied on May 7, the day after observing an "air circus" staged by Ninth Air Force for Third Army, one in which he went aloft for a flight in a Mosquito fighter. Patton promised Montgomery that he would do all he could to implement the proposals for air-ground cooperation despite current difficulties. His own "warm personal relationships with Air Force commanders…and the mutual understanding which we have," Patton declared, "will, I am quite sure, make our complete cooperation everything that you can desire."[59] Although collocating the air and ground headquarters would have to await movement to the continent, Patton promoted a Third Army–XIX TAC program of joint training that intensified in May.

General Bradley, at that time commander of the First Army, also criticized Allied air-ground training in the spring of 1944. He complained of the indifference shown by Ninth Air Force commander General Brereton when requested to participate in air-ground field exercises and training. "As a result of our inability to get together with air in England," Bradley said later, "we went into France almost totally untrained in air-ground cooperation." At the same time, however, he conceded that enemy rocket and buzz bomb launching sites and other high-priority targets demanded a heavy flying commitment from Brereton's forces until May. Yet, when in the final few weeks before D-Day, Brereton notified Bradley that his air forces had now been released for training with the army, Bradley told him it was too late.[60]

Important Allied operational flying commitments, which continued until the time of the actual invasion, must be judged the most crucial roadblocks to effective air-ground training in England prior to D-Day. These commitments conformed to tactical air power mission priorities—air superiority first, then isolation of the battlefield. By achieving them in the spring of 1944, the air arm insured that the invasion would succeed and that the close air support mission could become a major focus of tactical air operations on the continent. If in 1944 the best efforts of air and ground leaders to pursue joint training in England fell well short of the mark, it occurred for reasons other than doctrinal disputes or personal disagreements. Between Third Army and XIX TAC, however, considerable joint planning had taken place, and a wide variety of joint training contributed to better understanding on both sides.

Normandy: On the Job Training

Final plans for the great cross-channel assault in the late spring of 1944 called for the British Second Army and the U.S. First Army to land 176,000 troops on the first day at five designated beaches on the Normandy coast between the Seine River and the Cherbourg peninsula (**Map 3**).[61] British and Canadian forces assaulting Sword, Juno, and Gold beaches on the eastern edge of the channel landing zone in the Bayeux-Caen area were to move inland and converge on Caen, whose capture then would open the most direct path to Paris. American forces assaulting Omaha and Utah beaches on the western edge of the channel landing zone were to link up with their British and Canadian allies along the coast and then move west and north to capture the Cherbourg peninsula with its important port city. The British 6th Airborne Division would drop to earth northeast of Caen to protect the British flank, while the American 82d and 101st Airborne Divisions would perform a similar role on First Army's flank near Ste-Mère-Eglise.

In the channel, Allied naval forces were to provide transports for troops and supplies as well as fire-support ashore to neutralize enemy positions. Overhead, a continuous, orbiting Allied air umbrella would counter *Luftwaffe* attacks, while additional fighters would fly close air support missions to help the progress of the ground forces ashore. The Allies hoped the major air interdiction operation, intervention by the French Resistance underground army of 200,000, and fear of the real invasion at Calais would prevent the Germans from mounting an overwhelming counterattack against the first troops ashore in Normandy.

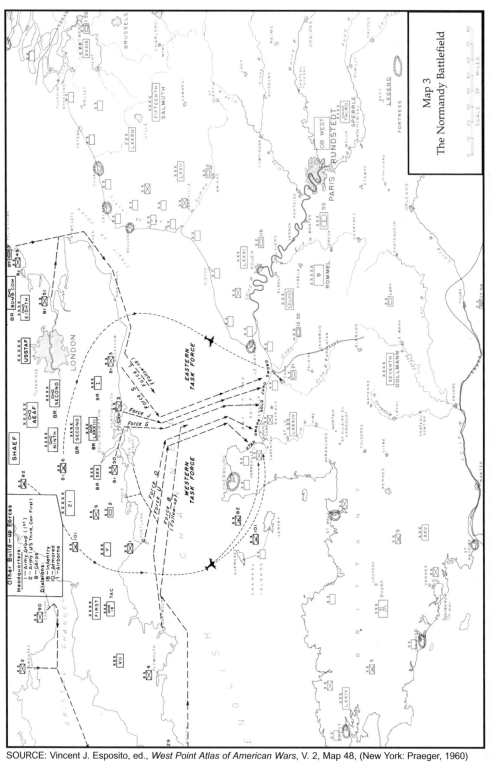

Map 3
The Normandy Battlefield

SOURCE: Vincent J. Esposito, ed., *West Point Atlas of American Wars*, V. 2, Map 48, (New York: Praeger, 1960)

The Allies also counted on some uncertainty and confusion among German commanders to aid in Overlord's success. Field Marshal Gerd von Rundstedt, *Wehrmacht* commander in chief in the west, favored a mobile reserve to thwart an Allied amphibious attack, unlike his nominal subordinate, Army Group B commander Field Marshal Erwin Rommel. Specifically charged with defending the channel coast with the Seventh Army in Normandy and Brittany, and with Fifteenth Army in the Pas de Calais region, Rommel advocated an extensive array of relatively simple coastal defenses as the best response. Rommel's experience in North Africa convinced him that Allied air superiority would render a mobile reserve ineffective.

Both *Wehrmacht* commanders, however, faced additional constraints from the Reich's Chancellor Adolf Hitler and his staff in Berlin, whose claims on military prerogatives embraced decisions on troop disposition and movement in the field—military prerogatives normally reserved to field commanders. In this regard, Allied leaders hoped their elaborate deception plan would convince Hitler to keep the stronger Fifteenth Army positioned near Calais well after D-Day to face the expected assault from Army Group Patton. In early June, the German Fifteenth Army contained 19 divisions, with five Panzer divisions back-stopping it. The German Seventh Army, on the other hand, comprised 13 divisions, but only six were stationed in Normandy, and only one Panzer division back-stopped them. Two of its Panzer divisions were still in southern France. As for the *Luftwaffe*, Allied intelligence officers believed that it could not play a decisive role during the invasion because the Allied air assault in late winter and early spring had left half of the estimated 400 *Luftwaffe* fighters in France nonoperational. Nevertheless, despite having massed the largest amphibious force in history against an enemy severely weakened after four years of warfare, an Allied success in securing a lodgement in Normandy remained far from assured.

No one realized the risks involved in Overlord more keenly than did Supreme Commander General Eisenhower, who elected to launch the invasion on June 6, one day later than planned and in spite of bad weather. D-Day events on Omaha beach, in particular, almost convinced Eisenhower and Bradley to call off the assault. High seas and poor visibility scattered American troops and they unexpectedly faced murderous fire from the crack German 352d Infantry Division, which, unbeknownst to Allied intelligence, had been in position for the previous three months. Despite suffering more than 2,000 casualties at Omaha, the Americans by nightfall had 34,000 troops ashore on a narrow strip of land less than two miles deep. German resistance at the three British beaches also proved tenacious, while American airborne units that landed behind Utah beach lost 2,500. Only at Utah did the Allies get ashore without difficulty. Tenacity and good leadership helped the Allies gain toeholds on all five beaches by the end of D-Day. During succeeding days, the Allies would continue to bring troops and supplies ashore and extend the lodgement area while the German High Command, still believing Calais to be the main landing site, held the Fifteenth Army in place for an invasion that never came.

The period in Normandy from D-Day, June 6, to August 1, 1944, served the Ninth Air Force in many ways as a practical laboratory in which airmen and ground force officers experimented with joint air-ground methods and techniques. In effect, they acquired on-the-job training. Initially, the Allies planned to control all tactical air support for the invasion from the Uxbridge headquarters in England. Accordingly, Leigh-Mallory's AEAF was authorized to direct the air effort by coordinating the responsibilities of the two tactical air forces, the Ninth and the Second TAFs. As the invasion began, Ninth Air Force officers planned their missions side-by-side with their 21st Army Group counterparts in the Uxbridge Combined Control Center.

In Operation Neptune, codenamed for the initial assault and lodgement on the Normandy coast, naval flagships and direction tenders provided an important intermediate communications link. Air representatives on board the USS *Ancon* and USS *Bayfield*, stationed off Omaha and Utah beaches, respectively, received requests for air support from air control parties on shore at each division and corps headquarters, and they passed them on to Uxbridge for action. Thereafter, although the combined control center provided flying control of strike aircraft by directing them to the general area, aircrews located and attacked their targets.[62] The air plan called for tactical air forces to fly four primary missions in support of the invasion force: five groups would provide beach cover; two groups, along with four from VIII Fighter Command, would fly convoy cover; five groups comprised a striking force against special coastal

Dicing shots of the formidable defenses at Normandy Beachhead, taken by the 10th Photo Reconnaissance Group one month before D-Day, provided the information needed to prepare the assault.

batteries and bridges; and six more groups remained on call, available to attack targets on the scene in cooperation with ground forces.[63]

The highly centralized Uxbridge control system proved unworkable from the start. For one thing, the USS *Bayfield* experienced communications difficulties and depended on the USS *Ancon* to relay messages. More serious, air support party officers on the ground could not transmit radio messages over the long distance directly to Uxbridge. Unable immediately to land the bulky SCR–399 high-frequency radio equipment, which possessed a range of 100 miles, planners had to substitute the 25-mile range SCR–284, a standard infantry radio, in its place. This meant unacceptable delays for immediate mission requests, which were supposed to be referred directly, and not to be relayed, from the English Channel to the combined control center for approval. That led Uxbridge officials to authorize the senior air representative aboard the USS *Ancon*, Col. Larry N. Tindal, IX TAC's operations officer, to assume additional responsibilities.

Initially, Tindal and his First Air Combat Control Squadron handled flying control and detection of enemy aircraft. After D-Day he passed targets from liaison officers in the forward areas and reconnaissance pilots directly to fighter-bombers that were available for his use. He also received word of mission results and passed it on to the appropriate ground units. In effect, the senior air representative performed the function of controller in addition to serving as the communications link for immediate, or call, missions. As air and

The D-Day assault.

ground leaders who served in North Africa already knew, responsive and effective air-ground operations demanded greater decentralization. The campaign ahead would demonstrate that centralized air command seldom functioned effectively, especially in emergency situations. In France, the reality of combat rather than doctrinal abstractions of FM 100–20 (1943) decided the conduct of air-ground operations.[64]

Although airmen flew their missions as prescribed by the tactical air plan, they found relatively little action on D-Day and the week after the landing. General Weyland's XIX TAC pilots participated in the first two assignments, beach and convoy cover, by escorting troop carriers, flying area patrol missions, and providing top cover over the assault area. On D-Day they sighted only three enemy FW 190s and easily drove them off. The *Luftwaffe*'s failure to contest the landing demonstrated for all just how overwhelming Allied air superiority had become. General Quesada's IX TAC groups, meanwhile, handled interdiction and close air support responsibilities. Army–air cooperation, the airmen's fourth D-Day mission assignment, proved especially interesting. The Army submitted only 13 requests for air support on D-Day, and the controllers refused five. The missions fell almost evenly between armed reconnaissance against transportation targets and dive-bombing of coastal batteries and gun positions farther in shore. Significantly, none of these requests originated from the air support liaison officers assigned to the forward units. Left mostly to their own devices, aircrews quickly realized the difficulty of locating and attacking targets in Normandy where one hedge-row so often looked like another.

The USS *Ancon* remained the designated control facility until June 10 when control passed to IX TAC's 70th Fighter Wing headquarters, which had arrived the day before at Cricqueville (site A–2), three miles inland from Omaha beach. On June 9, IX TAC personnel also arrived to establish their advance headquarters next to First Army headquarters at Au Gay. Henceforth, IX TAC would control all flying in support of First Army in Normandy, even though Weyland's XIX TAC pilots would remain assigned to his command. By June 13 this advance command post began assuming operational control through the 70th Fighter Wing and its fighter control center, although pre-planned missions continued to be handled by Uxbridge.

The Allies took a major step during the night of June 17-18, 1944, when they authorized IX TAC to operate the air support communications and control net at Au Gay and First Army to establish the bomb line. This consisted of an imaginary line just in front of the ground forces. All flying attacks between the ground forces and the bomb line became close air support and required army coordination and close flying control. Now IX TAC and First Army planned and controlled air support missions on the continent, while Uxbridge allocated the tactical air effort and handled only those missions the continent-based joint headquarters deemed beyond their capability. Meanwhile, a few days earlier on June 10, 1944, General Quesada's IX TAC also assumed operational control of all Ninth Air Force units operating from bases in Normandy. General Weyland, for his part, remained in England to command IX Fighter Command, which retained operational control of IX and XIX TAC units in the United Kingdom until they established airstrips in France. This arrangement continued until the end of July. In keeping with preinvasion aerial plans, Normandy would be a IX TAC show, with Weyland's XIX TAC in a supporting role.[65]

This new control system received a major baptism of fire at Cherbourg, the port the Allies eagerly sought as a supply depot. On June 21, VIII Corps requested massive air support for its final assault on the fortress city. With less than 48 hours to prepare closely coordinated attacks, Generals Brereton and Quesada decided to send all available Ninth Air Force bombers and fighter-bombers against German strong points and fortifications in a large area south and southwest of Cherbourg on the afternoon of June 22. First Army and IX TAC officers selected the targets and planned the missions. Preceded by strikes from ten squadrons of British Second TAF aircraft, Ninth Air Force sent one group of fighter-bombers over the target area every five minutes for an hour to bomb and strafe targets that the army identified by colored smoke. Tactics included dive-, skip-, and glide-bombing from heights as low as 200 feet. Medium and light bombers followed for a second hour against pinpoint targets. Despite the effort on that day, VIII Corps made little progress and failed to capture the fortress until June 26. Additional P–47 missions on a much smaller scale continued against Cherbourg until it capitulated.[66]

Armorers attach a 500-lb. bomb to a Thunderbolt.

The airmen expressed more displeasure with these results than the ground leaders did. Although Ninth Air Force officials agreed that the June 22 attacks helped hasten the capture of the city by 48 hours, their after-action report described planning deficiencies, poor use of the tactical force, and an inordinately high cost in terms of pilots lost and equipment and ordnance expended. Airmen at Uxbridge had prepared detailed plans without specific target information or army representation, which meant that the large area selected for attack did not permit sufficient concentration of forces against specific targets. Furthermore, the aerial attack occurred without on-the-scene ground-to-air control, which resulted in targets being missed or otherwise ineffectively attacked. Moreover, fighter-bombers attacked fixed fortifications, which the report's authors considered poor targets for tactical aircraft. They questioned this use of air power as flying artillery.

When measured against the results, they declared that the cost of the Cherbourg aerial operation—25 aircraft lost and an additional 46 severely damaged—seemed excessive. If the air attacks shattered enemy morale, at least for a short period, Allied ground forces failed to attack swiftly enough to take advantage of that demoralization. Therefore, the report concluded, thought should be given to moving forward ground elements within 500 yards of the bomb line, regardless of the risk. Yet, the challenge of coordinating swift Allied ground attacks after airmen had softened up enemy positions would continue to bedevil planners throughout the campaign.[67]

The Cherbourg operation made absolutely clear that major air-ground operations required extensive, coordinated joint planning and execution under close control of air liaison officers assigned with ground forces. It left open the question whether the use of light tactical fighter-bombers employed against fortified positions could be justified in terms of damaging enemy morale, if they proved unable to do serious damage to the actual fortifications. In any event, as a consequence of Cherbourg, the tactical air command–army joint operations team gained immediate prominence as the central agency for planning and conducting air-ground operations in Normandy.

Air-Ground Support System Refined

Just a few short weeks after the Cherbourg operation, IX TAC and First Army established an effective air-ground mission request system based on FM 31–35 (1942) and the North African experience. It would serve as the model for Third Army and XIX TAC, and for other future tactical air-ground support operations in Europe. (**Chart 4** depicts the close air support request system as it functioned in mid-July 1944.) The key feature involved close coordination between air and ground representatives at every level. This was achieved by collocating army and tactical air command headquarters in the combat opera-

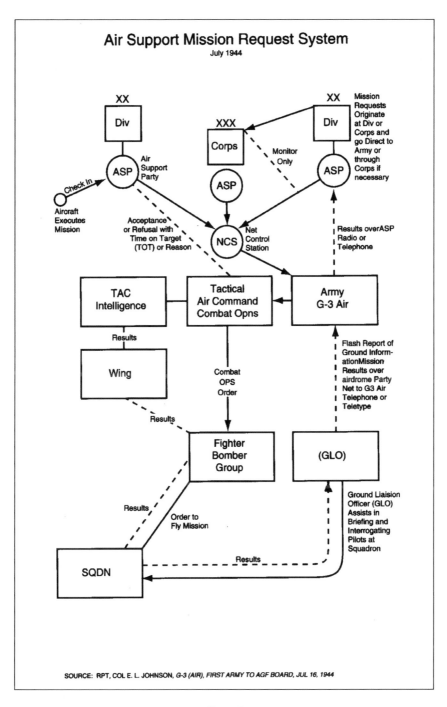

Chart 4
Air Support Mission Request System, July 1944

tions center, the nerve center directed by the tactical air command's combat operations officer. He worked side by side in a large tent with his army counterpart, the ground forces air intelligence officer, and his staff. Likewise, air intelligence personnel worked together to coordinate visual and photographic reconnaissance and artillery adjustment requests. Coordination continued throughout the system with air representatives, termed air support party officers, assigned to work with army air intelligence officials at all division and corps headquarters. Similarly, the army assigned ground liaison officers at wings, groups, and reconnaissance squadrons to work with their air force intelligence officer counterparts.[68]

This air-ground system is best understood by following the course of requests for preplanned and immediate air support missions.[69] As a rule, the army initiated preplanned requests at divisional level after discussion between the army operations officer and the air liaison officer; these two individuals determined the suitability of a given target for air action. The division request then went over army phone lines to corps headquarters, which acted as a monitoring or filtering agency responsible for analyzing specific requests for their impact on the overall corps situation. From the corps, the approved request travelled by means of an air force teleprinter or SCR–399 radio to the mobile communications van at the Joint Operations Center. A runner took the message to the army air operations officer assigned at the unit's combat operations center. The army representative went to the desk of the air combat operations officer and the two of them decided if the target could be attacked. If approved, they added it to the target list, which was presented at the regular evening joint air-ground briefing for operations the next day.

Meanwhile, the air force combat operations officer informed the requesting army unit through the air liaison officer radio net of the approved target and of the scheduled time of friendly aircraft over the target. If the target was not approved, the operations officer provided an explanation for its omission. After the evening briefing, the air combat operations officer prepared the operations order and sent it to a designated fighter-bomber group. There, the group operations officer normally selected the squadron to fly the mission and the type of ordnance to be used. Before the flight, the army liaison officer at that airfield briefed the pilots on the enemy situation, the location of the bomb line, and any features of interest to the air and ground forces.

A squadron of 12 fighter-bombers performed the basic close air support mission in Europe. Four flew top cover for the remaining two flights, each composed of four aircraft, which were assigned to dive-bomb the target. Before takeoff, the latter aircraft were bombed-up with two 500-lb. bombs each. About five minutes before the time-over-target, the flight leader checked in with the air support party officer at army corps or division headquarters on his SCR–522 VHF radio for any last-minute information on the target. The army marked these targets within the bomb line with colored smoke. After much experimentation, the air-ground teams eventually relied on red smoke as the best for visual identification. After their bombing runs, the pilots passed their visual reports to the air liaison officer at division or corps level; then all 12 aircraft either strafed in the target area or received permission to fly armed reconnaissance in enemy territory beyond the bomb line. After returning to base, both the air intelligence officer and the army liaison officer debriefed the pilots. The army liaison officer then sent a flash report by phone or radio to the army air section at the combined operations center. The air intelligence debriefing report went through air force channels to the wing and the Combat Operations Center, where it arrived approximately 30–60 minutes after the ground officer's flash message. The army air operations officer subsequently notified ground units of mission results.

Immediate request, or call, missions, were handled in the same manner but far more rapidly. Reconnaissance and fighter crews often spotted lucrative targets that required immediate attack. They passed the information to the operations center at division or corps level through either air liaison officer or wing command post channels, where army and air operations officers evaluated it. The tactical air command operations officer then either assigned designated alert aircraft to make the attack or diverted aircraft from a previous commitment to the newly chosen target. The latter often were airborne at the time. General Quesada estimated that immediate requests could be met by his aircraft within 60–80 minutes.

The request system and the entire air-ground joint planning effort turned on a joint meeting held each evening between key air and ground officers. In Normandy, Quesada normally attended these meetings; Bradley did so occasionally. The agenda and meeting format established by IX TAC and the First Army in July 1944 became the standard for joint American air-ground operations planning in the months that followed.[70] First, the weather officer analyzed weather for the next 24 hours both in England and in the prospective target areas in France. The air intelligence officer next assessed the past day's missions flown by IX TAC in support of army and Ninth Air Force requests. Then an army ground forces intelligence officer presented the previous day's enemy ground activities, including possible upcoming enemy action. The air intelligence officer returned to discuss targets based on intelligence obtained that day from visual and photographic reconnaissance reports, enemy prisoner interrogations, and a number of other sources. Based on this information, he suggested preplanned targets for the next day from the tactical air command viewpoint.

The army air operations officer then presented the Army's plan for ground operations the following day and submitted the target request list he had compiled from army corps requests. Normally, he also suggested retaining a small force of aircraft in reserve to meet immediate requests from corps and divisions. At this point, the air operations officer allotted tactical air command forces to the various missions identified in the meeting, on the basis of higher headquarters requests, the ground plan, the weather, enemy movements, and the availability of his air forces. After allotting these forces, the air operations section made flying group assignments for the various missions and this information was incorporated in the operations order sent to these units later that evening. The fighter control center located with 70th Fighter Wing headquarters at Criqueville performed flying control for all U.S. tactical aircraft.

Requests for reconnaissance missions functioned somewhat differently.[71] The divisions and corps submitted visual reconnaissance requirements to the army intelligence officer on duty at the Ninth Air Force combined operations center. To satisfy corps requirements, F–6 (P–51) reconnaissance aircraft flew the entire army front to a depth of 10–12 miles, four times daily. They also conducted regular visual reconnaissance in enemy territory to a depth of 200 miles. The air-ground team divided the area into three sectors to be flown four times a day. Pilots reported potential targets in the clear to the fighter control center by radio. These targets often became immediate requests. Army liaison officers with the air units also briefed and debriefed the reconnaissance pilots and passed the information on to the corps.

The camera-equipped F–5 (P–38) aircraft of the 67th Tactical Reconnaissance Group provided a variety of low-level photographic coverage of the target areas. In July 1944 they flew daily front line coverage to a depth of 10 miles to construct mosaics requested by the corps. They also performed automatic daily photoreconnaissance missions, which included covering specified airfields, marshaling yards, bridges, and targets that had been attacked previously. In addition to these and other pinpoint target requests, the F–6 aircraft furnished superb oblique photography requested by the corps headquarters for artillery adjustment missions. Army officers seldom complained about the quality of the aerial photography, but in the first few weeks they frequently found the delay in receiving it to be unacceptable.

The air-ground mission request system that operated in July 1944 might at first appear overly bureaucratic and involved. Initially, inexperience certainly produced its share of errors and delay. Nevertheless, observers in mid-July praised the system's effectiveness and observed that procedures adopted and equipment available had produced a level of competence and effectiveness that augured well for the campaign challenges ahead. Above all, the air-ground request system depended on the quality of the airmen and ground force personnel involved. To be sure, officers assigned to air-ground duty had to be skilled in the practices of their own service and familiar with air-ground procedures and methods. Beyond this, however, the influence exerted by an airman or a ground force officer involved in air-ground operations would disappear if he failed to understand or appreciate the other side's needs and concerns. Critical missions in support of ground forces, especially those missions that airmen judged the most dangerous, expensive, and least effective for tactical air forces to perform, depended on "teamwork, mutual understanding, and cooperation" among all of the affected air and ground officers.[72]

In the initial weeks of combat in Normandy, the leaders clearly did not always have the right people in the right positions. In one of the most perceptive reports on air-ground conditions in Normandy at this time, War Department observer Col. Edwin L. Johnson noted that First Army corps commanders relieved three of their four operations officers assigned to air-ground duty within two weeks of D-Day. Furthermore, the army replaced three of its 22 ground liaison officers assigned to duty with the air units. Although Johnson tactfully avoided discussing the reasons for the reassignments, evidence suggests that substandard abilities or poor attitudes accounted for the action. Why were these officers not identified and eliminated earlier? Perhaps only actual combat offered the opportunities for assessing personal abilities and for devel-

An F–5 with D-Day invasion markings.

oping effective procedures and creating the teamwork required to ensure successful joint operations.[73]

On the air side, available records do not show a similar turnover in air liaison officers assigned to army units in the first few weeks. Regardless, many had problems, if of a different sort. Numerous references allude to army commanders who seemed uninterested in and unwilling to accept advice from assigned airmen. A sizeable portion of this initial air liaison force consisted of nonflying observers and communications officers. However well qualified they might have been, they did not possess the credibility of rated pilots. By early August 1944, pilots filled most of the liaison officer billets, a solution made easier by a growing surplus of aircrew officers.[74]

Beyond the need for participants who understood the requirements of their air or ground counterparts, a number of other problems affected air-ground operations. The continental airfield construction program, for example, failed to meet established schedules. The IX Engineer Command's plan depended from the start on the progress of the Allied offensive, and bad weather and tenacious German resistance in the Normandy hedge-rows slowed the Allied advance. Moreover, supply channels operating from ship to shore and thence to proposed ALGs developed bottlenecks that seemed to defy all solutions. After the landing, planners also decided, correctly, that the overwhelming Allied air superiority called for more bases for fighter-bombers and fewer for fighters. That meant additional material had to be obtained to construct the longer runways for the heavier fighter-bombers (5,000 feet vs. 3,600 feet). The IX Engineer Command scheduled an ALG for each fighter-bomber group, with five to be completed by June 14, eight by the twenty-fourth, and twenty by mid-July. Although the engineers did not meet their schedule for June, by mid-July, only 45 days after the landing, they had 16 airfields completed in France. As of August 1, only two groups, including the XIX TAC's 36th Fighter-Bomber Group, continued to fly from British bases because French airstrips remained unfinished.[75]

For the air-ground program, these delays meant that many fighter-bomber groups—with their army liaison officers—operated from England well into July, where bad weather and overloaded communications channels often made the transmission of information to the ground force headquarters on the continent impossible. On the other hand, the engineers have been justly praised for their yeoman efforts under extremely challenging circumstances and changing requirements largely beyond their control. As an interim solution, the planners adopted the *roulement* system, whereby designated clutches of airfields received top priority for completion and servicing by mobile airdrome squadrons. In effect, these advance airfields became staging bases for several units pending completion of other, permanent airstrips. As a result of this novel policy, the XIX TAC was able to provide crucial air support to Third Army in its drive across France, even though the air bases remained as much as 300–400 miles behind the front lines.

**The flight leader of the 406th Fighter Group demonstrates both
the effectiveness and risk of low-level attack.**

Along with other air-ground operating problems that needed an immediate solution, airmen and their civilian research specialists experimented with a variety of equipment that became important in future operations. Among the more prominent, the ground-based SCR–584 radar was employed to control aircraft on blind bombing missions. Developed and used as a gun-laying radar, first at Anzio, Italy, in early 1944, its accuracy and potential for other functions led General Quesada to introduce it to guide aircraft that summer. Although achieving only limited success initially, it proved more effective after considerable experimentation in late fall under conditions of static warfare and bad weather.[76] In another first, P–47s dropped napalm bombs in the European theater on July 17 against camouflaged buildings near Coutances, France. The pilots reported a lot of smoke and the entire area ablaze. Napalm received its major test in the campaign to reduce the Brittany forts, after which it became a mainstay in the fighter-bomber arsenal employed against pillboxes, bunkers, and other enclosed fortifications.[77] In a final example of the use of new weapons, in mid-July the 406th Fighter Group's 513th Squadron installed five-inch high-velocity air-to-ground rockets. Developed by a research team at Caltech, an earlier model had been tested by IX TAC on ranges in England during the preinvasion period with little success. On the seventeenth, the squadron of 12 P–47s, mounting 48 rockets, tested the new weapon on the Nevers marshaling yard and achieved outstanding results against locomotives and rolling stock. Although the 406th's rocket squadron officially remained unpublicized well into August, German forces in Normandy came to fear its prowess. The 513th pilots, eventually known as XIX TAC's Tiger Tamers, gained a well-deserved reputation for destroying enemy armor with these rockets. Later in the campaign, Ninth Air Force authorized General Weyland to convert the remaining two squadrons in the 406th Group for rocket-firing ground support operations.[78]

Hedge-Row Fighting to a Breakout

During the so-called Battle of the Hedge-Rows in June 1944, Weyland's XIX TAC groups flew primarily interdiction missions as Allied air leaders mounted an extensive campaign to prevent major German reinforcements from reaching the French coast. These interdiction targets included the Seine and Loire rivers, rail and road bridges, marshaling yards, and supply dumps. Cherbourg proved to be the first major close air support operation for both IX and XIX TAC units. Thereafter, England-based units, directed by Weyland at IX Fighter Command's Uxbridge headquarters, focused on interdiction targets while, understandably, Quesada's IX TAC headquarters in Normandy directed the ground-support operation with fighter-bombers based mostly on the continent. Aircraft from both locations, however, continued to conduct the escort and beach patrol missions that pilots normally found the least challenging.[79]

By mid-July 1944, XIX TAC fighter-bombers had gained considerable experience flying from England and Normandy airfields to attack interdiction and close control targets. The more experienced 100th Fighter Wing groups arrived first on the continent, led by the 354th Pioneer Mustang Group, which was one of two tactical flying units that first deployed from England. By the middle of July, all four groups of the 100th Fighter Wing flew from Normandy landing strips under IX TAC operational control.[80]

The distinction between tactical interdiction and close air support, or cooperation, missions in Normandy was not always clear. The Ninth Air Force historian for example, identified attacks on bridges south of enemy positions at St. Lo on July 16 and 17, 1944, as air-ground cooperation rather than interdiction missions.[81] This example illustrates the difficulty of accurately assessing Phase II (interdiction) and Phase III (close air support) operations in Normandy and throughout the European Campaign. The AAF Evaluation Board made this point clear at the outset of its important postwar assessment of Phase III operations, stating categorically that "it is impracticable to distinguish in all instances between Second and Third Phase operations."[82]

Traditionally, evaluators have relied on the statistical records to measure the success or failure of tactical air power. Indeed, air operations in all theaters in World War II reveal a preoccupation among airmen with verifying and quantifying. Perhaps that reflected the larger issue of promoting the AAF's view of itself as a war-winning element with a grandiose postwar future. This is not to say that statistics are unimportant. Statistics, an Eighth Air Force report on tactical air operations in North Africa declared, provide a method for assessing mission accomplishment and serve to promote competition, better performance, and a sense of pride among fighter-bomber pilots.[83] Over-reliance on statistical evidence is, nonetheless, unwise. Tactical airmen in Europe found it impossible to compile accurate statistics regardless of their attempts at objectivity. "The results of individual interdiction missions are hard to assess," the Ninth Air Force historian observed, "and the assessment of the work done by the different types of planes employed is almost equally difficult."[84] Ninth Air Force mission records show that pilots often reported "unknown" damage to their targets or "no results observed." At the other extreme, pilots often made excessively favorable claims for their bombing prowess. More than likely, the truth lay in between. A Ninth Air Force report of aerial operations in France on July 29, 1944, reported fighter-bomber claims for 1,452 motor vehicles, 197 tanks, and 98 horse-drawn carts and wagons destroyed on traffic-congested roads. At the same time, however, the report conceded that "ground investigation of a portion of the roads subjected to attack indicated that, although inevitably exaggerated, such claims were not fantastic."[85]

Independent verification by ground forces or airborne reconnaissance seldom proved feasible, nor was it capable of providing absolute answers. Given the speed of the aircraft, the smoke often encountered in the target area, the flak menace, and visibility limitations under dive-bombing conditions, aircrew reporting of results could not be entirely accurate. Moreover, it often proved difficult to distinguish between damage caused by army artillery fire and fighter-bomber attacks. Weyland and other air force commanders recognized this dilemma early and made every effort to encourage aircrew accuracy and to verify pilot reports by means of reconnaissance photography and prisoner of war (POW) interrogations. Nevertheless, the problem of accurate reportage remained unresolved throughout the campaign in Northwest Europe.[86]

Even in instances when statistical evidence proved accurate and unequivocal, it remains questionable whether statistics represent an absolute means of determining tactical air power effectiveness. The effect of tactical air operations on the morale of both enemy and friendly troops was and is undisputed. German POWs repeatedly referred to the shattering effects that close air support had on morale, while Allied ground forces acknowledged that overhead friendly fighter-bombers were a real confidence builder. After the Cherbourg assault, for example, Ninth Air Force analysts concluded from enemy prisoner reports that "in any operation of this nature the morale effect is greater than the actual damage."[87] As the commander of the XIX TAC asserted following an air support mission in July, "the presence of our aircraft over the front line troops has had an immeasurable effect upon their morale. When our aircraft are over the front line the use of close in artillery and mortars by the enemy stops." Overemphasis on statistics could very well obscure the real significance of the morale factor.[88]

If tactical air power's effects could not be measured precisely, enemy and allied ground force leaders and their troops understood its impact well. They might sometimes refer to specific examples of physical destruction caused by tactical air, but they often described its psychological effects in demoralizing and disorganizing the enemy. Weyland recognized the psychological importance of air power and did not oppose sending fighter-bombers over a hesitant division to help it jump off. He also allowed his aircraft to patrol over ground forces to raise morale and keep the enemy's head down. Admittedly, overwhelming Allied air superiority allowed Weyland and his fellow airmen the luxury of flying morale missions without jeopardizing other responsibilities. Such missions always were frowned upon by more doctrinaire AAF officers who believed airpower should never perform functions best left to ground-force artillery units. Weyland, like Quesada and a host of other airmen in the tactical air commands, was a pragmatist on issues such as this and committed his forces in every way he believed they might support or improve Third Army's effectiveness in combat.

Leaders of XIX TAC spent much of July in Normandy on joint planning projects with Third Army personnel. The XIX TAC advance headquarters arrived on the continent on July 2 at Criqueville, which earlier was the home base for the 70th Fighter Wing (IX TAC's fighter control center) and the 354th Fighter Group. Three days later the forward echelon of Third Army headquarters arrived on Utah beach, and on July 6 its advance headquarters became operational under canvas approximately 15 miles south of Cherbourg, at Nehou. That very day, XIX TAC advance headquarters moved to join the Third Army headquarters' forward echelon at Nehou. Detailed planning for air-ground cooperation began immediately and continued during the complicated and lengthy three-week movement of army and air force operational and support units and personnel to the continent. Much of this planning involved establishing air-ground procedures, analyzing terrain for possible routes of advance, and allocating air support from fighter-bombers and reconnaissance aircraft.[89]

Third Army air intelligence personnel referred to this period in Normandy as a "command post exercise in realities."[90] Prior to August 1944, Third Army, like its XIX TAC counterpart, played a secondary role to the forces at the front. Yet, in addition to planning the forthcoming campaign with the XIX TAC airmen, Third Army sent two officers with knowledge of the air arm over to the IX TAC–First Army joint headquarters to gain experience under combat conditions. Also, a number of ground liaison officers already assigned to Third Army and Ninth Army worked with their First Army counterparts during June and July for the same reasons. The climax of joint training for XIX TAC and Third Army came on July 22, when Patton's command received a 12th Army Group directive for the Third Army's expected mission when it became operational. In response, Third Army and XIX TAC planners prepared an employment plan that became a two-day study for all concerned. Meanwhile, much depended on the results of Operation Cobra which was scheduled to begin on July 24.[91]

In contrast to the Cherbourg experience, Cobra resulted from meticulous joint planning and extensive efforts at coordination between Allied air and ground forces.[92] Cobra called for a concentrated air assault by both strategic and tactical air forces on German defensive positions concentrated in a 3,000 by 8,000-yard area between St. Lo and Periers at the foot of the Cotentin peninsula. The assembled aerial assault force consisted of 1,500 heavy bombers, nearly 400 medium bombers, and 15 groups of Ninth Air Force fighter-bombers. The object was to blast open a path for massed American ground forces to advance with four armored columns to the south and southwest where they could destroy and isolate enemy forces and break out of the Normandy beachhead.[93]

The difficulty of the earlier Cherbourg operation, the mounting of a successful ground offensive following an air assault designed to destroy and disorient the enemy without bombing friendly troops by mistake, impressed air and ground leaders. But as successful as Cobra eventually proved to be, it created what could be called a Cobra syndrome that would affect those who planned future ground offensives involving carpet-bombing near friendly troops. The tragic bombing of friendly troops by Allied heavy bombers flying at 12,000 feet produced a false start for Cobra on July 24. A second aerial effort on the twenty-fifth also caused substantial friendly casualties, including the former commander of Army Ground Forces (AGF), Lt. Gen. Lesley J. McNair, but it succeeded in destroying and disorganizing German forces. The next morning, VIII Corps' four mobile divisions massed along a one-division front, moved forward to exploit the gap in the enemy lines under the closest air-ground cooperative effort to date.

Quesada's adventure on the eve of this operation, when he obtained a Sherman tank and installed in it a VHF radio for communicating directly with aircraft, is now the stuff of Air Force folklore. Having proved his point to the satisfaction of Bradley, Quesada provided the lead tank in each armored column with a standard fighter-bomber SCR–522 radio, along with an experienced pilot to serve as an air controller. These air controllers then talked to continuing relays of fighter-bombers that had been dispatched to cover the advance of the columns throughout the day. Quesada's innovation in communications permitted what became known as armored column cover. This was the close air support helping to propel mobile armor operations in tactical warfare that would characterize the battle of France.[94]

Armored column cover succeeded immediately. At first, relay flights of four aircraft covered the advance of individual columns, sought out targets of opportunity, and struck those designated under the authority of the combat command commanders, directed by air force controllers. Coordination occurred entirely at the local level, with the IX TAC–First Army headquarters allocating air forces and identifying ground units to be supported. In three days, the air-ground team moved 30 miles and neared Avranches, southwest of St. Lo on the Gulf of St. Malo. The pace of advance convinced military planners to maximize the breakthrough and its opportunity for more rapid movement. They increased the force covering each armored column from four to eight aircraft. New flights arrived at hourly intervals to relieve those flights already operating in the target area. Although both IX and XIX TAC groups flew column cover missions in the drive beyond the St. Lo roadway, they performed other ground-support tasks, too. Designated squadrons remained on alert for immediate requests, while other units flew armed reconnaissance missions.[95]

With the American breakout proceeding so well, Patton grew restive. Officially, he and his Third Army had to wait until August 1, 1944, to enter the fray. At his urging, however, on July 28 Bradley named him acting Deputy Army Group Commander with operational command of all troops in the VIII Corps zone. This conformed to plans for VIII and XV Corps to operate under Third Army. For Weyland and Patton, the long wait had ended. The following day, on July 29, Weyland arrived from England and reviewed plans with Patton for operations scheduled to begin on August 1. Two days later both advance headquarters relocated to an apple orchard five miles northwest of Coutances. This would be the first of many joint moves as they prepared for mobile warfare on a grand scale.

In the past seven months, Weyland's and Patton's forces not only trained together, they fashioned an air-ground plan in which all could believe. At the same time, XIX TAC pilots and support personnel gained combat experience in support of the Allied landings in Normandy. During this period, the First Army–IX TAC air-ground team established a mission request and air-ground control system that worked. By the end of July 1944, air and ground personnel gained the necessary experience with procedures and equipment to fashion a very effective close air support system. Moreover, with an enemy now on the run and Allied air superiority well established, Weyland had every reason to feel confident. Yet, in the mobile warfare about to commence the air commander would face new air-ground challenges. To meet them, he would be forced to adopt and test new aerial practices that could not always be based on prior experience or doctrinal precepts.[96]

Chapter Three

The Battle for France

The battle for France created unprecedented challenges for Allied tactical air forces. Not even the famed mobile warfare in the deserts of North Africa could compare with the headlong dash of George Patton's Third Army from Normandy southeastward to the German border in the summer and fall of 1944. At the start of this campaign, O. P. Weyland and his staff could call on little combat experience beyond directing fighter-bomber operations from IX Fighter Command in England in June and July of 1944. Now, in France, Weyland decided how best to support Third Army in what quickly became a *blitzkrieg*. At one point in mid-September, the XIX TAC would perform a variety of missions at five different locations across a 500-mile front. To keep pace with and support Third Army, Weyland had to modify and adapt tactical air doctrine and conventional methods of communication and organization.

In all theaters of war, AAF doctrine called for centralized air control, for the concentrated use of air power, and for tactical missions flown in the prescribed order of air superiority, interdiction, and close air support. Yet these precepts, which applied most readily to positional warfare, failed in a fluid situation that called for selectively applying air power to support constantly moving ground forces dispersed over an expanding front. To direct aerial attacks on the enemy successfully in this kaleidoscopic environment, and to move and relocate air bases quickly, Weyland found it necessary to decentralize operations, disperse his forces, and delegate more authority to subordinates. In some cases he simply "threw away the book" and improvised as circumstances dictated. If the *Luftwaffe*'s weaknesses in 1944 permitted tactical airmen the flexibility to modify doctrine and improvise to solve operational problems, the demands of mobile warfare severely tested their solutions. In that testing, Weyland relied on the goodwill of the men in the air and on the ground, and on the good relationship already established between his command and the Third Army. In that relationship, cooperation and mutual respect became the keys to success for the XIX TAC–Third Army team.[1]

Exploiting the St. Lô Breakout: Blitz Warfare U.S. Style

On the morning of August 1, General Bradley met with General Patton and his staff and corps commanders to discuss how Third Army could best exploit the breakthrough which already found VII and VIII Corps troops moving forward 30 miles south of St. Lô. Having secured the base of the Cotentin peninsula at Avranches, Allied leaders realized their forces not only could swing west into Brittany and seize the Breton ports as planned, but by swinging east, they also could move around the German left flank toward the Seine River and Paris. Accordingly, Third Army received a three-part mission: first, drive south and southwest from the Avranches region to secure the Rennes and Fougeres area in eastern Brittany; second, turn west to capture the Brittany peninsula and seize the ports; and third, simultaneously prepare for operations farther to the east. To carry out this mission, Third Army gained the VIII and XV Corps on August 1, with the XX and XII Corps scheduled to become operational and join them on August 7 and 12, respectively. Under Maj. Gen. Troy H. Middleton, VIII Corps would exploit the breakthrough at Avranches and move westward into Brittany. While XX Corps, commanded by Maj. Gen. Walton H. Walker, readied its forces to move south later, Lt. Gen. Wade H. Haislip's XV Corps would push south toward Fougeres.

In this plan, XIX TAC's mission centered on supporting the VIII Corps' offensive with an initial force of three P–47 groups, the 358th, 371st, and 365th Fighter Groups, which at that time continued to operate under the control of General Quesada's 84th Fighter Wing. In early August, Weyland had no night fighter units and only one tactical reconnaissance squadron—the 12th Tactical Reconnaissance Squadron based at LeMolay in Normandy. The XIX TAC would receive additional flying groups based on the success of Patton's drive south and east.[2]

Maj. Gen. Troy Middleton, commander, VIII Corps, aboard the USS *Ancon*.

The first week of August set the tone for the first month and a half of mobile operations in France. Third Army and XIX TAC planners met on July 31 to confirm an earlier decision to move XIX TAC's advance headquarters with Third Army's forward command post during the forthcoming campaign. The emphasis on mobility began that day, when Patton announced that Third Army's command post would move immediately to a location five miles northwest of Coutances. Weyland agreed to join the army's command group at its new location the following day, on August 1. By late evening of the thirty-first, XIX TAC's advance headquarters was in place and ready for operations the next day. The air command's headquarters would move an additional four times during August and twice more in September. Shortly after midnight, Weyland called Ninth Air Force headquarters to declare his forces ready for operations and to review plans for the following day. It became a daily custom for the commander of the tactical air command to call General Brereton or, after August 6, Lt. Gen. Hoyt S. Vandenberg, his successor as commander of Ninth Air Force, on the Redline command net to discuss procedures, review the previous day's operations, and discuss the course ahead.[3]

During his conversation with General Brereton in the early hours of August 1, Weyland recommended reversing the locations of the 84th and 303d Fighter Wings. The latter, which arrived at Criqueville (A–2) from England on July 26, thus would be moved and positioned near Brucheville airstrip (A–16), 15 miles closer to the flying units it would control in Normandy when the command became operational (**Map 4**). The IX TAC's 84th Fighter Wing would maintain flying control of the three groups initially assigned to Weyland's command until the 303d Fighter Wing was in place and prepared to relieve the 84th. The XIX TAC's second wing, the 100th Fighter Wing, which had arrived at Criqueville earlier on July 4, would remain nonoperational until the command gained flying control of all assigned fighter groups. During mobile operations in France, the XIX TAC, unlike other commands, preferred to locate its fighter control center near wing headquarters and its airfields, rather than near the advance headquarters' combat operations center. Plans and directives originated at the combat operations center, but allocation of missions and flying control of the groups were wing responsibilities.

The XIX TAC's more decentralized organizational approach called for the wing, which the planners normally established between the advance and rear headquarters, to relay operational orders and reports to and from the flying groups and assist the rear headquarters. Rear headquarters handled administration, supply, training, and personnel matters. At the outset of the campaign, by making wing headquarters the center of the communications net, planners expected the XIX TAC advance headquarters to be able to move forward with Third Army's forward echelon headquarters and maintain communications to groups with a minimum of required new installations. As Weyland would soon learn, in the practice of mobile warfare, even more decentralization would be

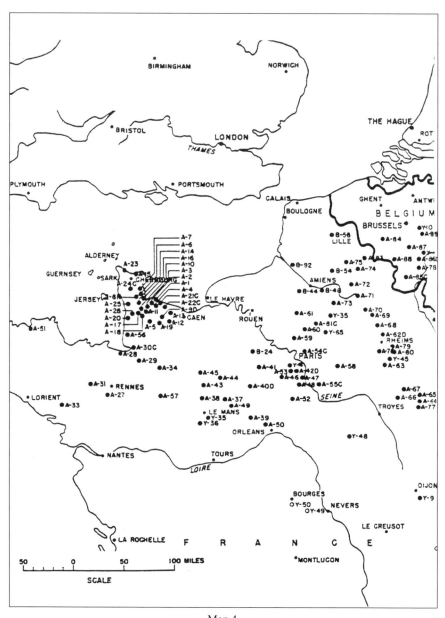

Map 4
U.S. Airfields in France, 1944-1945

Reprinted from: Rpt, AAF Evaluation Board, ETO, "Effectiveness of Third Phase Tactical Air Operations," pp. 327-328, AFHRA.

necessary if his advance headquarters was to keep up with Patton's headquarters *and* maintain reliable communications lines to his own forces.[4]

On August 1, 1944, however, Weyland faced other, more pressing command problems.[5] That day Ninth Air Force commander, General Brereton, left France for England to assume command of the First Allied Airborne Army. Before leaving, he called and informed Weyland that his deputy, Maj. Gen. Ralph Royce, would also be away temporarily and that Maj. Gen. David M. Schlatter would be setting up the Ninth's advance headquarters a few miles north of Coutances near the headquarters of the 12th Army Group. Consequently, Quesada, as commander of the IX TAC, would coordinate flying responsibilities and division of flying groups between the IX and XIX TACs. Quesada and Weyland could rearrange the wings as they saw fit without any need for formal orders. Anxious to have his own team in charge, after conferring with Quesada, Weyland assigned to the 303d Fighter Wing control over all XIX TAC fighter groups. That evening the 303d headquarters arrived near Brucheville (A–16) from Criqueville (A–2), to join the 84th Fighter Wing, which would remain there until it replaced Quesada's 70th Fighter Wing at Criqueville, when the latter moved south of St. Lô (**Map 4**).

During the initial week of combat operations, Weyland's command and control procedures evolved as his forces and responsibilities with Third Army grew. Only by August 8, 1944, when his command was at full flying strength with nine groups, did his two wings exercise extensive operational control. At least until mid-August, the 405th Fighter Group remained under IX TAC's 70th Fighter Wing for operational control. Early August would be a period of transition, one in which fighter-bomber groups moved from IX TAC to XIX TAC—and in some cases back again. The planners developed and refined organization and operational procedures in response to a growing Third Army and its requirements for ever greater tactical air support.

Although weather grounded Weyland's fighter-bombers in the morning of August 1, in the afternoon he sent the three groups covering VIII Corps on two types of missions. The 358th Fighter Group flew armed reconnaissance into the Brittany peninsula to explore the path ahead of VIII Corps' armored spearheads, while the 371st and 365th Fighter Groups provided cover for elements of the 4th and 6th Armored Divisions, respectively.

Armed reconnaissance normally involved squadron-size formations of eight or twelve P–47s armed with 500-lb. bombs and with armor-piercing incendiary .50-caliber ammunition for the aircraft's eight machine guns. The P–47s roamed well beyond the bomb safety line, the boundary within which all bombing was controlled by an air liaison officer. In enemy territory they searched for targets of opportunity, such as enemy troop concentrations or armored forces either fleeing or approaching the front lines. Patton's swift advance often caused the bomb line to change several times a day, frequently requiring pilots to update their maps while airborne.[6]

Crews arming P–47s with
500-lb. bombs and .50-caliber
ammunition.

The more highly publicized second tactical role, armored column cover (which was first used at St. Lô in conjunction with the Cobra breakout) became a standard feature of air-ground cooperation in the dash across France. General Weyland did not alter the original procedure significantly. He normally assigned one fighter group to each armored combat command and made it responsible for providing squadron coverage continuously during daylight hours. Air liaison officers attached to the armored columns controlled the missions either from tanks or other armored vehicles by means of SCR–522 VHF radio. Ordnance carried by the aircraft varied with the amount of enemy armor and German fighter opposition expected. In areas where enemy fighters were active, only a third of the aircraft were bombed-up. Where armor opposition was light, P–47 pilots carried fewer bombs and resorted to strafing attacks. The airmen considered strafing enemy forces the most effective form of attack during combat in France and German prisoners agreed.

It became common practice for Weyland's fighter-bombers to patrol as much as 35 miles in front of Patton's columns to search out and destroy potential resistance and keep the columns informed through the liaison officers of what lay ahead. The column cover force often performed armed reconnaissance in addition to a close air support mission, which made distinguishing between the two missions difficult for the statistical control section. Furthermore, the Third Army staff asked the airmen to report the location of the Third Army spearheads, which frequently outdistanced their own communications. In an air role reminiscent of the observation mission in World War I, it became customary for pilots to identify Allied ground units throughout the campaign, and the last section of the daily mission report listed all forward sightings.[7]

Because of the fluid tactical situation, close control and flexibility in planning became paramount. As a XIX TAC official observed, Patton quick-

An air-ground officer directs aircraft near the front lines (above);
a Ninth Air Force tactical liaison officer with the Third Army uses a radio
to direct fighter-bombers to enemy targets (below).

ly "turned the interdiction job inside out," requesting air power to prevent German troop movement out of, rather than into, the battle zone. In Brittany, for example, the fighter-bombers accelerated Third Army's rapid advance with column cover and armed reconnaissance missions, and thus prevented German counterattacks from developing. Crews for XIX TAC received explicit instructions not to destroy any bridges in the Avranches area, which already had become a bottleneck for Allied traffic. Except for the Breton ports, Patton's three armored columns bypassed any German strong points along the way that might impede the advance. If, as some critics have charged, Patton proved more adept at pursuit than destruction of the enemy's forces, it is hard to fault his tactics during the westward thrust in Brittany.[8]

For XIX TAC aircrews, Patton's *blitzkrieg* tactics meant that planning often took place in the cockpit while airborne, in response to swiftly chang-

**Night armed reconnaissance missions used tracers with
.50-caliber ammunition.**

ing requirements of Third Army troops. It also meant that tactical air power served as an air umbrella in highly mobile warfare, a coverage that FM 100–20 (1943) judged "prohibitively expensive" and effective only briefly and only in a small area. Doctrinal reservations aside, Weyland always defended his use of air cover for armored spearheads because the mobile warfare that Patton favored left too little time for artillery to be brought forward. Weyland and other tactical air leaders set aside established mission priorities in favor of a pragmatic response to mobile operations. General Weyland, however, would have been the first to agree that the existence of Allied air superiority, air power's first priority, made armored column cover possible by releasing large numbers of aircraft for close air support.[9]

At the end of August 1, 1944, the 4th Armored Division approached Rennes, 80 miles south of St. Lô. Its highly regarded commander, Maj. Gen. John S. "P" Wood, worried about a counterattack from a possible German column moving from the southwest. With XX Corps scheduled to move south through the Avranches bottleneck the next day, Weyland's forces found themselves stretched woefully thin because of commitments to cover the armored divisions and fly armed reconnaissance throughout Brittany and as far south as the Loire. Once again he contacted Quesada for support and received two additional fighter groups for the following day.

During the next four days of the Brittany Blitz,[10] between August 2–5, Patton's forces overran the entire Breton peninsula and laid siege to the port fortresses at St. Malo, St. Nazaire, Lorient, and Brest (**Map 5**). At the same time, XV and XX Corps moved rapidly south in the direction of the Loire River and swung east toward Paris. Ninth Air Force increased the aircraft in General Weyland's force accordingly. On August 2, he received the 363d Tactical Reconnaissance Group, the command's second P–51 group, and the 405th P–47 fighter group, which would gain a reputation as one of the Allies' top close air support groups. By this time, the 303d Fighter Wing had assumed responsibility from Quesada's 84th Fighter Wing for administration and control of the five XIX TAC groups and the command's fighter control center. Ninth Air Force's schedule of operations for August 2 reflected the rapidly changing situation as well as the flexible nature of tactical air power. It contained a long list of specific assignments for each of General Quesada's IX TAC groups supporting First Army. Weyland's five groups, however, could be assigned targets entirely "at the discretion of the CG [commanding general] of XIX TAC." The first stage of mobile warfare already compelled the air leaders to decentralize operational control.[11]

A host of problems had to be solved during the first week of August. The shortage of air support officers for ground units led the list. The very first request Weyland received on August 1 was a plea from VIII Corps to find two additional liaison officers for Brig. Gen. Herbert L. Earnest's Special Task Force A, preparing to attack along Brittany's north coast. One air support officer per armored division had proved insufficient because of the division's practice of creating combat commands or special task forces in pursuit operations. Because the air liaison function had not been included in the original personnel authorizations, the tactical air commands had to assign liaison officers to the ground units from their own organizations. Weyland managed to do this on August 1. Yet on the third, he needed to find three more officers for XV Corps' 5th and 7th Armored Divisions and its 28th Infantry Division. Faced with a shortage of experienced candidates at the time, he asked General Quesada for help, and IX TAC immediately supplied the needed officers. A

**Maj. Gen. John S. Wood,
Commanding General,
4th Armored Division.**

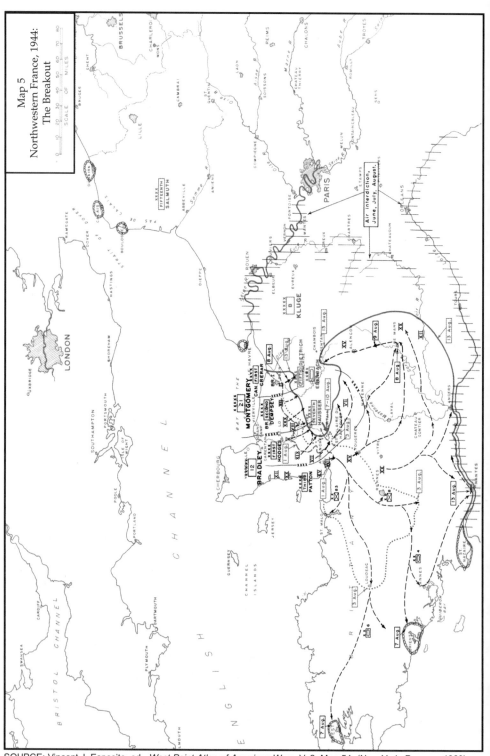

Map 5
Northwestern France, 1944:
The Breakout

few days later Weyland returned the favor, providing IX TAC additional air support needed to blunt a dangerous German counteroffensive at Mortain.[12]

Enemy night flying operations presented another challenge. Maj. Gen. Hugh J. Gaffey, Third Army chief of staff, approached Weyland on August 3, 1944, with a request for nighttime air cover for the Pontorson Bridge over the Sée River and for dams and roads in the Avranches area to quell nuisance nighttime shelling by the Germans in Northwest Europe. As in North Africa, night combat capability would prove a key weakness of Allied air forces throughout the campaign. Without a night fighter squadron, Weyland could only request that Ninth Air Force provide one as soon as possible. The Ninth responded by assigning one of IX Air Defense Command's two P–61 night fighter squadrons to cover this Third Army area of operations. Later in the campaign, when the *Luftwaffe* threat declined further, the air leaders would assign night fighters directly to the tactical air commands, where they increasingly flew interdiction rather than air defense missions.

Initial air-ground coordination also proved a problem. Several times during the first week of August, crews flying column cover for the 4th Armored Division in the St. Malo area complained that they could not contact the air liaison controller with the division. Officers at XIX TAC traced the problem to an overloaded C-channel, which pilots and the controllers used for all air-ground communications. Lieutenant John J. Burns of the 371st Fighter Group recalled that C-channel, despite being designated as the squadron channel, turned out to be a common channel for all of Ninth Air Force once close air support began in earnest. As a solution to the communications congestion, General Weyland's operations officers designated each of four channels for a specific function. They also encouraged better radio discipline whereby flight leaders would contact the ground station only when nearing the head of the column. Air-ground communications problems in Brittany declined significantly once the command introduced these procedures.[13]

As Patton's forces swept forward, Weyland had to move his headquarters, which involved relocating the advance headquarters' tents, vehicles, and communications and other equipment. On August 2, Third Army moved its forward echelon command post 11 miles north of Avranches, and XIX TAC followed suit the next day. That same morning, Weyland conferred with Ninth Air Force officers about constructing a clutch of airfields for the XIX TAC farther south in the Rennes area where the command could support ground offensives in the direction of Brest or eastward, depending on how events unfolded. General Royce wanted to send in engineers immediately and Weyland had to remind him that the area remained unsecured. The XIX TAC commander always coordinated airfield sites with the Third Army staff, and that evening General Gaffey concurred in the Rennes plan as well as in a proposal to establish a rearming and refueling strip near Avranches. Enemy activity and supply delays, however, prevented the engineers from beginning this work until August 7.

The IX Engineer Command's 2d Engineer Aviation Brigade (Provisional) handled airfield construction and maintenance for Weyland's command.[14] Normally its commander, Col. R. E. Smyser, Jr., would assign one of his aviation battalions to develop a single advanced landing airstrip with a runway 5,000 feet long and 120 feet wide. Understandably, the time required to complete the field depended on the site's initial condition. A new airfield normally took nine or ten days to complete, but the tactical air command's maintenance officers cautioned that the engineers tended to be over-optimistic by two or three days. Although the engineers refurbished former German airstrips that featured sod or concrete runways, Weyland preferred prefabricated bituminous prepared Hessian surfacing[15] for new runways during the good summer weather and Patton's rapid sweep east. A Hessian surface airstrip, which could be finished in about ten days, provided a firm, smooth, relatively dust-free surface and proved usable immediately after a rainstorm.

While the engineers worked on new airfields, the command's supply and maintenance officers located at the rear headquarters arranged through Ninth Air Force's Service Command to prestock these fields with ammunition, fuel, and other supplies. With the short distance from Normandy to the Rennes area, truck transportation and road congestion proved a lesser problem than the one that developed later, when the rapid drive eastward created severe bottlenecks and transport shortages. Normally, XIX TAC engineers considered a field operational after the runway and one taxiway had been completed. At this time, airdrome personnel, the real nomads of Ninth Air Force, arrived to rearm and service the aircraft until the fighter group's ground echelon arrived. Unlike British fighter squadrons, XIX TAC groups had their own maintenance personnel assigned to perform routine aircraft maintenance functions. The services of the command's two airdrome squadrons proved especially valuable for *roulement* operations, whereby a series of advanced landing strips could be used temporarily by squadrons whose home bases often remained far to the rear. This procedure increased the command's mobility, considerably extending the operational flying range of its units.[16]

As the XIX TAC prepared for its move to the Brittany airfields, Patton's forces already had advanced rapidly south and east. By August 5, 1944, XV Corps captured Mayenne, 20 miles east of Fougeres, and pushed on to Laval further south (**Map 5**). Patton's tactical interests lay clearly to the east, in the direction of Germany, not to the west in Brittany, which he had instructed VIII Corps to overrun with a minimum of force. He remained ambivalent about the need to "reduce" the French ports that proved so difficult to assault, yet which earlier seemed so essential as Allied supply bases for the campaign in Northwest Europe.[17]

The two commanders exchanged opposing views on this issue of fortified positions on August 5, when Patton requested aerial attacks on German gunboats that threatened his flank at St. Malo. Weyland declined to send fighter-bombers against such targets after learning that on the previous day the 358th Fighter Group had encountered extremely heavy flak from nearby pillbox defenses and ships in the harbor at St. Malo. Patton, perhaps mindful of the "short bombing" at St. Lô during Operation Cobra, did not want to call on heavy bombers, so Weyland requested medium bombers from Ninth Air Force. At the same time, the air force command also provided the night cover over the road south of Avranches that he requested on behalf of Third Army. This became Weyland's method of supporting Third Army operations: he supplied fighter-bombers whenever he believed the request sound, but otherwise he would refuse them and turn to Ninth Air Force for help with medium bombers. While conferring with Ninth Air Force leaders about medium bombers for Third Army, General Weyland received the good news that the 36th Fighter Group, flying P–47s at Brucheville, site A–16, (**Map 4**) had joined his command. Curry's Cougars, a favorite of his and the last of his original XIX TAC units to arrive from England, rapidly became a favorite of Patton's too, as attested by the letters of commendation and numerous references to shipments of Cointreau liqueur to the 36th Fighter Group from Third Army.[18]

Weyland had to have been pleased with the first five days of "Blitz warfare, U.S. style."[19] Despite the problematic nature of bomb damage assessment statistics, his groups tallied an impressive score of interdiction and close support target claims at a cost of only three aircraft lost. Armed reconnaissance and armored column cover missions clearly proved ideally suited for mobile operations, while the air-ground support system eliminated initial communications problems and continued to improve. He also could effectively command his forces and keep pace with Third Army's advance echelon. Planning was underway for his groups to displace forward, and maintenance and supply experienced no difficulty providing support. Although he dealt with many issues through established organizational channels, informal discussions with Patton and his staff often proved highly effective. With the combat situation changing almost hourly, informal decision-making and flexibility became essential to air operations.

As XIX TAC aircraft ranged south of the Loire—far ahead of the Third Army spearheads to the east—and west into Brittany in support of VIII Corps, General Weyland encountered growing command and control difficulties. While Patton needed to remain as close as possible to his advancing columns to oversee operations at the front, Weyland's focus shifted in the opposite direction. His operational capability depended increasingly on the aviation engineers who built new airfields and on the signals experts who provided his communications net. In numerous respects, the air arm became more ground based than were the ground forces. Command and control under these conditions would prove to be Weyland's greatest challenge and one he never completely mastered during the mobile phase of operations.

Army engineers handled airfield construction and maintenance for Weyland's advancing aircraft squadrons, laying steel mesh for emergency landing strips (top), and on occasion broom-massaging the airstrips (bottom).

Aviation engineers used heavy equipment in preparing fields for landing aircraft (top). They were also called upon to repair damage following enemy bombardment: this engineer battalion worked with air hammers on a bomb crater left by a 500-lb. bomb (bottom).

Mechanics hoist a severely damaged P–47 onto a trailer to be stripped of all usable parts (top); only a few miles behind enemy lines (right), these soldier-technicians are refueling, rearming, and checking planes for the next mission.

On a German airfield captured by the Allies, a mechanic checks out a P–51 Mustang.

A crane is used to transfer bombs from storage to be mounted beneath
the wing of a P–47 (top); and at a French railroad station, airmen load
crated bombs onto trucks destined for Ninth Air Force airstrips (bottom).

Supporting Patton's End Run to the Seine

On the Allied side, General Bradley's decision to allow Patton to operate in Brittany with minimum forces led to a major change in Allied strategy that took advantage of collapsing German positions.[20] In light of Third Army's initial success, on August 4, 1944, Allied ground forces commander General Montgomery, with General Eisenhower's approval, directed the Allied armies to strike east in force to destroy the German Seventh Army west of the Seine. Accordingly, while most of Patton's forces attacked to the east, First Army troops moved toward the road centers of Vire and Mortain while the British would attack toward Argentan, and the Canadians in the direction of Falaise (**Map 5**). The Germans, meanwhile, had not remained indifferent to the growing threat of encirclement. Back on August 2, Hitler directed Field Marshal Guenther von Kluge, his commander in chief in the west, to counterattack the Allies at Mortain with eight of the nine Panzer divisions available in Normandy. By doing so, Hitler hoped the *Wehrmacht* could reach the coast, regain Avranches, isolate Patton's army, and then move north to destroy the beachhead. If successful, the Germans could reestablish the conditions of static warfare that proved so successful during June and July. Von Kluge planned to attack by August 6 or 7.[21]

As Third Army's XV Corps prepared to encircle the German Seventh Army in the Mortain area from the south during the second week of August, XIX TAC assumed other support functions and expanded to its full complement of nine groups. On August 6, Ninth Air Force leaders decided to increase XIX TAC's striking power by dividing the fighter-bomber groups equally between the two tactical air commands. Until then most had been flying under IX TAC control. Ninth Air Force officers informed Weyland that XIX TAC would have operational control of the following nine groups beginning on August 7: the 36th, 373d, 406th, 371st, 405th, 354th, 358th, 362d, and 363d.[22] These comprised the command's original 100th and 303d Fighter Wings, now supplemented by the 371st and 405th P–47 groups. Weyland was particularly pleased to gain the 354th, a crack Mustang fighter group, and the 406th Fighter Group, whose rocket-firing 513th P–47 squadron had performed so effectively against tanks during the St. Lô breakout. At the same time, Weyland sought to simplify command and control procedures by having only one wing, the 303d, control all of these groups until the units moved to new airstrips farther afield.

On the evening of August 7, 1944, Weyland met with General Gaffey and other members of the Third Army staff to discuss the growing threat of a German counterattack, which they expected to occur east of Avranches near Mortain (**Map 5**). The XIX TAC aircrews had been overflying the Avranches bottleneck on return flights since August 2, and were keeping Third Army well informed of German concentrations developing in the Mortain area. After the meeting on the seventh, Weyland called Quesada, whose IX TAC held primary responsibility for the area threatened, and offered to divert his fighter-bombers to the crisis area at any time, and place them under the control of Quesada's command. Three Panzer divisions did, in fact, attack early the following morning and the IX TAC commander called to accept the offer. He asked only for the 406th's rocket squadron and P–51s for top cover. During the day's fighting, the XIX TAC pilots claimed 18 enemy aircraft shot down and much German ground equipment destroyed.

By August 7, 1944, General Walker's XX Corps units had reached the Loire River and began moving east. The XIX TAC now began its celebrated airborne "watch on the Loire," although it is not clear precisely when Patton requested Weyland's forces to guard his flank or when the air commander responded that he could do so, providing he had good weather. Patton did not worry too much about the exposed southern flank of the Third Army, noting in his diary that "our air can spot any group of enemy large enough to hurt us and I can always pull something out of the hat." Weyland's forces had been flying armed reconnaissance in the Loire region since August 2, and the 12th Tactical Reconnaissance Squadron had been doing the same. Once his fighter-bomber groups and the 10th Photo Reconnaissance Group moved into the Rennes and Le Mans areas in mid-August, the 10th added to the schedule a daily photo reconnaissance milk run over the Loire by A–20s of the 155th Night Photo Squadron. The watch on the Loire became a fixture on the mission charts well into September as Patton's southern flank grew to nearly 500 miles long— from Brittany in the west to the Mosel River in eastern France.[23]

On August 8, 1944 the Third Army command post moved again, this time to St. James, eight miles northwest of Fougeres (**Map 5**). The principle of collocating headquarters for joint operations continued when Weyland joined Patton the same day. Weyland left the command's B-echelon in place with the fighter control center under Colonel Ferguson at Beauchamps, the previous site above Avranches, until he could be assured of effective communication. He had good reason for concern. The following morning he learned that during the evening the enemy had sabotaged his land lines, normally the most reliable and secure means of communication, in what would become common practice in the days ahead. Wire and signal equipment shortages also contributed to the communication problem. Although Weyland could contact Ferguson by VHF radio, the situation proved far from ideal. The commander of the tactical air command vowed his advance headquarters would never again outrun its landline communications net to its forces. Meanwhile, Colonel Ferguson's small echelon, which had been left behind, maintained contact with the groups and controlled air operations.[24]

For Weyland and his staff, the best solution seemed to be to move the fighter-bomber groups forward to the Rennes area below the fighting at

Avranches and closer to Third Army's front line divisions that most needed air support. Being closer to the front lines would provide less flying time en route and, consequently, more time over target. Furthermore, the weather in Brittany was better because it did not suffer as much from the fog and mist of Normandy that often restricted flying in the mornings. Much of General Weyland's time during the second and third weeks of August involved arrangements for moving to the Rennes sites as quickly as possible. By August 11, the engineers had repaired the concrete runway at Rennes (A–27) and the sod field at a second German site, Gael (A–31) (**Map 4**). The 354th and 362d Fighter Groups and 100th Fighter Wing moved in that day, with the 12th Tactical Reconnaissance Squadron due at Rennes the next day. Conditions proved far from ideal at these new airfields. The 354th complained about the rough surface at Gael and Weyland agreed with their assessment when he visited there a few days after the field became operational. He also disapproved of the hordes of civilians on the field and he took steps to alleviate both hazards. With communications now secure, he decided to move the command's B-echelon down to St. James to consolidate operational control at advance headquarters once again. The fighter control center would remain with the 303d Fighter Wing at Beauchamps until it could be brought forward to the Le Mans area.

General Weyland had suggested Le Mans as the next site for forward airfields during a Ninth Air Force commander's conference on August 9. At that meeting he asked for a microwave early warning (referred to as MEW) radar, the new, large, 60-ton ground radar that could track and control intercepts of enemy aircraft and control friendly airplanes out to distances of 200 miles, well beyond the range of conventional forward directional post radar. General Quesada's command obtained one of the five existing MEW radars for use in Normandy ten days after D-Day. Although Ninth Air Force possessed a second radar, it remained in England to assist in defending against the V–1 flying bombs, which the Germans began launching against England on June 13, 1944. Weyland declared that he, too, needed a MEW radar in view of not only the renewed German air threat associated with the Mortain buildup, but also XIX TAC's widening range of reconnaissance missions. A lack of early warning, he argued after suffering the loss of several aircraft, was "costing planes, crews, ground soldiers, and equipment."[25]

Civilian technical experts in the European theater took a contrary position. Radar, they argued, played a rather small role in the battle of France because of the speed of the advance and the good weather. Pilots normally could navigate to their targets even when out of range of fighter control sets, while the sets themselves generally lacked organic transport and were not very sturdy. Although these reasons were doubtless valid, General Weyland, aware how important General Quesada considered the new radar, remained convinced of the requirement. In fact, IX TAC had the only available MEW radar, which it credited with playing a large role in helping its fighters destroy 160 enemy aircraft from D-Day to the beginning of September. General Weyland failed on four different occasions to obtain the MEW radar, but in the third week of September he succeeded. The XIX TAC received a set for its newly formed provisional tactical control group in the Metz area just in time for the Lorraine Campaign.[26]

It is difficult to precisely evaluate XIX TAC's effectiveness during the second week of operations. In terms of statistics, its groups continued to add to their impressive totals of enemy targets destroyed and damaged, while mission and sortie rates set record highs. These became the first of the heady days of Third Army's headlong advance that often averaged 20 miles a day. During the drive, Weyland's airmen flew column cover for the armored spearheads moving east while continuing to support ongoing operations in Brittany, and other patrols roamed well beyond Paris searching out the *Luftwaffe* in the air and the *Wehrmacht* on the ground.

A number of special days stand out in the record-setting operation. On August 7, the *Luftwaffe* appeared in force for the first time since August 1, and according to pilot reports of the ensuing engagements, it lost 33 aircraft. Significantly, the 36th Fighter Group claimed six after the ground controller released its aircraft from covering the XV Corps and vectored them to Chartres airfield following a reconnaissance pilot's report that he spotted enemy aircraft at that site. This type of reconnaissance and fighter-bomber teamwork would continue to improve in the weeks ahead. On another occasion, the 362d Fighter Group demonstrated in missions east of Paris that, contrary to conventional wisdom, strafing with .50-caliber guns proved effective against tanks attacked from the rear (which housed the engine compartment). On August 8, during their third mission of the day, the P–47 pilots attacked seven Panzer tanks, claiming three destroyed and four damaged, before proceeding on to other lucrative targets. Nevertheless, the 362d would have to work much harder to top the 406th Fighter Group's 513th squadron, the Tiger Tamers, which consistently led the command in claims of Nazi armor damaged and destroyed.[27]

Tactical air power demonstrated flexibility in other ways as well. When General Gaffey asked Weyland to see whether the 4th Armored Division, which had moved beyond its HF and FM communications range of headquarters, required help, Weyland obtained the information needed through his air liaison communications net (it was between 20–25 miles from Brest at the time) and notified army headquarters. General Patton also often asked the air arm to check out suspected counterattacks, which Weyland did with alacrity, scrambling or diverting aircraft to the target area. If the threat did not require immediate attention, he responded by sending a reconnaissance plane to have a look, and then followed it with fighter-bombers if necessary. In short, XIX TAC provided Patton an on call, close air supporting service.[28]

General Patton harbored no doubts about the effectiveness of his air support. Characteristically, following a visit from RAF Air Chief Marshal Arthur

Tedder, General Spaatz, and other prominent airmen on August 9, General Weyland recorded in his diary that Patton seemed "well satisfied" with the support of XIX TAC. A less happy aspect of the meeting, however, found these officers expressing renewed interest to Weyland in the seizure of Brest and other Brittany ports in the near future. Patton and Gaffey discussed this prospect with Weyland that evening over drinks. Neither the Third Army leaders nor Weyland were enthused over the prospect of static, siege warfare. The air commander knew that fixed fortifications represented some of the most difficult and dangerous targets for fighter-bombers, and his later evaluations of XIX TAC operations invariably stressed this point. Cherbourg should have been proof enough for those in doubt. On the other hand, tests at the AAF's Proving Ground Command at Eglin Field, Florida, in January and February 1945, demonstrated that fighter-bombers with 1,000-lb. bombs stood the best chance against the hardened defenses of the V–1 and V–2s. In the case of Brest, Spaatz and Tedder clearly reflected the views of General Eisenhower's headquarters, and although expressing reservations, Weyland "agreed to render ourselves [XIX TAC] available." It is likely that Patton later wished he had argued Weyland's case with the senior airmen.[29]

On August 11, 1944, with the encirclement of the German Seventh Army near Argentan well underway from the south, General Patton ordered units of XV Corps to push on toward Falaise after the capture of Argentan. The XIX TAC supported the offensive with 36th and 362d Fighter Groups' P–47s, which provided day-long air coverage of the advancing columns. Both Patton and Weyland looked forward to a crushing victory. At the same time, Weyland's forces continued to support the other, ever-widening Third Army fronts: in the east toward the Seine, in the west in Brittany, and in the south along the Loire.[30]

Between August 12–19, the Third Army and the XIX TAC attempted to close what their historians referred to as the Argentan Trap. On August 8, the day after the German counterattack began, General Bradley proposed that First Army hold at Mortain while units of First and Third Armies moved north to meet advancing Canadian and British forces, thereby preventing a German escape to the Seine. Bradley worried that Patton's force of four divisions might be too weak to halt the German retreat, while a failure to establish a clear meeting between the converging American and Canadian troops could result in confusion and much loss of life. Consequently, in one of the war's most controversial decisions, on August 13, Bradley ordered Patton to halt XV Corps' drive and hold near Argentan. Yet when the Canadian drive stalled at Falaise on August 16, a 15-mile gap remained between the two Allied lines. With the jaws of the trap open until August 20, an estimated 50,000 German troops escaped eastward through the so-called Argentan-Falaise gap. Eventually this force would join 200,000 additional German soldiers west of the Seine and the Allies would be unable to prevent their crossing. Patton, meanwhile, received permission from Bradley to send part of the XV Corps to the Seine in an additional attempt to encircle retreating German forces.[31]

The *Luftwaffe* could do little to assist the pell-mell German retreat. Despite using between 30–40 night fighters and bombers in operations against Allied ground targets, close support of German Seventh Army forces proved nearly nonexistent. By mid-August 1944, German air leaders could muster only 75 single-engine fighters for daily operations on the western front. Although the *Luftwaffe* could still achieve a figure of 250 sorties on August 15, this sortie rate could not be sustained despite reinforcements that allowed for several full-scale efforts of 250–300 sorties per day later in the month. The rapid Allied advance forced the *Luftwaffe* to abandon bases in France for more secure, more distant sites in Belgium. By the end of August, the *Luftwaffe*'s single-engine fighter force in Northwest Europe totaled only 420, 110 of which flew from French bases. Equally alarming, accumulated losses and insufficient training of new pilots after early 1944 resulted in a largely inexperienced force that found itself generally outmatched by Allied aviators. Pilots for XIX TAC reported the *Luftwaffe* now preferred to attack only when it clearly outnumbered its opponent, but the inexperience of the *Luftwaffe* pilots still gave the Allies the upper hand.[32]

With Allied troops holding the shoulders of, and causing severe losses within, the Mortain-Falaise-Argentan pocket, tactical air had good hunting as the Germans felt compelled to clog the roads even in daylight in their desperate attempt to flee. For XIX TAC pilots, though, the opportunity proved less rewarding than they desired. The Ninth Air Force had established boundaries that focused Weyland's forces on protecting Patton's right flank, where they could "blast away at armored columns east and south of Paris." One can appreciate the dismay of Curry's Cougars, who watched other Ninth Air Force units line up for what became known as harvest time in Argentan on August 17.[33]

Weyland, meanwhile, faced a major crisis in joint operations. The dilemma first appeared on August 11 when General Gaffey, Third Army chief of staff, recommended moving the two command posts forward to Le Mans. Weyland quickly rejected the idea because the site farther east would not be situated along the north-south communications axis of 100th Fighter Wing or near the proposed location of the 303d Fighter Group (**Map 5**). If Third Army moved directly to Le Mans, he said, XIX TAC would have to operate there with a liaison detachment. He suggested Laval as the next location instead. Both air and ground advance headquarters moved to Laval the following day, on August 12, with Weyland finally directing Colonel Ferguson's B-echelon to deploy to St. James. So far so good. Then, given the rapid pace of his sweep to the east, Patton announced that Third Army's forward echelon had to move to the Le Mans area on the fourteenth. The army commander had little choice. Spearheads by XII Corps had already reached Orleans, while XV Corps arrived earlier at Argentan, and then sent several units toward the Seine. Meanwhile, XX Corps was moving rapidly toward Chartres. In the west, VIII Corps continued to struggle against the Brittany ports while keeping a modest ground watch on the Loire (**Map 6**).

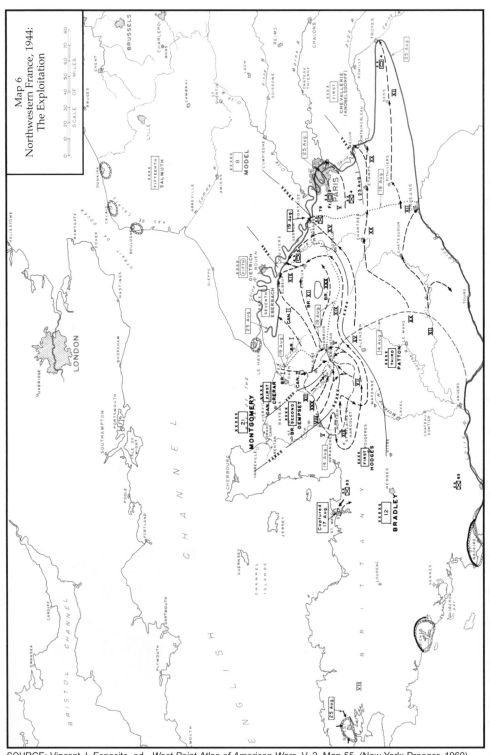

Map 6
Northwestern France, 1944:
The Exploitation

Weyland explained that he could not join Patton immediately in Le Mans and still retain effective control of his forces. The Army commander agreed that XIX TAC's advance headquarters should not move without adequate communications for command and control. Weyland's makeshift solution was to move deputy chief of staff Colonel Thompson, another officer, and a small signals unit to the Third Army's command post as the air command's so-called X-Ray detachment.[34] This plan called for Thompson's unit to link the two headquarters through a single cable that had been rushed forward, while retaining the air liaison party VHF radio net as backup. The X-Ray detachment performed a liaison function only; control of operations remained with General Weyland at the forward echelon in Laval. The headquarters B-echelon, which controlled the fighters, also would move to Laval from St. James as soon as effective communications could be established. Now XIX TAC had four separated headquarters elements—rear headquarters at Nehou and three advance headquarters echelons at St. James, Laval, and Le Mans—an example of tactical air's flexibility in Europe. Contrary to the emphasis on centralization called for in air force doctrine, highly mobile operations demanded ever greater decentralized control of the supporting air resources.

To accommodate this decentralization, the Third Army staff split its air operations section into two echelons as well.[35] The army's air operations officer and the administrative echelon remained with Patton's forward command post. There, the air operations officer posted the daily air situation for General Patton, coordinated missions for army support, and kept the ground echelon that remained located at XIX TAC's combat operations center apprised of General Patton's wishes and intentions. For his part, Colonel Thompson kept General Weyland informed of the army's intent. Even so, Weyland normally

The Chateau near Laval that served as the command post for Weyland's rear headquarters.

flew from Laval to Patton's command post in Le Mans every other day to confer personally with Third Army's staff. The decentralized system eventually functioned reasonably well, but at the start it faced major problems.

With decentralization there is always a tendency among the components, in the friction of war, to act independently. Effective command and control in these circumstances become more difficult to ensure. General Weyland immediately confronted this challenge. It is not entirely clear whether Third Army's air intelligence and operations officers at Le Mans bypassed only Weyland at Laval, or how much coordination they carried out with Colonel Ferguson at B-echelon's location in issuing orders to air units, but in Weyland's view they misused the system. This struck at the core of AAF doctrine on control of air power and General Patton's agreement with his air commander. Two days after moving to Le Mans, on August 16, Weyland visited Third Army headquarters and met with assistant chief of staff Maj. Gen. H. R. Gay (Patton and Gaffey were away at the time) and the Army air intelligence and operations officers. Afterward, he reflected, we "straightened out the confusion" of Army intelligence (G–2, Air) and Army operations (G–3, Air) officers who had been "laying on missions direct." Weyland clearly felt compelled to make his highly decentralized air command and control system function effectively—under the air commander's direction.[36]

By August 16, 1944, elements of the Third Army reached the Seine, and spearheads had moved within nine miles of Paris's western suburbs. The front lines now stretched 100 miles from Weyland's Laval headquarters and even farther from his fighter-bomber bases. This meant that Colonel Smyser's engineer battalions already needed to prepare sites in the Le Mans area before they had finished those in the Brittany group. Two days earlier, on August 14, Weyland had met with General Vandenberg and his deputy, Brig. Gen. Richard E. Nugent, regarding the next airfield cluster needed by the command. The generals agreed that construction on the first of four Le Mans fields would begin the next day. Weyland met with his staff on the fifteenth to arrange for the new deployment. They decided that the 100th Fighter Wing should handle the forward airdromes at Le Mans, while the 303d Fighter Group would operate those in the rear area at Rennes. The forward direction post radar system would be located at Rennes for flying control. The command's operations officer, Colonel Ferguson, would manage the move. Everything now waited on the progress of the engineers.[37]

The following evening, General Weyland attended his first XIX TAC joint operations briefing and first combined operations conference in several days. In fact, it is doubtful whether he found time in the days before separating his advance headquarters into two and then three echelons to be present at these evening briefings, since he normally met with General Patton and his staff on fast-breaking events during the evening hours. From mid-August forward, however, Weyland routinely attended the XIX TAC evening planning briefing.

Col. Russell A. Berg,
commander, 10th Photo
Reconnaissance Group.

After the evening meeting on August 16, Weyland conferred with Col. Russell A. Berg, recently designated commander of the 10th Photo Reconnaissance Group. The XIX TAC had just gained this group, which would provide much needed visual and photographic data for the air-ground team. Its arrival represented an additional challenge to his aviation engineers in their constant effort to find the optimum operational locations for command units. Weyland wanted to locate Berg's group, most of which was then only en route from England, at Chateaudun, the big German base approximately 150 miles east of Rennes. However, because the engineers did not expect it to be fully operational until August 27, the 10th's squadrons would use the Rennes airfield in the interim. The 155th Night Photo Squadron, flying F–3 (A–20) aircraft, arrived to join the 12th Tactical Reconnaissance Squadron on the eleventh, followed by the second F–6 (P–51) unit, the 15th Tactical Reconnaissance Squadron, on the twelfth. By August 15, the group reached full-strength with the addition of the 31st and 34th Tactical Photo Squadrons, which flew F–5 (P–38) reconnaissance aircraft.[38]

In addition to making Chateaudun the focus of the command's reconnaissance effort—at least until the command moved forward again—General Weyland viewed that base as the major *roulement* site for the entire area. Chateaudun could provide short-term support and serve as a staging base to increase the range of the fighter-bombers. The importance of reconnaissance had risen dramatically since the Normandy Campaign, and the Chateaudun location would enable the 10th Photo Reconnaissance Group to make a major contribution on all fronts. Reconnaissance data reported by pilots and acquired through photography became the primary source of intelligence for command operations during the summer of intense mobility. Although the fighter control center provided the tactical air command headquarters radio intercept, or Y, information from the 3d Radio Squadron (Mobile), Detachment C, the records are sketchy on its value before the Ardennes Campaign. Nevertheless, Weyland realized the importance of his radio intercept source of intelligence on enemy air movements and refused to release his Y-service to the new XXIX TAC when the latter became operational in September 1944.[39]

Meanwhile, on August 16, the Third Army steamroller overran Chateaudun, Dreux, Chartres, and Orleans; it reached the Seine at Mantes-Gassicourt and Vernon northwest of Paris three days later. The XIX TAC continued to find good targets in the area of German retreat. The 36th Fighter Group, in fact, had its biggest day of the month here on August 13 when it claimed the destruction of 400–500 vehicles west of Argentan. Allied officials estimated that, of the nearly 14,000 German vehicles lost in the retreat from Falaise, air attacks accounted for 60 to 80 percent.[40]

The command also dealt with what appeared to be a resurgent *Luftwaffe*. Once redeployed from its Paris airfields, the *Luftwaffe* attempted to protect German ground forces moving toward the Seine. On August 15 and 16, the *Luftwaffe* lost 26 fighter aircraft in action near Dreux against the 354th's Mustangs and P–47s of the 373d and 362d Fighter Groups. Perhaps it was fitting that the 36th Fighter Group, which had been deprived of participation in the lucrative Mortain corridor attacks, played a key role in the final act to the west when the first of the fortified ports in Brittany fell on the seventeenth. Curry's Cougars circled the St. Malo fortress area until the Germans accepted the surrender ultimatum that day.[41]

The Allies now turned their attention to the Seine River. As early as August 13, Weyland had requested information from the Third Army chief of staff concerning likely German crossing points on which his pilots could focus. Third Army's intelligence assessment concluded that the Germans would attempt to hold open the corridor to the Seine. Could the U.S. First and Third Armies arrive in force and in time to prevent the Germans from escaping across the river?

From the Seine to the Meuse

Third Army's XV Corps secured a bridgehead over the Seine at Mantes-Gassicourt on August 19, with orders to follow the left bank to Elbeuf and Vernon and cut off the enemy's escape route. On its right, XX and XII Corps moved rapidly toward Fontainebleau and Sens, respectively. Meanwhile, VIII Corps prepared to launch an offensive against the remaining German-held Breton ports by the twenty-fifth (**Map 6**). With First and Third Army troops continuing to pull up to the Seine on August 20, General Eisenhower earlier decided to abandon the original limits set for the lodgement area. Instead of waiting to build up the logistic base, American forces would cross the Seine in force and relentlessly pursue the disintegrating German army and prevent it from regrouping at the German border. At the same time, the Supreme Allied Commander rejected General Montgomery's proposal on August 23, for a "single front" approach in the north, one in which the British general would direct a methodical advance through Belgium and on into the Ruhr. In its place, Eisenhower adopted the so-called broad-front strategy that permitted a second advance led by Patton's Third Army farther south toward the Saar. To temper Montgomery's disappointment, he added Hodges's First Army to Montgomery's northern advance—*and* accorded it priority for gasoline deliveries over Patton's swiftly moving forces.[42]

General Eisenhower based his decision to continue pursuing the Germans across the Seine partly on the spectacular success of Operation Anvil (also called Operation Dragoon), the amphibious invasion of southern France. On August 15, 1944, three divisions of U.S. VI Corps and an attached French armored force under the command of Lt. Gen. Alexander Patch's U.S. Seventh Army landed on the south coast of France between Cannes and Toulon. Seventh Army's objective involved freeing the port of Marseilles for Allied supply and protecting Eisenhower's southern flank farther north. While French troops invested the ports of Toulon and Marseilles, American divisions, soon aided significantly by French resistance forces, quickly fanned out in hot pursuit of German troops fleeing north through the Rhone River valley and into the foothills of the French Alps. This rapid Allied drive threatened to eliminate German forces in southern France and, by linking with Allied forces in northern France, block German troops in their headlong retreat from reaching the safety of the German border.[43]

As Allied forces attempted to envelop German forces at the Seine River, XIX TAC continued to provide column cover and armed reconnaissance support over all of the Third Army's expanding fronts. Yet Weyland's fighter-bombers were now spread dangerously thin in the east and south, which meant increased flying distances and less time to loiter. Moreover, the weather turned sour on August 19, and air operations in the Seine region became severely restricted. The command could fly only 16 missions on the nineteenth, a more respectable 36 on August 20, but none on the twenty-first. This came at a particularly inopportune time because the Allies, rejoicing that the Argentan pocket at last had been closed on August 20, also knew that the Germans had been sighted crossing the Vernon Bridge over the Seine that same day. Again, Ninth Air Force's weak night fighter force limited its ability to interdict growing and extensive German nighttime movements. In spite of the rain and low ceilings, XIX TAC's fighter-bombers did what they could by dropping delayed-fuze bombs at ferry slips.[44]

Some critics contend that Patton and his Third Army could have prevented the escape of the German Seventh Army across the Seine. If, as the argument runs, Third Army had not been so dedicated to headlong pursuit to the German border and instead elected to confront the enemy directly in what amounted to frontal assault, it could have destroyed the retreating German forces, possibly leading to a German surrender all along the line well before Christmas 1944. To be sure, on August 23, General Patton directed his staff to prepare two plans, one for pushing eastward below Paris with all due speed, and another, Plan A, calling for just such a move—a sudden swing north of the city to Beauvais to entrap the Germans and, in Patton's view, indeed bring the war to a swift end. Yet, the latter operation meant moving Third Army forces across the boundaries of the British and Canadian armies, interfering with the other Allied commands, and threatening General Eisenhower's broad-front strategy. This strategy called for all of the Allied armies to advance abreast against the retreating Germans, to share equally in the eventual victory. Submitted for approval, Eisenhower rejected Patton's Plan A the next day, the twenty-fourth.[45]

At the Seine, tactical air power, too, played a less than decisive role. Only a massive, concentrated air assault on the German forces there might have made a difference, but XIX TAC planners apparently never contemplated this in view of competing priorities, worsening weather, and perhaps the command's preoccupation with getting the Le Mans airfields ready. Still, postwar AAF evaluators of these close air support tactical air operations concluded: "Allied air forces, with more night reconnaissance and night air attacks, could have effectively prevented most of [the German equipment] from crossing [the Seine]."[46]

Before Eisenhower disapproved Patton's Plan A, on August 22 Generals Weyland and Patton met at 12th Army Group headquarters, where they reviewed the probable course of future operations. With leading elements of the Third Army moving forward rapidly against Melun, Louviers, and Troyes, they anticipated the highly mobile campaign would soon move beyond Paris to the German border. Weyland worried that Patton might not understand the range limitations that his fighter-bombers faced when called on to operate far to the east of their soon-to-be completed bases at Le Mans.[47] Even with *roulement* operations underway at Chateaudun, the great distances involved would limit the P–47s' effectiveness in supporting operations in eastern France. With a full bomb load and a 150-gallon belly tank, the Thunderbolt possessed a combat radius of approximately 350 miles. Yet, the distance from Chateaudun to Metz totaled nearly 300 miles, which meant precious little time for operations in the target area. The P–51, with bombs and an external fuel tank, however, had a combat radius of 600 miles, which made it the obvious choice for extended fighter sweeps and area patrols in eastern France and Germany.

The prospect of conducting extended operations over greater distances also meant that the command faced problems of increased strain on pilots, aircraft, and support agencies. As Weyland told Patton, XIX TAC confronted major difficulties supporting a continued advance without more advanced fighter bases, adequate supplies, and established communication. Even before his groups moved to the Le Mans bases, Weyland was looking eastward for potential airfields. Paradoxically, the extraordinary success of mobile air-ground operations now imperiled effective air-ground cooperation!

In the Paris region, Weyland responded to a variety of Third Army requests. The *Luftwaffe* took advantage of the bad weather on August 21–22 to attack the 79th Infantry Division's bridgehead across the Seine northwest of Mantes-Gassicourt. Responding to the Third Army chief of staff's request for help, General Weyland promised to triple air coverage in that area. The twenty-second proved to be a particularly good day for the command; its fighters claimed to have destroyed 20 enemy aircraft while losing only one of its own. In response to the increased threat from German fighters, P–47 crews preferred to leave the high-explosive bombs behind and rely on rockets (for the 406th Fighter Group) and strafing while on column cover assignments. Armed reconnaissance and armored column cover, meanwhile, continued to comprise the majority of missions during this period, highlighted by the air support of 4th Armored Division's Combat Command A, 12 miles east of Sens on August 23. In this instance, 362d P–47s, after flying armed reconnaissance ahead of the column, returned to disperse Bf 109s that earlier had strafed the ground troops. The *Luftwaffe* also continued to challenge XIX TAC in the forward area, while the two P–51 groups had success on area patrols east of Paris near Reims.[48]

With the arrival of General Charles de Gaulle's French forces, the liberation of Paris began on August 24. Third Army continued its major thrust east in the direction of Metz and Nancy, and its staff worried increasingly about its diminishing supply stocks. In the West, as VIII Corps prepared to attack Brest the next day, the protection of its southern flank remained the task of XIX TAC. In spite of bad weather, the command flew 12 missions on the twenty-fourth, including the 371st Fighter Group's armed reconnaissance flights between Tours and Orleans, flights that became known as "working on the railroad." The group claimed more than 200 rail and road vehicles destroyed or damaged from German forces retreating northward from U.S. Seventh Army troops. This, however, served only as a prelude to the eventful interdiction missions of early September.[49]

General Weyland remained busy with the Le Mans airfield program. He informed his staff on August 23 that the Chateaudun field was nearly ready for initial *roulement* flying, even though the airfields around Le Mans would not be fully operational for another four or five days. He requested that Ninth Air Force station a night fighter squadron there with his 10th Photo Reconnaissance Group, but the initial priority centered on *roulement* operations, in which he planned to turn around six fighter-bomber squadrons a day at Chateaudun. Perhaps Third Army would receive the support it needed farther east after all.

During the final week in August, both Third Army and XIX TAC leaders had reason to be optimistic. On August 25 Patton's forces enlarged bridgeheads across the Seine, while armored spearheads drove east. Units of XII and XX Corps approached Chalons, while the XX Corps reached Melun and the XII Corps captured Troyes. In the increasingly distant west, VIII Corps as promised, launched its long-awaited assault against the isolated Breton ports on August 25 (**Map 7**). Only the persistent shortage of gas and ammunition, and increased maintenance requirements for armor, clouded expectations of continued Third Army success. Near month's end, the 12th Army Group issued orders that called for Third Army to proceed to the Rhine and secure bridgeheads from Mannheim to Coblenz.[50]

On August 25, XIX TAC played a major role in ending the German fighter threat in France. Once again the pioneer 354th Mustang group led the way with claims of 49 enemy aircraft destroyed in a series of fighter sweeps north and east of Paris. Among those 49 was the record-setting 500th enemy aircraft shot down by the group since it arrived in the theater in late 1943. That day, Ninth Air Force forces counted 127 German aircraft claimed destroyed and 30 more damaged, at a cost of 27 U.S. aircraft. During the aerial fighting, American pilots observed Bf 109s dropping belly tanks, suggesting that the enemy had begun flying from Belgium and the homeland as Third Army approached the last network of German airfields remaining in eastern France. American pilots also observed increasingly inexperienced foes, who all too frequently made the fatal mistake of trying to turn with the agile P–51 in pursuit. After the shoot-out on August 25, German tactical air forces posed little threat to Third Army's advance.[51]

The next day Weyland initiated *roulement* operations at Chateaudun for squadrons of the 36th and 405th Fighter Groups assigned to fly close air support missions at Melun and Troyes. However, Weyland and his staff remained well aware of the need for air bases east of Paris. The day after Chateaudun opened for business, Weyland met with Ninth Air Force officers to plan the construction and distribution of new sites as much as 50 miles east of the French capital. Fifty miles represented the typical jump forward for the command. Once again, Weyland focused on establishing a *roulement* staging base as soon as Third Army could secure the area. Meanwhile, his intelligence officer, Colonel Hallett, drew up a rail interdiction plan to cut off the main escape route for German troops trapped south of the Loire.[52] On August 26, Third Army's staff enthusiastically endorsed the plan, and Weyland started the operation the following day by sending the 371st Group south, where it destroyed more than 200 enemy vehicles. The key question about the rail-cutting program would be whether the command could devote sufficient air power to the task in view of its other commitments. Reports from Brittany, where the 358th and 362d flew daily area patrols and furnished ground support, indicated the Allied siege of the Atlantic ports was progressing slowly. Ground forces there might require a larger commitment from the tactical air forces. Yet, the weather also threatened to weaken the effort when a cold front moved in from the

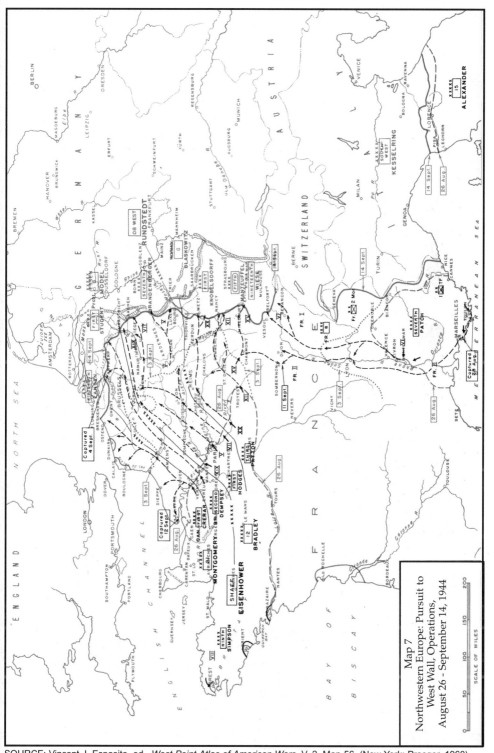

Map 7
Northwestern Europe: Pursuit to
West Wall, Operations,
August 26 - September 14, 1944

SOURCE: Vincent J. Esposito, ed., *West Point Atlas of American Wars*, V. 2, Map 56, (New York: Praeger, 1960)

Atlantic on August 28 and restricted operations for the remainder of the month.

In spite of bad weather on August 28, XIX TAC managed to fly its usual complement of fighter sweeps and close air support operations in the east and in Brittany. It also sent the 406th Fighter Group south of the Loire, where it had a good day against enemy air, claiming 14 aircraft destroyed. The next day, however, operations ceased entirely because of bad weather throughout northern France. Bad weather persisted on the thirtieth, when only two weather reconnaissance flights could be launched. Meanwhile, on August 29, XIX TAC moved its advance headquarters from Laval to the Foret de Marchenoir between Orleans and Chartres (**Map 7**). The command historian enthused that with this move "control of operations shifted far eastward."[53] Certainly a move of 100 miles proved necessary and helpful, but at month's end Weyland, ever the "fireman," had to spend most of his time in the East visiting potential sites for the next move forward. To increase support to the Third Army, he was determined to get *roulement* operations started at a Reims airfield immediately.

On August 28, 1944, Third Army crossed the Marne alongside First Army on a 90-mile front (**Map 7**), but its supply stocks were almost gone. Patton's staff described current supply levels of petroleum as alarming. No gasoline had been received that afternoon, and delivery was 100,000 gallons short of operating requirements. Moreover, logistics officers expected little improvement because General Bradley, 12th Army Group commander, adhered to Eisenhower's dictum and gave supply priority to the First Army. To keep up, Third Army enhanced its already notorious reputation for appropriating available fuel stocks and other supplies wherever it found them. Meanwhile, C–47s of the Ninth Air Force's IX Troop Carrier Command augmented the severely taxed Allied overland system by flying supplies to Beille and other airstrips near Le Mans, beginning on August 19 and continuing for the rest of the month. Although most of these C–47 deliveries ended up with Third Army, with priorities set otherwise, Patton's supply problems worsened.[54] The XIX TAC did not suffer from the fuel constraints experienced by Third Army. Although consumption of aviation gasoline and oil increased significantly following the Cobra breakout, the pipeline from Cherbourg and repaired railroad tracks and equipment provided the airfields with bulk fuel from sizeable accumulated stocks (with 2 million gallons in reserve). Where bottlenecks occurred or the pipeline and rail network could not keep pace with the swift advance, XIX TAC relied on deliveries by truck or C–47 aircraft.[55]

Even short of supplies, Patton's forces continued their relentless advance, now within 100 miles of the German border. On August 30, his intelligence section warned that the Germans would stand at the city of Metz to enable defenders to reinforce the Siegfried Line. Clearly the army needed to reach the Mosel River and pierce the German line of fortifications before the defense could entrench itself. Yet, it seemed as if the fates had combined to thwart Patton at the climactic moment of the campaign. On the thirtieth, he was told that Third Army would receive no further gasoline shipments at all until September 3. Bad weather and competing tactical air priorities also conspired to restrict armor operations.[56]

By the end of its first month of combat, Third Army had crossed the Meuse and swept past Chalons, over the American battlefields of the First World War (**Map 7**). Moving well ahead of initial schedules, Patton's forces had conducted widely dispersed mobile operations in France that left "uncovered" a southern flank nearly 500 miles long. Yet, the pace slowed as the army outdistanced its supply system. In fact, by August 31, XX Corps captured Verdun, but its Sherman tanks had no more gas. Generals Patton and Weyland nevertheless remained confident that Third Army and XIX TAC would win the race against time and break into Germany itself. After all, as one Third Army staff officer asserted, they had only one more river—the Mosel—to cross.[57]

For General Weyland and members of XIX TAC, the great drive across France in August 1944 would remain the high point of the command's service in Europe. The very next month, an account of its first month's exploits entitled *Twelve Thousand Fighter-Bomber Sorties* received wide distribution in Washington military circles. The command also made available an unclassified version for the public.[58] Although the end of mobile warfare had not yet arrived, September would indeed bring a change in the nature of the fighting in eastern France. At the end of August, however, the participants could not yet foresee this change. With the promise of more supplies at month's end, Third Army was poised to launch a major assault against the Mosel River defenses, while the XIX TAC prepared to concentrate its forces in the East in support of this army offensive.

Protecting Patton's Southern Flank

Historians debate the effect of operating responsibilities in the Loire and Brittany in September on XIX TAC's ability to provide close air support for Patton's offensive on the Mosel. In the East, was Third Army denied the concentrated air support it required? Attention had focused on fuel and ammunition shortages, but did a shortage of aerial support also contribute to the halting of Patton's forces?

At the beginning of September 1944, XIX TAC's mission embraced air support responsibilities on three fronts: in eastern France it flew armed reconnaissance and column cover missions in support of Third Army's drive toward Metz; along the Loire River it kept watch on Patton's flank and flew interdiction sorties against German forces retreating from southern France; and, lastly, in Brittany it played the key tactical air role in the sieges of the Breton fortified port facilities. It operated air bases from Brittany to the Le Mans area. As it prepared to move forward again, General Weyland's strike force consisted of the 10th Photo Reconnaissance Group and two wings of four fighter-bomber groups each. Only the 363d Fighter Group, the second P–51 group, no longer appeared in the command's original nine-group lineup of August 7. Given the *Luftwaffe's* inability to contest air superiority, the 363d had been redesignated at the start of the month as the 363d Tactical Reconnaissance Group and was being reequipped with F–6 aircraft for reassignment to the soon-to-be established XXIX TAC.[59]

Among the three fronts, in terms of operational commitments, the Loire front proved to be the least burdensome for the command. Weyland dispatched daily reconnaissance flights and armed reconnaissance missions south of the river when good targets could be found. To support his intelligence officer's interdiction plan, he also scheduled a daily rail-cutting mission in the Dijon-Belfort region, the point of exit for German troops retreating from southern France. Often his air groups attacked targets of opportunity on these missions and rearmed and refueled at one of the *roulement* staging bases, thence to fly "on cooperation" with the ground forces for the remainder of the day. Although the southern flank did not become a major combat front for the army in September, it remained important because of the potential threat from German forces remaining in the south. Patton garrisoned the north bank of the Loire River thinly with elements from VIII Corps and relied entirely on his air arm to alert him to and blunt any tactical threats from the Germans in this quarter. The air arm, in turn, greatly benefited from Ultra intelligence on German locations and movements south of the Loire. From the beginning, the "watch on the Loire" became largely an air force show, and it marked a historic milestone for tactical air power.[60]

September opened with a major victory for XIX TAC pilots flying south of the Loire. The rapid drive of Third Army beyond the Meuse and the advance of General Patch's Seventh Army northward from the Mediterranean precipitated a general German retreat up the Rhone valley toward the Belfort escape hatch. As a result, command pilots on armed reconnaissance and fighter sweep missions in the Nancy and Bourges regions found numerous choice targets in the *Wehrmacht* traffic jam. On September 1 the command tallied the largest interdiction mission score of the entire campaign in France when its aircrews claimed more than 800 motor vehicles destroyed or damaged. Curry's Cougars led the way with claims of 311 motor transport and 94 armored vehicles knocked out, and an ammunition dump set ablaze for good measure.[61]

The XIX TAC kept up the pressure on harassed German troops with its modest surveillance and armed reconnaissance force. The effort paid dividends early in the afternoon of September 7, when one of the 155th Night Photo Squadron's F–3s flying the Loire spotted a long enemy vehicle column near Chateauroux on its way toward the Belfort Gap (**Map 7**).[62] The 155th

Ultra operatives busily intercepted communications of the German troops who used Enigma machines such as this to encode their transmissions.

pilot radioed in his sighting and the 406th Fighter Group arrived shortly thereafter. Once it expended all of its ordnance and ammunition, the group left to reload, leaving vehicles overturned and burning. Then the 406th aircraft returned again to complete the destruction of the column. Final claims totaled 132 motor transport and 310 horse-drawn vehicles destroyed. This mission served as the most outstanding example of reconnaissance-fighter-bomber coordination that, by September, had developed into a routine but very effective system.[63]

On September 9, 1944, information reached Army authorities that *Wehrmacht* elements remaining in the area south of the Loire would likely surrender with a gentle nudge, and U.S. Ninth Army commander Lt. Gen. William H. Simpson and Maj. Gen. Robert C. Macon, commander of the 83d Infantry Division, assumed this responsibility after Third Army had declined it. That evening Simpson visited General Weyland at XIX TAC headquarters and outlined his plans to force a surrender, plans in which the XIX TAC figured prominently. Weyland's forces would fly reconnaissance overhead, along the route of the Germans' march to the Loire River, but would not interfere with their movement. If the enemy troops refused the surrender terms offered,

**Field Marshal Bernard L. Montgomery with
Lt. Gens. Omar Bradley and William H. Simpson.**

Some of the 20,000 German prisoners who were surrendered to
General Macon, commander of the 83d Infantry Division, and
General Weyland, XIX TAC, on September 16, 1944, in a formal
surrender at Beaugency Bridge. The surrender was forced largely
by the campaign of isolation by XIX TAC fighter-bombers.

however, then the fighter-bombers would return to attack them. Two days later,
on the eleventh, Weyland learned that the German commander of this hastily
assembled composite force, Maj. Gen. Botho Elster, had agreed to the terms
and marched his troops under U.S. Army escort through country controlled by
the French Resistance to the Loire River and a formal *Wehrmacht* surrender at
the Beaugency Bridge.[64]

General Simpson called Weyland on September 16 and generously invited him to attend the surrender ceremony at 1500 hours local time. It proved to
be a busy day for the XIX TAC commander. He arrived at Chalons to join
Generals Simpson and Macon at the Beaugency Bridge on schedule and was
pleased to hear that the XIX TAC's aerial presence overhead received primary credit for compelling the surrender. Never before had an air commander
been present or received such laurels when one ground unit surrendered to
another. On his return to Chalons, Weyland received a call from General
Vandenberg asking for information and requesting his presence that evening at
Ninth Air Force headquarters in Versailles. Once again the XIX TAC commander took to the air, this time flying westward for dinner with Vandenberg
and his deputy, General Nugent. At a press conference, Weyland described the
role his command had played in convincing the German troops to surrender.[65]

The command's own analysis of the Loire victory acknowledged that the
Germans' flight south of the Loire did not result exclusively from the aerial
interdiction missions on September 1 and 7, or from Colonel Hallett's rail-cut-

ting program which forced the *Wehrmacht* onto the highways where it became even more vulnerable. Equally important, on September 11, the U.S. Third and Seventh Armies linked up, blocking the Belfort exit to Germany and trapping these forces. Constant harassment from the French underground also took its toll on the German troops. Tactical air power, nevertheless, contributed an important element in forcing the surrender, if it was not a sufficient cause in its own right. For the first time air forces not only had secured an army's flank, but aerial pressure and the threat of renewed aerial attack led directly to the surrender of the enemy ground force. *Wehrmacht* General Elster made that abundantly clear afterward. The persistent fighter-bomber attacks, he said, had been the key factor in the decision to surrender his 20,000-man *marschgruppe*. The XIX TAC mission of guarding Third Army's flank and contributing to the ultimate surrender of opposing ground forces has been lauded as an unprecedented example of tactical air power's flexibility and diversity.[66]

A Decision in Brittany

In spite of XIX TAC's unprecedented achievement on the Loire front, General Weyland remained convinced that the diversion of his command's assets in Brittany during this period precluded even greater successes. "The fruits of the program of interdiction and harassment," he said, "would have been considerably larger had it not been interrupted by concentration of the fighter-bomber effort at Brest."[67] Indeed, the command's major focus in early September centered not on the Loire or Meuse fronts, but on Brittany where the fortress city of Brest, after many weeks, still represented a major "potential" port for Allied supplies. Whatever its potential, by this time Brest clearly had become a secondary Allied objective 300 miles from the main front. Under the command of an experienced General Middleton, VIII Corps had made little progress since opening its siege offensive back on August 25. Initially, Middleton simply had been allocated insufficient forces and ammunition to succeed against the 30,000 determined defenders—almost twice the number estimated—who remained well protected within an elaborate defensive complex that included concrete pillboxes, casements, gun emplacements, and a host of additional obstacles. After VIII Corps failed to capture the garrison by September 1, the planned completion date of the siege, military officials decided that more effort would need to be devoted to the embarrassing problem.[68]

On September 2, 1944, General Vandenberg notified the XIX TAC commander that Allied leaders had identified Brest and the other Breton fortified sites still holding out as an urgent priority. These sites would be attacked by all available bombers and fighter-bombers. Weyland, Vandenberg continued, had been named operational commander for the tactical air effort, an effort that would include not only every fighter-bomber group in his command, but others from General Quesada's IX TAC as well. General Vandenberg directed Weyland to coordinate the Brittany air effort with General Middleton, the VIII Corps commander. Earlier, Middleton had criticized what he considered sub-par air support from the XIX TAC. Yet, when Weyland raised the issue with Patton the corps commander denied it, and nothing more came of the incident. Weyland could have anticipated support from Patton. The Third Army commander judged Middleton at this time to be a complainer and procrastinator who, like Montgomery, required more of everything before beginning an assault. In fairness to Middleton, his assessment of the tactical difficulties at Brest proved accurate, and later Patton would come to consider this most capable infantry leader among his best corps commanders. In any event, in early September, Middleton had all the air power he needed, or so it appeared. When Weyland contacted the VIII Corps after Vandenberg's call on the evening of September 2, however, he learned that American ground forces could not follow up immediate fighter-bomber attacks because insufficient supplies of ammunition made it impossible to mount coordinated air-ground attacks.[69]

The Ninth Air Force operations order for September 3, 1944, nonetheless, called for an "all out attack" which, as it turned out, totaled 24 of the 34 missions and nearly 300 of the 500 sorties flown on that day.[70] Weyland spent the day coordinating the effort and trying to obtain updated target lists for his pilots from army air intelligence and air liaison officers in Brittany. On the following day, when bad weather forced cancellation of air operations at Brest, he turned his attention to improving support for Third Army in eastern France. Leaving the Brest operation in the capable hands of his combat operations officer, Weyland left on the morning of September 5 for the Third Army front with three specific objectives in mind: investigate potential new airstrip locations; discuss air support for the forthcoming offensive; and convince Patton that XIX TAC planes assigned to Brest would better serve Third Army in the east.

First, Weyland wanted to reconnoiter potential airfield sites in eastern France personally. Before leaving Chateaudun, he spoke with Ninth Air Force headquarters and requested five fields in the Reims area and several near St. Dizier for his groups then at Rennes and Le Mans, respectively. He also discussed using two airfields much closer to Third Army's Mosel front— Coulommiers (A–58) and Melun (A–55) near Paris—as rearming and refueling strips (**Map 4**). In fact, on the trip to Third Army headquarters on September 5, he stopped off to visit his airdrome squadrons in the vicinity. General Weyland also wanted to discuss Third Army's resumption of operations with Patton's staff. Because air and ground leaders customarily consulted on upcoming major assaults, Weyland had ample reason to fly to Chalons and consult with the staff on the air role in Third Army's joint plan for an offensive against the Mosel defenses.[71]

Early on the afternoon of September 5, Weyland conferred with Generals Patton and Gaffey and with General Haislip, commander of XV Corps. The

Haislip forces would attack in the direction of Luneville on the right of XII Corps, which had taken up positions opposite Nancy. Facing Metz, the XX Corps prepared to attack the next day, on the sixth, in an effort to pierce the Siegfried Line—*provided* its forces received sufficient gasoline supplies. Although operations reports for the first three days of September confidently alluded to securing bridgeheads and performing active reconnaissance to the east, Third Army basically had stalled. The situation began to improve when supply allocation rose and gas allowances increased on September 4. Of the 640,000 gallons requested that day, supply depots delivered 240,265. On September 5, air and rail shipments of 358,840 gallons proved sufficient for General Patton to order immediate resumptions of the advance.[72]

During the planning conference with Patton and his staff, Weyland also raised the third issue. He informed Third Army leaders that air support in the east would be restricted because all XIX TAC groups were reassigned to the Brest operation. It is not clear whether he asked Patton directly for help to reduce this commitment, although such a request probably would have been unnecessary. From early in the campaign, Patton considered Brittany a back-water of the war. On September 5, the day of his meeting with Weyland, he doubtless experienced relief now that VIII Corps and the Brittany Campaign, on the fifth, had become the responsibility of the newly formed Ninth Army. Whatever his feelings, higher authorities had committed his fighter-bombers to support non-Third Army missions. After the meeting, Weyland remembered that Patton agreed to seek release of the fighter-bombers in Brittany so they could support Third Army's attack to the east and into Germany. The XIX TAC commander certainly cannot be faulted for seeking Patton's help to escape or reduce a commitment that neither favored. Weyland knew perfectly well that the Brittany fortifications represented high-risk, low-yield targets for his fighter-bombers, despite AAF evaluations that suggested P-47s would have better success than medium or heavy bombers. Moreover, the air com-mander, like the ground commander, considered Brest a costly diversion from far more urgent military tasks.

General Weyland and his staff always maintained that the command's commitment to the Brittany Campaign, especially for two pivotal weeks in early September, prevented it from giving Third Army the vital support it needed during the final push to the German frontier. Third Army officers felt the same way. As for the Brest Campaign itself, it is hard to disagree with the military historian B. H. Liddell Hart, who concluded that "the diversion to cap-ture the Brittany ports brought [to the Allies] no benefit."[73] Senior airmen sub-sequently deplored the use of air power at Brest as "wasteful and ineffec-tive."[74]

There is much merit to the criticism. Despite 31 battalions of allied artillery available at Brest at the start, as days turned into weeks, the pressure mounted for more and more air support. One must remember, however, that army planners in the late 1930s had designed army divisions for speed and mobility, which meant that medium rather than heavy artillery became the standard issue. As part of the compromise that would build up the air arm in the early 1940s, army leaders planned to rely on air power to augment artillery fire. Air leaders quite willing, even eager, to accept the expansion of aerial forces later seemed much less willing to accept the trade-off that would employ the fighter-bombers as flying artillery.[75]

After Brest became Ninth Air Force's primary objective on September 3, Weyland sent fighter-bombers from the two tactical air commands against every conceivable target holding up the ground advance there. These included dug-in troop positions, heavily fortified coastal batteries, and reinforced concrete pillboxes and fortress walls. On occasion he resorted to the air umbrella, the practice frowned on by doctrinaire air force leaders. Weyland's air umbrella in Brittany provided continuous four-plane air patrols to support each division. Nevertheless, VIII Corps ground forces made little progress until September 14, when accumulated attacks on seacoast batteries, specific targets in the city center, and constant pressure from the ground forces at last forced the defenders into the inner ring. Here, in the final assault, P–47s identified and attacked individual fortified houses in what amounted to house-to-house fighting.[76]

The postwar AAF Evaluation Board analysis proved highly critical of the indiscriminate use of air power at Brest, which it attributed to the absence of an air liaison or other advisory officer at VIII Corps headquarters. As a result, planners had inadequate knowledge about the effects of various bombing techniques, bomb fuzings, and related procedures. The evaluators also deplored the lack of coordination by target officers to produce an integrated target plan for the operation. General Weyland's difficulties in obtaining targets for his aerial forces certainly reflected this weakness. It seems surprising to find many of the same coordination problems that first appeared at Cherbourg reappearing at Brest.[77]

The tactical air experience at Brest, however, also revealed a positive side, at least by the later stages of the operation. Air-ground coordination, in particular, improved steadily during the campaign. Unlike the Cherbourg operation, air liaison officers now provided a VHF controller link that proved invaluable. Missions directed by the division air liaison officer who coordinated the use of fighter-bombers on airborne alert with division artillery batteries proved especially effective. In contrast with air operations in North Africa, air superiority and sufficient forces allowed the air-ground team to use the air umbrella effectively. Normally the P–47 groups flew 12-ship squadron-size missions and relied on three types of ordnance: two 500-lb. bombs, one 1,000-lb. bomb, or napalm-filled tanks. Brest was the first major test of napalm employed on the continent, and the jellied gasoline bomb rapidly became a popular and effective weapon when used properly. At Brest, fighter-bombers dropped 133.2 tons of the firebombs. Airmen found that napalm proved most destructive when used on targets already partially destroyed and on deep shelters because of its adverse effect on the ventilation system. The use of napalm in attacks with ground forces in close proximity to the target suggests that air and ground forces had achieved a high level of coordination. Near the end of the assault on Brest, which fell on September 18, 1944, the XIX TAC historian could declare with good reason that "close air-ground cooperation was paying big dividends."[78]

Although the command lost only 12 aircraft during the entire September operation in Brittany, in terms of future value, the operation proved far too costly for the Allies. The German defenders destroyed the port facilities when VIII Corps troops finally overran the fortress complex on September 18. By that time the main Allied war effort had moved far to the east. Allied leaders decided not even to rehabilitate the Breton ports, relying instead on port facilities in Antwerp, Belgium. General Weyland, with some justification, could complain bitterly: "While this enormous air effort was being concentrated on such a small area, Third Army's eastward-pushing spearheads were covered very thinly with fighter-bombers...."[79]

Back on September 8, 1944, just three days after their joint planning meeting at Chalons, Generals Gaffey and Gay asked Weyland for more air support of Third Army's Mosel crossing. Evidently Patton had been unable to secure a reduction in XIX TAC's commitment in Brittany, and the air commander explained how SHAEF's current air requirements for Brest affected the level of air support that he presently could furnish for the ground advance at the Mosel.[80] In fact, on September 6, the day after the planning meeting at Chalons, the command sent six of its eight groups on 33 of the day's 37 flying missions to Brest. This heavy concentration of air power in Brittany continued for the next two days. After that, however, the effort would decline to three groups on September 9 and 10, and normally two groups thereafter until the fall of Brest on the eighteenth. During this period, Third Army always received air support from at least two groups, and after September 12, it normally claimed about two-thirds of XIX TAC's daily mission allotment. Weather also played a role in allocating the air effort. Bad coastal weather at Brest could, as it did on the sixth, result in aircraft being diverted to Patton's front. Then, too, Patton carefully retained his airborne watch on the Loire River flank.[81]

Third Army probably received more air support than Patton could have expected after the Brittany assault began in earnest on September 3. Certainly he could have benefited from additional air support in September, but probably interdiction, not close cooperation sorties over his columns, would have proved most helpful. With the pause in mobile operations, his artillery now could support front line troops preparing to cross the Mosel. Tactical air support to isolate the Mosel battlefield seemed likely to produce the greatest dividends. Weyland recognized this, and the mission logs for mid-September show that armed reconnaissance rather than armored column cover missions predominated. It is here, with interdiction targeting, that the Brest commitment most seriously affected Third Army's potential for success. It is hard to avoid the conclusion that a major interdiction program in the Mosel-Rhine region, designed to prevent an intensive German buildup along the Mosel, offered the best role for tactical air power at the time. No amount of tactical air power, however, could move an army that literally had run out of gas at the end of August, an army that remained largely stationary the entire first week of September. Logistic constraints rather than insufficient air support proved to be Patton's real Achilles heel.[82]

Final Pursuit to the Mosel River

By September 18, 1944, with Brest captured and the Loire flank secured, the command could devote its full force and attention to Third Army's Mosel front. As important as the Brest and Loire operations became, General Weyland realized that his chief objective continued to be one of support for Third Army's main offensive. This meant moving his groups to Chalons and St. Dizier airfields in time to concentrate his air power in force on Third Army's front. Could XIX TAC relocate its groups to airfields in eastern France in time to affect favorably Third Army's operations? Weyland directed the majority of his time during the month of September to that end and his personal touch was evident throughout the relocation process. On September 6, the day after personally examining potential airfield sites, he joined General Quesada at Ninth Air Force headquarters in Versailles, where they, along with Generals Vandenberg and Nugent, allocated new airfields between the two tactical air commands.[83]

The XIX TAC received four fields in each region. Weyland approved of the selection, but later he would lobby—unsuccessfully—to be given the Reims-Champagne airfield as well. The main problem was that only two of the fields, Conde-sur-Marne (A–76c) and St. Dizier (A–64), could be used immediately (**Map 4**). Weyland had already chosen these as his *roulement* and emergency rearming and refueling fields in the forward area, and on the evening of September 6 he directed Colonel Ferguson to have the command's two airdrome squadrons move in, and the Ninth Air Force's service command representative to stock the fields with sufficient gas.

As for the other sites, five needed to be surfaced with square-mesh tracking material and the remaining two required extensive rehabilitation. The plan called for the St. Dizier cluster to have two of its fields operational by September 10, and two more by the thirteenth. The engineers expected the Chalons sites, with the exception of the *roulement* base, to be operational by

Maj. Gen. Richard E. Nugent,
assistant chief of staff for
operations, Ninth Air Force.

the eighteenth. That schedule, as Weyland learned, however, did not reflect operational availability. Vandenberg allowed only two of Weyland's groups, the 371st and 405th Fighter Groups in Normandy, along with the 100th Fighter Wing headquarters at Le Mans, to relocate to the St. Dizier area on September 10 (**Map 7**). The remaining six groups would have to remain in place farther west until the Brest Campaign's conclusion.[84]

Weyland also wanted to move his advance headquarters to Chalons as soon as adequate communications facilities could be established. The 405th and 371st Fighter Groups would be controlled by the advance headquarters until the 100th Fighter Wing became operational, while the 303d Fighter Wing would continue to control groups in the rear area until they moved forward. Complications arose in early September, when authorities decided to create a new command, the XXIX TAC, commanded by General Nugent, from units currently assigned to the IX and XIX TACs. General Nugent's command would support U.S. Ninth Army operations on First Army's left flank. From General Weyland's forces, the planners selected the 303d Fighter Wing for transfer, along with two as yet unnamed fighter-bomber groups. Nugent's new command would become operational on September 14,[85] and understandably he wanted the 303d available on the fourteenth. Weyland objected because his widely separated fields of operation required more decentralized command

and control arrangements than the IX TAC and he declined to give up the wing as long as the Brest Campaign remained active. As it turned out, General Vandenberg allowed the 303d to remain with the XIX TAC one more day, until September 15.

On September 10, the St. Dizier airfield became operational, and the 10th Photo Reconnaissance Group arrived from Chateaudun to fly missions from its new site. Ninth Air Force agreed to use medium bombers to augment resupply of the Third Army and declared the bomber resupply mission top priority. St. Dizier was the field selected. This troubled Weyland because it meant his own units' operations would be shorted, and the runways would suffer damage from the heavier airplanes. Yet, Third Army clearly needed special help for its worsening supply plight. As it was, airmen did not deliver the first bulk gas to St. Dizier until the twenty-first.[86] September 10 also proved memorable for another reason. On that date XIX TAC moved its advance headquarters to Chalons. The command historian confidently proclaimed that this move finally ended the communications problems between the two headquarters. Although another two weeks passed before the relocation could be completed, joint planning no longer had to include the X-Ray echelon, and at Chalons, Patton and Weyland were only 15 miles apart (**Map 7**).

While Weyland moved his forces to forward airfields as rapidly as possible, Patton confronted his supply problems. Supply shortages for the Third Army began to occur in mid-August.[87] The gas situation emerged as the most serious of all in early September. Even when fuel began arriving for the Third Army as promised after the third—by air, road, and rail—the stocks never reached the levels required. Ammunition stocks also had been seriously depleted, especially for XII Corps divisions attacking in the Nancy area. By September 12, Third Army had to request its entire airlift allocation be used for ammunition requirements.

Despite shortages of ammunition and fuel, Patton's forces continued a limited offensive, and on September 7, XX Corps units reached the Mosel south of Metz and forced a crossing. By September 9, elements of the corps established bridgeheads north and south of the city and U.S. artillery had begun shelling the forts. At the same time, XII Corps launched a coordinated assault to outflank Nancy. The corps could not capture the city, however, until September 15, while the Metz forts proved impervious even to shelling by 8-inch howitzers, medium guns. Even though all three corps had reached the Mosel, determined enemy resistance made it difficult to maintain bridgeheads. Progress became slow in all zones of the front.

Weyland realized the urgency of the situation. On September 12, he met with General Gay and 12th Army Group officers about the requirements involved in transporting his air groups to their new locations in eastern France. They had to come by rail from three different areas (**Map 7**), he explained, and it would take four trains to transport ground elements of two groups. The assistant chief of staff promised to ask Patton and Gaffey for rail priority. Given the transportation bottleneck and Third Army's own desperate needs in September, it was not surprising that XIX TAC ground echelons improvised the move via a combination of rail, road, and air transport.[88]

The relocation experience of the 36th Fighter Group proved typical.[89] It had only been at site A–35 on the outskirts of Le Mans for 12 days when, on September 19, the command notified it to pack up for the journey to Conde-sur-Marne (A–76), 160 miles to the east (**Map 4**). The base was already famil-iar to aircrews as a rearming and refueling base for the longer missions from Le Mans. Unit personnel performed the now-familiar task of packing up tents and equipment and splitting into advance and rear echelons. The air echelon left on the nineteenth, with the rear following in stages. Most of the equipment made the journey by train, while the majority of the personnel arrived by C–47 aircraft. The group took nine days to complete the move, which must be con-sidered admirable given the enormous transportation problems that existed throughout the Allied area in September. On the other hand, the nine days in transit loomed large for a command in a race against time.

Solving the enormous transportation problems that existed throughout the Allied area in September 1944 must be credited to the personnel of the Transportation Section, rear headquarters, Chalons, France.

The group historian declared the field at Conde-sur-Marne, nine miles northeast of Epernay, to be a virtual wilderness. What made the most impression on the new arrivals proved to be the mud, which they considered even worse than they remembered in England. On the other hand, at least the forward deployment meant better air support for the Army and it ended the practice of landing at forward fields to refuel, then flying the mission, and later landing at one of the eastern airstrips because of bad weather. The 354th Fighter Group historian recounted how, in past *roulement* operations, half the group might be grounded at forward bases or at their home base because of bad weather, with some continuing to fly missions from the staging sites for several days. For all its hardships, however, the *roulement* system clearly allowed XIX TAC to provide air support quickly to front line units, and it ensured the flexibility and mobility of tactical air power during the exploitation phase of combat in France.[90]

With Brest about to fall on September 17, 1944, General Weyland directed his combat operations officer, Colonel Ferguson, to have all XIX TAC groups moved forward and ready by September 25, for "all-out" operations in eastern France against German forces on the Mosel.[91] Yet would there still be time to make a difference against German defenses growing stronger by the day? From September 19–25, most of XIX TAC's missions consisted of armed reconnaissance flights against transportation targets in the Rhine and Mosel River valleys.[92] Despite these mission assignments, there is no record that General Patton complained that the air command now emphasized interdiction rather than close air support. With his artillery available on an increasingly static front, it made good sense to send the fighter-bombers to try to isolate the battlefield. During this period, however, poor weather interfered with strike missions, and tactical reconnaissance missions continued to report heavy enemy traffic moving into the Mosel region unhindered.

If General Weyland began to emphasize armed reconnaissance in late September, he did not neglect close air support missions. Many of these supported the celebrated 4th Armored Division, now engaged in heavy combat outside Nancy. Its division commander, however, General Wood, offered Weyland his only other encounter over command authority. One of XIX TAC's communications officers, Lieutenant Kiljauczyk, was temporarily serving with the 4th Armored pending reassignment. General Wood flatly refused to release Kiljauczyk on the grounds that XII Corps retained authority in such matters. Weyland, who did not brook lightly challenges to his authority, promptly telephoned the Third Army chief of staff, General Gay, who just as promptly settled the question in Weyland's favor. To their credit, General Patton and his staff invariably supported their air commander.[93]

Appropriately, the operational highlight that closed this period involved the same 4th Armored Division. Early on September 24, General Gaffey called Weyland and requested emergency air support for the division's Combat

Command B, which had come under heavy armored counterattack near Nancy. Despite poor weather, Weyland dispatched two squadrons of the 405th Fighter Group with 500-lb. bombs to rescue the force. Afterward, increasingly bad weather forced them to land at Etain and Weyland took the crews over to meet with a grateful Third Army staff. The following day, the 4th Armored Division sent the command a proper message of thanks, confirming that the P–47s had knocked out six Panzer tanks.[94]

On September 22, 1944, both air and ground advance headquarters began moving from tents to covered quarters at Etain, which meant that joint operations would be conducted together for the first time since early August. Circuit problems, however, cut out communications between Chalons and Etain, delaying the arrival of the bulk of XIX TAC's advance personnel and communications equipment until the twenty-fourth. By this time, Colonel Ferguson had met his commander's directive of having all groups in place for the all-out effort on September 25. Unfortunately, bad weather made the twenty-fifth the first totally nonflyable day of the month. That morning, General Patton, with General Weyland in attendance, addressed his staff, announcing that Third Army would go on the defensive until sufficient fuel and ammunition could be obtained.[95] Typical of Patton, this would be an aggressive defense, one in which limited attacks would be made to improve positions, while the troops prepared to resume the offensive and attack on the Nancy-Frankfurt axis when ammunition and supply permitted. The Third Army–XIX TAC team had lost the race against time and the mobile warfare of the summer and fall came to an end.

The French Campaign Reviewed

O. P. Weyland's report on XIX TAC's performance during the drive across France boldly asserted that aerial operations on fronts 350 miles apart proved "entirely practical because of the flexibility and range of air power."[96] The airmen made this possible in large part by decentralizing operations farther than established doctrine recommended or than planners originally intended. At one time, XIX TAC had groups based in three different areas and used *roulement* practices to stage from several others. At the same time, while the command echelon maintained air force control of its far flung units with diverse responsibilities, its task became increasingly difficult through late September. Too often, perhaps, General Weyland found himself a fireman scurrying back and forth, attempting to maintain control and ensure effective operations.

Air force tactical doctrine prescribed that control of air assets remain concentrated in the hands of the air commander, especially at the theater rather than the army level. Except for overall tactical air priorities, however, General Weyland held that control at the army level, and only occasionally did army interference demand his attention. During the battle of France, in only two instances did Weyland consider his authority as the air commander endangered. One occurred when Third Army operations officers at Le Mans attempted to direct close air missions; the other involved the assignment of the XIX TAC communications officer serving with the 4th Armored Division. Neither situation involved Patton or his immediate staff. In both cases, at Weyland's request, Third Army's chief of staff acted promptly to settle the matter. The ability of XIX TAC to respond rapidly to Third Army's changing combat situations during the exploitation phase overcame tendencies by army officers to extend their authority into the air arena. From the beginning, the battle for France emerged as a joint operations campaign that required and received a high measure of cooperation and personal involvement. If the Allies enjoyed overwhelming air superiority and possessed the organization and forces to make joint operations function effectively, personal respect and trust among partners proved decisive, as the XIX TAC–Third Army team demonstrated.

Air-ground cooperation, of course, began at the top. The professional relationship between Weyland and Patton was one of admiration and mutual respect. Although Patton's ability to improvise is well documented, Weyland, too, showed that in the drive across France he could react to and meet changing situations with an equivalent flexibility of thought and action. However inexperienced in combat he may have been on arriving in England, Weyland proved himself a fast learner under fire. The XIX TAC commander emerges from the record as the tactical air commander in fact as well as in name. When ground authorities requested supporting action beyond the capabilities of his forces, Weyland quickly refused, while asking the Ninth Air Force to furnish the supporting action needed. Normally, these requests involved the use of medium or heavy bombers and night fighters. Only during the initial assault against heavily defended Breton ports in late August did Patton appear to disagree actively with his air commander, who opposed the use of his fighter-bombers in the attack. In this case, however, Weyland's hands were tied by senior Allied leaders once they set air priorities and decided on maximum use of air power to accelerate capture of the forts. A few days later, both Weyland and Patton worked together to free tactical air and reduce its commitment in Brittany during the major effort against the ports in early September 1944.

During the first two weeks of the campaign, Weyland met with Patton nearly every day. Normally, the Third Army inner circle consisted of Patton, chief of staff Gaffey, and assistant chief of staff Gay, although corps commanders attended planning meetings that involved major offensives. Third Army headquarters also conducted a regular morning briefing that Weyland attended as often as possible. Beyond this, however, Weyland's diary reflects frequent conferences and informal discussions with Patton and Gaffey on fast-breaking developments that called for air force assistance. Weyland normally would suggest the course of action and, once a course was approved, immediately contact his combat operations officer, Ferguson, to arrange the details.

The fast pace of combat in France in the summer and fall of 1944 meant that planning and decision-making frequently became more fluid, unstructured, and highly personalized. Only by mid-August did Weyland regularly attend the XIX TAC–Third Army nightly joint operations meetings. Even when the two headquarters were separated after August 14, Weyland did not rely entirely on his X-Ray liaison unit at the Third Army command post; instead he daily discussed with Patton and his staff current and future plans by phone or teletype. As often as possible, he flew his Stinson L–5 light plane or a P–47 aircraft from a XIX TAC airfield to Third Army's headquarters to discuss matters personally. Along the way, he invariably reconnoitered prospective airfield sites and visited his operating units.

If mobile warfare called for flexibility in action on Weyland's part, it also compelled him to modify doctrine over the course of the campaign. Although close air support remained third in priority for AAF tactical air forces, XIX TAC gave "first priority [to] cover of the armored units." Moreover, that support most often appeared in the form of air patrols dedicated to specific army units—the exact patrols that were found so objectionable in North Africa because they prevented the concentration of air power.[97] This close support of the armored forces and infantry divisions did not diminish the role of interdiction, as armed reconnaissance mission results demonstrated. Moreover, Allied air superiority, the first aerial priority, made possible the dual emphasis on isolation of the battlefield and close support of the ground forces in the first place.

If mobile land warfare called forth tactical air power's special capabilities, it also exposed its limitations. The extended lines of communication and the pace of the campaign put a tremendous strain on all elements of the command. The technology of the World War II communications network proved especially sensitive and General Weyland repeatedly had difficulties establishing and maintaining good circuits from advance headquarters to the wing headquarters and the fighter control center. The signals network depended on the fate of the airfield siting and construction program; both served to restrict

General Weyland often flew in a Thunderbolt from one headquarters to another to coordinate activities.

XIX TAC's efforts to keep up with a rapidly advancing Third Army. In Northwest Europe, as in other Atlantic and Pacific theaters, air power was built on the ground.

By September 1944, concern over aircraft shortages also arose within the command. Although the XIX TAC never had to curtail operations because it possessed too few aircraft, it had to adjust aerial operations to account for the uneven flow of replacement airplanes. For added flexibility, General Weyland set squadron size at 12 rather than at 18 aircraft, a 33 percent reduction. Moreover, the command, which normally possessed eight groups, found that flying more than two group missions daily (or a total of 72 individual aircraft sorties) could not be supported adequately, given the aircraft loss rate of 114 in August and 72 in September, when combined with the uncertain arrival of replacements.[98]

On the other hand, fighter-bomber groups never lacked for sufficient numbers of combat pilots during the drive across France. In fact, groups complained that they had too many pilots for available positions. Although aviator losses for the command totaled 64 in August and 92 in September, the August and September pilot replacement figures were 162 and 281, respectively. Fatigue became a concern. The strain of continuous combat encouraged the command to rotate pilots back to the states for recuperation normally after 200 combat hours. In doing so, Ninth Air Force policy, perhaps reflecting the overabundance of fighter pilots in the theater, required that such pilots be reassigned to other commands upon their return. Combat losses, rotation, and the heavy influx of new, inexperienced pilots led to a decline in the number of experienced group, squadron, and flight leaders, and this proved the most serious and persistent problem for the command.[99]

By September 1944, XIX TAC support units also felt the strain of the long lines of communication and difficulties in transportation. Aircraft maintenance seemed less affected than supply. The command's assistant maintenance and supply officer believed that maintenance in the command was the best in Ninth Air Force because of the coordination between service teams, depots, and the tactical units. The supply saga proved to be different, however. For the move to Chalons, which began on September 10, 1944, and took two weeks to complete, the supply section found itself short of truck transport and had to resort to the expedient of pooling group vehicles and of securing help from available rail and air transport.[100]

On balance, the conduct of mobile warfare on several fronts presented XIX TAC a challenge it never entirely mastered. Even the air commander's resort to extremely decentralized command and control and a rearrangement of mission priorities could not provide all of the air support wanted in Third Army's *blitzkrieg* across France. If, as the command declared, it proved capable of supporting diverse ground operations on widely separated fronts, it invariably found that concentrating its air power on one particular front caused a restriction in its coverage on other fronts. This became most evident in

September when the Brest Campaign in the west demanded substantial tactical air involvement at the expense of air operations in eastern France. Even with command of the air assured and substantial aircraft available, warfare's competing priorities overtaxed General Weyland's available forces; these events remind us that tactical air forces represent a costly, limited resource. Only late in the month could he muster his forces and concentrate them on Third Army's front. By this time, however, the plan of the air-ground team was thwarted by a combination of bad weather, limited night flying capability, Third Army supply shortages, and a new type of combat: positional warfare.

General Patton did not always appreciate the limitations of tactical air power. As General Weyland recalled, after their early successes the Third Army commander seemed to believe that the XIX TAC was capable of anything.[101] An overstatement, perhaps, but it reflected Patton's faith in the army–air team, a faith that never faltered. Even when chances of success on the Mosel diminished sharply in late September, he still found time to send an Associated Press reporter to Weyland to give the XIX TAC the publicity Patton thought he deserved, and "link 3d Army–XIX TAC as a team."[102] Indeed, for the peppery, judgmental Third Army commander, over the course of the campaign, General Weyland had proved himself and his command in the face of formidable and constantly changing operational challenges. In late September 1944, however, both men confronted another, more vexing assignment. Static warfare now would challenge the XIX TAC–Third Army team as never before. The Lorraine Campaign was about to begin.

Chapter Four

Stalemate in Lorraine

Of all U.S. Third Army's World War II campaigns, Lorraine would prove by far the most difficult and frustrating. In early September 1944, however, victory fever remained high and both officers and troops believed that Lorraine would fall quickly in General Patton's drive to the Rhine River. By month's end, numerous obstacles conspired to thwart the best efforts of Third Army and the XIX TAC; the air-ground team found itself embroiled in fighting similar to the positional warfare of World War I on the western front.[1]

Autumn's Changed Conditions

In the fall of 1944, Patton's route for invading Germany south of the Ardennes increasingly claimed less Allied attention. With few key military objectives, it hardly compared with British General Montgomery's northern approach through the Ruhr industrial area, and in the context of General Eisenhower's broad-front strategy (**Map 8**), Allied leaders viewed Lorraine as a secondary front. Natural terrain and man-made defenses favored the *Wehrmacht*, and because the land rises from west to east, the Third Army would have to fight uphill throughout much of the region, cross many rivers and small streams, overrun numerous fortified towns, *and* breach two major defensive systems, the Maginot and Siegfried Lines.[2]

Among the German defensive systems, the Maginot Line would prove somewhat less troublesome. The French sited and built it looking eastward. The Siegfried Line, or West Wall, however, looked westward and remained a formidable challenge for the invaders. Despite recent neglect, the fortifications extended three miles deep in places and included numerous interconnected concrete pillboxes, troop shelters, observation posts, and antitank obstacles. Moreover, American troops in Lorraine dealt not only with reduced supplies of ammunition and gasoline, but also with increasingly determined German defenders able to take advantage of fortified positions and foul weather in the fall. As if these were not enough challenges, General Bradley's 12th Army Group, committed to the "northern approach," ordered Patton on September 10, 1944, to overrun the province of Lorraine and penetrate the Siegfried Line with an army reduced from four corps to two, the XXth commanded by Lt. Gen. Walton H. Walker, and the XIIth led by Maj. Gen. Manton S. Eddy. The

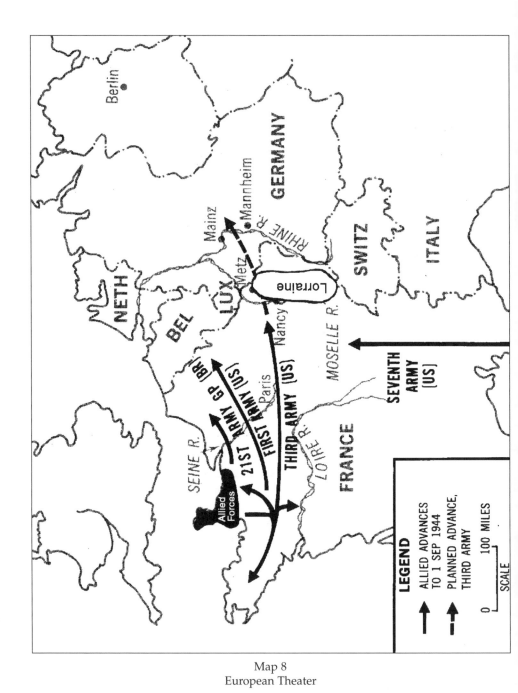

Map 8
European Theater

Reprinted from: Christopher R. Gabel, "The Lorraine Campaign: An Overview, Sep-Dec 1944," (Ft. Leavenworth, Kan.: U.S. Army Command and General Staff College, 1985), p. 2.

October combat quickly became a stalemate, with Third Army ground forces fighting limited engagements to improve their positions while building the supply base for a major offensive in early November that, they hoped, would take them through the Siegfried Line and on to the Rhine River.[3]

The Lorraine Campaign encouraged XIX TAC officials to consider the capabilities, and especially the limitations, of tactical air power. Above all, the airmen in Lorraine sought to use air power to break the stalemate on land. Weyland, as commander of the XIX TAC, became the key figure in the planning of air support in three joint operations undertaken by the Third Army against German border defenses during this period: first, Operation Madison, the assault on Metz and the Mosel defenses in early November; second, Operation Hi-Sug, the first major attempt to break through the Siegfried Line in early December; and finally, Operation Tink, the most ambitious air and ground operation of its kind, which the Allies planned to begin at the very time the Germans launched their Ardennes counteroffensive known as the Battle of the Bulge. Throughout the nearly three-month period in Lorraine, General Weyland proved to be a resourceful and pragmatic commander, one intent on providing maximum support for the ground forces. In that effort, doctrinal pronouncements did not dictate field operations. Air superiority, interdiction, and close air support received the attention he thought they deserved, but not necessarily in that order. If the way in which Weyland mixed the mission priorities during the campaign largely satisfied the needs of the ground commanders whom he supported, it frequently did not meet the expectations of tactical air purists.

Like Third Army, XIX TAC faced a radical readjustment of operations in the fall conflict. With army elements drawn abreast in September on a 135-mile front along the old French fortress line from Thionville to Epinal, mostly static action on a single front replaced the mobile operations of summer (**Map 9**). The new combat conditions were not entirely unfavorable. The long, good-weather flying days might be gone, but static warfare meant an end to decentralized operations that compelled Weyland to support multiple fronts far from home bases. As mobile as tactical air power could be, he had learned through experience that the air arm could not keep pace with General Patton's breakneck advance across France when communications links unravelled. Now the command consolidated its forces, which enabled communications, maintenance, and supply echelons to catch up near the Marne River region in close proximity to Third Army. Air bases could be clustered within 50 miles of Third Army's front lines, which reduced flying time to the target area by 50 percent. With the ground forces able to bring their medium and heavy artillery into position, the airmen could leave a large portion of the close support mission to army gunners and thus devote more of their effort to isolating the battlefield in a concerted Allied program of air interdiction.[4]

By late September 1944, the *Luftwaffe* had become especially ineffective in Third Army's zone of responsibility. During the month, the Allied onslaught

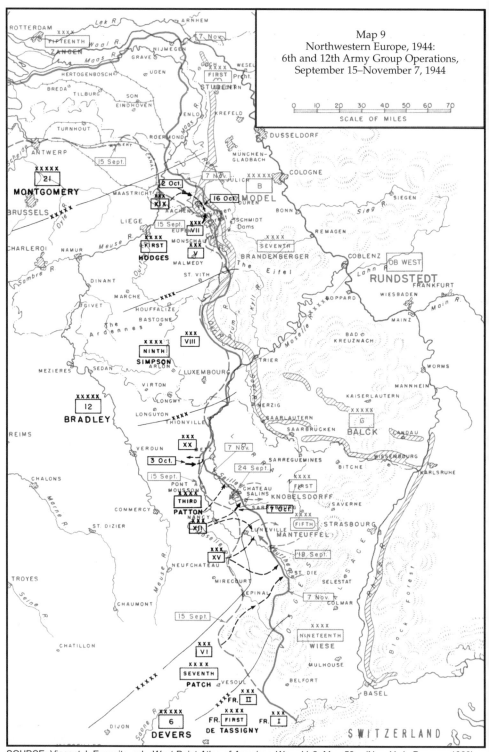

Map 9
Northwestern Europe, 1944:
6th and 12th Army Group Operations,
September 15–November 7, 1944

SCALE OF MILES

SOURCE: Vincent J. Esposito, ed., *West Point Atlas of American Wars*, V. 2, Map 59a, (New York: Praeger, 1960)

forced *Luftwaffe* leaders to give up air bases first in France and then in Belgium and to withdraw their remaining forces into Germany. The dislocation produced by Allied attacks, the loss of unified command and control, poor servicing facilities, and fuel shortages at the new bases in Germany meant that serious operations would have to await a rebuilding of the force. Moreover, at month's end, Hitler redirected the air force's primary focus to the overhead defense of the Third Reich against Allied strategic bombardment, rather than to support the *Wehrmacht* on the ground in the west. As a result, only 350 single-engine fighters covered the approaches to the Rhine, while the remaining western front command's 500 fighters moved to bases in northeast Germany to help defend Berlin and the oil industry. By transferring aircraft from the eastern front as well, the aerial force defending the Reich numbered 1,260 single-engine fighters, or nearly 65 percent of the total available single-engine fighter force.[5]

As the weather worsened with the onset of winter, XIX TAC's sortie figures plummeted from a high of 12,292 in August to 7,791 in September 1944, then skidded to 4,790 in October and only 3,509 in November. Third Army's slowdown in September and the worsening weather also permitted the Germans to build up their defenses. For XIX TAC pilots this resulted in the worst flak concentrations they had experienced thus far in the conflict.[6]

Like Patton's Third Army, Weyland's command also fought the Lorraine Campaign with reduced forces. On September 23, 1944, when General Bradley directed Third Army to assume a "defensive attitude,"[7] Weyland still possessed all eight fighter-bomber groups comprising 288 aircraft, as well as having the 10th Photo Reconnaissance Group from the summer campaign in place in eastern France. By October 1, however, XIX TAC strength had declined to five groups and 180 fighters: the Pioneer Mustang 354th Fighter Group and four Thunderbolt units. The latter included the 358th Orange Tails, the 362d Maulers, the 405th Raiders (perhaps the command's premier close support group), and the celebrated 406th Tiger Tamers. In early November, the command also lost the 358th Fighter Group to XII TAC, which supported General Patch's U.S. Seventh Army on Patton's right flank in the Alsace area of France. The only addition made to the command prior to the Ardennes emergency of mid-December was the 425th Black Widow (P–61) night fighter squadron that was assigned on October 7.[8]

During the Lorraine Campaign, General Weyland directed air operations from Etain, where XIX TAC advance headquarters moved on September 22, 1944. Administrative and support responsibilities continued to be exercised through rear headquarters located at Chalons under his chief of staff, Colonel Browne. The rear headquarters remained at Chalons throughout the fall and early winter, but advance headquarters followed Patton to Nancy on October 12, where it remained until January 1945 (**Map 9**). The most significant change in the fall came not in command organization but in flying control. With win-

Gen. O. P. Weyland
awards an Air Medal
to Col. Roger Browne,
his chief of staff.

ter's weather impending, the equipment, organization, and procedures for navigating and bombing assumed central importance for the command. Indeed, in the campaign to come, the establishment in late September of a provisional tactical control group to replace the fighter control center would prove a crucial decision.[9]

Refinements in Command and Control

During the drive across France, a fighter wing operated the fighter control center far removed from advance headquarters. General Weyland became convinced that this method of command and control was inefficient. Establishing a tactical control group to perform the functions of navigation and operational control at Etain solved the problem of divided responsibility, and it brought together all aircraft warning units, the fighter control squadron, and the Y-service radio intercept detachment in a single advance headquarters. Elements of the group operated from a tactical control center located directly behind the front, close by advance headquarters. In short, with consolidation of forces at the Third Army front, decentralization came to an end. Communications now would be centralized and positioned more directly under the command's control.[10]

Radar also became important once the command undertook to support position warfare in bad weather. Earlier, wing personnel at the fighter control center had used an area control board to plot and handle aircraft movement. Now, the tactical control center delegated this function to *five* fighter director post radar facilities in the XIX TAC flight control system (**Chart 4**). Each forward director post facility consisted of two British radars with their rotating antenna arrays and control and communications trucks. While personnel used one radar to control aircraft, the other swept the area of coverage to provide early warning. Field orders passed from joint combat operations centers to the control group's tactical control center, where communications officers made flight control assignments for each of the director posts based on their radar coverage capability and handling capacity. The command sited the director posts so that close air support coverage could be provided all along the Third Army front. Data from the forward radars and radio equipment were transmitted back to the tactical control center, which maintained a complete picture of all scheduled missions and unknown and hostile tracks in the command area. This control proved especially important for, and effective in, diverting fighter-bombers to targets called in by reconnaissance aircraft. In this capacity, the director post units provided vectors to fighter-bombers on close cooperation missions to bring the aircraft to a specific point where the ground air liaison officer took over. Likewise, reconnaissance aircraft could be vectored to specific targets or general areas designated in the field order. Although these director posts proved their usefulness late in the drive across France, General Weyland and his staff considered that their limitations in range, radar resolution, and in the amount of control facilities available posed serious handicaps for fall and winter flying conditions.

The answer appeared with the arrival in late September of the American-built MEW radar AN/CPS-1, which supplemented the four forward director post radar facilities in the XIX TAC communications network. This huge, 60-ton radar offered a high-power output (3,000 mc), very short wavelength (10-cm wave), and a rotating antenna which resulted in superb coverage and excellent capability to accurately locate individual aircraft over a 200-mile front in all directions. MEW radar operators used two sets of indicator tubes. Half consisted of B-scans, which observers watched to report all aircraft in their assigned sectors to the tactical control center. Controllers handled the remaining tubes, known as planned position indicator tubes, to track assigned close air support formations from takeoff to landing.

A Direction Finder (D/F) Fixer Station at each radar site identified the formation and its bearing or position taken on all VHF transmissions. When correlated with blips on the MEW's planned position indicator tube, the D/F Fixer MEW could furnish a close air support formation leader with a variety of flight and target information. With its British height-finder radar, the MEW also could provide range, azimuth, and altitude of aircraft at ranges approaching 200 miles. The microwave radar's resolution and inherent accuracy were greater than any other Allied search radar. During intermittent testing in its first month of operation, the XIX TAC controllers found the new microwave radar to be accurate to a range of one-half mile with an azimuth error of one degree, which they considered acceptable for initial operations.[11]

During August 1944, General Weyland had lobbied hard for improved radar that would provide long-range control of his aircraft far from their operating bases. Its introduction was delayed by difficulties in finding and converting one of the few alternate systems available. Only one of the five preproduction models had been modified in the spring of 1944 for mobile operations in Normandy, but it remained with General Quesada's command. A second MEW radar facility was operating as a fixed station on England's south coast to control nighttime aerial operations and to track incoming V–1 flying bombs. To answer Weyland's need for an offensive system, technicians made this model mobile, or at least transportable in vans, and sent it to the continent on September 8. After a test exercise at Chateaudun, where it performed well, the command moved it east to Nonsard, near Etain, on the twenty-second. Clearly, Weyland also based his decision to reorganize the flight control function in September on the timely acquisition of this long-range radar.[12]

The MEW radar immediately became the key element in XIX TAC's operations for flight control and as a device to direct reasonably accurate aircraft bombing in bad weather. Records for October 1944 indicate that it controlled about half of the command's daytime missions and all of the night photo and night fighter aircraft flights. In nighttime flying, it performed a ground controlled intercept (GCI) function. The night missions were unprecedented for the tactical air forces and only the radar system made possible the command's new night offensive capability. In a conference with Ninth Air Force officers on September 27, Weyland learned that the tactical air commands would likely receive night fighter squadrons of P–61s. Although the Black Widows had been operational since early summer, their effectiveness was less than desired because the tactical commands did not always know when or where they would be airborne. With the arrival of the 425th (P–61) Night Fighter Squadron in early October, XIX TAC controllers now had the ground equipment needed to operate night defensive patrol and offensive

A P–61 night fighter equipped with rockets.

intruder missions. Better command and control measures could not, however, alleviate the fundamental and ever-present problem of too few night fighters available to seriously impede German nighttime movements.[13]

Not surprisingly, the command experienced initial technical and operator problems with its new and unfamiliar equipment. As a line-of-sight instrument, optimum location of any radar is crucial, a fact made clear at the first site when communications officers discovered a blind spot to the southeast. Although siting processes proved to be slow, by November 20, the AN/CPS-1 had been moved five times. Technicians estimated its antenna life would not exceed ten movements from place to place, which became an incentive to develop effective siting techniques and procedures as quickly as possible.

Although the command remained enthusiastic about the new MEW radar and control facility from the start, the same could not be said for the SCR–584, a 10-cm microwave close control radar system. General Quesada's IX TAC had experimented with the short-range SCR–584 for close control in a number of operations in Normandy. This radar promised to provide more accurate navigation control, what airmen referred to as last-resort blind bombing. The set, however, with only a 30-mile practical operating range, required more personnel than the more powerful MEW radar and it proved more difficult to operate. When conducting a mission, a formation would rendezvous at a given altitude over a specified point with the lead aircraft positioned 500 feet ahead of the formation. Once the SCR–584 locked on to the lead plane, the pilot could take his formation to the assigned target. Course deviations en route could be made without difficulty because a moving spot of light on the underside of a horizontal map always indicated the plane's position to the controller. Under static conditions and with adequate operator training, a modified SCR–584 later became a useful addition to winter operations during the Ardennes Campaign. During the winter, however, the XIX TAC long-range MEW radar received an additional close-control modification, after which the command preferred it to the SCR–584 system for both winter flying and the mobile conditions of the drive across Germany in the spring of 1945.

After paying a visit to XIX TAC to observe installation of the long-range microwave radar in late September 1944, David Griggs, a technical advisor with the U.S. Strategic Air Forces in Europe, urged Weyland to acquire a number of new devices, including a ground-controlled (blind) approach (GCA) system to aid aircraft landing in poor weather, as well as an SCR–584, which he predicted could achieve blind bombing accuracy of 200 yards at a range of 30–35 miles. He admitted that "we have yet to learn how to make the most efficient use of it operationally" and recommended the command accept civilian experts from Ninth Air Force's Operational Research Section to monitor the MEW radar and the SCR–584, when the latter became available.[14]

In early October 1944, Weyland requested that his staff study the Griggs proposals and recommend a course of action. In contrast to officers at

Quesada's IX TAC, those at XIX TAC seemed wary of the civilians, perhaps because of the extravagant claims made for the new technology. Although Weyland's chief of staff Colonel Browne favored the new equipment and civilian operational research personnel, he told General Weyland that the senior XIX TAC intelligence, operations, and signals officers would accept an "ORS [Operational Research Section] in this Command as a necessary evil. No one wants it particularly but we all feel that it may do some good." As it was, the scientists and engineers proved their worth, especially after December 1, when British Branch Radiation Laboratory scientist J. E. Faulkner arrived to coordinate all radar-related activities of the command. In any event, with the addition of the MEW radar, the XIX TAC could now conduct effective long-range armed reconnaissance and escort missions in Northwest Europe under winter weather conditions. At the end of September, meanwhile, the XIX TAC prepared for operations in support of Third Army's assault on German defensive positions in the Mosel region.[15]

Stalemate along the Mosel

On the western front in early September 1944, General Eisenhower believed Allied armies could reach the Rhine River before constraints on resupply became critical or German defensive actions proved decisive. United States First Army patrols crossed the German border near Aachen on September 11, 1944, while Allied forces in southern France linked up with Eisenhower's northern troops in pursuit of what appeared to be a thoroughly beaten enemy. On the eastern front, Soviet armies had conquered the last areas of Russian territory from the Germans and slashed into Poland. Overhead, operating almost at will, British and American strategic bombers pounded Germany day and night. The Third Reich indeed appeared on the verge of collapse. By the end of September, however, the Allied optimism disappeared.[16]

To begin with, Montgomery's bold plan in the north, labeled Operation Market Garden, called for crossing three rivers in the Netherlands to outflank the West Wall, while employing an airborne-assisted assault. Approved by Eisenhower, British and American airborne troops were to seize a narrow corridor 65 miles deep and hold it, while Montgomery's British Second Army raced through on its way to the Zuider Zee. The airborne portion of the operation began on September 17 and proved successful. Stiff German resistance, however, slowed the British ground forces, while nearby German Panzer units isolated the northernmost British airborne troops at a small bridgehead north of the Lower Rhine, at Arnhem, the celebrated "bridge too far." Facing an increasingly desperate situation, on September 25 and 26, 2,000 British paratroopers, all that remained of an original 9,000-man force, retreated to the south bank of the Rhine. Though most of these surviving paratroopers managed to reach Allied lines, Operation Market Garden failed entirely. Montgomery's forces had stalled and they neither outflanked the West Wall nor achieved a position for a strike against the Ruhr.[17]

Allied armies farther south also experienced the brunt of renewed and tenacious German resistance. General Hodges's U.S. First Army found itself too greatly extended to exploit the West Wall penetrations achieved at Aachen and in the Ardennes. In Alsace, the 6th Army Group made only limited gains against *Wehrmacht* troops who used the forested foothills of the Vosges Mountains to good advantage. Patton's U.S. Third Army drive bogged down when his troops encountered determined German defenders at the Mosel River and the fortified city of Metz. By month's end, the Allied assault in the west had stalled everywhere; it became increasingly clear that a sustained, renewed offensive would have to await replenishment of supplies. Montgomery's troops captured Antwerp on September 4, 1944, the Belgian port city crucial to an Allied logistical buildup, but his forces neglected to clear all of the Schelde Estuary of its German defenders. Despite being surrounded and isolated, elements of Gen. Kurt Student's battle-seasoned *First Parachute Army* now blocked passage of Allied shipping into and out of the port. Allied military leaders, it must be said, at first failed to see the threat that this situation posed and days passed before General Eisenhower pressured Montgomery to clear the Schelde Estuary of its German defenders. Newly promoted to Field Marshal,[18] Montgomery in mid-October finally turned his full attention from Operation Market Garden to the challenge on the Schelde. Much to the surprise of the baton-wielding British commander, despite intense assaults, the tenacious Germans retained control of the port approaches for three more weeks, until they surrendered on November 8. Even then, until the last mines were located and cleared from estuary waters, Antwerp's port facilities remained closed to Allied vessels until November 28, 1944![19]

In the south, Omar Bradley's directive in late September 1944, called for U.S. Third Army to assume a defensive posture and hold its position in Lorraine until supplies reached levels that would permit a major offensive (**Map 9**). Never content simply to hold a position, Patton advised Third Army leaders on September 25 that a "defensive posture" did not imply an absence of contact with the enemy. Rather, while consolidating, regrouping, and rotating personnel, Third Army would pursue "limited objective attacks" against the enemy.[20] The XIX TAC supported these modest attacks and conducted an interdiction program against the *Wehrmacht*, while preparing for the impending, major joint offensive.

During one of these attacks in late September 1944, General Eddy's XII Corps found itself engaged in a sometimes desperate tank battle at Arracourt, while to the north in the Gramecey Forest, a grim, close-quarters infantry struggle continued for control of the bridgehead there (**Map 10**).[21] On September 26, while XII Corps consolidated its position northeast of Nancy

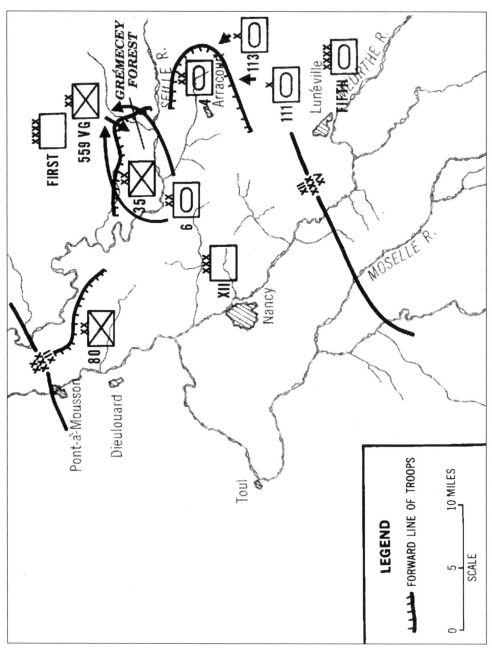

Map 10
German Counterattacks Against XII Corps: September 19–30, 1944

Reprinted from: Christopher R. Gabel, "The Lorraine Campaign: An Overview, Sep-Dec 1944," (Ft. Leavenworth, Kan.: U.S. Army Command and General Staff College, 1985), p. 18.

and fought off heavy enemy counterattacks, General Patton ordered General Walker in the south to capture the fortified town of Metz and sweep to the Rhine. This would prove much too large a limited objective for two supply-short infantry divisions and one armored division spread along a 40-mile front. Earlier, Patton's forces assaulted the outlying forts to the southwest of the city on a small scale, but using only the Michelin road maps available to them at the time, they had no idea of the challenge they faced.

As it turned out, when French archival maps and drawings of the Maginot Line arrived from Paris in early October, Third Army leaders learned that the old Metz fortress complex consisted of *43* interconnecting forts surrounding the city on both sides of the Mosel River. Many held up to 2,000 personnel and housed heavy artillery in steel- and concrete-reinforced turrets. These heavily defended forts also would prove an equally tough target for XIX TAC fighter-bombers. On September 26, for example, while Walker's forces prepared to attack Fort Driant five miles southwest of Metz, the 405th Fighter Group, the Raiders, flew in bad weather to bomb the fort using 1,000-lb. bombs and napalm. The results offered little encouragement to those hoping for a quick victory (**Map 11**).[22]

On September 27, the first good flying day in several weeks, the 5th Infantry Division's probing attack at Ft. Driant met fanatical resistance. The 405th Fighter Group's six-mission supporting effort again had little effect in spite of accurate bombing and correspondingly high praise from the ground forces. Next day, XIX TAC stepped up its effort by sending squadrons from four groups against the Metz forts for a total of 13 missions and 156 sorties. The command preferred using squadron-sized missions and continued this practice for most of the fall campaign. Under conditions of fewer daylight hours and limited forces, XIX TAC provided maximum flexibility by allowing a fighter group to divide its forces, if necessary, among close support and interdiction missions. It also became customary at this time for each squadron in a group to be assigned to support a particular army division.

The Metz mission results of September 28, 1944, did not please General Weyland. Using pillboxes and turrets as aiming points, his pilots had bombed accurately, yet had apparently produced little damage. Ninth Air Force became especially interested in the effect of napalm on the Metz targets and Colonel Hallett, XIX TAC's intelligence officer, undertook a study of firebomb results during this attempt to subdue Ft. Driant's defenders. His investigation of attacks on the twenty-eighth revealed that the 5th Infantry Division reported large fires lasting as long as 30 minutes. When a reconnaissance patrol attempted to move forward shortly after the bombing, however, German defenders in the fort kept it pinned down by heavy and accurate automatic weapons fire. Unfortunately, Hallett's findings proved typical for fighter-bomber attacks in support of assaults against fixed, fortified defenses. The only note of encouragement was that the attacks often stunned the defenders and temporarily silenced the guns.[23]

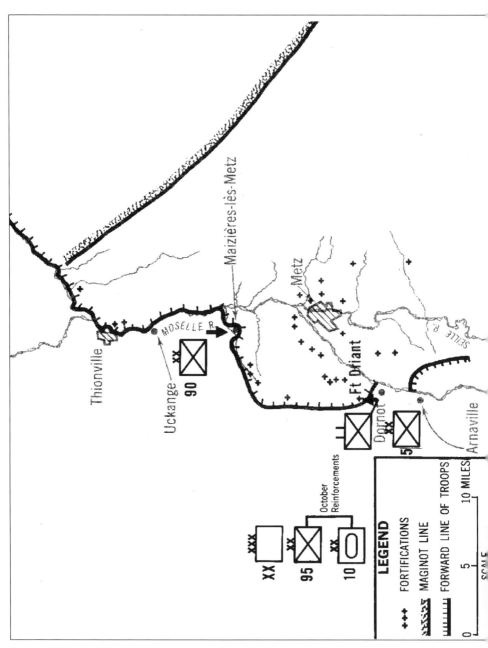

Map 11
XX Corps Operations: October 1944

Reprinted from: Christopher R. Gabel, "The Lorraine Campaign: An Overview, Sep-Dec 1944," (Ft. Leavenworth, Kan.: U.S. Army Command and General Staff College, 1985), p. 25.

General Weyland and his staff expressed their frustration at the evening briefing on September 28. After assessing mission results, Weyland concluded that the forts were "not a proper target" for fighter-bombers. As in the case of Brittany, his arguments focused on the high level of effort and cost for the limited results achieved. On the previous day the command lost six aircraft to flak and he expected the flak threat to worsen. For Weyland and his staff veterans, it must have seemed like a rerun of the Cherbourg and Brest Operations. They believed the Metz fortifications required bombing by heavy and medium bombers. General Weyland's air support efforts in the weeks ahead invariably turned to coordinating heavy and medium bombers of the Eighth and Ninth Air Forces for his joint air-ground plans.[24]

Later in the evening of September 28, 1944, Patton's chief of staff Gaffey called Weyland to request priority support next day for Manton Eddy's XII Corps, whose 35th Infantry and 4th Armored Divisions came under heavy counterattack at Arracourt. Weyland promised Gaffey a squadron arriving overhead every hour and he gave that assignment to the 405th Fighter Group. The Raiders responded with 96 sorties and, in the words of the Army historian of the Lorraine Campaign, "nearly leveled the village and cut up the German reserves assembling there, thus weakening still further the ability of the enemy to exploit an attack that had been initiated successfully." The *Wehrmacht* counterattack was blunted.[25]

In the weeks ahead, General Weyland found his reduced command assuming new missions, straining the forces available for each assignment. For example, the command assumed responsibility for supporting XV Corps, which had been transferred to the U.S. Seventh Army, on Third Army's right flank, until aircraft of the XII TAC under Brig. Gen. Gordon P. Saville could be based closer to the Lorraine front. Support for the 5th Infantry Division at Metz decreased to only two squadrons of Curry's Cougars in the 36th Group. A Ninth Air Force directive on September 25, established rail-cutting as the first priority for fighter-bombers. This interdiction program intensified in October, but it would be hampered by continuing bad weather and the relatively small number of aircraft that Weyland had available and which he was willing to commit to the effort. On September 29, the other groups of XIX TAC flew fighter sweeps against German airfields or armed reconnaissance against rail interdiction targets. Along with close support of XX and XII Corps efforts, these three missions—close air support, interdiction, and fighter sweeps—comprised the bulk of XIX TAC's flying in the Lorraine Campaign. Bad weather on the last day of September prevented all flying and the winter weather ahead threatened an effective interdiction campaign against German ground forces. With the XIX TAC grounded, Third Army might rely on its artillery for close support to continue its limited-objective attacks. The interdiction rail-cutting program, however, received a setback every day of bad weather. Only continuous air attacks on transport held the prospect of keeping

German supply lines shut and the Third Army battlefield isolated. The European weather worsened.[26]

General Weyland faced bad flying weather and conflicting aerial priorities throughout the October 1944 buildup. As part of a major Allied bombing effort, Ninth Air Force announced an expanded interdiction campaign on October 2 against rail traffic, marshaling yards, and bridges on the Rhine and Saar rivers. At the same time, XIX TAC was expected to furnish close air support to the Third Army because, for General Patton, any defensive stance on the ground involved limited-objective attacks against Germans. In that cause, Maj. Gen. S. LeRoy Irwin's 5th Infantry Division struggled to take Fort Driant during the first two weeks of October, suffering an incredible 50 percent casualty rate before Patton conceded failure. As early as October 3, with both Patton and Weyland observing, General Irwin's forces breached perimeter defenses of the fort assisted by strong air support from the 405th and 358th Fighter Groups, *after* medium bombers from the IX Bombardment Division had first stunned the German defenders.[27] Third Army lauded the support of both fighter groups.

It was one thing to penetrate Ft. Driant's outer defenses and quite another to gain access to its underground, interconnected defensive network. German officer school candidates, who happened to be battle-hardened former NCOs, led a ferocious German counterattack which halted the American forces. Intense fighting continued around the fort until October 12, when Patton reluctantly directed his forces to withdraw and maintain a containing operation. Elsewhere along the front, however, Patton's so-called defensive operations escalated. The XX Corps' 90th Infantry Division continued methodically to reduce Maizieres-les-Metz, the town six miles north of Metz that blocked the only unfortified approach to the city. Other units laid siege to other Metz fortresses, while forward units pressed ahead to enlarge bridgeheads across the

Brig. Gen.
Gordon P. Saville,
commander,
XII Tactical Air Force

Mosel north and south of the city. During Third Army's buildup for the planned November offensive, it continued to rotate troops out of the front line for training in the reduction of fortifications (**Map 11**).[28]

General Patton became increasingly frustrated with the lack of forward progress during October 1944. At the army's morning briefing on October 13 he urged his air commander to clobber the Driant fort in retaliation for the casualties it had inflicted on his 5th Infantry Division. Weyland turned that task over to his operations officer, Colonel Ferguson, but little aerial retaliation occurred prior to the major offensive in early November. The command flew only one bombing mission against the Metz fortifications during the last two weeks of October. Directed against three small fortified towns south of the city, it involved but one squadron from the 405th Fighter Group on the twenty-second. Weyland considered interdiction targets more important than the fortifications, and General Patton, who seemed to have recovered from his frustration, did not pressure the air arm further.

Both Patton and Weyland could agree that the key to unlocking the Metz fortress complex lay in a massive bombing effort in conjunction with a major land attack. Earlier, on October 2, 1944, Weyland and his staff had met with General Vandenberg, Ninth Air Force commander, to discuss responsibilities and procedures for use of the medium and heavy bombers in tactical operations. They decided to request heavy bombers for the planned offensives in the First and Third Army areas and they agreed on 48 hours' notice to complete necessary arrangements. Even at this early date in the Lorraine Campaign, air leaders had begun long-range planning for the joint operations to come.[29]

Meanwhile, XIX TAC concentrated on the rail interdiction program, with General Patton's full support. On October 5, Ninth Air Force revised target assignments for its medium bombers and fighters with inner and outer lines of interdiction. It divided the targets among tactical air commands accordingly. The XIX TAC's allotment consisted of eight rail lines in Third Army's sector from Coblenz to Landau and ten lines east of the Rhine. On October 7, Patton lifted the ban on bridge destruction, although it was not until after the nineteenth, when Ninth Air Force again directed all four tactical air commands to make interdiction their top priority, that mission results showed a pronounced number of bridge targets attacked.[30] The XIX TAC historian on October 7, 1944, claimed the "all out campaign against RR traffic was paying dividends" because the enemy had resorted to barge traffic on the Rhine-Marne canal. Understandably, policing this canal also became a major command activity and command pilots achieved good success, especially after the 362d proposed and carried out a lock-destroying mission. Nevertheless, reconnaissance reports after the first week in October indicated German traffic continued to be heavy west of the Rhine, which tempered initial optimism.[31]

Army chief of staff General Marshall visited Third Army headquarters on October 7, 1944, and praised the accomplishments of the Third Army–XIX TAC team. He also attended what General Weyland referred to in his diary as a special briefing. In fact, Weyland, too, attended these special briefings either in General Patton's personal van or the Third Army chief of staff's office prior to the regular Third Army morning staff briefing. These particular briefings normally occurred every morning and, as only became known publicly many years later, involved Ultra communications intelligence. By early October, Patton had received Ultra assessments for more than two months. Ultra specialist Maj. Melvin C. Helfers joined Third Army at its Knutsford headquarters shortly after Patton's arrival in England, but remained on the sidelines and unknown to Patton until his information, so vital to Third Army operations, was brought to Patton's attention. This occurred on August 6, when Ultra forecast a German counterattack in the direction of Patton's troops at Avranches. Armed with this information, Major Helfers convinced Third Army's intelligence chief, Col. Oscar W. Koch, that Patton must be briefed on this German plan. Duly impressed by the Ultra data, Patton expressed surprise that he had not been informed earlier of Helfers's intelligence role at Third Army. In any event, the next morning the General summoned Helfers to personally conduct the first of what became routine Ultra briefings for Patton and a few other select Third Army officers.

Although General Weyland began attending the Third Army Ultra briefings consistently only in early October, he had been receiving Ultra data on *Luftwaffe* plans and dispositions since mid-June, while he was still in England. During operations in France, his fireman duties in support of Third Army's offensive often precluded regularly scheduled briefings from his own Ultra specialist, Maj. Harry M. Grove. In addition to meeting with General Weyland when feasible, Major Grove provided the XIX TAC's intelligence chief, Colonel Hallett, with daily updates on German air force activities. By mid-October, and with the Lorraine Campaign well underway, Weyland brought Colonel Browne, his chief of staff, and Major Grove to the Third Army Ultra briefings when *Luftwaffe* data proved especially important.[32]

There is little disagreement about Ultra's importance in supplying Third Army with the enemy's ground order of battle information on a regular basis, but its usefulness for the tactical air arm appears more questionable. General Quesada has argued that Ultra's main contribution was "to instill confidence and provide guidance to the conduct of war…rather than the tactics of the war." No doubt this came from following changes in the *Luftwaffe's* air order of battle. Indeed, Ultra allowed Allied intelligence officers to follow the major *Luftwaffe* recovery, redeployment, and first serious use of jet fighters in the fall. Though one can argue that Ultra's information provided knowledge of strong enemy concentrations, which meant heavy flak areas to avoid, the airmen seem to have relied on the Y-service radio intercept operation for their best intelligence of immediate *Luftwaffe* plans. Beyond this, tactical and photographic reconnaissance assured the command of systematic coverage of the battle zone, weather permitting.[33]

Despite a weak *Luftwaffe* presence on Third Army's front, General Weyland remained determined to guard against a possible resurgent air threat. The command's intelligence chief, Colonel Hallett, studied the problem and on October 6, 1944, he advised the combat operations officer that the presence of 350 German fighters at 30–40 airfields in the Saar represented a force that could not be ignored. He suggested that higher headquarters develop a coordinated plan of attack. Failing this, XIX TAC should hit all of the airfields within range of its fighter-bombers. Hallett awaited pictures from the 10th Photo Reconnaissance Group, whose efforts had been hampered by the weather, before he prepared the final target folders. Unknown to Weyland's intelligence chief, the *Luftwaffe* had already begun building up its forces for a counterattack that Hitler began planning as early as mid-September. On October 8, Weyland sent three groups against some key German airfields where tactical reconnaissance reported a major buildup. Led by P–51s of the 354th Fighter Group, command pilots attacked five airfields with impressive results. They claimed seven aircraft destroyed in air combat, 19 more on the ground, and possibly an additional 26 damaged. Although General Weyland continued to worry about the *Luftwaffe* threat, his forces did not strike German airfields purposefully again until the end of the month. The command focused on interdiction, but bad weather continued to hamper that effort. Following the attacks against German air forces on October 8, for example, air operations had to be scrubbed for the next two days.[34]

General Weyland used the nonflying time to deal with support problems. Airfields, especially, needed attention. The persistent rains of September and October 1944, along with heavy use of command fields by heavily laden C–47 transports resupplying Third Army, had taken their toll on runways and taxiways. On October 8, Weyland inspected the airstrip at Etain, which he wanted as the future base of the 362d Fighter Group and the 425th Night Fighter Squadron. The C–47 landings had ruined the runway, and the previous evening's rain forced engineers to abandon their attempt to lay Hessian strip, the bituminous surface used most frequently during the drive across France. The engineers required three or four dry weather days to complete a runway, and rain fell nearly every day. General Weyland strongly argued for switching to pierced steel plank surfacing, but Ninth Air Force refused, citing availability and shipping weight. A steel-plank airfield required 3,500 tons of material, while only 350 tons of Hessian proved sufficient to cover the same field. At Vitry, rain in October softened the runway to the point where it became unserviceable. Consequently, the 358th Fighter Group Orange Tails moved to Mourmelon, home of the 406th Fighter Group. From the command's viewpoint, however, two groups operating from a single base placed an undesirable strain on personnel and facilities. Weyland also lobbied to have a pierced steel-plank field laid at a future site near Metz for two groups, and in this case he succeeded.[35]

By late October 1944, pierced steel-plank runways also experienced rapid deterioration and required considerable maintenance. Officials referred to reduced operations resulting from these conditions, although the record is not specific or entirely clear how seriously the problem affected operations. The engineers knew, however, that the incessant rains loosened the grading and soil compaction. The solution seemed to be a crushed rock base for all airstrips, but this meant finding rock in sufficient quantity, crushing it and shipping it efficiently in spite of its enormous weight. If the rains of October created one set of operational problems, the cold weather expected in November would intensify difficulties with the Hessian-surfaced fields because the cold would crack the tar seal, thus permitting propeller wash to blow the stuffing loose. Had they been granted three or four more days of good weather in early October, the engineers declared, they would have been able to winterize all XIX TAC airfields before the onset of severe weather. The command's experience in October underscored an oft-forgotten axiom that "air power begins and ends on the ground."[36]

Despite the rain and mud in October 1944, the command's aircraft maintenance operation experienced no major difficulties, something that could not be said for supply. Although the supply situation improved with the establishment of dumps in the forward area, key problems affected the command throughout the winter. Back in September, the command reported shortages of replacement P–51 aircraft and related spare parts, yet repeated requests for resupply were not met. By November, the 354th Fighter Group, for example,

The lab of the 10th Photo Reconnaissance Group processing recce photos.

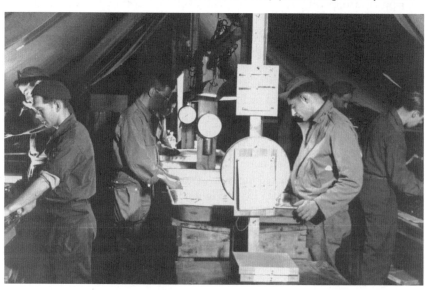

reported a shortage of 30 aircraft in the group. Given the Eighth Air Force's priority claim on P–51s for bomber escort duty, no solution appeared in sight. The P–51 problem doubtless contributed to a decision in November to convert the Pioneer Mustang group to P–47s. Although officials attributed this conversion to the need for more fighter-bomber support and reduced air defense requirements, the adverse effects of insufficient replacement aircraft on the XIX TAC mission doubtless contributed to the decision.[37]

The flow of P–47 planes and parts, meanwhile, remained uninterrupted during October and November. By mid-October, all groups had at least the prescribed 70 aircraft; by the end of October, the new P–47D-30 model with its improved electrical bomb release began arriving. Soon it became the dominant Thunderbolt model in theater. The only subsequent improvement involved installation of the underwing pylons for rocket launching. The 362d Fighter Group was next in line after the 406th for five-inch rockets, but a shortage of parts delayed the conversion. By the end of October, only one squadron of the 362d completed this modification.[38]

Finally, the XIX TAC commander had to deal with pilot replacement. The problem was not that the command received too few fighter pilots—although only 99 pilots arrived in October 1944 to fill the 162 vacancies, the surplus of 63 from the month before balanced the allotment. The main difficulty involved the experience level of the newly arriving airmen. Early in the month the command historian observed that new pilots had very little flying time in fighters and appeared especially weak in gunnery and bombing. Furthermore, the command had neither the facilities nor sufficient gasoline to train these replacements properly. Although General Weyland complained to General Vandenberg, Ninth Air Force did little until December 10. That day Weyland evidently had had enough; he refused to accept 11 replacement pilots who collectively had almost no training in fighter operations. Ninth Air Force approved his decision and promised to look into the stateside training program.[39]

Planning an Offensive

While XIX TAC carried out a variety of missions in support of Third Army's limited-objective attacks and worked to improve the command's logistics and control functions, General Weyland and his staff joined their colleagues at Third Army headquarters in planning a major offensive. The logistic situation remained the key hurdle. During mid-October 1944, while Patton's forces continued fighting house-to-house in Mazieres-les-Metz and consolidating their positions in the XII Corps area, Third Army supply officers worked diligently to build up supply depot stocks through a rigorous conservation and rationing program, highlighted by a 25 percent reduction in the gasoline issue.[40]

While Third Army focused on logistics, the XIX TAC concentrated on its rail interdiction program. Once the heavy overcast lifted on October 11, 1944, for example, the command followed the practice of designating one group, usually the 405th Fighter Group, for close air support, while the other four flew armed reconnaissance missions. After October 23, however, the command stopped flying scheduled ground force support missions and devoted its entire effort to armed reconnaissance, escort, and at times, fighter-bomber sweeps of German airfields.

Waiting to take the offensive while his supply base was replenished offered no comfort to General Patton. On October 18, he advocated a major offensive even if it had to be undertaken on a shoestring. At the morning briefing, his staff suggested two alternative plans for enveloping Metz and pushing on to the Siegfried Line. Although in attendance, Weyland made no comment when the Third Army commander called for an immediate offensive, but he personally considered it ill-advised to attack before all major army elements were fully equipped and prepared. Despite the co-equal intent of published doctrine, Weyland and Patton were not on an equal footing in rank and Weyland never pretended otherwise. In any case, the joint planning process was officially underway. Armed with Third Army's plans, on October 19, Weyland prepared a directive for his staff to develop an air plan for the offensive. At the same time, another air plan called for sending fighter-bombers against the Etang de Lindre Dam in what would prove to be an impressive XIX TAC first.[41]

The dam-busting idea had been raised a few days earlier, on October 13, 1944. The dam lay three miles southeast of Dieuze and right in the path of XII Corps' proposed line of advance. The corps staff feared that the enemy might destroy the dam during their assault and cause the Seille River to overflow, isolating forward elements and forestalling the entire Third Army advance. This dilemma foreshadowed another that would confront Allied armies in the north on an even larger scale in November, when First and Ninth Armies on their way to the Rhine needed to cross the Roer River. Germans on the high ground at Schmidt in the Huertgen Forest controlled two dams on the upper reaches of the little river which, if opened, could flood the low-lying plain and forestall the Allied advance. In Lorraine, XII Corps wanted the Seille River dam destroyed in support of its limited-objective attack. Because of the precision required, the planners canceled the original request for heavy bombers in favor of fighter-bombers.

Weyland assigned the task to Col. Joseph Laughlin, the aggressive commander of the 362d Fighter Group, which frequently received the command's most challenging missions.[42] Colonel Laughlin and several officers spent hours at headquarters in Nancy studying large-scale photographs taken by the 31st Photo Squadron and diagrams and specifications obtained from local records. They even consulted a professor from the University of Nancy. The

High-level strategy dictated breaching the Etang de Lindre Dam at
Dieuze, France, before the Third Army offensive in November, preventing
the Germans from releasing the water between Patton's advancing
troops and thereby separate them from supplies after the attack had
begun. The photo below shows the extent of the breach and how
successfully the 362d's Thunderbolts carried out their mission
in spite of a difficult target defended by very heavy flak.

preparation paid off handsomely. On October 20, with Colonel Laughlin in the lead, two P–47 squadrons armed with 1,000-lb. armor-piercing bombs, dove from 7,000 to 100 feet in the face of heavy flak and scored at least six direct hits. The bombs made a 90-foot break in the dam; the resultant flood waters engulfed the town of Dieuze and isolated German units in the area. The XII Corps used the disruption caused by the flood to launch a successful limited-objective attack three days later.[43]

The next day, October 21, 1944, the 405th Fighter Group flew missions in support of three different corps. One of them, bombing a town and troop concentrations, assisted XII Corps' 26th Infantry Division in its limited-objective attack 22 miles east of Nancy that elicited high praise from the ground controller. General Weyland had to be encouraged when General Spaatz visited the air command that day and remarked that "the Third U.S. Army–XIX TAC team is the finest we have yet produced." Even if Spaatz's declaration was intended only to boost morale, the record of this air-ground team already merited praise.[44]

Although bad weather severely curtailed flying during the last week of October, team officials continued to work on the joint plan for Third Army's offensive. Scheduled to begin on November 5, 1944, the Third Army plan called for crossing the Mosel north and south of Metz, entirely bypassing the strongest forts, and pushing on to the Rhine River. Metz would be taken later by XX Corps through encirclement and infiltration.[45] On October 22, Weyland's intelligence and operations chiefs presented the air plan, which the air commander discussed the next day in a joint meeting with General Patton, the Third Army staff, and the two corps commanders. Essentially the air proposal called for a large preliminary air assault to neutralize the forts and strongpoints. Heavy bombers would pound the outlying Metz forts while medium bombers hit smaller forts, supply dumps, and troop concentrations in two key areas. The XIX TAC fighter-bombers would attack all known command posts in the vicinity as well as fly armed reconnaissance missions against all road and rail traffic and enemy airfields in close proximity to Third Army's front. (At this time, General Weyland did not know what would be the size of the bombing force available for Third Army's use.) Army leaders expressed satisfaction with the plan, and Weyland indicated he intended to request two additional fighter groups for tactical support. The planners dubbed this offensive Operation Madison.[46]

Despite the fact that Generals Patton and Weyland had agreed on the joint plan, the path ahead during the next week and a half was far from smooth. For one thing, higher authorities reminded them immediately that the Third Army sector of the Allied front continued to be judged second in importance to the First Army area opposite Aachen. Originally, Allied plans called for the main effort against the Siegfried Line to be led by General Hodges's First Army. Now that Aachen had been secured, Hodges's plan called for an attack toward Cologne south of the Ruhr, also beginning November 5. Politics and prestige, however, never seemed far removed from Allied decision-making and Field Marshal Montgomery delayed returning an American infantry division borrowed earlier from the 12th Army Group. Under these circumstances, General Bradley, 12th Army Group commander, postponed First Army's offensive and decided to allow General Patton to begin Operation Madison on the fifth. First Army would then launch Operation Queen, an attack against the Roer River defenses, a week after the initiation of Operation Madison (**Map 9**). At the end of October a decision between the two planned offensives had not yet been reached.[47]

Meanwhile, Third Army's supply shortfalls continued. Even though ammunition and rations stocks improved, available gas reached only 67 percent of the level requested. General Weyland had his problems, too. Meeting with Ninth Air Force Commander General Vandenberg on October 27, he learned that not only would XIX TAC not receive two additional fighter groups for Operation Madison, but the command instead would lose another group, this time to General Saville's XII TAC for its operations in southeastern France. Moreover, as the Ninth Air Force commander explained, General Bradley's focus on First Army in the north meant dividing the fighter groups that remained: six for General Quesada's IX TAC and four each for General Weyland's XIX TAC and General Nugent's XXIX TAC.[48]

Weyland objected vigorously, but to no avail. The next day, he met with his wing commander, Brig. Gen. Homer "Tex" Saunders and Colonel Ferguson, combat operations chief. If the decision could not be overturned, they recommended relinquishing the 358th Orange Tails. Still upset, Weyland expressed displeasure to General Patton later that day in a formal memorandum. The proposed fighter group allotment, he asserted, "appears most inequitable, and if it goes through we are in a bad way." The ratio of fighter-

General Patton (right) is removing a new pistol from his holster to show Gens. Hodges (left), and Bradley (center).

bomber support for the offensive, he averred, penalized Third Army because the IX and XXIX TAC groups would be supporting proportionally smaller ground forces. He reminded General Patton that all of the Ninth's 13 bomber groups remained under centralized control and could be shifted easily to influence the action in any area. The rapid shifting of fighter support, divided among three tactical air commands, under the circumstances could not be depended upon to meet exigencies. He considered it essential that XIX TAC be allowed at least five groups for Operation Madison. "I contend," he said, "that First Army can still have priority without robbing us."[49]

Patton promptly called General Bradley on the matter. Then he, General Weyland, and Col. Paul D. Harkins, Third Army's deputy chief of staff, drove to Luxembourg on October 29 to discuss the issue further with Bradley and Ninth Air Force officers. Their argument did not prove convincing. As Patton confided to his diary: "tried to move a fighter-bomber group for Weyland but lost all the air guys to First and Ninth Armies." The 358th Fighter Group prepared to transfer prior to the offensive, even though XII TAC would not play a significant role in Operation Madison. In the end, Ninth Air Force allowed the Orange Tails to fly one last operation for XIX TAC after all.[50]

The bad weather ended temporarily and October 28 and 29 became two of the best flying days of the month. The command used its good fortune to concentrate on interdiction targets: rail and road bridges both east and west of the Rhine. The armed reconnaissance missions brought out the *Luftwaffe* this time, and the 354th Fighter Group Mustangs again set the pace in air encounters. Attacked by more than 100 Bf 109s near Heidelberg, the pioneer group tallied claims of 24 destroyed and eight damaged in aerial combat, while losing only three of its own. Weather again forced cancellation of the interdiction program the last two days of the month. By now the command began focusing on bridges rather than rail cuts, and it ended the month claiming 17 bridges destroyed and 22 damaged. The command admitted, however, while the bridges proved to be suitable targets, the program achieved only limited success. General Weyland did not question sending squadrons of 12 aircraft, each armed with two 500-lb. general-purpose bombs, against each bridge. The bridges, however, proved to be heavily defended by flak batteries and very difficult targets to hit. As later studies would show, the fighter-bombers would have had greater success against bridges if they had been armed with the larger, 1,000-lb. bombs. Moreover, like the rail-cutting program, the airmen needed better flying weather to bomb the German-held bridges consistently. Too often mission reports revealed that pilots flew against secondary targets because of overcast conditions in the original target area. When the command reviewed its flying effort for October 1944, it was not surprised to find that only 12 days had been completely flyable, 12 partially flyable, and seven totally nonoperational. Forecasters predicted the weather in November would be worse.[51]

As October drew to a close, Weyland looked back on a month in which his command contended with bad weather, strengthened German defenses, Third Army's inability to mount a sustained offensive, and requirements that called for a battlefield interdiction program and a variety of additional missions—and all had to be managed with reduced aerial forces. At month's end, however, plans for Operation Madison, aimed at crossing the Mosel and driving for the Rhine, neared completion. Patton seemed determined to attack the Germans entrenched in Lorraine even though the offensive was viewed elsewhere as a secondary attack and even though his ground forces were short-handed. Third Army supply officers still believed a major offensive could not be sustained at this time, but D-Day remained set for November 5, weather permitting.[52]

From Metz to the Siegfried Line

Throughout the week preceding Operation Madison, General Weyland met daily with the Third Army staff on matters of coordination, timing, and target priorities. As the air commander on the air-ground team, he played a crucial role in the planning and execution of the joint operation. On November 1, 1944, for example, two officers from Eighth Air Force Bomber Command visited Weyland to discuss Madison targets for their heavy bombers. Next day he attended a conference at Third Army headquarters, where a visiting General Bradley received a detailed review of Operation Madison. Bradley told Patton that First Army could not be ready to attack until the tenth; Patton replied that his Third Army could attack on 24 hours' notice. Bradley gave him the "green light" to launch Operation Madison on November 8.[53]

During this conference, Third Army supply officers happily noted that the logistics situation continued to improve, especially as a result of bulk gasoline shipments delivered by rail. How much of this improvement represented unauthorized supplies purloined from other commands remains unclear. Patton seldom interfered with the innovative activities of his supply officers, who continued to enhance a notorious reputation for "requisitioning" army materiel originally destined elsewhere. After other ground officers discussed various minor changes in the assault plan, Weyland presented the air plan to Generals Bradley and Patton. He discussed the various adjustments that had been made in terms of lines of attack and specific targets and he explained realistically what could be expected from his forces with his command reduced from five to four groups of fighter-bombers. With bad weather anticipated and the shorter flying days of winter to contend with, the ground forces would receive about 25 percent of the aerial support they had received in the summer. Consequently, the timing of various parts of the operation would be essential if air support were to achieve its objectives. Clearly Weyland attempted to make a case for receiving air reinforcements now that Operation Madison would lead the Allied assault on the western front.[54]

Gasoline for Patton's Third Army was flown from England in C–47s
(top and center), then moved by truck and rail to supply dumps near his
armored columns.

On November 3, 1944, Patton, Weyland, and their staffs conferred again at Third Army headquarters on target priorities and the timing of attacks for the various infantry and tank units. Late that morning, General Weyland revised the air plan to include maximum bomber support. Afterward, Ferguson and Hallett flew to Ninth Air Force headquarters with the published plan to request full heavy bomber and medium bomber support from the fifth through the eighth of November, and possibly to the ninth, as well. The air proposal called for heavy bombers to attack ten forts commanding the road approaches to Metz and the medium bombers to strike four forts in the Metz area, eight supply dumps, and German troop concentrations in the Bois-des-Secourt and Chateau Salins areas about 12 miles east of Nancy. Fighter-bombers would attack nine command posts using 500-lb. general-purpose bombs with delay fuzes and napalm, where available. Additionally, the fighters would bomb eight German airfields on D-Day. Weyland considered this plan extremely ambitious, especially for the fighter-bombers, and he continued his effort to obtain more groups.[55]

If the weather proved unsuitable on November 5 and no improvement occurred by November 8, the ground forces would attack early on the eighth without initial support from the heavy and medium bombers. Although the Third Army staff always preferred to attack with air support, it would delay, but seldom cancel, an offensive if the air arm proved unavailable. Nevertheless, if bad weather persisted, the air leaders would still attempt to have bomber support available for later use against specific forts, well out of range of the advancing troops.[56]

With the onset of static warfare during September 1944, the emphasis on reconnaissance had shifted from visual or tactical reports to photographic coverage. By the end of the month, the F–5s (P–38s) of the 31st and 34th Photo Reconnaissance Squadrons were working overtime flying daily photo cover to a depth of nine miles behind enemy lines, as well as obtaining vertical and oblique coverage of Mosel River crossing points and pinpoint photos of fortifications. In addition, the F–5s continued their program of bomb damage assessment and airfield coverage missions.[57]

In October 1944 the challenge for the 10th Photo Group's F–5s increased markedly as poor flying weather created a large backlog of requests and the group lost its 34th squadron to the 363d Reconnaissance Group; this left only one squadron to handle the load. The 31st Photo Reconnaissance Squadron's historian provided a good description of the effort. "One day in October, when the weather broke, the unit flew 36 missions totaling 80 targets and 4,000 square miles of mapping." This occurred in only five hours of photo daylight. By the end of October, the overworked squadron completed 90 percent of the air-ground basic photo coverage plan, which consisted of a combination of areas and routes in a zone from the front lines to the Rhine River.[58]

Before the November offensive, the reconnaissance pilots provided photos of each Metz fort as well as photo coverage of the terrain that surrounded the city of Metz. The photographs and interpretation reports were included in the target folders that XIX TAC sent to the bomber commands for study. Patton took a personal interest in this process. When he learned, on October 31, that bomber crews had not received the required target folders, and with the unhappy consequences associated with the short bombing in Operation Cobra vividly in mind, he had intelligence officers prepare to rush them by car to Ninth Air Force and the IX Bombardment Division headquarters in Luxembourg. The XX Corps also received vertical and oblique shots of all planned crossing points, and all targets scheduled for attack by the fighter-bombers were photographed and analyzed as well.[59]

With everything ready, General Weyland flew off to Mourmelon on November 4 for a farewell address to the 358th Orange Tails. Bad weather in the target area on November 5 and two subsequent days, however, forced cancellation of the strikes planned for medium and heavy bombers. Meanwhile, although the XIX TAC could only fly on the afternoon of the fifth, it made the most of its attacks on German airfields. The 354th Fighter Group racked up the day's top score with claims of 28 German aircraft destroyed and 16 damaged with no loss of its own.

The Allies, meanwhile, consolidated XII TAC and a recently equipped French First Air Force into a new tactical air force, the First Tactical Air Force (Provisional). Its commander, former Ninth Air Force deputy commander, General Royce, arrived at Nancy on November 5 to complain personally to Weyland about what he considered the lack of cooperation from XIX TAC. Apparently he expected to receive at XII TAC the 405th Fighter Group that he preferred rather than the 358th that Weyland had assigned him and he made plain to Weyland his profound displeasure. He also criticized the proposed basing arrangement for his air force. Weyland patiently explained that the initial mix-up, whereby Ninth Air Force had mistakenly assigned the 405th to Royce, had been sorted out and that Royce's command would receive new

An F–5 from the
31st Photo
Reconnaissance
Squadron.

orders assigning the 358th Fighter Group to the XII TAC. Weyland told Royce that his command had been cooperating extensively with XII TAC in support of XV Corps. In fact, Weyland declared, "we have been doing their missions." Nothing further occurred over the unit transfer issue, although the question of support for XII TAC resurfaced later in November and again in January, when the Germans launched a diversionary offensive in Alsace. This incident involving Royce remained one of the few instances of overt disagreement among the tactical air commanders. Such isolated cases do not detract from the cooperation that generally characterized relations among the airmen.[60]

Air defense against the debilitated *Luftwaffe* became another issue of special concern to General Weyland. As the officer responsible for air defense of the Third Army area, prior to the offensive he convened a meeting to discuss coordination of antiaircraft artillery fire in the so-called inner artillery zone, the designated area within which Third Army gunners could fire freely at unidentified aircraft. Participants included the chief of Third Army's antiartillery units and several XIX TAC officers: Col. Don Mayhew, the tactical control center commander, Colonel Ferguson, the operations officer, and representatives from the night fighter and night photo squadrons. They wanted to assure themselves that everyone concerned had detailed information on all aircraft scheduled to pass through the artillery zone and obtain agreement on the proper safeguards. All too often army gunners fired on friendly aircraft because air defense personnel had not been forewarned or because an aircraft had not conformed to flight plans. At the same time, no one wanted to waste valuable, limited night fighter sorties on intercepting what frequently turned out to be friendly aircraft, unknown to the ground controllers flying in the area. Air-ground coordination required constant attention, and the challenge to the air defense system became especially acute later during the Battle of the Bulge in December 1944.[61]

The XII Corps opened the Madison Offensive at 6:00 a.m. on November 8, despite the lack of bomber support and the misgivings of General Eddy, who was ordered by Patton to either attack or "name his successor." By the end of the first day, Eddy's troops progressed two to four miles along a 27-mile front in absolutely atrocious weather and against stiff German resistance (**Map 12**). Later that morning the weather improved enough for limited fighter-bomber operations and the XIX TAC made the most of it. Enemy nerve centers attracted over half of the day's 471 sorties. Highlighting these command post raids was an attack by the 405th Raiders that scored direct hits on the 17th SS Panzer Division headquarters at Peltre, southeast of Metz. Subsequent interrogations and investigations revealed that a number of high-ranking officers had been present when the fighter-bombers demolished the structure, and German operations suffered disruption for two weeks following the attack. The other groups also had good success on the eighth, although at day's end XIX TAC squadrons found themselves scattered at bases all over the forward area as a result of the weather.[62]

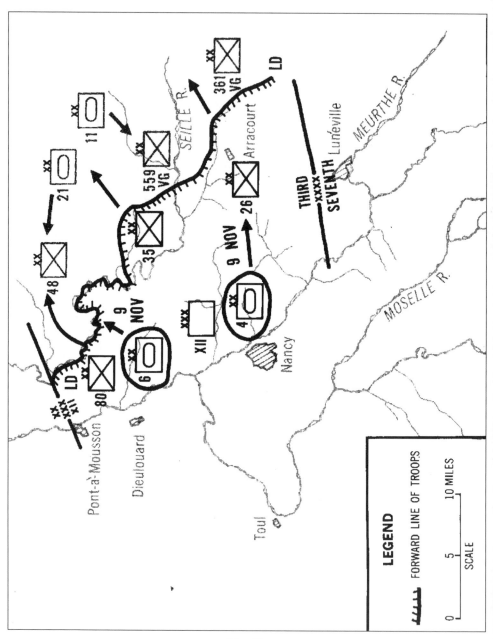

Map 12
XII Corps Attack: November 8, 1944

Reprinted from: Christopher R. Gabel, "The Lorraine Campaign: An Overview, Sep-Dec 1944," (Ft. Leavenworth, Kan.: U.S. Army Command and General Staff College, 1985), p. 26.

Maj. Gen. Ralph Royce, commander, First Tactical Air Force (Provisional)

The cost to XIX TAC, however, proved high. The 362d Fighter Group suffered most when a German force estimated at 40 FW 190s bounced one of its 12-ship squadrons. Although the Mauler pilots shot down 11 enemy aircraft, they lost three of their own. Another of the group's aircraft crashed on a strafing run in extremely poor weather. The command had established poor-weather flying parameters at a minimum 3,000-foot ceiling with broken clouds and a visibility of three miles. For takeoff, the XIX TAC considered a 1,000-foot ceiling acceptable. Now, however, much of the target area had ceilings down to 1,500 or 1,000 feet. That evening at the command briefing, Weyland acknowledged the problem, but he asserted, given the importance of the offensive, that the command would take "calculated risks on weather" as a matter of policy.[63]

General Weyland's expressed concerns about fighter resources and the postponement of Operation Queen, the Allied plan for First Army in the north to attack toward the Roer River defenses, convinced Generals Bradley and Vandenberg to provide Weyland with additional fighter support for Madison. On November 8, the XIX TAC received three fighter groups and the return, for one week, of its old 358th Fighter Group. In fact, despite its administrative transfer to XII TAC on the fifth and Royce's displeasure, General Weyland might well have been the beneficiary of further tactical assets after November 11 had the poor weather held. This was not to be, and when the weather improved on November 16 and Operation Queen began, additional fighter-bombers could not be spared.

On November 7, 1944, General Vandenberg convened a conference at Luxembourg City on how to best use the medium bombers. Army and air officials in attendance decided to strike at tank obstacles in the Siegfried Line. On November 9 large numbers of heavy and medium bombers attacked in force. To prevent the bombing of friendly troops, Third Army used radio marker beacons to identify its forward positions, and artillery lobbed two flak lines of red smoke 3,000 feet below the bombardment formation. The medium bombers had the most difficulty with the weather. Only 74 of the 514 bombers dispatched actually bombed their assigned targets, which were German troop concentrations, barracks, and tank obstacles. Of the 1,223 heavy bombers attacking, 679 used seven forts as aiming points in the 5th Infantry Division zone south of Metz, 47 attacked Thionville, 34 others hit Saarlautern, 432 bombed the Saarbruecken marshaling yard, and 31 attacked targets of opportunity. Patton considered the attack "quite a show and very encouraging to our men." He also attributed the participation of the heavy bombers on his army's front to the good relations he shared with the leading airmen. Generals Spaatz and Doolittle observed the bombing with him, and Patton told his diary that "the show was largely a present to me from them."[64]

With direct dive-bombing hits, two squadrons from the 405th Fighter Group demolished this command post of the 17th SS Panzer Grenadier Division at Peltre, France.

A cutaway of a German FW 190.

Most of the heavy bombers had to bomb through an overcast ranging from 6/10 to 10/10 cloud cover. Evaluators considered this a major reason why the forts themselves received little material damage. In early December 1944 ordnance and engineer officers conducted a study for the AAF Evaluation Board of the air attacks during the November campaign. Relying on photographic records, personal examination of the forts attacked, and interviews with American and German ground force personnel in the assault area at the time, the survey determined the air attacks did very little material damage to the forts, but the bombing destroyed other strongpoints, disrupted communications, cut roads and railways, and generally left the enemy confused and dazed.[65]

As the study of Phase III close air support operations concluded, "It was the intensity of the attack, rather than the pin-point accuracy, that achieved the results of materially aiding the attacking ground forces."[66] The lesson once again proved that ground forces had to move forward as rapidly as possible after the bombardment to take advantage of the enemy's shocked condition. The same problem recurred a few days later, in Operation Queen, when Allied ground forces withdrew to a safety zone two miles from the target area and could not move forward fast enough to prevent the German defenders from reestablishing their positions after the war's heaviest air bombardment in support of ground forces. The Cobra syndrome and fear of short-bombing continued to haunt Allied air-ground operations.[67]

Operation Madison proved successful from the air force's standpoint. Assisted by the air assault, XX Corps bypassed the Metz fortifications and pushed across the Mosel River. On the second day of the offensive, XX Corps attacked north and south of Metz, after the Mosel flooded its banks and left mud ankle-deep in most places. Despite the hostile elements, the Americans established bridgeheads over the Mosel and captured eight more villages. The next day, 11 more towns fell, and Patton's troops forced the surrender of the important Fort Koenigsmacher, southeast of Thionville. For Third Army personnel, the weeks of patient training in October paid off. The tactics of bypassing the strongest fortified positions and reducing them later with high explosives and gasoline proved very effective.[68]

By the third day, on November 10, 1944, the enemy began a general but "fighting" withdrawal in the region. The movement offered good targets for XIX TAC fighter-bombers, which provided effective support through November 11. In most cases Weyland's fighter groups supported a specific frontline division *and* with only group-sized missions. During the initial drive of Operation Madison, fighter-bomber pilots perfected what they termed village busting tactics. Standard practice soon called for successive waves of an attacking squadron in flights of four to carry three different types of ordnance: four aircraft came each armed with two 500-lb. general purpose bombs; four came with fragmentation bombs; and four came with napalm. The flights attacked targeted villages in that sequence, with the first wave opening up the houses, the second creating kindling in the structures, and the napalm dropped by the third ignited the material exposed by the bombs. As one command official dryly observed, "this [bomb] combination worked quite successfully," and ground controllers offered lavish praise. Unfortunately, the operational reports are silent on whether civilians or soldiers occupied the houses attacked, or to what extent the airmen experienced moral qualms about attacking the villages. Following the attack, bad weather set in to restrict air support on November 10 and 11, and made the following three days totally unfit for flying.[69]

Mission Priorities and Aerial Resources

With Third Army's offensive off to a good start, General Weyland returned to one of his favorite concerns, the *Luftwaffe* threat to the Third Army's area. He had good reason to worry. Throughout October and November 1944, Ultra analysts continued to monitor the *Luftwaffe* buildup, which resulted in a single-engine fighter force that expanded from 1,900 to 3,300 aircraft by mid-November.[70] This represented an increase of nearly 70 percent over the numbers available in early September. Weyland attempted to enlist the aid of heavy bombers in the counterair mission. Even before the Eighth Air Force bombing on November 9, he had convinced officials to direct bombers against

16 airfields identified by his intelligence section on November 10. The result, however, proved disappointing: pilots hit only 2 of the 16 fields. Nevertheless, he repeated his request for the heavy bombers and also lobbied for the use of Eighth Air Force fighters.

The seriousness of his concern was perhaps best demonstrated on November 12, when he convinced General Patton to relieve all fighter-bombers that day from close air support missions, which permitted them to be applied against counterair targets. Weyland could never implement the consistent program of pressure on the *Luftwaffe* he desired. The weather, the limited availability of medium and heavy bombers, and the continuing high-priority rail and road interdiction program took precedence. Although it is tempting to speculate on whether a more sustained effort against the *Luftwaffe* might have crippled it for the future Ardennes assault, such a diversion of resources might well have rendered the interdiction program ineffective.[71]

As it was, interdiction received only 50 percent of the effort that Weyland devoted to close air support of Patton's Third Army. The statistical record for November suggests that scheduled close support sorties totaled 1,387, while the figure for armed reconnaissance was 697. The command flew armed reconnaissance missions against what officials termed targets of opportunity. On the other hand, they recorded pinpoint targets separately and the figure for this third category reached 532 sorties. Statisticians, however, reported all three in official command statistical summaries under the heading "dive bomb." Understandably, the vast majority of close air support missions in November occurred in conjunction with Operation Madison. It is also clear, in spite of Third Army's reliance on its own artillery for a significant portion of its close fire support, that fighter-bombers continued to play a major role, especially in large offensives. Once again, competing mission priorities made it difficult, if not impossible, to make interdiction the overwhelming priority on a consistent basis.[72]

Then, too, the effectiveness of the interdiction program is enormously difficult to measure. Too often bad weather in the target area prevented accurate aircrew reporting or later assessment of bomb damage results by means of reconnaissance flights. In any case, at this stage no one could expect a fighter-bomber pilot to achieve the kind of pinpoint bombing in bad weather often unachieved by aircrews of a later generation with much improved technology. Although mission reports increasingly mention that pilots dropped bombs through the overcast under the direction of ground control, the targets normally proved to be large area concentrations beyond the bomb line. Although the MEW system could direct aircraft within range of the target, the pilot still needed to acquire it visually for accurate bombing. After December 1944, accuracy would improve markedly when the command acquired the SCR–584 and a close control device for the MEW system.[73]

Bad weather days in mid-November compelled General Weyland to deal with a number of mission support issues. The problem of soggy airfields now headed the list. Rainfall amounted to twice the norm during the month, and on two occasions the Mosel overflowed its banks. The 354th Fighter Group had the most difficult situation. October rainfall made its airfield at Vitry largely unserviceable and a second flood on November 8 effectively eliminated all operations from the site. As a result, the group flew from St. Dizier after November 13, until the engineers readied the field at Rosieres (A–98) later in the month (**Map 4**). The most shocking news for the Mustang group, however, came on the thirteenth, when it learned that P–47s would replace its P–51s. To say that group pilots were not pleased is an understatement of the first order. The group's historian termed November 13 a "Black Letter Day," and morale took a nosedive. Three months later, the group historian asserted that the pilots, for the most part, still preferred the P–51 because of its additional speed and better handling qualities.[74]

General Weyland had little choice in the fate of the 354th Fighter Group. In mid-November his job was to convert the group as soon as possible. Transition training began immediately, one squadron at a time. At Weyland's insistence, the P–47s were to arrive before all the P–51s left so at least two squadrons would remain operational at all times. Training lasted about a week and a half for each squadron, with the last squadron finishing on December 17, 1944. Although one might expect the new P–47 group to be less proficient than its sister groups, operations records do not bear this out. The 354th Fighter Group came in for its share of praise over the next two months and Weyland thoughtfully commended the group on its first outstanding P–47 group mission. Whether the XIX TAC benefited in the winter fighting by having a P–47 rather than a P–51 unit is doubtful. In any event, when the air-ground team prepared for mobile operations in March 1945 the spare parts availability for the P–51 aircraft again improved, and the 354th reconverted back to the P–51s. Even so, one officer asserted that the reconversion occurred largely because of the serious morale problem in the group.[75]

The severe November rain and mud, meanwhile, forced other groups to change bases as well (**Map 13**). On November 5, the 362d Fighter Group began its move from Mourmelon to Rovres, near Etain and Verdun, where it was joined by the 425th Night Fighter Squadron. Later in the month the 10th Photo Group, with one exception, moved its squadrons and photographic facilities from St. Dizier to Conflans to escape the elements. The exception proved to be the 155th Night Photo Squadron whose A–20s could operate more safely on St. Dizier's concrete runways in bad weather. Although the command made the moves in response to the terrible weather, it now had all three groups positioned farther forward and better able to support Third Army operations. The ground advance in Operation Madison had widened the distance from the Marne bases to the front lines from 50 miles in September 1944, to as much as a 100 miles in November. Fortuitously, these groups also would be well-sited to support the Ardennes counterattack in December.[76]

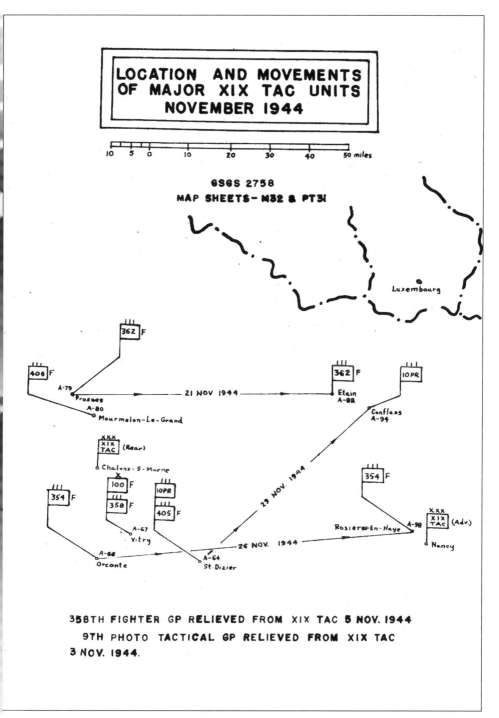

Map 13
Location and Movements of Major XIX TAC Units: November 1944

Reprinted from: XIX Tactical Air Command, "History," Operations, November 1944, AFHRA.

General Weyland still found the aircraft replacement situation in November unacceptable. The critical P–51 shortage could be alleviated through the conversion program, but the single squadron of P–61 Black Widows had declined to 14 aircraft from its authorized strength of 18, and prospects for replacements in the immediate future seemed poor. As a result, he proposed to Ninth Air Force that A–20 Havoc light bombers be exchanged for their P–70 night-fighter variant for intruder operations. Ninth Air Force disapproved the request. Weyland also failed to convince Ninth Air Force headquarters to support another ambitious plan. To compensate for winter conditions, he asked General Vandenberg in a November 14 letter to increase the number of aircraft authorized for fighter groups by 25. In a lengthy argument he noted that bad weather and shortened daylight hours had reduced the sortie rate to less than 50 percent of the summer figure. At the same time, the groups now received a steady flow of pilot replacements in numbers capable of sustaining a much higher loss rate. Each squadron, he said, could man 24 aircraft, or 72 per three-squadron group. Moreover, because of the low sortie rate under winter conditions, available maintenance personnel could support a 100-aircraft group, which meant that 72 aircraft could be sent on missions when weather permitted.[77]

Ninth Air Force declined to raise the number of authorized aircraft, citing the eventual need for additional logistics personnel in assembly and maintenance at the base air depot as well as in the tactical and service squadrons. Headquarters Ninth Air Force had little interest in trying to change authorization for maintenance personnel, let alone aircraft, and instead it suggested reducing the flow of replacement pilots rather than increasing the number of airplanes. Although Weyland's proposal seems imaginative and reasonable for the situation in the fall, he could not foresee the strain an emergency such as

A–20 Havoc at a Ninth Air Force Base in France.

the Ardennes Offensive would put on his facilities and personnel. Indeed, late in December 1944, his command maintenance and supply officers described maintenance as poor. As a result of the heavy battle damage suffered by most aircraft in the intense effort to halt the German attack, depots and service teams became overburdened with no end in sight.[78]

The nonflying days in November also provided General Weyland time to confer with XII TAC to the south on support requirements. Here the cooperative spirit and the theme of flexibility predominated. He agreed to a request from General Saville that the XIX TAC assist XII TAC with two groups to support Seventh Army's planned offensive on November 15–17, with the proviso that XIX TAC receive help from Ninth Air Force to the same extent. When Ninth Air Force authorities in Luxembourg did not approve this arrangement, Weyland declined to send his two groups, but he still promised Saville help if he got "in a jam." Unexplainably, when Ninth Air Force subsequently agreed to provide Saville's command four groups instead of two, XII TAC declined them because it "expected bad weather on the 14th."[79]

Autumn weather in Lorraine was awful. One member of the 362d Fighter Group described the move to Rouvres on November 5 in terms reminiscent of the First World War:

> When the last remnants of the Group splashed up the quagmire roads into this churned up sea of mud that was to be our new site and possibly our winter home, the unanimous opinion was expressed that web-feet and fins would be requisitioned next....Living conditions in the immediate future looked very dismal and bogged down.[80]

The slow pace of the campaign and the many days when the weather prohibited flying led to inactivity and boredom that could be relieved only slightly by contact with the dour Lorrainers. Typical was the attitude of the 405th Fighter Group historian who concluded his commentary on his outfit's experiences in November by noting that "all in all, it was an unremarkable month, characterized only by its dreariness and monotony."[81]

The weather finally improved somewhat on November 15, 1944, and the command sent a squadron each from the 405th, 406th, and 362d Fighter Groups to support XII and XX Corps as well as fly armed reconnaissance. General Eisenhower visited the command that day and, like many before him, dutifully paid tribute to the outstanding partnership of XIX TAC and Third Army, and to General Weyland personally. Also on this day the 358th Fighter Group departed officially for XII TAC, which left the command with four fighter groups, its lowest number since it became operational.[82]

Fair weather—a ceiling of 5,000–7,000 feet and visibility between two and three miles—made November 17 the biggest day in the air in a number of

As the Ninth Air Force–Third Army operations advanced, air-ground teamwork became more sophisticated. Air and ground coordinators shared VHF radio facilities in relay stations near the front (top) and were also installed in mobile radio stations in 3/4-ton trucks (bottom), receiving messages from communications officers (top, opposite page).

Air-ground operations and liaison officers directed fighter-bombers directly overhead to targets from information relayed to them (center).

Effectiveness of counterflak artillery also increased through air-ground teamwork, using liaison planes for spotting flak positions and directing fire to officers in ground units (right).

weeks. Weyland sent all groups on two missions, totaling 317 sorties. Two groups furnished Third Army close air support, with the 406th Fighter Group flying in support of the 10th Armored Division in its push beyond Fort Koenigsmacher and the 405th Fighter Group supporting the 6th Armored Division in the XII Corps zone. Weyland tried to visit Third Army's corps and division headquarters as often as time permitted. On November 17, he happened to be visiting the 6th Armored Division, where he conferred with an appreciative General Eddy. Weyland also encountered his disputant, General Wood, commander of the 4th Armored Division, soon to be relieved after the stress of combat proved too severe. Their earlier disagreement over control of a XIX TAC officer seemed behind them, and indeed, Weyland had little trouble in Lorraine with the corps and armored division commanders who understood the constraints imposed by the weather, and invariably appreciated XIX TAC aerial assistance when the weather made flying possible. Even most infantry division commanders, whose troops generally received less air support than their armored division counterparts, expressed satisfaction with XIX TAC's effort on their behalf.[83]

On November 18, General Weyland visited XX Corps, which had nearly completed its encirclement of Metz with the able support of the 406th Fighter Group. With the 405th Fighter Group assigned expressly in close support of XII Corps units, only the 354th and 362d Fighter Groups could attack interdiction targets. The 354th and 362d had a field day. Tactical reconnaissance had reported heavy rail traffic west of the Rhine, and the two groups combined to destroy nearly 500 railroad cars, the highest number of claims in the command's history. According to reports, they also counted destroyed nearly 300 motor vehicles, 26 armored vehicles, 74 locomotives, 42 horse-drawn vehicles, 32 gun positions, and 19 buildings.[84]

November 19, 1944, proved to be another good day, but a costly one. As Third Army cut the exits from Metz, fighter-bombers swooped down to within a hundred yards in front of the American patrols to strafe the retreating enemy. The command lost 13 aircraft and 8 pilots, and officers now considered Third Army's zone of operations the worst for flak concentrations since Caen back in the early stages of the Normandy fighting. The command lost 62 aircraft shot down in November, exactly twice the October figure. Ironically, despite the higher losses, the XIX TAC took important steps to reduce the flak menace. For one, the command's intelligence section maintained a detailed flak "library" and display map showing all known flak concentrations. The daily intelligence report also described each new flak sighting to pilots.[85]

The major development, however, proved to be the antiflak program initiated by the ground-pounders of XII Corps. As General Weyland explained at a press conference in December 1944, "this was not at our request, but that started in the XII Corps—I did not even think of it, but somebody in the XII Corps saw that when bombers came over, the [XII Corps] artillery would open on the flak positions. Undoubtedly, this saved many planes and lives." Indeed, the Army directed antiflak artillery to fire on all known enemy gun positions when fighter-bombers operated in their area. The new procedure called for the artillery to be alerted when aircraft assigned to close air support missions in the area were airborne, then a liaison plane served as artillery spotter and directed fire on the German flak positions. In one of the XIX TAC combat reports, an official judged the XII Corps artillery support very effective and "most popular with the pilots."[86]

The effectiveness of counterflak artillery fire increased as the result of a major advance in air-ground teamwork that occurred during the latter part of the Metz operation, when Third Army corps and divisions adopted the "combined operations office" used at the command. Now, air and ground officers shared the same room and received facilities and equipment previously unavailable. Technicians furnished VHF air-ground equipment for the new offices, which provided good integration of the air effort into the ground operation. Ground personnel, for their part, ran a land line to the artillery fire direction center, which made target marking and, especially, antiflak fire considerably more effective. Even with improved air-ground cooperation, however, the massive concentration of light flak on the Siegfried Line and the increase in close support missions in November produced a high fighter-bomber casualty figure for the month.[87]

After November 19 the weather closed in again for five straight days, as Third Army forces led by the 95th Infantry Division (a unit comprised of those Patton liked to call "the Iron Men of Metz") completed mop-up action inside the ancient city on November 22. Third Army officers proudly boasted that they commanded the first military force to capture Metz since 451 AD. Some might criticize the length of the operation and remind Americans that the Prussians had occupied Metz during the Franco-Prussian War, but Third Army's two-month siege remains impressive in view of the region's worst flooding in 20 years and limited air support. Critics, including German officers, have been less kind to Patton for following his own broad-front strategy of dividing his armor and using it as infantry support rather than forming it into a concentrated battering ram to break through the Maginot and Siegfried Line defenses in early November. As it was, after Metz fell, six forts still remained in German hands and General Patton made the decision to invest them while continuing eastward. By the end of November, his forces had crossed the Saar at Saarlautern and Dillingen against stiff resistance to hold a continuous front of 25 miles inside Germany, while only four of the Metz forts remained in enemy hands (**Map 14**).[88]

The high Third Army casualty rate of 22,773 attested to the grim fighting in Lorraine, 90 percent of which came from infantry units. Losses in infantry units became so severe that draftees from noncombat positions had to be involuntarily retrained as infantry. The cold and soggy November fighting

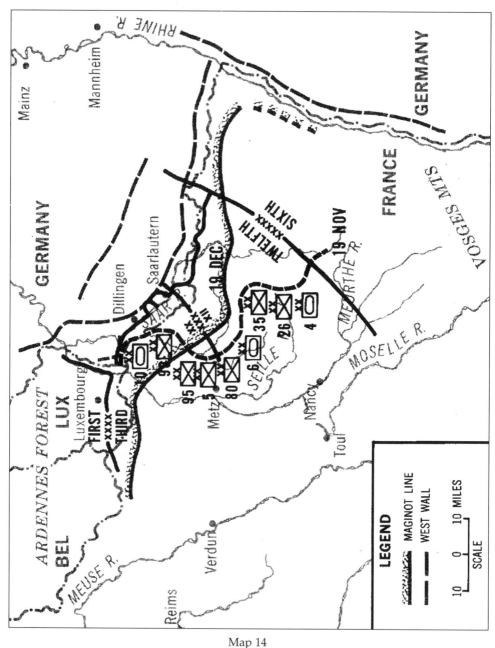

Map 14
Third Army Operations: November 19–December 19, 1944

Reprinted from: Christopher R. Gabel, "The Lorraine Campaign: An Overview, Sep-Dec 1944," (Ft. Leavenworth, Kan.: U.S. Army Command and General Staff College, 1985), p. 29.

also produced a trenchfoot problem of monstrous proportions. Fully 4,587 cases appeared at division clearing stations, and an estimated 95 percent of the individuals afflicted proved useless to the Army until the following spring.[89]

For General Weyland's forces, it became the same old story of limited flying. After Metz fell, the command had only two more good flying days in November. On November 25, XIX TAC pilots flew 220 sorties divided generally between the two groups supporting advancing ground units and two flying armed reconnaissance/interdiction in the Rhine and Saar valleys. The next day only the 406th Fighter Group flew ground support missions, but its targets included 14 towns that subsequently fell to XX Corps' assault. In a perceptive comment on air-ground effectiveness on November 21 General Patton observed, "The impetus of an air attack [for ground forces] is lacking due to [the] fatigue of [the] men. I have attempted to get at least an infantry division out of action for a rest." The brutal conditions of fighting in Lorraine seemed to hamper the air-ground team at every turn.[90]

While weather prohibited flying the last four days of the month, Weyland turned his attention to the problem of the Siegfried Line defenses. The XX Corps found, to its unpleasant surprise, that cities like Saarlautern had actually become part of the West Wall. American forces discovered the Siegfried Line to be unlike the Metz or Maginot Line systems of huge underground forts and artillery positions. Third Army now confronted a line of Dragon's Teeth—tank obstacles, extensive barbed wire, well-positioned pillboxes with overlapping zones of fire, and fortifications that included cities such as Saarlautern and Dillingen. Even though the German forces opposite Third Army were reduced to one-quarter the size of the American attacking force, the tenacious defenders remained in well-prepared positions and fought hard to protect their homeland. Fighter-bombers could only offer modest assistance against such fortified defenses.[91]

The key problem was how to get Third Army forces across the swollen Saar River in the face of the entrenched Siegfried Line defenders. Given Third Army's situation, General Weyland again decided to coordinate heavy air bombardment with the advance of the infantry units. Planners termed this plan "Hi-Sug." An earlier attempt to breach defenses at Merzig through an aerial assault on November 19 failed overwhelmingly. There, XIX TAC employed an air plan that called for eight groups of medium bombers to soften up the bridgehead area. Only four groups completed their bombing runs, however, and although accuracy proved good, the 9th Bombardment Division lost 13 aircraft and eight pilots. Once again, for fear of short bombing, the ground troops had been positioned so far back from the Saar River that they failed to attack the German defenses until 48 hours *after* the bombing. Weyland judged the air effort as "absolutely wasted."[92]

The lesson repeated in the Merzig bombing proved a telling one in the Northwest European campaign. When medium or heavy bombers carpet-bombed a defensive area, the ground forces needed to move forward immediately after the last bomb had fallen and close with the stunned defenders. For the Hi-Sug plan, Third Army decided to cross the Saar River near Saarlautern at the end of November, with forces directed to move forward to within 2,000 yards of the river prior to the air bombardment. The bombers would carpet-bomb the eastern side of the river in the proposed bridgehead area.[93]

General Weyland served as the major liaison figure for air support in the joint planning process. On November 27 he requested of Ninth Air Force heavy as well as medium bomber strikes. Although he did not get the heavy bombers for the assault, Ninth Air Force promised full use of the medium bombers. During Third Army's morning briefing on November 29, General Patton approved Weyland's plan to have medium bombers strike the Siegfried Line. As always, air-ground coordination and timing would be critical. Weyland assured the ground leaders that medium bombers could be employed as soon as Third Army ground forces were ready, and Patton's staff responded by saying XX Corps was prepared for the assault any time from November 29 to December 2. Patton wanted to attack the following day, but later on November 29 his staff notified Weyland that XX Corps would not be ready for the bombardment until December 1. Although this meant that targets in the northern area of the offensive had to be scratched, the plan still looked promising (**Map 14**).[94]

On November 30, the air-ground team held a joint planning meeting at Third Army headquarters where it reviewed the plan to use medium bombers and further examined and established last-minute timing changes in detail. The XX Corps would lead off, with the 95th Infantry Division's Iron Men attacking across the Saar River in the vicinity of Saarlautern, while the 90th Infantry Division performed a holding action. In the XII Corps zone, the main effort would be made by the 26th Infantry and the 4th Armored Divisions, with the 80th Infantry Division to follow. If XX Corps encountered trouble on its front, it would hold the enemy's key forces while XII Corps troops broke through the gap below Saarlautern in the enemy's weakened sectors.

The air plan called for medium bombers employed over three days, with the first day's bombing of Siegfried Line defenses to be accomplished visually before 2:00 p.m. Should bad weather occur on the second and third days, Third Army agreed to continued bombing using the Oboe radar blind-bombing method. That evening, at the XIX TAC briefing, General Weyland explained that the entire 9th Bombardment Division force would be allocated to the Siegfried Line breakthrough operation now scheduled for the following day, December 1. He also told his staff that Third Army, reflecting confidence in the bombers as well as the urgency of the operation, had overcome its doubts and now agreed to accept Oboe bombing at any time.

General Patton's willingness to permit use of a blind-bombing system, which was more effective against large area targets, suggests how important aerial bombardment support had become for the Army commander. Even so, his troops would attack without air support if necessary. Before that evening's XIX TAC briefing, Patton met with Generals Gaffey, Gay, and Weyland on the subject of the air plan. Although he desired air support, Patton declared that the 90th and 95th Infantry Divisions would attack on December 3, with or without the benefit of aerial bombing.[95]

General Weyland remained confident that Operation Hi-Sug, his third joint operation of the Lorraine Campaign, could overcome the stiff German defenses, the bad weather, and the friction of war to burst open the Siegfried Line and permit Third Army to move rapidly on to the Rhine River. If so, he could put behind him a frustrating period for his command.

Assault on the Siegfried Line

The air-ground assault in Lorraine in early December 1944, was the only major Allied offensive on the western front at that time. First and Ninth Armies in the north continued to clear the Huertgen Forest after many weeks of grim infantry fighting and high casualties and labored to build up their forces along the Roer River for a major offensive in mid-December. The river would remain a major barrier until American troops could wrest control of the dams on its upper reaches from the Germans. In Alsace, Lt. Gen. Jacob L. Devers's 6th Army Group achieved greater success, forcing retreating Germans from French soil and reaching the Rhine River. Only a large bridgehead of enemy forces west of the Rhine near Colmar, the Colmar pocket, remained to impede the Allied drive.[96]

General Patton's high expectations for Operation Hi-Sug rested in large part on the massive bombing assault scheduled for December 1, and he, General Weyland, and their respective staffs devoted considerable effort to ensure that air-ground coordination proved successful. At midmorning on December 1, 1944, Weyland called the Third Army commander to tell him that eight groups of medium bombers were on their way. The XX Corps had been notified as well. Shortly thereafter, General Patton called back requesting that XX Corps receive priority from the fighter-bombers, too, and Weyland informed him that this had already been done. Indeed, XX Corps units began crossing the swollen Saar River supported by three of four bomb groups that flew 96 of the 123 total sorties for the day.[97]

By midafternoon the early optimism began to fade. Because of radio failure, Weyland learned that only four of the eight bomb groups had bombed their targets. The air commander then conferred with General Patton and Colonel Harkins, his deputy chief of staff, who informed him that, in any case, XX Corps had not been in position that morning to follow-up the bombing and establish its bridgehead on the east bank of the Saar. Despite the laborious planning of the past days, ineffective air-ground coordination once again prevented success.

General Weyland agreed to try again the next day and Patton promised to get the necessary target information and current front line locations from XX Corps by 7:30 p.m. that evening. Weyland then contacted Ninth Air Force to again request the bombers and to assure bomber pilots that the target information would be delivered at about 8:00 p.m. Director of operations at the Ninth, Col. George F. McGuire, responded favorably but suggested that, because 12th Army Group established flying objectives for the medium bomber effort, it would help if Third Army contacted General Bradley's headquarters. Weyland, determined to avoid repeating the first day's mistake, never hesitated to call on General Patton for crucial assistance, and he considered assistance crucial in this instance. He asked the Army commander to "needle" higher headquarters to ensure the support of Ninth Air Force and Patton said he would call Bradley immediately. As these machinations on December 2 illustrate, the medium bomber force also had other competing priorities and represented a limited resource.[98]

At that night's XIX TAC briefing, the airmen announced that 10 groups of medium bombers, approximately 360 airplanes, would strike the Siegfried Line the following day, while the fighter-bomber force would be strengthened by the loan of two groups from IX TAC and XXIX TAC. They assigned to the fighters armed reconnaissance missions and other missions to disarm strongpoints and blunt counterattacks in support of the ground advance.[99]

During the Hi-Sug attack on December 2, 1944, the TAC commander and his combat operations officer (using call signs Ding Bat 1 and Ding Bat 2) observed the medium bombing from a P–47 and P–51, respectively. This time all medium bomber groups struck the targets assigned and General Weyland found only one group that appeared to have bombed off-target. This time XX Corps troops had moved to within 2,000 yards of the Saar River and followed up the bombing effectively, despite heavy resistance. The 95th Infantry Division's crossing on December 2 received air support only from the 406th Group, although the group did good work against what the army considered the highest concentration of enemy flak it had ever faced. However, the 406th Fighter Group achieved its bombing claims at a high cost: five aircraft lost to flak. Using napalm and fragmentation bombs, the 406th fighter-bombers struck artillery positions under the close control of the air liaison officer who maintained contact with the division artillery officer. The latter directed effective artillery smoke to mark targets in the Siegfried Line and the pilots claimed five gun positions destroyed. It represented another example of a successful air-ground cooperative effort that turned on placing the combat operations office at division level.[100]

Despite the close support from medium bombers and fighter-bombers, the 95th Infantry Division came under intense enemy artillery fire from the Siegfried Line fortifications for the next few days as its forces struggled to cross the overflowing Saar River. In the face of severe winds, the veteran 405th Fighter Group failed repeatedly to lay smoke bombs on the hilltops and enemy observation posts to screen the crossing. General Weyland followed the events closely and held out hope that the army would make the grade. The tenuous bridgehead did hold, but the XX Corps became bogged down in house-to-house fighting in Saarlautern that would last for two weeks. Meanwhile, XII Corps pushed steadily, if slowly, northeast toward the Saar, while at the same time mopping up enemy activity in Saar-Union.[101]

While close air support of the advancing infantry units accelerated on December 2, XIX TAC also decided to support Third Army's drive with a renewed interdiction program against rail targets on December 2. The air-ground team did not doubt the need for a major effort. Weyland remained convinced that he could cover the ground troops sufficiently and also engage in interdiction operations to isolate the battlefield. Tactical reconnaissance pilots reported heavy rail traffic west of the Rhine since late October. Third Army intelligence specialists, meanwhile, began to monitor and analyze rail traffic in their area in mid-November. Observations and reports of rail traffic for the period November 17 to December 2 showed, among many sightings, 300 trains active on November 17, 84 on November 18 and 19, and 46 on November 26. This rail traffic, intelligence officers concluded by December 2, suggested "a definite buildup of enemy troops and supplies directly opposite the north flank of Third U.S. Army and the southern flank of First U.S. Army." Subsequent analysis of rail traffic on December 9, 14, and 17, cited a continuing, heavy volume of traffic directed toward the Eifel region, a hilly, densely wooded region of Germany north of the Mosel River between Trier and Coblenz. In early December, Third Army intelligence officers began to warn of a possible German spoiling offensive in their sector or from the Eifel.[102]

The XIX TAC interdiction program in early December, however, could hardly do more than minor damage to the enemy. Even though it received priority attention, mission reports from December 1–16 show the command flew interdiction and close air support missions in equal proportion. As the November program demonstrated, the competing priorities of the command made concentration of aerial forces on any single mission next to impossible. The ferocity of the fighting in the Siegfried Line called for flying ground support missions on every day possible.[103] While the interdiction and close support missions assisted the slow-moving offensive, it became clear that Operation Hi-Sug had not achieved the overwhelming breakthrough sought by the air-ground team and the military stalemate on the Siegfried Line continued. Weyland immediately began working on plans for a more elaborate operation, a massive air assault that would require even closer coordination between XIX TAC and Third Army forces.

On December 5, 1944, Weyland attended an important conference at Supreme Headquarters Allied Expeditionary Forces (SHAEF) in Paris. Allied conferees addressed the question of how best to use air power against the Siegfried Line. Particular interest centered on the potential effectiveness using strategic bombers in a tactical role, a proposition long considered doctrinal heresy by strategic airmen. Predictably, attendees representing strategic bombers opposed using heavy bombers for anything except strategic bombing. First and Ninth Army representatives wanted to divert heavy bombers for use against dams on the Roer River. Weyland argued that if the heavy bombers were made available, they would be effective in a tactical role, in coordination with a major offensive in which the ground forces would be moving forward. Evidently his argument helped, because Eisenhower requested that General Spaatz, commander of United States Strategic Air Forces in Europe (USSTAF), assist Third Army with the support of heavy bombers even though Allied leaders continued to view Patton's front as secondary. At the same time, it was clear Third Army would have to make substantial progress against the Siegfried Line or go over on the defensive. The Ninth Air Force commander, General Vandenberg, concurred and when Spaatz said he would visit Nancy, Weyland assured him that XIX TAC already "had a plan to use the heavy bomber effort."[104]

The next day, December 6, General Spaatz and General Doolittle, commander of Eighth Air Force, arrived at XIX TAC headquarters to confer with General Weyland and his staff. Weyland explained the Third Army's situation on the Siegfried Line and the air plan to get them through it, while Colonel Hallett discussed the targeting objectives for the heavy bombers. Spaatz and Doolittle accepted the plan in principle, after which they met with General Patton and together approved Weyland's joint plan of attack. Unlike previous heavy bomber operations, this plan called for attacks on the Siegfried Line in the vicinity of Zweibruecken by the heavy and medium bombers for three consecutive days. Troops from XII Corps would move forward while bombing of deeper targets continued. Five target areas would be hit initially by heavy bombers and safety would be assured by detailed coordination with antiaircraft artillery units, the use of marker panels, and by Eighth Air Force radio communications. Fighter-bombers would be employed to keep the enemy off balance and break up any counterattacks.[105]

General Weyland considered his plan the best solution to date for solving the dilemma of the time lag between the carpet-bombing and infantry advance. Previously, Operation Queen, and initially Operation Hi-Sug, failed because the infantry took too long to reach the target area after the bombing. Clearly coordination, timing, and a host of other potential problems had to be clarified for Weyland's plan to succeed. For example, the planners needed to coordinate operations with Seventh Army and XII TAC, and Doolittle and Spaatz agreed to visit General Devers, the 6th Army Group commander, and General Royce, his air commander. Both accepted the XIX TAC plan "in principle." Meanwhile, General Weyland set to work on other requirements such as developing target folders with current photos of the targets and coordinating air defense measures. The latter became an issue because of the proposed move to the Metz airfield of the command's 100th Fighter Wing in the near future. Weyland always favored keeping the same army antiaircraft units to defend the same air units when they moved to a new airfield. For the upcoming offensive, he sought to ensure that air defense units would be provided adequate communications for control of the inner artillery zone or, failing that, that these zones would be curtailed for the offensive. He met with key air defense officers from 12th Army Group and Third Army on December 8 and they promised to have their ground antiaircraft controllers well-briefed.[106]

Meanwhile, the Hi-Sug ground offensive continued. At Metz, Fort Driant fell to XX Corps troops on December 7. Now only Fort Jeanne d'Arc remained in enemy hands. General Walker's troops also continued to enlarge their bridgeheads at Saarlautern and Pachtern. In the XII Corps sector, troops engaged in house-to-house fighting in the southern part of Saargumeines and corps artillery shelled Saarbruecken (**Map 15**). The XII Corps received priority air support at this time and Weyland's command continued its general practice of assigning one group to cover one particular front line army division. On December 8, for example, the 405th Fighter Group supported the 35th Infantry Division's attempt to consolidate its four Saar River crossings near Saargumeines, attacking towns and marking artillery targets with smoke, while the 362d Fighter Group repelled counterattacks threatening the 80th Infantry Division. Both groups received letters of appreciation from XII Corps for their

Generals Spaatz, Patton, Doolittle, Vandenberg, and Weyland (left to right) at the advance headquarters in Nancy, December 1944.

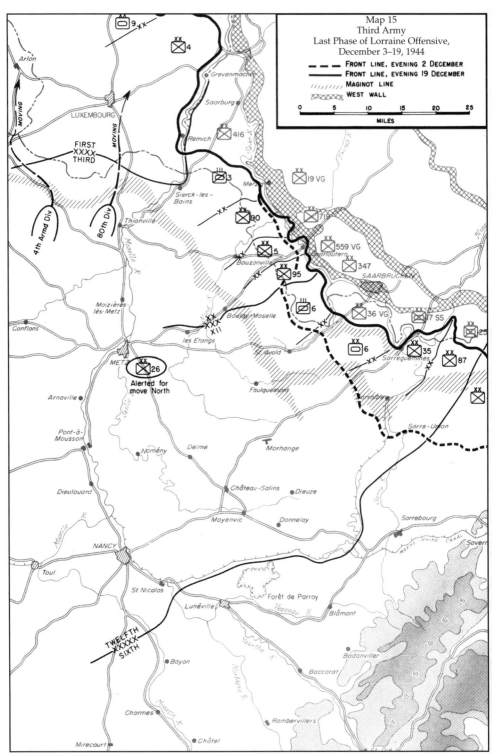

SOURCE: H.M. Cole, *The Lorraine Campaign*, Map 49, (Washington, D.C.: GPO, 1950)

aerial assistance, but progress proved slow in the face of German delaying actions which included land mines, booby traps, persistent counterattacks, and the ever-present mud and rain.[107]

Bad weather set in again on December 9, 1944, and XIX TAC severely curtailed air operations for the next three days. Even so, with the 90th Infantry Division in trouble, the command responded despite the poor weather. On the ninth, for example, it flew only 56 sorties, including a 362d Fighter Group mission to drop blood plasma in wing tanks to troops of the 90th pinned down in their Saar River bridgehead. Invariably, during December two fighter-bomber groups flew close air support missions for the same corps: the 362d supported XII Corps operations while the 406th provided coverage of XX Corps units. Meanwhile, the 405th Fighter Group, which had flown more ground support missions than any other group during the Lorraine Campaign, now assumed the burden of flying armed reconnaissance missions. The Raiders had no trouble adjusting to this role.[108]

Not surprisingly, General Weyland concentrated on the forthcoming combined operation during the lull in the air war. Perhaps a measure of his personal association with the joint operation is expressed in the name adopted for it: Tink, his wife's nickname. It was a busy time for the planners. On December 10, Seventh Army and XII TAC officials visited Third Army, where all acknowledged that the forthcoming XIX TAC–Third Army offensive would have first priority. Another coordinated attack, termed Operation Dagger, would follow in the Seventh Army area within four days of the start of Operation Tink. They further agreed that Generals Saville and Weyland would go to SHAEF to receive final approval for their plans, while General Patton would meet with his Seventh Army counterpart, General Patch, on December 13 to decide final timing of the attacking forces. After the December 10 meeting, Patton described the expectations of the Allied planners. Previous tactical carpet-bombings, which had been confined to a single day, had not proved entirely effective. Allied leaders believed that the three day air blitz on Zweibruecken planned in Operation Tink would catch the enemy off guard.[109]

On December 11, officers from Strategic Air Forces Headquarters in England arrived to discuss Operation Tink, after which Weyland called Spaatz to request RAF Bomber Command's support as well. General Spaatz promised to attend the meeting at Third Army headquarters scheduled for the thirteenth. On December 12, the XIX TAC's chief of staff flew to London with the air plan, issued only that day, to coordinate the Eighth Air Force bomber contribution. "D-Day" was set for December 19.

Improved weather on December 12 also brought a request from Patton and General Walker, XX Corps commander, for special support for his troops closing in on the final Metz fort. Bombing of the fort by six groups of medium bombers was originally scheduled, but it had to be scrubbed because of bad weather. Weyland promised an extra effort from his forces to take up the slack,

Dicing, or low-level, photo taken across the Saar River at the
Siegfried Line (top) by a 10th Photo Reconnaissance Group F–5 provided
vital information needed for Patton's troops in breaching the
formidable defenses (bottom).

and the 406th Fighter Group responded with five missions on the twelfth. Fort Jeanne d'Arc finally surrendered that day.[110]

The next few days were filled with various planning meetings for Operation Tink. Generals Patton and Patch together with Generals Vandenberg, Weyland, Saville, and a number of other key figures met on December 13 to examine air-ground plans and procedures in detail. Although Tink remained first priority, Seventh Army would attempt to sneak through the German defenses in the Vosges under Tink's momentum, assisted by Ninth Air Force's medium bombers (**Map 9**). All air support for XII TAC and Seventh Army would be coordinated though XIX TAC, thereby ensuring that centralized control of the air forces would be maintained.

With the plan in good order, General Weyland spent December 14 and 15 visiting his units. On the sixteenth, he arrived back at Nancy, where he convened a meeting for representatives from all participating air organizations to confirm reconnaissance areas and towns selected for interdiction attacks. In the evening of December 16, General Weyland, in what appears to have been little more than an afterthought, penciled a brief notation in his diary about events reported to the north of Third Army, "German offensive started in First Army area." One can only speculate whether at this early point he appreciated the significance of the assault and what it might mean for Operation Tink. The weather was good on December 16 and aircrews happily described a "field day" flying against German targets west of the Rhine, reports reminiscent of those in the heady days of August in France.[111]

At the Third Army morning briefing on December 17, 1944, army briefers reported that First Army and VIII Corps were "very surprised" at the German counterattack in their zone. Not only had the *Wehrmacht* caught them off guard, the enemy marshaled a larger striking force than anyone had expected. General Weyland promised to send two fighter groups north to support

Generals Patton and Patch

A squadron commander in the 354th Fighter Group checks last-minute details with his flight leaders before a mission against German supply lines.

VIII Corps throughout the day. In fact, December 17, with a total of 356 sorties, turned out to be the busiest flying day for the command since November 8, when Operation Madison began. All four groups flew in support of the beleaguered VIII Corps troops in the Ardennes region near Bastogne.[112]

The XIX TAC issued the revised air plan for Operation Tink on December 17. It confirmed that this attack would be the largest tactical air operation of its kind yet attempted. Medium bombers from the IX Bombardment Division and heavy bombers from Eighth Air Force and RAF Bomber Command would bomb both specified areas and 34 individual targets during three consecutive days. Moreover, Eighth Air Force fighters would fly 14 armed reconnaissance routes and bomb 26 supply depots. Fighter-bombers from XIX TAC would attack all communications centers behind the point of assault immediately following the main bombardments. In the confusion, the ground forces expected to be able to move forward with less opposition. Tink, indeed, was an ambitious plan.[113]

Bad weather on December 18 restricted flying to two groups, the 354th on loan to IX TAC and the 362d in support of XII Corps. General Weyland now confided to his diary that "First Army is in a flap" over the German counterattack and that his Siegfried Line assault, Operation Tink, had been postponed from December 19 to 22. After the briefing next morning, on December 19, a special meeting took place at Third Army headquarters. General Patton's staff announced that the 4th Armored and 26th Infantry Divisions had been ordered to move north, if required, to relieve VIII Corps. In that event, Weyland concluded, Operation Tink would be canceled because Third Army would have insufficient forces to exploit an air bombardment. Patton was to meet that day with Eisenhower and Bradley at Verdun and would subsequently advise Weyland of the final decision.[114]

That afternoon General Weyland called General Vandenberg. He urged the Ninth Air Force commander to continue with Operation Tink and hoped that it would be unnecessary to divert ground forces. Yet, early the same evening Patton called to say that "Tink was scrubbed." Official notice from SHAEF arrived later, and with the severity of the situation in the Ardennes becoming clear to all, Weyland immediately requested three additional fighter groups and a second reconnaissance group to help Third Army pull the "First Army's chestnuts out of the fire."[115]

Although Operation Tink never occurred, it offered perhaps the best coordinated air proposal for propelling ground forces through German Siegfried Line defenses in the Lorraine Campaign. It also provided a good means of assessing General Weyland's role as its key planner and liaison officer for air support. Operation Tink could have represented "what might have been" for Generals Weyland and Patton. On December 20, however, the air commander had little time to brood about cancellation of his plan. The Ardennes emergency required everyone's full attention.

Lorraine in Retrospect

The Lorraine Campaign ended in mid-December 1944. General Patton captured the sentiments of those he led for Secretary of War Henry L. Stimson in one of his own colorful epigrams:

> I hope in the final settlement of the war you insist that the Germans retain Lorraine, because I can imagine no greater burden than to be the owner of this nasty country where it rains every day and where the whole wealth of the people consists in assorted manure piles.[116]

General Weyland certainly was no less frustrated by the three months of static warfare. The high hopes of September 1944 had unquestionably turned sour and the unpleasant weather seemed to match the progress of the campaign. Nothing that Weyland could command in the air seemed able to alter that stalemate. In terms of the weather, the terrain, the forces, and the fortifications, the Lorraine Campaign in many ways represents a case study in the limitations rather than the capabilities of air power.

All the while, in response to requests from Generals Patton and Vandenberg, Weyland assigned and shuffled mission priorities to meet the most crucial needs as he perceived them. With air supremacy seldom contested by the *Luftwaffe*, he directed most of the command's flying toward interdiction and ground-support targets. For air power purists, he may have favored close air support missions too often at the expense of interdiction. Nevertheless, Weyland always responded first to the needs of Patton's troops in combat. Normally he handled this responsibility with two fighter groups, which left the other groups free to apply against the remaining missions. Most of these consisted of armed reconnaissance sorties, but bomber escort, leaflet dropping, fighter sweeps, and at times, air alert required attention. Force size continued to be a constant headache. To be sure, commanders seldom, if ever, believe they have sufficient forces. Yet, given the competing responsibilities, and with the exception of supporting the infantry and armor units, Weyland's command was far too small to concentrate on any assignment in force. In Lorraine, the command had sufficient resources to cover the ground support mission only because Third Army itself had to fight with reduced forces and suffered from the tyranny of logistics.

Most of all, with the size of his command, Weyland found it impossible to defeat the weather, which became the air-ground team's worst enemy. A liability for the Allies, the abundant bad weather was always a comfort to the enemy. On bad-weather days, the fighter-bombers did not fly effectively; sometimes they did not fly at all. This left the German defenders free to move supplies to the forward area and dig in from Metz to the Siegfried Line, ably protected by heavy flak concentrations. Even in the best of times, with more air firepower, the dug-in and reinforced strongpoints often proved impervious to fighter-bomber attack. Weyland knew this, and so did the enemy. Little could be done until both air and ground forces received reinforcements, and their mission in Lorraine became more urgent. This was the promise of Operation Tink and the reality of the Ardennes emergency.[117]

On the other hand, tactical air operations made gains during the campaign. Air-ground cooperation improved considerably as a result of counter-flak procedures and the combined operations offices situated at Army corps and division headquarters. The air arm also demonstrated that it could be effective in aiding the advance of the ground forces in spite of unfavorable conditions. Numerous letters of appreciation from the ground units attest to aircrew success in attacking German strongpoints, repelling counterattacks, and creating better tactical mobility for the troops.

Radar and communications developments during the three months accounted for much of the gains. Like so many aspects of the command, air-base movement became routine, in spite of the weather, while tactical air power proved itself able to react immediately and adjust to new situations. Such adjustments, for example, might involve the rapid movement of an entire group from one base to another, or involve reconnaissance aircraft leading fighter-bombers to an immediate target and coordinating army antiflak artillery fire.

Early in the campaign Weyland recognized that larger air attacks were required to break the stalemate on the ground. For him the answer lay in long-range, jointly planned offensives propelled by a heavier concentration of air power. If the four air-ground operations he helped develop—Operation Madison, Merzig, Hi-Sug, and Tink—proved less than completely successful, they nevertheless were well-conceived. In December, he became absolutely convinced he had found the answer to the stalemate and a return to mobile warfare in Operation Tink. Although it was a complex plan, requiring closer coordination among the various air and ground participants than any previous offensive, Weyland remained confident that thorough preparation, teamwork, and close cooperation would ensure success.

Above all, through all the frustrating experiences of the Lorraine Campaign, Weyland and Patton maintained close cooperation between the air and ground forces. Although other Allied air-ground teams cooperated effectively in the fall campaign, XIX TAC and Third Army developed a special relationship under adverse conditions. The official Army historian of the campaign declared, "one outstanding feature of the Lorraine Campaign was the cooperation between the XIX TAC and the Third Army."[118]

Near the end of the Lorraine experience, General Patton met the press with his air commander. He explained the Third Army's "method of air-ground tactical cooperation" for the correspondents assembled so that they might describe it accurately for the public back home:

> No operation in this army is contemplated without General Weyland and his staff being present at the initial decisions. We don't say that we are going to do this and what can you do about it. We say that we would like to make such an operation—now how can that be done from the air standpoint?[119]

Third Army staff members, General Weyland added, understood "not only the capabilities…of air but also [its] limitations.…Third Army does not look upon the XIX Tactical Command as a cure-all." He then turned to the heart of their relationship. "Our success is built on mutual respect and comradeship between the air and ground [team] that actually does exist. You can talk to any of my boys about that.…My boys like the way the Third Army fights. My kids feel that *this is their army* [emphasis added]."[120] The mutual respect, even affection, that promoted this kind of cooperation, coupled with Weyland's pragmatic approach to using tactical air power, surely accounted for much of the air-ground team's success.

The cooperation between the XIX TAC and Third Army air-ground team had grown and prospered, remarkably under the most disconcerting conditions of static warfare in Lorraine. That cooperation would be put to the test under far more desperate circumstances in mid-December 1944—in the Ardennes.

Chapter Five

The Ardennes

The German surprise attack in the early morning hours of December 16, 1944, quickly turned into far more than the spoiling action about which Third Army intelligence officers had worried for the past several weeks. Instead, three Nazi armies launched a 20-division assault along a 60-mile front opposite the Ardennes forest region in southern Belgium and northern Luxembourg. Defenders of this area held by First Army's VIII Corps was comprised of, as one observer phrased it, "dirt farmers and shoe salesmen." The success of the German onslaught ended General Eisenhower's own ambitious plan for a winter offensive. Planned offensives by First Army in the direction of Cologne and by Third Army in the Saar had to be abandoned to combat the German menace at the Allied center, a bitter struggle that became known as the Battle of the Bulge.[1] When Eisenhower met with key Allied officers at Verdun three days after the initial German attack, he declared the grave military situation to be "one of opportunity for us and not [one] of disaster." Although his audience may have found it difficult to embrace such a view at that moment, Eisenhower's perception proved absolutely correct. In the end, Germany's Ardennes Offensive, Operation Herbstnebel (Autumn Fog), ended in overwhelming defeat, leaving West Wall defenses woefully depleted before a renewed Allied attack.[2]

The Ardennes Offensive also provided Allied air power with an opportunity to demonstrate its capability in a defensive emergency. Never before in northern Europe had tactical military forces been called on to meet a major threat without benefit of extensive prior planning between air and land commanders. It would prove a test worthy of tactical air power and of the air-ground teamwork demonstrated a few months earlier in France. Although the Allied aerial response was applied theaterwide, Weyland's XIX TAC faced challenges at the cutting edge of Patton's celebrated counterattack to relieve Bastogne and drive German forces out of the Bulge.[3]

Weyland played a pivotal role in directing tactical air operations in the southern half of the Bulge. Yet, popular attention is fixed most often on Patton's dramatic 90-degree turn north, and in the air, on Quesada's direction of air support in the northern area of the Bulge. Nevertheless, for both Third Army and its air arm, the Battle of the Bulge in many ways represented their greatest triumph of the European Campaign.

Operation Autumn Fog

On December 16, 1944, in the initial confusion and fog of battle, the true nature of Operation Autumn Fog remained unclear. If Allied leaders had correctly identified Adolf Hitler rather than Field Marshal Gerd von Rundstedt as the architect, they might have better reacted to a surprise attack of such a size and stunning boldness. Since September, Hitler had brooded about a German counterattack out of the Ardennes against Allied forces reminiscent of Operation Fall Gelb, the invasion of France in mid-1940. If in late 1944 German forces could reach the Belgian port of Antwerp, 100 miles in the distance, they would split the Allied line and be in position to destroy American and British troops to the north by trapping them against the English Channel and North Sea. If less than completely successful, so audacious an assault would nevertheless gain precious time and disrupt the anticipated Allied offensive against the Siegfried Line.[4]

Operation Autumn Fog called for the main attack to be delivered in the north along the Malmedy-Liege axis to Antwerp by the Sixth Panzer Army, led by SS Gen. Sepp Dietrich. It had the narrowest front of the attacking forces, and much would depend on access to the road network to sustain the drive (**Map 16**). In the center, General von Manteuffel's Fifth Panzer Army had the task of seizing the key road communications centers of St. Vith and Bastogne, and of pushing on to the Meuse River before turning north. To the south, the Seventh Army, commanded by Gen. Eric Brandenberger, would provide flank

**Field Marshal
Gerd von Rundstedt
with Adolf Hitler**

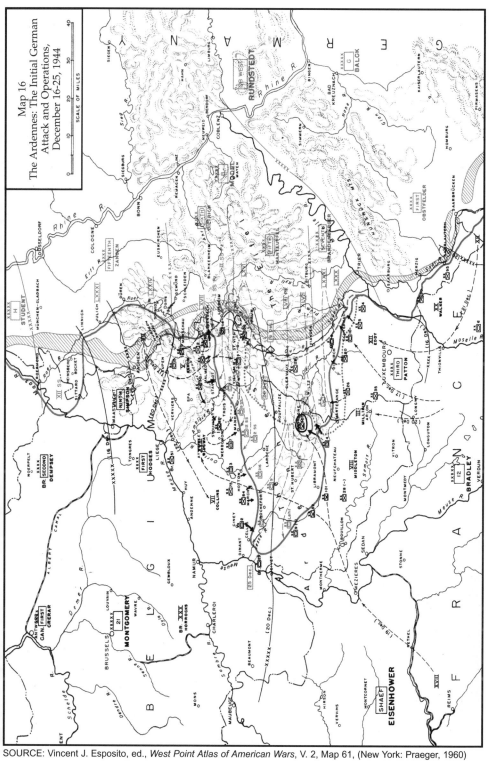

Map 16
The Ardennes: The Initial German
Attack and Operations,
December 16-25, 1944

SCALE OF MILES

SOURCE: Vincent J. Esposito, ed., *West Point Atlas of American Wars*, V. 2, Map 61, (New York: Praeger, 1960)

protection to the Fifth and expand into northern Luxembourg. To further the drive, the Germans formed special parachute units to seize key road junctions and serve as blocking forces, while Lt. Col. Otto Skorzeny's U.S.-uniformed guerrillas would sow confusion behind Allied lines and take control of the Meuse bridges. The *Luftwaffe's* aerial striking force, meanwhile, had been secretly expanded to some 2,400 tactical aircraft for the campaign and moved to bases in the Rhine valley. The mission was to provide close air support for the attacking armored and infantry units in the breakthrough area. Whether an air force by now trained largely in air defense interception tactics could achieve success in ground attack operations without first attempting to gain air superiority remained to be seen. Like the entire operation, much would depend on deception, surprise, and the weather.[5]

The failure of Allied intelligence to comprehend the marshaling of German forces has remained one of the most controversial aspects of the campaign. Although it is difficult to avoid blaming American and British commanders and their intelligence officers, one must admire the German deception operation that included a massive buildup in the Eifel region without the Allies suspecting its true nature. The Allies identified Dietrich's headquarters near Cologne in the fall, and the Germans made every effort to give it a defensive

Gen. Hasso von Manteuffel, commander, Germany's Fifth Panzer Army

appearance against First Army's expected offensive. Then, at the last minute, Dietrich's Sixth Panzer headquarters secretly moved to the Eifel. Similarly, the Fifth German Army moved into the heavily wooded Eifel under a cover plan that called for counterattacking the First Army's offensive to the north. Only top-level *Wehrmacht* officers knew the true nature of the plan, while their forces developed elaborate measures of camouflage and followed strict radio discipline. By mid-December 1944, sufficient fuel and supplies had accumulated and forecasters predicted a spell of much-needed foul weather. In the course of three nights, the attackers quickly moved into place and prepared to strike. The deception achieved complete success.[6]

In hindsight, many indications from Ultra and other intelligence sources pointed to an impending German offensive. In mitigation, it is often argued that bad weather prohibited sufficient air reconnaissance of the buildup area, especially on the eve of the assault. Despite terrible weather, however, tactical reconnaissance flights from at least one of the two photo reconnaissance groups covered the Eifel and the Rhine River valley on all but one day preceding the attack. On five of those days, including December 14 and 15, all flights reported heavy road and rail traffic into the region. As for the XIX TAC, it experienced only two days before the sixteenth when flying proved impossible, and its focus on armed reconnaissance missions provided sufficient opportunity to appreciate the heavy rail traffic west of the Rhine. Even with inconsistent reports, there could be little doubt of a major deployment taking place. Third Army analysts had studied rail movement since mid-November 1944, and understood the direction and general size of the rail transport activity, but they thought about the movement mainly in terms of a German spoiling attack that might be launched from the Eifel against either the First or the Third Army front. Moreover, the Germans communicated over land lines and avoided the radio. Thus, Ultra intercepts remained silent on the Germans' true purpose for the buildup, and with a traditional army officer, von Rundstedt, assumed to be in charge, it made perfect sense to overlook the Ardennes as the center of German interest. Not only did its hilly terrain seem especially unsuitable for armor operations in winter, but the Germans could hardly be expected to attack through the Ardennes a second time.[7]

Given the inability of the Allies to be strong everywhere on the western front, they weakened what appeared to be the most secure sector, the center. It would have taken more to alter Allied preconceptions about German intentions than the intuition of General Patton, who in late November 1944, recorded in his diary, "the First Army is making a terrible mistake in leaving the VIII Corps static, as it is highly probable that the Germans are building up east of them."[8] Indeed, as one authority on the Ardennes Offensive remarked, "the Americans and British had looked in a mirror for the enemy and seen there only the reflection of their own intentions."[9] In fact, on December 16, 20 divisions from three German armies confronted only four Allied divisions deployed along an 80-mile front between Monschau on the north and Trier on the south. When it struck that day, the *Wehrmacht* directed the brunt of its attack against the line held by a combination of recently arrived green or else battle-weary troops of General Middleton's VIII Corps (**Map 16**). German artillery barrages followed by a heavy infantry assault broke the line of the Allied defense for rolling armored spearheads. The next few days became desperate ones for the Allies.[10]

The Allied Response

On December 16, 1944, Allied air forces possessed a significant numerical advantage over the *Luftwaffe*. Ninth Air Force had deployed in the field nearly 1,000 fighters and fighter-bombers in three tactical air commands; two were mostly to the north, in Belgium, while the XIX TAC was south of Luxembourg, in France (**Map 17**). Fighters from other Allied air commands brought the Allies' total to just over 4,000 available front line fighter aircraft, nearly double the available *Luftwaffe* deployment. Much would now depend on how Allied air leaders used their superior force.[11]

The official Ninth Air Force account of the campaign asserts that the tactical air forces pursued three objectives in reacting to the German offensive on December 17: first, maintain air supremacy and prevent the *Luftwaffe* from supporting German ground forces; second, destroy the enemy's main combat elements, such as the tank and artillery forces that propelled the advance; and third, strike at the enemy's means of supply, including bridges, rail yards, supply depots, and communications centers to isolate the breakthrough area. This final objective drove enemy supply lines farther back from the battle area and made them more vulnerable to subsequent Allied air assault.[12]

In the emergency, close air support, which claimed third-priority in the tactical mission hierarchy, took precedence over interdiction.[13] One might argue that, at first, close air support even held priority over air superiority in the desperate attempt to blunt the German drive and confine it to manageable proportions. At the same time, the Ninth Air Force did not need to specifically target the German air force in the Ardennes region because the *Luftwaffe's* determination to provide cover to its attacking forces reopened the contest for air supremacy in the battle zone. Thus, close air support missions almost invariably resulted in first-priority counterair contests as well.[14]

This was certainly the case for General Weyland's forces on December 17. His response to the call for assistance was immediate and overwhelming. Taking advantage of unexpected good weather, every group in the command flew what they termed ground-force cover missions in support of VIII Corps units. At day's end, the fighter-bombers had flown half of their 356 total sorties in support of ground forces in the Ardennes breakthrough area, west of the

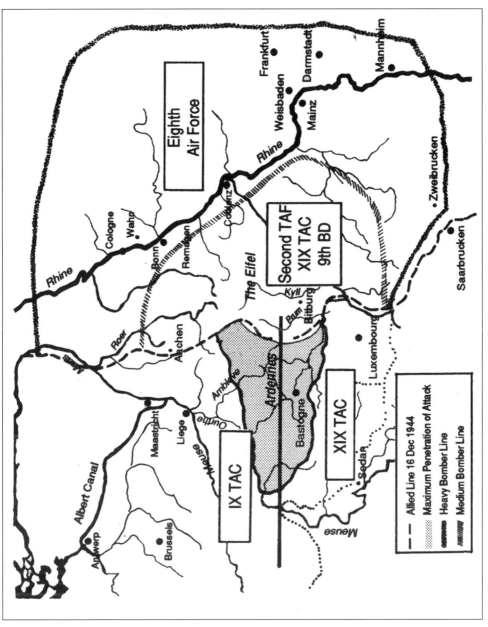

Map 17
Air Assignments for the Ardennes Counterattack December 1944

Reprinted from: Col. William R. Carter, "Air Power in the Battle of the Bulge: A Theater Campaign Perspective," *Airpower Journal*, III No. 4 (Winter 1989): 23.

Our and Sauer rivers along the German border. The remaining sortie figure reflected close support and interdiction missions in support of limited-objective operations by XX Corps and XII Corps, which at this time continued preparations for the soon-to-be canceled Operation Tink.[15]

The *Luftwaffe* made a strong presence on that December day with an estimated 600 sorties flown in support of the armored breakthrough and airborne landings. Both sides suffered high losses. Weyland's fighters claimed 24 enemy aircraft destroyed for a loss of nine of their own. General Quesada's forces, which had major responsibility for supporting First Army operations, claimed 49 destroyed and another 35 damaged. Even the reconnaissance pilots got in on the action when the 15th Tactical Reconnaissance Squadron's crack pilot, Capt. John H. Hoefker, returned with three and a half planes claimed. Ground air defense units tallied an additional 54 aircraft shot down. The next day, the *Luftwaffe* appeared in force again at the Ardennes front and once more suffered heavy losses—50 to Allied fighters and 51 to antiaircraft fire. After December 18, the *Luftwaffe* would never again attempt another large-scale air support effort for its ground forces in the Bulge.[16]

The Allies achieved immediate air supremacy in the battle zone less by conscious design than as a by-product of the close support missions. Not that the German Air Force did not remain a menace. Instead of fighter-bombers, Allied air leaders assigned medium and heavy bombers the counterair mission of striking nearby *Luftwaffe* bases. Nevertheless, fighter-bombers frequently attracted *Luftwaffe* attention while supporting ground forces or while on interdiction missions beyond the Ardennes. In fact, the experience of the 406th Tiger Tamers proved representative. Its 513th Fighter Squadron, flying a ground support mission on December 17, received orders to assist P–38s in a dogfight with six FW 190s. After jettisoning their bombs, the Thunderbolt pilots entered the fray and claimed three enemy aircraft destroyed. Of course, this encounter meant that the 513th aircraft did not bomb targets in support of ground forces, a dilemma that persisted throughout December when the *Luftwaffe* remained most active.[17]

The outstanding aerial effort on December 17, however, could not be repeated for the next five days because the Germans received the bad weather that facilitated their plans. Like Lorraine, weather became a determining factor in the air portion of the Ardennes Campaign. Only a squadron-sized mission on December 18 and 19 by the 354th Fighter Group broke the frustrating pattern. Yet, the 354th Pioneers found the *Luftwaffe* dangerous on both occasions. On the eighteenth, one of its squadrons attacked a force of 12 FW 190s bombing First Army troops east of Duren. Although it claimed four of the enemy aircraft destroyed, it lost two P–47s of its own. The next day an estimated 70 FW 190s attacked another Pioneer squadron after bombing a marshaling yard, and the American pilots counted nine enemy fighters down at a cost of three of their own. Despite the losses, General Weyland was pleased with the performance of his newly equipped P–47 outfit; that evening he lauded the Group "on [a] fine beginning with P–47s." All further flying by the command until December 23 supported XII Corps, which remained in position opposite the Zweibruecken area prior to its emergency redeployment north.[18]

While bad weather during the next five days prevented effective aerial operations, Allied leaders developed their strategy, prepared the necessary command and control measures, and readied their forces for a counteroffensive. On December 18, General Eisenhower alerted Patton to postpone Operation Tink and be prepared to counterattack against the expanding German salient. The situation on the ground quickly became critical for VIII Corps, as a German Panzer corps rapidly moved to reach the key communications center of Bastogne before the 101st Airborne Division arrived there in

4th Armored Division vehicles move past wrecked American equipment, Bastogne (above); tanks of the 4th Armored Division in the Luxembourg area used as artillery fire on German positions (below)

force. The Germans lost that close race the next day, the nineteenth, but they captured Houffalize 18 miles to the north. By December 21, they would surround the 101st Airborne Division, elements of the 10th Armored Division, and various other units at Bastogne.[19]

Early on the morning of December 19, Patton directed his 4th Armored and 26th Infantry Divisions to begin moving into the III Corps area 30 miles north.[20] Later that day, he joined Eisenhower and Bradley at Verdun, where the Supreme Commander outlined his plan, first to blunt and then turn back the assault (**Map 16**). The western tip of the German attacking force was to be prevented from crossing the Meuse. With the northern and southern shoulders of the salient confining the width of the breakthrough, the Allies would seal the northern part of the Bulge and counterattack in the south. Allied leaders adjusted the boundaries accordingly. General Devers's 6th Army Group would move up to replace Third Army's XII Corps in Lorraine, while Patton assumed command of VIII Corps and headed north with two attacking corps. Once his forces had secured Bastogne, he would attack northeast in the direction of Houffalize and eventually cut the salient in two.[21]

At this meeting, Patton electrified those present by promising to move his forces northward and be positioned to counterattack within 48 hours. Although he had directed his staff to prepare for this eventuality, it nonetheless meant shifting an entire army, solving enormous logistics problems, and arranging complex movement schedules during brutal winter weather. Patton and the men of his command succeeded, and the move remains today as one of the great feats of military history. As his biographer observed, "it was an operation that only a master could think of executing."[22]

General Weyland did not react as swiftly. On that day, December 19, he still hoped to salvage Operation Tink. Like many others, he had been slow to appreciate the gravity of the German attack. One can also understand his reluctance to abandon the plan he had helped fashion and believed would lead to a breach of the Siegfried Line. Certainly his conversation with General Quesada that afternoon, when they used special encrypted communications for the first time, could have left him in little doubt about the seriousness of the situation. That evening, after General Vandenberg notified him of Operation Tink's cancellation, he requested reinforcements for his command—three additional fighter groups and another reconnaissance group. He soon received nearly all of the forces that he requested.[23]

Ninth Air Force planners, meanwhile, continued developing an air plan based on requests from 12th Army Group, which focused on attacking German armored elements, isolating the Ardennes-Eifel region from rail support, harassing road traffic inside and outside the Bulge, and eliminating resupply facilities immediately beyond the Ardennes. This basic plan would remain unchanged. It called for medium bombers to concentrate on supply facilities such as bridges, railheads, and communications centers with the objective of forcing enemy supply points back to the Rhine River. Although fighter-bombers would help, their main assignment would be close support to meet the immediate threat, the front line Panzer force; they would also fly armed reconnaissance against road and rail targets from the Ardennes to the Rhine River. The planners viewed air superiority as essential and likely to need more attention because of the increased *Luftwaffe* presence, although they did not at first address this issue specifically. Eventually, they relied on Eighth Air Force bombers and fighters to handle much of the *Luftwaffe* counterair threat (**Map 17**).[24]

With the cancellation of Operation Tink, December 20, 1944, proved to be the key planning day for a counterattack by the Third Army–XIX TAC team. At a morning conference at the Third Army command post, Patton distributed the new order of battle: XX Corps would remain deployed along the Saar; XII Corps would reinforce the blocking force at Echternach; VIII Corps would strike the salient from the west; and while III Corps attacked from the south with 4th Armored Division advancing north to Bastogne, the 26th Infantry Division would move toward Wiltz, and the 80th Infantry Division toward Diekirch. Third Army units, Patton explained, had already begun to regroup to wheel the army's axis of advance from northeast to the north.[25]

Armed with Patton's plan, Weyland met with key staff members and decided to revive X-Ray, the command's small mobile command post that permitted close air-ground coordination, and move it with the Third Army command post from Chalon to Luxembourg City the next day. This time, chief of staff Col. Roger Browne would head X-Ray, while Colonel Thompson remained in command of the rear headquarters at Chalon. General Weyland would operate advance headquarters from Nancy with his combat operations officer, Colonel Ferguson. Much, of course, would depend on the pace of the battle and General Patton's location.[26]

At the same time, Weyland directed his signal officer, Col. Glenn Coleman, to work with Ninth Air Force to extend land lines from the Metz airfield, already scheduled to become operational later in December, to the Luxembourg City headquarters and other XIX TAC bases. They also discussed additional communications problems, especially new radar locations, and they decided to leave the MEW radar at its present location at Morhange, east of Nancy, until Third Army shifted the bulk of III Corps forces north. Then the MEW radar, which offered the best range and precision of available radar systems, could serve as the primary navigation and warning radar for the command's operations in the Bulge.[27]

That evening SHAEF informed Weyland of the new air and ground command arrangements based on Eisenhower's decision to divide the Ardennes sector into northern and southern halves for better command and control. Field Marshal Montgomery would command Allied forces in the northern sector, while in the south, General Bradley retained control of Patton's Third Army along with a sprinkling of First Army units. In the north, the two American air commands, IX and XXIX TACs, would be subordinated to the British Second Tactical Air Force commanded by Sir Arthur Coningham (**Map 17**). Coningham, however, left General Quesada free to apply both British and American fighter-bombers as he saw fit. This arrangement for the air forces avoided the kind of friction that developed later between Montgomery and American ground commanders over the British Field Marshal's methodical and extended preparations, and over his subsequent claims to have "saved the American side" in the Ardennes emergency.[28]

In the press of events, when Weyland contacted the Ninth Air Force chief of staff on December 20, 1944, regarding reinforcements, he learned that his request the previous evening had not reached Vandenberg. Weyland stressed its importance in light of the SHAEF message, and a short time thereafter he spoke to Vandenberg personally. The Ninth's commander did not commit himself at this point, but suggested they meet in Luxembourg City in two days, on December 22.[29]

Once again General Weyland turned to General Patton for assistance. The next day he drove to Luxembourg City and, after assuring himself that his staff had XIX TAC's "Spitfire X-Ray" ready for operations, conferred with Patton on the aerial reinforcement issue. Patton readily agreed to prime Bradley, and he delivered on his word. Next morning, on December 22 at 12th Army Group headquarters in Luxembourg City, Bradley, Patton, Vandenberg, and Weyland reached agreement on Weyland's request for additional units. Since Third Army would make the main effort against the Germans in the Bulge, Weyland argued, tactical resources needed to be divided more equitably among the air commands.[30]

The outcome pleased General Weyland. Within the week he expected to receive three fighter-bomber groups from IX TAC: the 367th (a P–38 group) and the 365th and the 368th (two Thunderbolt groups). The 365th would go to the Metz airfield when the engineers had it ready, and the other two groups would go to Juvincourt, at least temporarily. Two tactical reconnaissance squadrons from XIX TAC would join the 10th Photo Reconnaissance Group at Conflans. This would bolster the reconnaissance capability of the command by 50 percent, and the air leaders expected the emergency to call for a maximum effort from these units. At this early date, the planners at 12th Army Group Headquarters discussed the likelihood of each tactical air command temporarily receiving a P–51 group from Eighth Air Force to handle escort duties and perform counterair missions. The XIX TAC group was later identified as the 361st Fighter Group, a P–51 unit, and the command based it at St. Dizier. With these additional units, XIX TAC would have a striking force of eight groups totaling 360 airplanes— its most potent arsenal since the summer campaign in France. Moreover, the locations of the new bases improved the effectiveness of the force because all were within short striking distance of the Ardennes and the Saarland.[31]

Yet, the transfer of these aerial units had not been cleared beforehand with IX TAC's commander, General Quesada, the primary loser in the realignment. When Weyland saw Vandenberg the next morning, he learned that both IX TAC and Second TAF (RAF) vigorously protested the transfer. In view of the deteriorating situation on the ground in the northern sector at that time, Quesada's dismay was understandable. Nevertheless, Vandenberg explained, the transfers would take place as planned. Despite the disagreement, Quesada's objections did not alter the close personal relationship between the two American air commanders or affect tactical air power's effective response. The rapid transfer of units between commands demonstrated its flexibility.[32]

The basic command, control, and organizational arrangements were completed on December 22, 1944, the sixth day of the German offensive. General Weyland immediately began coordinating support for the new air units with his maintenance and supply officers, and he approved a new tactical reconnaissance plan that comprised ten areas generally encompassing St. Hubert within the western portion of the Bulge, Cologne, Mainz, and St. Avold in Lorraine.[33]

The command's preparations for a counterattack during the initial week of the offensive proceeded smoothly. Weather remained the major uncertainty. Group histories for this period reflect the intense preparations to attack and the frustration and anxiety of waiting for the weather to clear. Moreover, for the first time on the continent, the command also had to worry seriously about *Luftwaffe* air raids. By December 22, Third Army reported 78 *Luftwaffe* raids. Most seemed to be nuisance strikes, such as the attacks on Rosiers and Metz, two of the XIX TAC airfields. Although these raids caused little damage, they nevertheless heightened the tension and compelled planners to take action to thwart the air threat in their rear area.[34]

Meanwhile, despite the bad weather, German ground forces experienced problems executing all phases of their plan. In the north, U.S. V Corps troops

P–38 of the 367th Fighter Group

exercised unexpectedly stiff resistance along the Elsenborn Ridge, and Dietrich's armored forces found themselves delayed and confined to only two of the four needed roads. Likewise in the south, VIII Corps grimly held on for three days opposite Echternach, thereby delaying the Seventh German Army's drive to break through to the southwest. In fact, both northern and southern shoulders continued to resist and confine the width of the German attack. As a result, the Fifth German Army in the center assumed the main burden of the offensive, as it had more success breaking American defense along the Schnee Eifel ridgeline with its two Panzer corps in the lead. Even here, tenacious pockets of resistance delayed General von Manteuffel's forces. St. Vith held out until December 23, forcing the Germans to deal with severe traffic congestion and supply backups. For an offensive scheduled to reach the Meuse River while operating on two and a half days' worth of supplies and five days' rations, these delays proved critical.[35]

By December 22 at XIX TAC, officers and enlisted men realized that German forces had encircled Bastogne and were regrouping for a fresh assault. Although 4th Armored Division's three combat commands moved northward, their pace slowed in the face of heavy snow and ice, and the German forces in their path. The fighter groups eagerly sought to get into the battle—none more so than the 406th Fighter Group that had developed such good rapport with the 101st Airborne Division when these paratroopers arrived at Mourmelon in late September 1944 to recuperate after their rough experience in Operation Market Garden. The 406th Fighter Group expected to take the lead at Bastogne just as soon as the weather broke.[36]

Paratroopers of the 101st Airborne Division, supported by firepower of the 4th Armored Division, Bastogne

Victory Weather

Seven days after the Nazi breakthrough, on December 23, 1944, the Allies awoke to a Russian High, a high pressure system from the east, which brought clear skies and cooler temperatures throughout the region.[37] Now the planes could fly and tanks could roll during what the American side would call five days of victory weather. For Weyland's forces, the next five days, from December 23–27, proved the most active in the command's operational experience and provided a superb example of tactical air power's effect on a land battle under emergency conditions.[38]

On December 23, the XIX TAC swung into action, lacking only the 361st Fighter Group, which Eighth Air Force had yet to deploy to the continent. The airplanes flew in close support of VIII Corps forces at Bastogne and of Third Army's advancing armored columns, by now within six miles of the beleaguered town, although facing increasingly stiff German resistance. The 362d Fighter Group flew six missions in support of the III Corps forces, but it also supported XII Corps with two missions and, for good measure, sent 15 aircraft to escort C–47 Dakotas on a mission to drop supplies in parapacks to the American troops isolated at Bastogne. Characteristic of flying during the Bastogne period was the 362d Fighter Group's high mission rate. The XIX TAC's average of 57 missions per day for the five-day period was among the highest in the command's history.

During the emergency operation, ground support personnel serviced, reloaded, and returned the aircraft to action as fast as they possibly could. Tactical reconnaissance pilots played a particularly crucial role, keeping all roads and railroads entering the Bulge under continuous surveillance. It became increasingly routine for these pilots, having called in targets to the control center, to lead fighter-bombers to them. This saved time, allowing more fighter-bomber missions to be flown during these short December days. Sortie figures for the tactical reconnaissance squadrons reflect their important contribution. They flew 26 successful sorties on the 23rd, but with the addition of the two squadrons from XXIX TAC, they averaged 70 for the remaining four days. No unit proved more important than the night photo squadron, which flew 99 sorties in December, its largest number to date, acquiring urgently needed nighttime photos of highway traffic and communications targets.[39]

The missions of the other groups on December 23 included escort for 263 C–47s to Bastogne, specific close support, armed reconnaissance of the Bulge and the Eifel region near Trier, and coverage of the weakened Saar front opposite XX Corps. Moreover, because Third Army leaders worried about XII Corps' right flank, the 10th Photo Reconnaissance Group flew a daily mission in the Trier-Merzig area looking for any signs of a buildup and excessive bridge-building. In effect, the command again protected Patton's right flank much as it did in France the previous summer.[40]

These five mission types characterized the entire Ardennes period. Of the five, close air support in the Bulge received the most attention as Allied air forces attempted to slow the German drive and protect American units under attack. During the five days of victory weather, close support sorties outnumbered armed reconnaissance sorties by two to one (1,124 to 509). Again, however, the wartime records defy precise analysis. Many aircraft that initially set out on a ground support mission ended flying armed reconnaissance after being released by the ground controller. Likewise, pilots flying armed reconnaissance often had targets in the St. Vith, Malmedy, and Bastogne areas in close proximity to friendly ground forces. Then, too, fighter-bombers on escort duty for bombers and C–47 transports frequently bombed and strafed targets of opportunity after completing their escort missions.[41]

Targets of opportunity abounded. Following the Bulge Campaign, in February 1945, the command's operational research section analyzed the effort devoted to targets of opportunity from December 15, 1944, through January 31, 1945. They included in this category targets attacked on armed reconnaissance missions and on missions that originally had assigned targets but that ended attacking targets of opportunity. During the five-day Bastogne emergency, the command's daily sortie rate for targets of opportunity averaged 71 percent of the total 2,846 sorties flown. In view of the emergency, controllers often diverted aircraft to "hot targets." Researchers reminded the command of the difficulty of compiling precise and accurate information, and cautioned that "the number and type of such targets cannot be determined…[precisely]…, since operations following December 15 have involved the attacking of such a wide variety of targets, most of which might well be classed as targets of opportunity."[42]

Both the scramble and escort missions also demonstrated that the airmen still considered the *Luftwaffe* a major threat. During the Ardennes Offensive it became standard procedure to escort and fly cover for all medium bomber flights. At times, the fighters and bombers failed to properly rendezvous, however, and the bomber-force leader then had to decide if the importance of the target required that his unit proceed unprotected. That option ceased on December 23, 1944, when a large force of about 500 B–26 Marauders and A–20s, after failing to contact their fighter escort, chose to fly on and strike vital bridges west of the Rhine. On this mission that force lost 37 aircraft, 31 to enemy fighters and 6 more to flak.[43] The arrival of P–51s from the Eighth Air Force on December 24 relieved the XIX TAC of a considerable escort responsibility, and from that date until the end of the Ardennes Campaign, the P–51-equipped 361st Fighter Group flew the majority of medium bomber escort missions, allowing the rugged P–47s to concentrate on what they did best—bomb and strafe.[44]

The command's concerns about the *Luftwaffe* threat during the fight for Bastogne were well-founded, as the B–26 losses on December 23 made plain. The urgent need of forward *Wehrmacht* troops for aerial protection from the massive Allied fighter-bomber assault during the five days of late December brought the *Luftwaffe* out in force. It averaged nearly 600 sorties per day and a further 200–250 at night from an assortment of night fighters, fighter-bombers, and bombers. The desperate situation now faced by German troops in the Bulge required the *Luftwaffe's* entire effort, which meant that Allied bombers could attack rearward supply and communications sites virtually unmolested. Indeed, the vigorous appearance of the *Luftwaffe* on December 23 and resultant loss of B–26 medium bombers prompted Ninth Air Force to take swift counterair action. It possessed one division of heavy bombers on loan from Eighth Air Force for use in its interdiction program east of the Rhine River. On December 24, Ninth Air Force dispatched them to carpet-bomb 14 airfields in the Frankfurt and Cologne areas.[45]

By month's end the Allied heavy bombers and fighters had exacted a severe toll from *Luftwaffe* forces. From the approximately 1,000 enemy sorties flown over the battle lines west of the Rhine on December 23, Allied airmen forced that daily rate steadily downward until December 27, the last good-weather day of the period, when the *Luftwaffe* managed only about 500 sorties—some 50 percent of the number flown four days earlier. Moreover, it became increasingly difficult for *Luftwaffe* aircraft to penetrate Allied defenses and reach the Ardennes area from bases in the Rhine valley. The American air counteroffensive had pushed German air support, like other supporting elements for German ground forces in the Ardennes, steadily eastward away from the front lines. The *Luftwaffe* withdrawal put greater strain on its already depleted fuel supply. Although the *Luftwaffe* might inflict severe losses on the Allies, it could neither protect the *Wehrmacht* ground troops, especially during daylight hours, nor blunt the Allied air and ground counterattack. Moreover, the massive Allied air response during the days of good weather resulted, for the first time, in widespread reports of *Luftwaffe* pilots using any excuse available to return early from their missions.[46]

Claims of aircraft destroyed by XIX TAC for this five-day period were the highest in its history. On December 23, command pilots counted an impressive 34 enemy aircraft shot down in air encounters. Although claims of so great a number of enemy aircraft vanquished in a single day would not again be made, by the twenty-seventh, when the weather began closing in once again, the command could claim a total of 84 enemy aircraft killed and 35 damaged. During the same five-day period XIX TAC also suffered its highest loss rate. Of 93 aircraft lost in combat during December, 47 occurred during the period from December 23–27. The worst losses occurred on December 26, the day after Christmas, when the XIX TAC lost 14 aircraft, although six pilots parachuted safely into friendly territory. By the end of December, General

Weyland once again had to discuss the rate of the flow of P–47 replacement aircraft with General Vandenberg.[47]

Participants described the concentration of flak in the Ardennes as the greatest in the war to date. Allied intelligence explained that two large, self-propelled flak units had been sent forward under fuel and movement priority to secure key towns and crossroads. By the time they reached the point of farthest advance, five miles from the Meuse River, all communications junctions had heavy flak protection. Understandably, the command suffered most of its losses from flak. Of the 93 aircraft lost in December, flak accounted for 42 and probably 22 more as well. In January 1945 the statisticians attributed 35 of the 50 aircraft shot down to flak.[48]

Capt. Richard Parker, 405th Fighter Group (left); flak-spattered P–61 (below)

Most of the tactical air command's losses during the Bastogne operation occurred among the P–47 groups, the 362nd, 405th, and 406th Fighter Groups, which flew the majority of close air support missions and had the highest sortie rates. These three groups accounted for 42 of the 69 pilots lost in December, and 47 of the 81 aircraft lost in combat. What at first is most surprising are the aircraft abort statistics. Although the figure for the month was 6 percent, that for the period, December 21–31, was only 4.23 percent. Moreover, the record shows mechanical reasons responsible for only 1.59 percent of the aborted flights. Yet this record occurred during the most intense flying period of the month, which suggests that the emergency elicited a special effort from the maintenance and support people, and that the command permitted aircraft to fly with problems not otherwise tolerated.[49]

Along with 11 aircraft lost on December 23, one other disturbing incident occurred on that day. Intelligence officers reported that pilots of 362d Fighter Group P–51s, in a dogfight near Trier against what they later claimed were enemy FW 190s, tangled with and shot down one of the Orange Tail P–47s from the 358th Fighter Group. By the end of the month, the problem of what authorities referred to as friendly fire incidents involving both aircraft and artillery units would become a major issue of concern for Ninth Air Force and 12th Army Group.[50]

Support Facilities and the Aerial Relief of Bastogne

While XIX TAC pilots pressed their attacks during the days of victory weather, General Weyland spent much of the period dealing with a variety of operational support issues. On December 23, the topic of airfield status headed the list, with discussion focused on the Metz airfield. Weyland's chief engineer, Colonel Smyser, promised to have the Metz field ready for one fighter-bomber group on December 25, and for another one on January 1. As usual, the engineers' hopes proved too optimistic. By this time, they constructed all fields with pierced steel-plank to avoid the damage from weather that forced the command to abandon six airfields in the fall. Even with pierced steel-plank runways, however, the engineers needed to lay a rock base first. They also had learned from experience that they could not declare a field operational when only the runway and little else had been completed. An operational airfield needed useable, all-weather hardstands, service roads, and taxiways *before* the aircraft arrived.[51]

The Metz airfield, which lay within 25 miles of the Saar valley, was closer to enemy lines than any other XIX TAC base. For this reason General Weyland wanted to ensure that it had adequate air defense units in place. He called Ninth Air Force's air defense chief about protection for the three new fighter-bomber groups that were on their way to XIX TAC. Weyland learned that Metz already had an antiaircraft battery in place, and the air defense chief promised to check on Juvincourt and put a battery at Mourmelon. By December 25, Weyland had arranged for two antiaircraft batteries at each airfield. Third Army continued to report nightly visits from the *Luftwaffe*, and Weyland could not afford to take the aerial threat lightly.

On December 24, with the air defense situation apparently well in hand, General Weyland and his staff turned their attention to airfield facilities. That day he visited Juvincourt, where he found that the 367th Fighter Group had just arrived, "glad to join XIX TAC." Although the group's sincerity is not to be doubted, the unit could hardly be pleased with the new field. The 368th Fighter Group had been scheduled to move from Juvincourt to the Metz complex, but it flew from Mourmelon until the Metz field could be readied. Hardstand problems at Mourmelon required that the group remain at Juvincourt along with the 367th. The heavy flying of the next few days considerably strained the support facilities of a base not designed to service two groups simultaneously.[52]

After conferring on December 24 with his 100th Wing commander, Brig. Gen. "Tex" Sanders, Weyland decided to establish what he referred to as a rear wing at the command's rear headquarters at Chalons. This, he explained, would improve operational control of the groups in the Marne area, while the 100th Wing, which had moved to Metz, would handle support for the forward bases in Lorraine. The command declared the rear wing operational on December 27, 1944, which in effect, meant that Weyland had further decentralized command and control. Despite the shorter flying distances, the new arrangement proved similar to the one used for mobile warfare in France. Extremely decentralized tactical air operations had been associated with widely separated facilities or fast-paced mobile warfare in France. Now, however, although the front was relatively stable, Weyland established three headquarters echelons and two wings. He could rely on experience, good communications links, and his tactical control group located with the advance headquarters to ensure efficient command and control.[53]

The next four days proved relatively quiet along the Saar and Mosel fronts as the battle for Bastogne, farther to the north, intensified. Responsibility for the city's aerial defense belonged to Weyland's command, and relieving Bastogne would always retain a special place on the command's honor roll. The Bastogne mission illustrates the various ways the tactical air force could contribute to support troops in a defensive situation. None proved more important than the escort mission to protect Allied transports supplying the garrison. In this instance, no one questioned the number of sorties that might have been used for other missions. Bastogne, which held up the XLVII Panzer Corps, had to be defended at all costs. Led by the 406th Fighter Group, three groups flew a total of 95 sorties on December 23 when escorting 263 C–47 cargo craft to the city. The size of the escort force varied from one to two squadrons, depending on the number of transports that required protection. Frequently, the fighter-bombers flew armed reconnaissance or close support missions after completing the escort assignment. This, for example, occurred on December 23, when a squadron from the 362d Fighter Group performed its escort responsibilities and then went on to strike a German command post and bivouac area.[54]

A single squadron provided escort protection on December 24 to a transport force flying to Bastogne because the transports numbered only 161. Yet the squadron from the 354th Fighter Group failed to rendezvous with the transports and went on to attack its secondary target, a marshaling yard near Mayen, 16 miles west of Coblenz. The next day, a four-plane flight from the 405th Fighter Group flew the only escort mission, one that proved significant. In the initial fighting east of the city, most of the 326th Airborne Medical Company had been captured. With medical needs critical, a Third Army physician volunteered to go into the besieged perimeter in a L–1 light plane. He did so without incident under the protection of the 405th Fighter Group. The number of escort missions increased to five on December 26, the day the Third Army broke the siege, and to three on December 27, before the weather turned nasty again. If the results of the operation are measured in losses, as well as how well they ensured the survival of the garrison, the relief operation succeeded. Of the 901 C–47s involved over the five-day period, 19 from the IX Troop Carrier Command were lost.[55]

Along with the escort mission, much of the command's close support effort during this period focused on Bastogne, either in support of VIII Corps troops surrounded inside the town, or in support of III Corps forces driving north to rescue the trapped VIII Corps units. Attacks on close-in targets that defenders could not shell because of ammunition shortages proved particularly effective. While all groups participated at one time or another during the five days, General Weyland assigned specific groups almost exclusively to these two corps. The 362d Fighter Group covered the advance of the III Corps' 4th Armored Division, while the 406th Fighter Group flew the close support mis-

C–47 used for supply drops to besieged troops at Bastogne

sion for VIII Corps in the Bastogne area. During the height of the battle, from December 24–26, the 406th Fighter Group averaged 17 missions a day in support of VIII Corps. Losses were heavy, with seven 405th Fighter Group aircraft shot down on December 26 alone. Although the 362d Fighter Group suffered fewer losses, none was more difficult to accept than the death of Maj. Berry Chandler, commander of the 379th Fighter Squadron, inadvertently shot down on December 26 by III Corps antiaircraft fire. That same day Weyland received a personal call from Maj. Gen. John Milliken, III Corps commander, thanking the 362d Fighter Group for its magnificent support in breaking through to the city's defenders. Weyland promptly passed the corps commander's message on to the group hoping it would help atone for the loss of Major Chandler.[56]

The *Luftwaffe* appeared again in force on December 26, mostly in the IX TAC sector. Even though General Weyland's Y service, the command's intelligence communications intercept operation, had predicted an air attack on Bastogne consisting of between 400 and 500 aircraft, nothing of the sort occurred. Later command reports affirmed that the Y service made a valuable contribution during the Ardennes Campaign, but the record shows little more than two Y reports, both of which proved to be false alarms.[57]

The Bastogne emergency also elicited a major effort from the 10th Photo Reconnaissance Group. Responsibility for battlefield coverage of the area fell primarily to F–6 (P–51) pilots of the 15th Tactical Reconnaissance Squadron, who proved adept at spotting enemy armor columns preparing to attack the perimeter, leading fighter-bombers to attack targets, and at adjusting artillery fire for the gunners. Normally the F–6s, rather than the unarmed F–5s (P–38s) of the 31st Photo Reconnaissance Squadron, flew photo missions in high-flak areas. Bastogne was not, however, a routine situation for the group. The 101st Airborne Division trapped in Bastogne requested photos of the area in order to conduct accurate counterbattery artillery fire. A P–38 pilot volunteered to fly in the photos, which the group gathered from its photo library and delivered in a drop-tank. The pilot had to come in low and slow to drop the tank accurately to the encircled troops. Although he succeeded, the 101st wanted more current prints. The next day the 31st Photo Squadron flew 20 missions to get them. Again, volunteers came forward to fly the dangerous delivery mission, but two separate drop attempts ended in failure when German flak downed both planes. The experience of the P–38 pilots well represents the extra effort airmen displayed during the Bastogne emergency.[58]

Only in the area of night fighter support of Bastogne did air power prove deficient. Generally, IX TAC's single night fighter squadron patrolled the Bulge area, while XIX TAC's 425th Night Fighter Squadron flew patrol and intruder missions in the Eifel and Saar regions. Reviewing the operation, the 12th Army Group Air Effects Committee concluded that "generally, night fighter activity within the area was inadequate."[59] Yet this was a major theaterwide weakness of the tactical air forces.

On December 26, Third Army broke the German encirclement at Bastogne. At 1:00 p.m., General Patton called Weyland to request a maximum effort in front of the 4th Armored Division for its final push to Bastogne. Weyland immediately directed his combat operations officer, Colonel Ferguson, to lay on extra missions. That afternoon, the 362d Fighter Group flew nine missions in support of III Corps, while VIII Corps forces received eight from the 405th Fighter Group and 18 from the 406th Fighter Group. The extra effort paid off. Elements of the 4th Armored Division made contact with the 101st Airborne Division at an outpost two miles south of the city later that day. By December 27, the last day of victory weather, the task became one of keeping the Bastogne corridor open. That did not promise to be easy.[60]

F–6s, 10th Photo Reconnaissance Group (above); tank commander of an M–7 tank directing fire from a self-propelled 105-mm outside of Bastogne (below)

Protecting the Corridor, Dealing with Friendly Fire

By the end of December 1944, the German drive in the Ardennes had stalled and the most forward units were forced back (**Map 18**). Panzer forces had reached Celles, within five miles of the Meuse, as early as December 24, before stiffening resistance from British and American troops and a lack of fuel halted their advance. At year's end, Third Army was involved in heavy fighting in the III Corps area where Patton's corridor into Bastogne had been widened to approximately five miles and the Bastogne-Arlon highway cleared. In the VIII Corps sector, units advanced to within three miles of linking up with First Army's forward elements, and they fought hard to repel counterattacks west of Bastogne. The XII Corps units, meanwhile, conducted a seesaw battle for Echternach at the southern hinge of the Bulge, where their pace slowed in the face of bad weather, rough terrain, and German artillery concentrations. While Field Marshal Montgomery continued to gather forces in the north in preparation for his major offensive planned for January 3, 1945, General Patton acted to protect the Bastogne corridor and readied his forces to move farther northeast to St. Vith by way of Houffalize to cut off German units to the west. Bad weather and German intransigence combined to slow progress everywhere.[61]

Bad weather in late December certainly weakened XIX TAC's efforts to cover ground units in the Bulge and to undertake an ambitious interdiction program to cut the enemy's lifeline. Along with directing the air campaign to support the Third Army, General Weyland also confronted issues of air defense that stymied his best efforts. From December 26, 1944, until January 3, 1945, when bad weather forced a two-day cancellation of flying, Weyland's forces continued to support the Third Army corps as much as possible and in the same manner as it had done so previously. The 362d and 406th Fighter Groups largely flew in support of III Corps and VIII Corps operations, respectively, while the 405th Fighter Group covered the XII and XX Corps fronts. This left the three new groups and the 354th Fighter Group available to focus almost exclusively on the interdiction program developed by Ninth Air Force. Although in later years General Weyland provided no special reason for this division of labor, one must assume that he considered the command's longest serving P–47 groups best qualified to fly close air support missions because they were more accustomed to working with Third Army's units and their air controllers. Nevertheless, all four groups flew "cooperation" missions with the ground forces on occasion, especially in late January 1945, when the Germans on the hitherto static Lorraine front increased their pressure on Saarlautern in XX Corps' area and began a mass exodus from the Bulge.[62]

The theaterwide interdiction plan developed by Ninth Air Force and 12th Army Group sought to break down the German forward supply system by reducing the enemy's road capacity in the Bulge itself, while simultaneously destroying the road and rail system in the Eifel and communications centers east of the Rhine. The planners divided bomber targets geographically into an inner and outer zone to be attacked by medium and heavy bombers, respectively. By the end of December the interdiction effort began to produce results. Towns in the Ardennes had become favorite targets as chokepoints and reports of rubble blocking traffic became commonplace. In the Eifel, where the XIX TAC and the IX Bombardment Division had been concentrating on rail bridges and marshaling yards, intelligence analysts considered the rail network useless. Ultra intercepts confirmed their assessment, which described the chaos on both sides of the Rhine River. Shipments of German materiel faced delays of a week or more now that supplies had to be off-loaded at the Rhine for movement westward. With the rail system in the Eifel largely destroyed, the fighter-bombers turned their attention to the road network, while the medium bombers used larger bombing formations to attack key bridges. This aerial interdiction effort gradually isolated the battlefield.[63]

Mission assignments reflected renewed emphasis on interdiction for the seven-day period beginning December 27 when the new groups began flying in force for Weyland's command. Except for one 368th Fighter Group seven-plane attack on a tunnel on January 2, 1945, the three new fighter-bomber groups exclusively flew armed reconnaissance. Nearly half of the 361st Fighter Group's missions were fighter sweeps that produced attacks on targets of opportunity. For the six flyable days during this period, interdiction sorties averaged 78 percent of the total for the command. As always, operations of the tactical air arm reflected the ground situation, and after Bastogne, the XIX TAC could afford to cover the ground forces with fewer missions and devote a larger share to interdiction targets. Its flexibility enabled it to adjust with ease to the new requirements.[64]

Although the *Luftwaffe* seldom appeared during the final days of December 1944, Third Army continued to report nightly German air raids. During the five days of victory weather, the raids rose to more than 100 per night, but they declined to approximately 50 by month's end. Although airfields occasionally reported attacks, damage never proved severe, and Third Army air defense units always reported destroying at least a portion of the attacking force. Nevertheless, the German strikes made air leaders like Weyland sensitive to a threat he could do little to contain. Certainly his night fighter force was woefully inadequate for the task.[65]

General Weyland's single P–61 night fighter squadron, like IX TAC's, could only be described as understrength, short of spare parts, and battle weary. Altogether, the squadron flew only 111 sorties during the last week of the month which accounted for 14 enemy aircraft destroyed at a cost of 3 of their own. The 425th Night Fighter Squadron seldom could sustain a consistently high sortie rate. One night the number might be 20 and another night 5; the bad weather and hazards of night flying combined with equipment short-

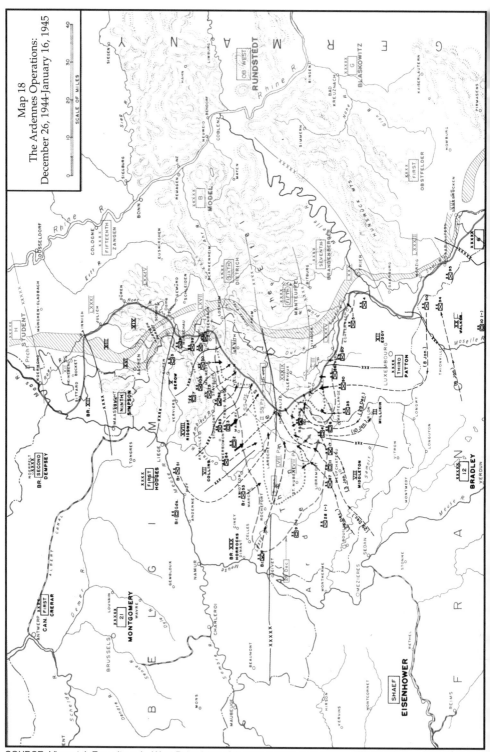

Map 18
The Ardennes Operations:
December 26, 1944-January 16, 1945

SOURCE: Vincent J. Esposito, ed., *West Point Atlas of American Wars*, V. 2, Map 62, (New York: Praeger, 1960)

ages to limit the Black Widow's effectiveness. Even with the XIX TAC controlling all night flying with its best radar, the MEW system, periodically either the controller or pilot would fail to make positive contact with one another, or the aircraft's radar would malfunction. Apart from this, the airmen found the counterair intruder mission especially challenging because enemy airbases often proved too widely dispersed or beyond the range of available AAF aircraft. Nighttime disorientation and uncertainty could kill, too. The most unfortunate example of this occurred on December 27, 1944, when General Weyland learned that a Third Army air defense battery shot down a P–61—the second such incident. Although the gunners bore part of the blame, in this case the pilot mistook another base for his home one and inadvertently wandered into the army's inner artillery zone.[66]

Despite the handicaps, however, neither tactical air command wanted to give up its night fighters. With their enormous fire power of four 20-mm cannon, napalm bombs, and eight 5-inch rockets, when properly applied, the P–61s had a terrifying effect on enemy morale. For air leaders, the answer lay in more aircraft and spare parts. On the last day of the month, Col. Robert M. Lee, operations deputy at Ninth Air Force, called to ask whether the XIX TAC would be interested in a British Mosquito squadron from the Mediterranean theater to supplement its night force. Weyland gladly accepted the offer, but when he heard that a P–61 squadron would become available as well, he suggested that IX TAC receive the Mosquito squadron because of its proximity to RAF bases. Ninth Air Force disagreed, and the Mosquitoes of the 421st Night Fighter Squadron arrived at Etain to join the 425th Night Fighter Squadron on January 13, 1945. The XIX TAC night fighters remained, however, a small but gallant force arguably faced with the most demanding mission in the command. Their small numbers limited them to a harassment role having little impact on German operations.[67]

This issue of friendly fire—of American gunners on the ground mistakenly shooting at American aircraft overhead, or American aircraft mistakenly attacking other Allied aircraft or bombing or strafing American forces on the ground—became so serious it could not be ignored. Losses to friendly fire persistently occurred during the Allied campaign in the Mediterranean, and the problem never had been solved. If carpet bombing errors by heavy bombers employed in tactical operations such as Cobra produced the most spectacular and notorious mistakes, the problem proved even more acute in the far more numerous fighter-bomber close support operations. During fighter-bomber bombing and strafing in proximity to friendly ground forces, opportunities for error were ever-present. Large- or quick-reaction military operations like the Ardennes Offensive demanded greater close air support, attracted more attention to real or imagined *Luftwaffe* intruders, and magnified the problem across the front. Pilots frequently complained about trigger-happy infantry gunners, while the latter reported that too often Allied fighters attacked them instead of the enemy.

Although General Weyland's responsibilities included air defense of the Third Army area, he did not control all air defense units. In the tactical control center, the air force controller worked closely with the liaison officer of the 38th Antiaircraft Artillery (AAA) Brigade (which protected the airfields) to coordinate night fighter patrols, inner artillery zones, and the so-called blank check areas, for which the controller specified certain times for firing. Army-controlled air defense units, however, remained coordinated with, but not fully integrated into, the air force warning system. General Weyland sought to answer the problem by stressing positive identification and radar control of fighter-bombers, and enforcement of procedures governing local air defense. This meant ensuring that all elements in the system received comprehensive aircraft movement information. All too often, for example, Eighth Air Force aircraft, flying through friendly artillery zones, were surprised when fired upon, and were then chagrined to learn that the artillery controller had no knowledge of their flight plan.[68]

The air defense problem demanded constant attention. Every major joint operation required detailed coordination on air defense procedures, while each time one of his air units moved to a new location, Weyland needed to confirm that the site had adequate protection from the Third Army's 51st AAA Brigade. His challenge increased in winter and during the intense Ardennes fighting. Heavy snows made target identification more difficult, especially in the breakthrough area where airmen worried about an imprecise bomb line, about friendly troops positioned on three sides of the enemy bulge, and about the fake target-marker panels deployed on the ground by the Germans.[69]

The XIX TAC thoroughly investigated every friendly fire incident reported. Its records for the winter months on the subject are reasonably comprehensive and show an inadvertent firing-at-aircraft incident nearly every day in the month of December 1944. Perhaps Third Army gunners can be forgiven when, for the first time in the conflict, they experienced substantial and recurrent *Luftwaffe* raids. On the ground, most friendly fire reports originated with Third Army units and concerned strafing attacks by friendly aircraft. Normally the battalion headquarters sent these field reports to the commander of the 38th AAA Brigade, who passed them on to Colonel Ferguson at XIX TAC. He usually turned them over to the command's capable inspection team of Lt. Col. Leo H. Johnson, Air Inspector, and his chief investigating officer, Chief Warrant Officer (CWO) Samuel L. Schwartzberg. On occasion, Ninth Air Force also contacted General Weyland with a request to investigate an incident that might have involved the command's fighter-bombers. The inspectors' investigation reports reveal an impressive comprehensiveness and objectivity. Not unlike contemporary air accident investigation procedures, the inspectors collected reports from all parties, examined various types of evidence including film when available, reconstructed the missions of all groups that flew on the day of the incident, and interviewed all parties concerned. If XIX TAC pilots proved to be at fault infrequently, the friendly fire investigative reports

**Col. James Ferguson (far left) and General Weyland (far right)
at a press briefing**

nevertheless appear thorough and convincing. Throughout the Allied drive into Germany, friendly fire continued to bedevil the air-ground team's best efforts to eliminate it.[70]

The problem of friendly fire had been building for some time, as Weyland's concern over the losses of Major Chandler, the night fighter, and the 362d Fighter Group incidents attest. The issue came to a head for both the air and ground leaders during the last two days of December 1944, when Luxembourg's capital served as the advance headquarters site for Generals Bradley, Patton, and Vandenberg. Apparently on December 30 Ninth Air Force controllers called for help when two German Bf 109s appeared overhead. Two P–51 and two P–47 aircraft arrived five minutes after the German aircraft left. In spite of attempts to identify themselves, anxious American gunners guarding a bridge on the city's outskirts shot down a 405th Fighter Group P–47 and the pilot perished. The incident deeply disturbed General Weyland, who sent a sharp message from his Nancy headquarters to Colonel Browne at X-Ray. He "requested" all Allied antiaircraft batteries be prohibited from firing on any aircraft except those positively identified as belonging to the enemy and clearly observed to be strafing or bombing.[71]

The following day, on December 31, the P–47 affair at Luxembourg City took center stage in an exchange of messages among key air and ground leaders. Its seriousness became evident when Weyland reported that General Vandenberg had taken the matter to Bradley, and that Bradley or Patton would send a message of regret to the 405th Fighter Group because, as General Weyland pointed out, we "do not want bad feeling[s]." Later that morning, Vandenberg called Weyland about a report from Third Army concerning a P–47 strafing attack on one of its convoys between Thionville and Luxembourg City, asking him to investigate the charge. In this instance Vandenberg identified the 362d Fighter Group as the probable culprit, but subsequent investigation showed the Maulers to be elsewhere at the time of the incident.[72]

In the early evening, Colonel Browne informed Weyland that Generals Spaatz, Doolittle, Patton, and he had conferred that afternoon at Third Army headquarters in Luxembourg City about the issue of army firings on Allied planes and of fighter-bomber attacks on U.S. ground forces and installations. In the first case, they believed the chief culprit to be a rumor circulating widely in the Third Army area to the effect, that in the words of General Patton, "the Germans are flying our P–47s." Besides official refutation, the conferees had no solution to this problem, but they reiterated that there would be no bombing whatever permitted within the bomb line except under control of an air support officer. Air units also needed to do a better job of crew briefing and always rely on radar control. Most interesting and portentous of all, they

From left to right: General Weyland; Col. Roger Browne, XIX TAC chief of staff; Brig. Gen. Homer L. Sanders, commander, 100th Fighter Wing; and General Patton

decided to prohibit all flying operations the following day, January 1, 1945, in the XII and XX Corps areas, where the most recent incidents had occurred. Evidently they thought this would help cool tempers and allow everyone time to review procedures.[73]

Yet friendly fire incidents continued throughout the Ardennes Campaign. In mid-January 1945, it would reach a point where the XII Corps commander wrote personally to General Weyland. He worried that if accidental aerial attacks on his forces continued, relations between the air and ground units would collapse. Only the end of the campaign and the intense flying associated with it seems to have reduced, but not eliminated, the difficulty.[74] By New Year's Eve, 1944, certainly both air and ground leaders were alert to the issue. The fighter-bombers would not fly over the XX Corps area the next day, and Third Army gunners were admonished to be less trigger-happy. The *Luftwaffe* could not have chosen a better time for an air assault against XIX TAC and Third Army installations.

The *Luftwaffe* Responds

At 10:30 a.m. on January 1, 1945, while XIX TAC's forces carefully avoided flying in the XII and XX Corps zones, 15 Bf 109s attacked the Metz airfield. They approached at low-level, "on the deck," in flights of three and strafed the field from all four directions of the compass. Their assault destroyed 20 command aircraft and damaged 11 more, but the Germans suffered severe losses as well: the Metz air defense battery claimed 12 of the 15 attackers; Third Army units reported that they shot down 6 of 10 other fighters over the Metz area during the airfield attack. The fog of battle, however, produced a number of less praiseworthy incidents elsewhere in the Third Army area. In his diary that evening, General Patton noted three P–47s had chased a staff car with General Gaffey, 4th Armored Division commander, into a ditch, while his own Third Army antiaircraft gunners took aim and holed the airplane in which AAF Generals Spaatz and Doolittle were returning to First Army headquarters at Liege, Belgium, after their December 31 meeting that addressed the friendly fire problem![75]

Although the *Luftwaffe* struck only the Metz airfield in the XIX TAC area of France, this attack was part of a coordinated strike of between 750 and 800 fighter aircraft against 16 Allied airfields in Belgium and Holland. The Allies counted 134 aircraft destroyed and a further 62 that required major repair, while German fighter chief Gen. Adolf Galland reported a loss of 220 aircraft in the operation. The *Luftwaffe's* bold New Year's Day raid originally had been planned to begin the Ardennes Offensive. Coming as it did this late in the campaign, the attack provided hard-pressed *Wehrmacht* forces in the Bulge no relief and it further decimated the *Luftwaffe*. Afterward, Hitler directed his attention

Damage caused by the *Luftwaffe* raid on January 1, 1945

to the 6th Army Group front in Alsace. To support the German offensive north of Strasbourg during the first week in January, the *Luftwaffe* diverted between 400 and 500 aircraft from the Ardennes Operation south, opposite the Alsace region. Along with a host of aircraft serviceability problems, bad weather during much of the first half of January prevented the *Luftwaffe* from flying more than about 250 sorties per day in both operational regions.

The poor reaction of air defenses to the *Luftwaffe* raid at Metz troubled Weyland and his staff the most. Despite significant claims against the attacking force, none of his planes on five-minute alert got off the ground and the Ripsaw microwave radar control provided no warning until just a few minutes before the low-flying Bf 109s struck. Although not mentioned, the Y service intercept operation appeared equally ineffective against an enemy that required only six minutes' flying time from German-held territory and came in on the deck under radio silence.[76]

In light of the *Luftwaffe's* tactics, the inability of the air defense units at Metz to respond more rapidly does not seem surprising. Nevertheless, the *Luftwaffe* threat called for immediate countermeasures. At 1:00 p.m. that afternoon, Weyland chaired a conference with his staff to discuss ways to improve the air defense system. The group decided on a number of specific changes, including keeping two flights on air alert and warning all units to be aware of possible repeat air attacks as well as parachute landings. Members of the command needed little encouragement, and the unit histories are replete with stories of one immediate response: the digging of slit trenches to protect personnel against air attack.[77]

Weyland did not want the 368th Fighter Group to make its scheduled move from Juvincourt to Metz until Ninth Air Force had a third air defense battery in place at the latter base. After the Metz attack, it became standard practice for all airfields with two groups assigned to be protected by three air defense batteries. As for the lack of adequate warning, he wanted General Sanders, the 100th Wing commander, to work with the tactical control group on measures to improve early warning effectiveness.[78]

How active was the early warning radar on January 1, 1945? At the beginning of the German offensive, the MEW radar operated at Morhange, east of Nancy. When Third Army shifted north, however, the radar facility also moved to Longwy, 12 miles southwest of Luxembourg City, to provide coverage over the Bulge. The site was selected by Weyland and key technical officers using maps and a transit. They even had one of the SCR–584 radars set up to check permanent echoes. The expert from the operational research section later stated that the new location gave superb low-level coverage of the target areas and bases, and the command considered it the best of all microwave radar locations on the continent. Yet this move, which began in late December 1944, took five days to accomplish; the new site could not be occupied until January 4. Although the MEW radar's precise status on the morning of January 1 remains unclear, it is likely that it was not completely operational, and other radars with less range had to provide coverage.[79]

Weyland and his staff also addressed a fundamental weakness in the air defense network. The air commander explained that he wanted to examine the possibility of incorporating what Third Army called the Mosel inner artillery zone—the entire army artillery system—into the air force warning net. Significantly, after this incident coordination through the tactical control group improved. Yet problems continued, and air force analysts believed the system could not be entirely effective until all air defense units, including those at the front, could be brought under air force control. On the basis of postwar analysis of this problem, Weyland seems to have had more success than most air commanders. An important Ninth Air Force report, for example, described the controversy between air and ground forces resulting from lack of clear responsibility for AAA in certain areas. It advocated integrating all AAA into the air force defense system as well as air force control of all air defense components.[80]

Weyland did not remain content with improving defensive measures. That evening he urged General Vandenberg to have the Ninth Air Force's medium bombers strike German airfields in the southeast with fighter-bombers to follow later that night or the next morning. The Ninth Air Force commander, however, decided that the "time was not ripe" and suggested that the P–51s be used for the attack as an alternative. He also recommended that Weyland consider operating 361st Fighter Group P–51s farther east and giving P–38s more of the bomber escort mission. Unless the P–51s got more shooting, he said, Eighth Air Force wanted them back. Weyland accepted the proposal, and the 367th Fighter Group P–38s flew escort missions on 10 of the remaining 14 flyable days in January.

The day after this discussion, the 361st Fighter Group flew fighter sweeps along the Rhine in addition to an escort mission. The command, how-

Radar installation established by XIX TAC Signal Section

ever, targeted specific German airfields only on January 5, and the 354th Fighter Group attacked them with disappointing results. The 361st Fighter Group may not have had many opportunities to fly fighter sweeps and area cover missions at that time. It flew escort missions on seven of the remaining operational days in January, and its interdiction and counterair missions occurred largely in the same Rhine and Mosel River region rather than farther east, as Vandenberg had suggested. On the other hand, Eighth Air Force's criticism might have been muted because much of the XIX TAC escort effort supported Eighth Air Force bombing missions.[81]

The discussion of P–38 and P–51 roles reflects the command's concern for the *Luftwaffe* threat as well as the dilemma of escort duty. Although the XIX TAC planned to have the 367th P–38 Group converted to the more durable P–47D, it was not unhappy with the performance of the P–38s in the Ardennes Campaign. Almost exclusively flying armed reconnaissance missions outside the breakthrough area, the P–38s avoided the higher flak concentrations in the Bulge. With five aircraft lost in December and three in January, the group had a lower loss record than any of the command's P–47 groups, and it was second only to the 361st Fighter Group in this respect. Ultimately, the command divided the escort mission between the two groups, while also assigning P–51s to the counterair role and both groups to interdiction missions. Neither flew close support "cooperation" missions until January 22, when the 367th Fighter Group joined a shoot-out at the Dasburg bridge.[82]

Did General Weyland overreact to the surprise attack on January 1, 1945? In hindsight, perhaps yes. At the time, however, air superiority remained the key mission priority, and doctrine recommended repeating counterair attacks and maintaining "air defenses in the theater...continuously to provide security from hostile air operations."[83] Weyland was especially sensitive about the *Luftwaffe* threat from the time of the Lorraine Campaign, when raids in Third Army's area increased, and Ultra and tactical reconnaissance began observing the buildup at airfields in the Rhine valley. His responsibilities for air defense in the Third Army zone made him particularly anxious to plug possible holes in the defensive system.

On the other hand, Weyland allowed the German air threat to become a key focus in command tactical air planning and operations long after it clearly had become little more than an annoyance. In fact, January 2, 1945, proved to be the last day for which Third Army reported *Luftwaffe* raids of any consequence. Beginning on January 5, army records show only reports of V–1 and Me 262 sightings, but no attacks on Third Army positions. For its part, the *Luftwaffe* appeared in strength on only two additional occasions during the month, once on January 14, and again two days later. In both instances, the action occurred well to the east of the Third Army front, responding to Allied interdiction missions in the Eifel. Moreover, tactical reconnaissance pilots observed the first signs of German withdrawal from the Bulge as early as January 5, and by the second week in January, Ultra confirmed that armored forces were being withdrawn and moved eastward to confront the Soviet offensive launched in Poland on January 12, 1945. In effect, the *Luftwaffe* could be expected to devote even less attention to attacks in the Bulge and, especially, in the Allied rear areas.[84]

Nevertheless, the daily air alert and air defensive patrol missions remained prominent until the end of January. The 405th Fighter Group began patrolling on January 2, with 16 aircraft flying in flights of four throughout each day. Bad weather on all but two of the days from January 3–13, delayed full implementation of the patrol program, but after January 13, patrols flew every flyable day until January 26. Although all but one of the P–47 groups participated, the 405th flew the vast majority. Usually flights of four aircraft carried out the mission, repeating it from three to five times during the day. Seldom did they return to base with anything to show for their efforts. During this period the equivalent of twelve, 12-plane squadrons performed aerial patrol duty and could not be assigned ground support or interdiction missions. Whether these flights would have made a substantial difference in the interdiction program is questionable. Nevertheless, frequent bad weather and competing priorities limited interdiction missions in any case, and argued for devoting maximum emphasis to isolating the battlefield on the few good days available.[85]

Furthermore, given the concern of Weyland and other air leaders about the *Luftwaffe's* continuing potency, it would seem to have been more profitable had they redirected much of this defensive patrol effort into offensive operations by attacking airfields in the Rhine valley. Doing so may have helped fill the gap left by the Eighth Air Force bombardment division, which in the first week of January 1945, had been withdrawn from supporting Ninth Air Force to supporting 6th Army Group requirements in its area. Even if the XIX TAC's counterair missions proved uneventful, the fighter-bombers could still strike targets of opportunity. As understandable as General Weyland's concerns were, this diversion of scarce aerial resources does little to enhance his reputation as an otherwise highly capable commander. Weyland, like many others during the Ardennes Offensive, seems to have overcompensated, impelled "by a nervousness far greater than the transient emergency warranted."[86] Although AAF doctrine supported taking adequate defensive measures, in this instance Weyland's use of combat air patrols unwittingly confirmed another doctrinal proposition: an "air umbrella in orbit over friendly forces is wasteful." Certainly aircraft assigned to defensive patrol responsibilities would have been more effectively employed elsewhere after early January 1945.[87]

Consolidating Support Elements and Flight Operations

While providing support to Patton's troops farther south in the Saar and flying interdiction missions, the XIX TAC continued supporting Third Army's slow, difficult drive to link up with Allied troops in the northern half of the Bulge. Although the German drive was blunted by the first of the year, the Allies knew there would be no headlong retreat from the Bulge. Their attention the first week in January 1945, centered on the western Bulge area and the lower Saar (**Map 18**). On Third Army's Bastogne front, VIII Corps continued its attack from the west, while III Corps widened the corridor to Bastogne and fought off counterattacks as it slowly pushed northeast farther into the German flank. On January 3, First Army launched Montgomery's long-awaited offensive against the northern flank of the salient. The best advance occurred northeast of Vielsalm, where the 82d Airborne Division attacked on a six-mile front. Like Patton's drive northward, it made slow but steady progress in the face of dug-in German armor, horrendous ice and snow, and extreme winter temperatures of nine degrees Fahrenheit.[88]

Farther to the south, the Germans launched a diversionary attack on 6th Army Group's front in Alsace-Lorraine in conjunction with the New Year's Day air strike (**Map 19**). Forewarned by Ultra, General Eisenhower, under great pressure from French General De Gaulle to hold the city of Strasbourg, planned to fall back to prepared defenses in the northern sector as French forces defended the Alsatian city. Despite initial German gains, the Allied troops held. Soon neither side found itself strong enough to make any significant progress until the Russian offensive forced Hitler to move several German divisions from the western to the eastern front.[89]

American reinforcements for General Devers's 6th Army Group consisted primarily of increased air support. Ninth Air Force, meanwhile, protested

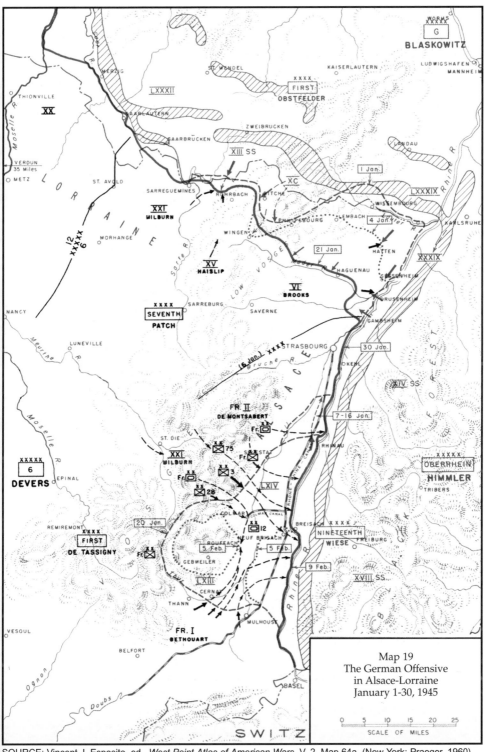

Map 19
The German Offensive
in Alsace-Lorraine
January 1-30, 1945

SCALE OF MILES

SOURCE: Vincent J. Esposito, ed., *West Point Atlas of American Wars*, V. 2, Map 64a, (New York: Praeger, 1960)

SHAEF's decision to direct bombers south from the Eighth Air Force heavy bomber division, which had been playing a key role bombing targets in the outer interdiction region, to support operations in the 6th Army Group sector. To analysts at 12th Army Group and Ninth Air Force, "this diversion [to support 6th Army Group] was of secondary or even minor importance, and it was with dismay…[that we]…saw SHAEF transfer top priority for bombardment to that area." From the standpoint of the Ninth Air Force and 12th Army Group, this diversion seriously threatened the success of their interdiction program. At the same time, Vandenberg asked Weyland on January 2 what he could spare for XII TAC, and that day the XIX TAC commander diverted four squadrons to help in the Saar and Palatinate regions with armed reconnaissance missions.[90]

The Ninth Air Force air plan continued to target enemy armor and pursue an elaborate interdiction program focusing on bridges and supply centers. Weyland's forces had just begun flying intensive interdiction against bridges on the first two days of January 1945 when freezing drizzle and rain, along with a 600-foot overcast and 1–2 miles of visibility, shut down operations for two days. Between January 3 and 14, the XIX TAC pilots could fly on only two days; they flew 191 sorties on January 5 and 325 on January 10. The remaining days were socked in. The heavy snow that arrived on January 3 helped make the January snowfall in northern Europe the heaviest in 175 years. All told, the XIX TAC had only seven operational days in the month compared to 13 for December. Under these conditions it became impossible to maintain a consistent interdiction effort.[91]

On January 5, 1945, operations continued with the 362d Fighter Group supporting III Corps and the 406th Fighter Group backing VIII Corps, while the command flew four armed reconnaissance missions for XII TAC. That day also witnessed one of the most spectacular flights of the Ardennes period. General Patton had been concerned for some time about the XII Corps' right flank and the XX Corps' area opposite Saarburg, in the Merzig-Saarbruecken region. Reports appeared with increasing frequency that German engineers had a major bridge-building program underway in this thinly held sector. To study the strong points and bridges and to assess the severity of the threat, the Third Army commander asked for photographs of the area.[92]

Thus a low-level F–5 (P–38) dicing run in a high-threat area was ordered. Capt. Robert J. Holbury of the 31st Photo Reconnaissance Squadron volunteered to fly the mission despite a ceiling of less than 600 feet of solid overcast. After a particularly hazardous flight that included flying below 25 feet and dodging high-tension wires as well as flak, Holbury returned on one engine, with a vertical stabilizer shot off and with his aircraft peppered by shell holes. He also returned with 212 superb pinpoint and oblique photos showing three traditional bridges, a pontoon bridge, and barges strapped together. Although this threat did not require reinforcing the XX Corps front, Third Army wanted the German bridgework destroyed whenever the weather permitted.[93]

After an Ultra briefing on January 9, Patton became increasingly concerned about Merzig-Saarbruecken as a possible site of another major German offensive, and General Weyland agreed to have his fighter-bombers attack the region as soon as weather permitted. Consequently, when the weather improved on January 10, the 362d Fighter Group flew three squadron missions against the bridges, piers, and barges that had been photographed on January 5. The pilots achieved only mediocre results, and though claiming one direct hit and a number of approaches damaged, the bridges remained serviceable. Soon a spirited contest developed between Weyland's fighter-bombers and Ninth Air Force medium bombers to see which group could knock out the heavily defended bridges.[94]

General Weyland took advantage of the nonflying period to move his headquarters closer to the action. Procedures called for moving in two stages in order to maintain communications. Weyland and the initial A headquarters party arrived in Luxembourg City on January 8 where they set up communications with Third Army and Ninth Air Force headquarters' command posts and Weyland's units early the following morning. Colonel Ferguson, however, remained at Nancy and maintained control of operations throughout the ninth. That evening he closed up shop and moved his B party to Luxembourg the next day. The plan worked to perfection. The absence of flying made the communications transition much easier because there were no flight operations to handle. Now Third Army and the XIX TAC had their air and ground headquarters again completely collocated.[95]

On January 11 and 12, 1945, atrocious winter weather forced the command to cancel most missions. During this period Weyland used the time to good advantage. On January 10, he learned that his command would receive a radar ground-control approach system by February 1. (His initial request was made in early October 1944.) One of the specialists, an SCR–584 expert, worried about the command's slow progress with the two modified SCR–584 systems, termed battle area control units (BACUs), which it had received in late December. At this time the command's BACUs functioned only as navigation devices. Operators of the two systems worked with the air liaison officers assigned to Third Army's XII and XX Corps. The system vectored close air support flights either to a target selected by the liaison officer at corps headquarters or to a point forward where the air control officer operating with the ground unit took control and directed the attack.[96]

Only in February 1945 did the command begin what it referred to as last-resort blind bombing with the SCR–584 radar, after it received two additional sets that had been modified earlier for ground control intercept operations. The SCR–584, however, proved difficult to operate effectively. As one of the research technicians assigned to the command stated, "picking up the correct aircraft formation, locking on and staying locked on, and controlling the aircraft through a good bomb run was difficult and the crews and controllers had insufficient training to do the job well."[97]

Dicing mission photo of the Saar River

After much practice, the system proved useful as both a navigation and an area blind bombing aid in late February and March, when static conditions and little movement prevailed. After March 1945, however, fast-paced mobile conditions would make it impossible for the SCR–584 radar equipment to keep within range of the bomb line, and Weyland ordered it withdrawn. In fact, the command continued to prefer the MEW radar, especially after it received a close-control unit for the system at the end of December 1944. Along with its ease of transport and longer range, microwave radar procedures proved far simpler for the controllers to master.[98]

On January 12, 1945, Weyland accompanied General Gay on a visit to units of VIII Corps and to the headquarters of both VIII and III Corps. Weyland and his officers visited army commanders in the field periodically to discuss air-ground issues, particularly as part of the joint planning process and to promote good relations. In this instance, Weyland discussed plans for future operations with Generals Middleton and Milliken, who reported that enemy counterattacks had diminished amid more signs of withdrawal.[99] Indeed, by January 15, 1945, VII Corps in the north had cut the key St. Vith-Vielsalm road, and Patton's forces and First Army units had also severed the St. Vith-Houffalize road and converged on Houffalize (**Map 18**). To the east, III Corps had taken Wiltz and now approached the Clerf River line, while XII Corps still battled for the town of Echternach and exerted pressure on the German line of withdrawal. Although German forces fell back on St. Vith, they continued to counterattack fiercely. Allied forces also confronted the by now customary impediments of heavy snow and ice, mines, road blocks, and booby traps. Nevertheless, the outlook appeared promising. Intelligence analysts predicted that the Germans would attempt to move the armored forces out of the Bulge for duty in either Alsace or on the eastern front and replace them with infantry units. If so, the Allies expected to turn the retreat into a rout.[100]

Clearing the Bulge

During the last half of January 1945, the XIX TAC enjoyed one of its most successful operational periods of the entire campaign. A month after the Germans began the Ardennes Offensive, the Allies finally had them on the run. Although Ultra picked up the first signs of a German retreat on January 8, only when the weather cleared on January 13, did the Allies fully realize that the Germans had decided on a general withdrawal from the Ardennes salient.[101] The question became whether German delaying tactics and the winter weather could prevent the Allies from isolating substantial parts of the enemy's forces before they could withdraw into the Eifel. The retreating Germans had to travel during daylight hours on main roads that became increasingly congested. Fleeing under these conditions, the *Wehrmacht* offered ideal targets to Weyland's fighter-bombers. Four consecutive days of good flying weather provided more than one-third of the month's total claims of 10,525 ground targets destroyed or damaged in operations reminiscent of the previous summer. In terms of the number of sorties flown, January 14 was, in the words of the XIX TAC commander, the "biggest day since summer." His command flew 61 missions and 633 sorties both within and outside the breakthrough area for what proved to be the second-best claims day of the month. With the 354th and 406th Fighter Groups seeing most of the action in the III and VIII Corps areas, the remaining groups flew armed reconnaissance missions against bridges and command posts throughout the Eifel region. The day's score included 410 motor vehicles, 174 railroad cars, and 45 buildings destroyed.[102]

Although the command's claims remained unsubstantiated, the effort that resulted in them nevertheless contributed significantly to the Allied cause. The coordination between ground and air that occurred during this four-day period, and between reconnaissance and fighter-bomber aircraft and artillery counterflak units, reached a new level of effectiveness. One of the best examples of this teamwork occurred on January 14, 1945. Two F–6 (P–51) pilots of the 12th Reconnaissance Squadron, flying an artillery adjustment mission at Houffalize, spotted 50 armored vehicles entering the city. After observing good results from the artillery fire, they called the tactical control group, which vectored a squadron of 354th Fighter Group P–47s to the scene. The reconnaissance pilots then led the fighter-bombers to the targets and directed artillery counterflak fire on enemy gun positions while the P–47 pilots completed their bombing runs. During the ground advance, XIX TAC fighter-bombers again charted the way from village to village in operations reminiscent of the Lorraine Campaign.[103] Although the type of teamwork displayed on January 14 occurred periodically in France and more frequently during the Lorraine fighting, by early 1945 it had become commonplace among all the tactical air and ground commands. When First and Third Army linked up at Houffalize on January 16, Third Army gave much of the credit over the previous three days to the air support of the airborne village destroyers.

The only significant variation in aerial operations appeared in the ordnance loads. By this time 500-lb. incendiary and 100-lb. white phosphorus bombs had been added to the inventory. The fighter-bombers dropped both napalm and incendiary bombs in record numbers, especially during the five days of victory weather in December. Often armorers replaced the fragmentation bomb with a 500-lb. general purpose bomb that was fuzed to detonate instantaneously. It combined good fragmentation effect with outstanding shock effect and proved to be the best answer for concealed armor, vehicles, and personnel. Later, with the enemy on the run in the open, fighter-bombers flew strafing missions loaded only with .50-caliber ammunition.[104]

On January 15 and 16, 1945, the command focused on attacking German front line troops in the Bulge and on any movement along the road and rail networks leading out of the salient. Except for the heavily defended Saar River bridges, which continued to defy destruction, XIX TAC pilots achieved impressive results. The overall objective remained to isolate the battlefield and disrupt any attempt at orderly withdrawal. Colonel Hallett, the command's intelligence officer, developed his own interdiction target plan to supplement the Ninth Air Force target listing. It proved especially useful when aircrews needed secondary targets to attack.[105]

The intense effort during the four-day period from January 13–16 brought out the hard-pressed *Luftwaffe*. With 14 German aircraft claimed destroyed and 3 more damaged, the sixteenth proved to be the command's best day of the month in the air against the *Luftwaffe*. It lost five of its own in these encounters, an improvement over the results of two days earlier when it experienced 11 losses in air combat. The 368th Fighter Group, with six losses, suffered the most. On that day, some 50 Bf 109s and FW 190s attacked ten aircraft from the 397th Fighter Squadron returning from an armed reconnaissance mission near Neustadt. Normally the American fighters managed to out-duel the *Luftwaffe* even when severely outnumbered and surprised. During the Ardennes Campaign, however, American pilots reported *Luftwaffe* aviators fought aggressively and often with greater skill in defense of the homeland. Although these reports referred primarily to the first two weeks of the Ardennes Offensive, even in mid-January, after the transfer of 300 aircraft to the Russian front and the increasing use of inexperienced pilots, the *Luftwaffe* could still mount an occasional large and dangerous foray.

In the January 16 incident, 397th Fighter Squadron pilots apparently became complacent and violated one of Weyland's cardinal maxims for air combat: "The iron law of a flight is that the element will be maintained, for the lone bird is the dead bird." If, as some commentators explained, the enemy air attacks on January 13 and 16 represented the last desperate flailing of a *Luftwaffe in extremis*, they also reinforced Weyland's belief that *Luftwaffe* capabilities required him to retain his air defense patrol missions unchanged. As events transpired, these would be the only occasions during the month when the *Luftwaffe* appeared in strength to menace Allied fighter-bombers.[106]

On January 17, 1945, the XIX TAC historian asserted that the "Belgian Bulge had been reduced to a mere bump."[107] Although correct, judging from the map, another week passed before the Allies eliminated the Bulge completely. The German position admittedly had become desperate. During this last phase of the battle, German forces made every effort to disengage and withdraw within the Siegfried Line defenses, hoping to hold Allied forces in place in the west while the Panzer forces shifted to the east. The British, American, and French forces, of course, remained equally determined to prevent their escape.

After the two U.S. armies met at Houffalize, First Army units pressed on toward St. Vith. On Third Army's front, VIII Corps and III Corps forces forged

German Bf 109

Troops of the 4th Armored Division in the Ardennes (above); 101st Airborne Infantry Division troops move through Bastogne towards Houffalize (below); Enemy tanks and motor vehicles destroyed by Ninth Air Force fighter-bombers (facing page)

62294 A.C.

Staff, XIX Tactical Air Command

ahead toward the Clerf River with their goal the Our River that separated Luxembourg from the Eifel (**Map 20**). To create more pressure on the southern shoulder and narrow the escape route at the base of the breakthrough area, XII Corps started an offensive on January 17 in miserable weather and without the protective shield of air power. Air support for the corps' right flank became a major priority, and when the weather cleared on January 19, Weyland's forces flew five armed reconnaissance missions in the Echternach area and three more in the Trier area. By January 20, XII Corps units came within two miles of Vianden at the international border between Luxembourg and Germany. Bad flying weather on January 20 and 21, however, once again restricted the level of air support to two armed reconnaissance squadron flights near Trier. Meanwhile, as Patton had supposed, XX Corps encountered a determined German counterattack against the 94th Infantry Division at Saarlautern. In this situation, corps artillery provided most of the close support firepower, while the 365th Fighter Group contributed by flying armed reconnaissance along the Saar River from Saarbruecken to Merzig.[108]

General Weyland spent January 19 and 20 visiting his units before returning to Luxembourg City the next day. There he discussed current operations and force movements with General Quesada and Maj. Gen. Samuel E. Anderson. At this meeting, the air leaders decided to transfer the 365th Fighter Group back to the IX TAC, and the 361st Fighter Group to an Eighth Air Force wing. This decision to readjust unit strength certainly reflected the confidence the commanders had in the current state of the air war. Weyland explained to his colleagues that he also intended to move the 406th Fighter Group farther forward to replace the 365th Fighter Group at Metz, and likewise, to move the

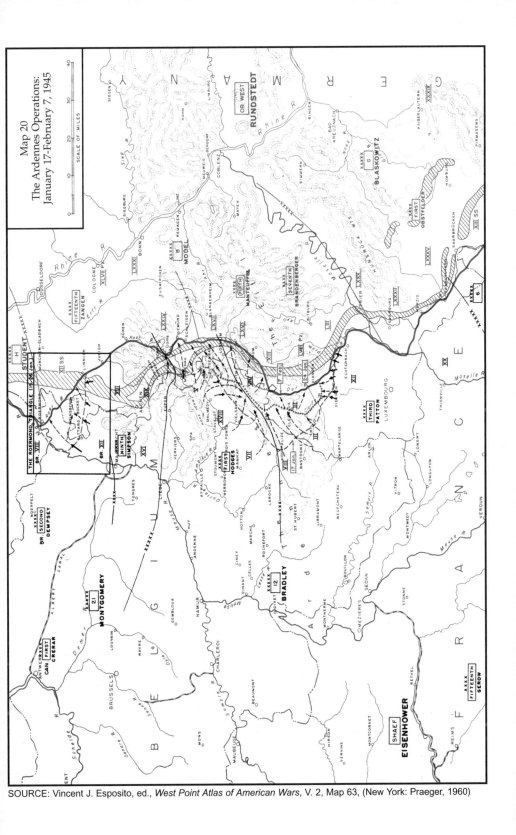

Map 20
The Ardennes Operations:
January 17–February 7, 1945

SOURCE: Vincent J. Esposito, ed., *West Point Atlas of American Wars*, V. 2, Map 63, (New York: Praeger, 1960)

367th Fighter Group to St. Dizier to replace the departing 361st Fighter Group. None of the moves, however, transpired before the end of the month, after the Ardennes Campaign ended.[109]

For its part Ninth Air Force sent medium bombers and every fighter-bomber available against bridges along the Rhine and Mosel rivers, but especially those over the Our River, at the point of initial German penetration into Belgium. With the enemy retreat accelerating and Allied ground forces working to narrow the escape routes, the vital Our River bridges became the focus of Ninth Air Force attention.[110] On January 22, medium bombers obliterated the approaches to the Dasburg bridge, creating a monumental bottleneck for the Germans, and a magnificent opportunity for Weyland's fighter-bombers. An unexpected break in the weather on January 22 enabled the command to fly 57 missions and 627 sorties primarily against clogged traffic west of the Our River. At 1:00 p.m., reconnaissance pilots reported heavy transport traffic in the Bulge in front of XII Corps, and every available fighter-bomber flew to the area with reconnaissance pilots leading the way. Weyland, on hearing this news, informed Generals Vandenberg and Patton of the evidence of a general withdrawal. In the words of the command intelligence officer, "the last remnants of the Ardennes bulge [were] collapsing like a punctured tire."[111]

Flying four missions in support of the 4th Infantry Division, the 368th Fighter Group achieved the day's best score. It, too, reported that the destruction of the Dasburg bridge had created a massive traffic jam on the west side of the Our River. Pilots said the congested scene provided a better shooting opportunity than the one encountered in the final closing of the Falaise Gap. The 368th Fighter Group was joined by squadrons from all other groups except the 406th and 361st Fighter Groups that were attacking rail targets near Trier, and the 365th, which supported the 94th Infantry Division against the ongoing German counterattack. Only the five planes lost from the 362d Fighter Group dampened the day's enthusiasm.[112]

Aerial claims processed on January 22, 1945, totaled 1,177 trucks, tanks, and other motor vehicles destroyed and another 536 damaged, twice the figure for the previous high day on September 1, 1944. The XIX TAC's record day for claimed destruction of enemy transportation became a major news story picked up and broadcast by the BBC and NBC. Congratulatory messages arrived immediately from Generals Arnold, Spaatz, and Vandenberg.[113] General Weyland told his officers and airmen:

> For information on who did it, look in your own ops flashes. Germans claim great strategic withdrawal with only one army NYR [not yet reported]. Yesterday was [a] beautiful example of tactical cooperation between recce, fighter control, ground control and fighters. I am plenty proud of you all.[114]

The good hunting continued through the morning of January 23, before snow and low ceilings reappeared. Of the four groups not grounded for weather, three returned to the scene of the slaughter for even more impressive claims. Because the intensity of the flak in the Dasburg area now proved to be some of the heaviest in the Bulge fighting, the 354th Fighter Group reported that it had to bomb at 5,000 feet. Meanwhile, the 365th Fighter Group again flew in support of XX Corps, conducting armed reconnaissance in the Trier and Neunkirchen areas and flying two air patrol missions near Metz.[115]

A special mission to test the efficacy of a new reconnaissance target-spotting method set up by General Weyland proved less successful. During the euphoria of January 22, he proposed that his reconnaissance aircraft lead 16 A–26 Invaders to strafe targets at low-level in the Dasburg area of the Bulge. A replacement airplane for the twin-engine Douglas A–20 Havoc, the Douglas A–26 medium bomber had arrived in the European theater late in 1944. On January 23, Lt. Howard Nichols of the 15th Tactical Reconnaissance Squadron rendezvoused with the first flight of five bombers at Luxembourg and led them to the target area 28 miles to the north. The units arrived too late to master the weather and the flak, and two of the bombers took hits and crashed behind Allied lines. Nichols returned to lead six more bombers back, but he promptly observed two more shot down and several others severely damaged by flak. The mission was a disaster. Although officials knew the A–26 should not be risked in low-level operations against heavily defended targets, Weyland apparently believed that surprise and good work by his reconnaissance "spotter" aircraft would overcome the problem.[116]

Even though the experiment of using light bombers on a low-level mission failed in this instance, the reconnaissance pilot performed as planned. Reconnaissance pilots not only served as the eyes of the ground forces and the intelligence section, they also functioned as airborne controllers much like the Horsefly light-plane controller operation that Americans first developed in the Italian theater. There the largely static front proved more conducive for light planes employed in this role. In northern Europe, Weyland and his fellow commanders preferred to rely on fighters for tactical reconnaissance and airborne control operations.[117]

During the next six days, from January 23–28, 1945, Allied ground forces slowly overcame tenacious German defenses to close up to the Our River and, on January 26 created a bridgehead on the east bank inside Germany. The XIX TAC operations continued with major emphasis on interdiction in the Eifel near Prum and close air support for XII Corps troops facing German forces attempting to flee across the Sauer River. As usual, inclement weather limited the sortie rate and prohibited operations altogether on January 27.[118] On January 28, American patrols crossed the Our River in force, and General Weyland recorded that the "reduction of the Ardennes was officially completed." The next day, he said, XIX TAC would resume the offensive. Four days earlier he with Patton, his staff, and corps commanders had attended a conference at Third Army headquarters to discuss forthcoming offensive operations. Together, the XIX TAC–Third Army team prepared for the final drive.[119]

Ardennes in Retrospect

Reflecting on the Ardennes Campaign, the Ninth Air Force historian declared that "here, as never before, was the chance to apply sound principles of tactical air power."[120] He referred to the demonstrated deployment and employment of tactical air power quickly, in force, in an emergency. General Bradley echoed these sentiments in a report of his own. "Aircraft claims during that period [Bastogne] are impressive," he said, "not alone for the havoc created, but because they demonstrate the potential flexibility which permits the rapid massing on a limited target area."[121] Fighter-bomber response, indeed, proved to be swift, concentrated, and instrumental in helping first to blunt the offensive, then to force German troops back, beyond the Our River.

The aerial response, in fact, seemed drawn directly from a textbook and performed to perfection. The early days of the assault, however, reflect a somewhat less organized reaction to the crisis. With troops overrun or in retreat and the entire Allied center in danger of collapsing, air leaders faced a dire emergency. They responded on December 16 and 17, 1944, without FM 100–20 (1943) in hand for guidance. The theoretical priorities of air superiority, interdiction, and close air support were set aside in favor of bringing all available fighter-bombers to bear as quickly as possible in bombing and strafing the enemy. This is the very essence of tactical air power's flexibility. If the *Luftwaffe* put in an appearance, so much the better. During the course of the bad weather before December 23, the planners had time to prepare an air plan for victory and give proper attention to allocating effort among the three missions.

The initial reaction of General Weyland and his command also demonstrated just how much the applied doctrine, organization and procedures, and experience of the airmen had developed since the North African Campaign. In the Ardennes' crucible, Weyland's forces demonstrated the maturity tactical airpower had achieved. With hardly a pause, he and his staff redirected command forces from a focus of operations along the Siegfried Line to the Ardennes region with the smoothness of a well-functioning machine. Airplanes flew north to cover Patton's fire brigade and east to harry German supply lines, while Weyland resurrected his X-Ray liaison command echelon to ensure close coordination with the ground forces. Meanwhile, he marshaled support elements to make an extraordinary effort in maintaining the air assault. The urgency of the situation proved sufficient incentive to elicit an outstanding performance from all his forces up and down the line.

Certain problems and constraints could never quite be overcome. The winter weather made flying impossible at crucial points in the battle and it prevented a consistent harassment of enemy communications. It also delayed the well-orchestrated interdiction program to isolate the battlefield. Winter weather magnified the major weakness in the Allied tactical air arsenal—the night fighter force. This small, if heroic group of night flyers simply did not possess the assets or technology needed to consistently interrupt German movements of supplies and defensive reinforcements during the long hours of darkness. Without a significant night operational capability, the Ardennes Offensive was prolonged and the flak concentrations became the most hazardous of the war for Allied flyers. Air leaders understood the deficiency, but without sufficient resources little more could be done before the advent of the all-weather, fly-by-wire fighter-bomber of the future.

The winter weather and the urgency of the defensive operation also provoked friendly fire from anxious Allied personnel on the ground and in the sky. General Weyland acted promptly to improve communications between air and ground personnel, but better coordination among air defense agencies could only limit the problem as long as the flying hazards and tension associated with action in the Bulge continued. Even with better coordination, wartime conditions ensured that the friendly fire problem continued throughout the campaign, if at a lower level of concern.

As always, teamwork and cooperation among leaders of goodwill ultimately prevented any serial recurrence of the worst of the friendly fire incidents, as they did most other problems. Clearly the mutual respect and understanding between Generals Patton and Weyland continued unaltered. From the start of the battle it was a joint operation and remained so. Weyland or his X-Ray chief attended every Third Army morning briefing, and the integrated combat operations staff ensured continued joint planning and operations. Teamwork and cooperation also occurred in the combined operations office at corps and division level, as well as in the smooth and effective coordination that developed among and between reconnaissance and fighter aircraft, ground controllers, and artillery units. Moreover, Weyland always gave first priority to air cover for Patton's army, whether or not formal doctrine favored such extensive measures. Patton, in turn, never interfered with the basic air plan to support his forces in the Bulge and participate in Ninth Air Force's interdiction program. Only occasionally did the army commander request special reconnaissance or air support for troops in trouble, and Weyland's forces always responded.

Certainly, the XIX TAC could respond to Third Army requests more effectively with eight fighter-bomber groups instead of four. Unlike conditions in the Lorraine Campaign, Weyland possessed a force capable of decisive intervention in the battle zone. Yet, his responsibilities correspondingly increased, too. While three groups always provided close air support, three

Destroyed self-propelled gun near Dasburg, Germany

more concentrated on interdiction. This left two groups to fly escort, counterair, defensive patrol, and to strike the pinpoint targets that seemed to need attention on a regular basis. These six aerial assignments could and did change, but they limited the concentration of effort the command could apply to any single one.

Ninth Air Force, of course, continued to decide major force allocations. In the official recounting of the campaign, its historian reflected on the constant challenge of balancing competing priorities:

> There was always the difference of opinion on the tactical employment of air power. A request might call for immediate cooperation against a close target when overall commitments dictated continuation of a longer-range program. Many requests were beyond [our] capabilities.[122]

In hindsight, Ninth Air Force analysts concluded that perhaps too much initial effort had been devoted to bomber escort duties at the expense of close support. One might also question whether the airmen, given the intelligence information at hand, accorded more attention than the threat warranted to potential *Luftwaffe* attacks after the German drive had been blunted. If the actions of the XIX TAC commander clearly reflected the conventional wisdom of contemporary airmen, that wisdom ordered numerous aircraft on air combat patrol that otherwise might have been applied to offensive missions. Whatever the decisions on air priorities, the Allied tactical air power available then in northern Europe provided sufficient concentration of force for decisive intervention on the battlefield.

Chapter Six

The Final Offensive

The final offensive—which would strike at the Siegfried Line, and, if successful, press forward across the Rhine River—could be expected to differ considerably from either the Lorraine Campaign or the Battle for France. First and foremost, General Weyland's XIX TAC possessed important advantages not previously available. Above all, the command could rely on overwhelming air superiority—far more than at any time during operations in Northwest Europe. Weyland's aerial force numbered nearly 400 fighter-bombers in this Third Army sector alone. Intelligence estimated the *Luftwaffe* possessed at most only 700 fighters arrayed against all of the Allied armies and air forces deployed along the German border in the west. (Nazi war records later proved this Allied estimate to have been remarkably accurate.) Because of severe fuel constraints and the *Luftwaffe's* large-scale redeployment to the eastern front at the end of 1944, the Germans stationed only 600 single-engine fighters in the west. Moreover, not until early March 1945, when the Allies pressed their drive to the Rhine, did the overall German sortie rate increase from the late January figure of 250 to 300–400 per day, weather permitting. Even a major effort to protect airfields with turbojet aircraft and overworking Ju 87 aircraft in missions at night failed to slow the inexorable Allied advance.[1] With uncontested air superiority, Weyland could be expected to devote the bulk of his flying effort to the second- and third-priority aerial missions of interdiction and close air support, respectively.

The ground situation seemed equally favorable. After the Ardennes defeat, Third Army intelligence officers learned that units from both General von Manteuffel's Fifth Panzer Army and General Brandenberger's Seventh Army were moved to reinforce the eastern front and bolster German forces defending the Cologne area where the main Allied thrust was expected. General Patton's intelligence section predicted that enemy forces facing them in the Eifel region amounted to no more than five American-strength divisions.[2] In addition to numerical superiority, the Third Army–XIX TAC air-ground team also possessed the advantage of experience gained during six months of combat in all kinds of weather and terrain in northern Europe. It could be expected to react confidently to the challenges of fighting under conditions of mobile and static warfare, especially against a rapidly weakening enemy.

Nevertheless, the Siegfried Line defenses of concrete bunkers and pillboxes presented formidable targets for fighter-bombers. The airmen could expect little cooperation from the weather as the Eifel region was noted for its wretched winters. Weyland also knew, in the event of a breakthrough of the Siegfried Line, he would again face the formidable tasks of moving supplies and establishing forward airstrips rapidly enough to maintain pace with Patton's armored spearheads. All the while, the air-ground team would contend with an overarching Allied strategy that assigned only a supporting role to the Third Army with concomitant priorities in the climactic drive against Nazi Germany.

With the Ardennes emergency officially ended on January 28, 1945, General Eisenhower and his advisors returned to their grand plan for breaching the Siegfried Line, hurdling the Rhine River barrier and plunging Allied armor into the heart of Germany.[3] The Supreme Allied Commander favored advancing to the Rhine along a broad front, then holding at the river with a small force while the British 21st Army Group pressed the main Allied assault north of the Ruhr industrial area, under the direction of doughty Field Marshal Montgomery. A secondary attack led by General Patton's Third Army would follow to the south in the Frankfurt area. When the British and American chiefs of staff met on the island of Malta in late January and early February 1945, they endorsed Eisenhower's plan, but only after the Supreme Commander allayed British fears that he might wait to cross the Rhine until the entire west bank had been cleared. Moreover, to avoid unwanted procrastination mounting the offensive in the north, General Eisenhower promised to reinforce Montgomery's 21st Army Group with sizeable American air and ground units so it might be ready to cross the Rhine "in force as soon as possible."[4]

Although Allied leaders had their eyes on a northernmost Rhine crossing from the Low Countries, the immediate challenge in early February 1945, was to overcome the still formidable Siegfried Line defenses in the Rhineland. To achieve this objective, SHAEF developed plans for a series of consecutive Allied attacks from north to south that would bring the armies to the banks of the Rhine (**Map 21**). The main assault, termed Operation Veritable, would be led by Montgomery opposite the Ruhr. To give the offensive more punch, Eisenhower gave Montgomery, who had temporary command of General Simpson's Ninth Army since the Battle of the Bulge, units from Hodges's First and Patton's Third Armies.

General Bradley received permission to allow Hodges and Patton to continue attacking in the Eifel region only until February 1. Then priority for supplies and personnel would again shift to Montgomery's area to meet Operation Veritable's deadline for the attack on the eighth. Once the British field marshal's forces reached the Rhine and began preparations for the crossing, General Bradley could resume his Eifel offensive, now termed Operation Lumberjack. Shortly thereafter, General Devers's 6th Army Group in the south would launch an assault in the Palatinate, Operation Undertone. Despite Eisenhower's assurance to British leaders that Montgomery would lead the way, his broad-front strategy, which called for all Allied armies to

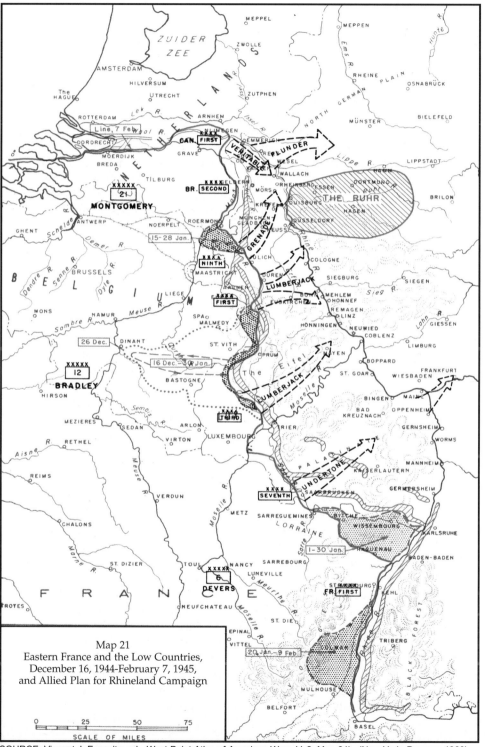

Map 21
Eastern France and the Low Countries,
December 16, 1944-February 7, 1945,
and Allied Plan for Rhineland Campaign

0   25   50   75
SCALE OF MILES

close to the Rhine before attempting to cross that barrier, seemed as much intact as ever.

Under the SHAEF plan, Montgomery would cross the Rhine to the north in the Wesel area as soon as possible and proceed along the main invasion route north of the Ruhr, sweeping across the north German plain (**Map 21**). He would be followed by the two American army groups, which would make secondary crossings in the Mainz-Frankfurt region and attack northeast through the so-called Frankfurt-Kassel Corridor. Once the two Allied forces linked up east of the Ruhr, Germany's industrial heartland would be encircled, and all hope of forestalling the Allied offensive eliminated. Understandably, Hitler appreciated the vital importance of the Ruhr, and the growing Allied threat served to reinforce his natural inclination to defend the area west of the Rhine with fanatical determination. Closing the Rhine would not be easy and the vagaries of winter weather, short supplies, and contemporary technology complicated the assignment.[5]

Operational Challenges and New Tactics

The need for improved accuracy in bombing and for bomb damage assessment was underscored in an incident involving destruction of the Bullay Bridge over the Mosel River. For months this structure eluded the best efforts of medium bombers and fighter-bombers to destroy it. Then, on February 10, 1945, a squadron from XIX TAC's 368th Fighter Group scored direct hits with several 500-lb. bombs. Despite Ninth Air Force's initial skepticism, reconnaissance later confirmed that the center span had collapsed into the river. At this point, an ebullient General Weyland could not resist sending photographs to General Anderson, commander of the IX Bombardment Division, with a suggestion that any targets he found too difficult for his medium bombers be referred to XIX TAC fighter-bombers. In an equally mordant reply, General Anderson asserted that his bombers had weakened the bridge for Weyland's "pea shooters," and he had photographs to prove it. Operational research specialists, he told the XIX TAC commander, had shown that fighter claims for bridges and rail cuts were actually inflated 70 percent.[6]

Later that month Nicholas M. Smith, chief of XIX TAC's newly formed operational research section, considered methods employed in the aerial bombing of bridges. He analyzed the probability of destroying double-trussed bridges with various size bombs and different fuzes. Initially he thought that bridge targets might require bombs too heavy for fighter-bombers; further study, however, suggested these aircraft might have better luck with the smaller bombs using different fuzing. Smith's analysis demonstrated that the probability of destroying trussed bridges with their numerous small redundant trusses increased with a larger number of smaller bombs fuzed contrary to the parameters used by the medium bombers. The bridge study was one of several important technical investigations undertaken by Smith and an associate, radar specialist Arnold C. McLean, to improve the command's operational performance.[7] Two other studies carried out by the command's operational research section in the late winter and early spring also deserve special attention. One involved an intensive effort to produce a bomb strike camera, and the other to develop an accurate blind bombing radar system. Their stories illustrate the promise, as well as the limitations, of technology applied at the front.

The bomb strike camera offered the prospect of improvements in bomb damage assessment and bombing accuracy, which might end the turmoil over pilot claims. Ninth Air Force had been interested in such a project since the late fall when the studies mentioned by General Anderson indicated that fighter-bombers made one rail cut in every eight or nine sorties rather than one in every three as claimed by the pilots.[8] Smith, the XIX TAC research chief, worked closely with Col. George W. Goddard in Ninth Air Force's Office of Technical Service after the Ardennes Offensive to develop more effective mounting arrangements and test various oblique cameras on P–47 aircraft. The key problem proved to be finding a workable mounting system. Hanging a

The Bullay Bridge, destroyed by the direct hits of the 368th Fighter Group

K–25 short focal-length, wide-angle, rear-facing camera from a wing support had to be abandoned after tests by pilots from the 371st Fighter Group showed that its field of view remained too small. The pilots also complained about the external mount and the need to fly straight and level after hitting the target. A belly camera mount experiment proved equally unrewarding, and research and testing continued throughout the spring.

In early May 1945, with the war nearly over, Smith and a XIX TAC intelligence officer exchanged visits with their counterparts in the Mediterranean theater where fighter-bombers successfully used an oblique camera mounted in a faired compartment in front of the left bomb pylon. At the same time, Colonel Goddard began experimenting with 70-mm cameras mounted in split vertical pairs. They were activated by the bomb release mechanism in order to obtain photographs in conjunction with the bomb bursts. Although the scientists could not produce an effective bomb strike camera system before the end of the European Campaign, their work continued and the outlook appeared promising.

The other major project studied by the operational research section during the last offensive focused on the SCR–584 ground-based blind bombing system discussed earlier in Chapter 5. According to conventional wisdom, when modified for close control, the SCR–584 could serve as an effective blind bombing system during important operations like the Ardennes counteroffensive. Its radar equipment would position the fighter-bomber over the target with sufficient precision to bomb effectively through cloud cover or at night.[9] Such was not the case, however, and like the search for a good bomb strike camera, accurate blind bombing remained out of reach throughout the campaign. As has so often occurred with new technology, the SCR–584 story is a fascinating tale of a technical system that never quite lived up to the initial predictions of its developers.[10]

When, in early November 1944, the XIX TAC received the first SCR–584 radar system, a BACU, officials decided to use it mainly as a navigational device to position aircraft close enough over a target to enable the pilot to acquire it visually. They assigned this unit and subsequent SCR–584 flying control units to the tactical air liaison officer at army corps headquarters, which had good land line communications. The system's first mission did not occur until December 2, and by December 10 it had controlled only ten missions, all navigational. At that time, a second unit had been installed near Metz, which was moved north to cover the Bulge in early January 1945. Between December 4, 1944, and January 10, 1945, it controlled a total of 16 separate missions, only two of which represented blind bombing runs. In fact, of the 26 missions controlled by the SCR–584 during this period, 10 could not be completed because of controller error; 14 of the remaining 16 proved to be navigational, not blind bombing, missions. Moreover, the average error in positioning the aircraft accurately amounted to an unacceptably high 3,500 feet.

In early January 1945, the command decided to employ the MEW and director post radars for close navigational control and to use the modified SCR–584 for blind bombing almost exclusively. Ninth Air Force, which strongly supported efforts to improve the system, wanted each tactical air command to have its scientific-military team work independently to improve system accuracy. It seems that the Ninth Air Force also received motivation from reports compiled by other tactical air forces that indicated better performance than the Ninth had been able to achieve. General Lee, Ninth Air Force deputy for operations, became concerned over statements made by General Saville, commander of the XII TAC. General Lee told General Weyland in a January 5 letter that Saville claimed aircraft in his command used the SCR–584 to bomb accurately through overcast within 100 yards of friendly troops without fear of hitting them. Given the difficulty of achieving this kind of accuracy even in daylight under optimum conditions, Weyland and his Ninth Air Force colleagues were more than a little skeptical. Yet the Saville report focused attention on improving the system, and testing continued from January until the end of the campaign.[11]

Upon investigation, McLean, the command's radar expert, determined that equipment limitations and inadequate controller procedures made it impossible to develop accurate control of aircraft for blind bombing with great accuracy. McLean introduced radar siting procedures that called for survey measurements to obtain proper station grid coordinates and antenna alignment. He also instructed controllers to compute range and bearing information mathematically rather than rely on large-scale maps. In all, the research technician discovered 12 common problems associated with the two types of plotting boards and three methods of blind-level bombing in use. Most could be minimized through an extensive training program for controllers. Indeed, SCR–584 system accuracy improved considerably by the time a third control unit arrived on February 27.[12]

After evaluating all available bombing data, McLean reported an average bombing error of 1,745 feet for the command. He advised Ninth Air Force that current accuracy and the size of bomb patterns made it unsafe to bomb any closer than 2,000 yards, or slightly more than a mile from front line troops. In early May 1945, after collecting reports from the other tactical air commands, Ninth Air Force research officials concluded, despite Saville's claims to the contrary, that it found no appreciable difference among the three commands in operational techniques and equipment used or in the results attained. As for other commands, Ninth Air Force consultant R. W. Larson disputed figures used by the British Second TAF specialists, who asserted that safe blind bombing could be done within a thousand yards of friendly troops. He also reported that Mediterranean theater testing now indicated that accuracies of 500 feet could be attained, but the authorities there had not yet issued a formal report.[13]

By war's end, Ninth Air Force recommended using the SCR–584 only for navigational purposes, not to direct blind bombing missions. Officials nonetheless expected much progress in future blind bombing through the use of radio beacons, or identification friend or foe (IFF) transponders, some already installed in General Quesada's aircraft as the fighting came to a close. The Ninth also directed that controller training continue after the war. Although important breakthroughs would have to await further developments in technology, the efforts of the airmen, scientists, and engineers represented an important element in the program to improve combat effectiveness for tactical air power.[14]

Like the Lorraine experience, static warfare along the Siegfried Line in February 1945, nonetheless offered XIX TAC several advantages that mitigated poor flying weather and heavily defended targets. The command now could test the cumbersome, ground-based SCR–584 blind bombing radar system. Indeed, communications in general remained uniformly excellent throughout the month and into March because neither the headquarters nor any of the flying groups changed station. In fact, only one fighter group, the 367th (which subsequently again changed locations on March 15), redeployed from St. Dizier to Conflans, bringing it 60 miles closer to the Third Army front lines.

Other operational considerations benefitted from the static situation as well. For example, flying distance from air bases in France to the target areas, normally less than 50 miles, increased loiter times over selected targets. The stable front and well-established bases also made it easier for the command to solve logistic challenges. By mid-February, however, the XIX TAC's heavy flying commitment threatened shortages of both 500-lb. general-purpose bombs and .50-caliber ammunition. Because 500-lb. bomb stocks could not be replaced immediately, armorers used a substitute, RDX Composition-B, a British-made, high-explosive bomb consisting of a mixture of TNT and wax. More popular with the aircrews and ground forces, however, was the M–47 100-lb. white phosphorous bomb, first used by the command at this time. Its 50-foot burst and shower of burning particles made it a superb antipersonnel incendiary, and its smoke provided airmen a good protective screen against flak. Although attacks west of the Rhine at Freillingen and Mayen during February produced excellent results, transportation problems also affected the supply of white phosphorous bombs, and the command decided to conserve a minimum for special missions.[15]

High consumption of the universally used .50-caliber ammunition created greater concern when priorities in ground transport were claimed by Montgomery's forces. The command increasingly relied on air resupply to alleviate the deficit both in February and in March 1945, when the situation again became acute with the advent of more mobile ground operations. By mid-March, ammunition stocks were nearly exhausted. On March 18, in fact, the 371st Fighter Group alone fired a record 300,000 rounds while flying in close support of XX Corps. In response to the ammunition crisis, the IX Air Force Service Command flew in 2 million rounds to the 1907th Ordnance Depot Company. Even though the command stressed conservation of ammunition, it could not hope to reduce strafing operations when the war became

P-51 Mustangs of the 354th Fighter Group

more mobile and fighter-bombers often flew with reduced bombloads. However, at no time in February 1945 or later did ordnance shortages adversely affect flying operations.[16]

The relatively static situation in February eased the burden of aircraft conversion for two XIX TAC groups. With earlier experience to follow, the command had no trouble providing the 367th Fighter Group with P–47s in place of P–38s, and the 354th Fighter Group with P–51s in place of P–47s. In fact, both conversions occurred faster than the 354th's conversion from P–51s to Thunderbolts back in November 1944.[17] For some time the command had considered standardizing its fighter-bomber force by reequipping its lone Lightning group with the more durable P–47s. Despite the P–38's superior low-level speed and maneuverability, the command preferred the Thunderbolt for dive-bombing and close support in the final offensive. The reconversion of the 354th Fighter Group from P–47s to P–51s no doubt became a consideration as well. Beginning in December 1944, each of the 367th Fighter Group's three P–38 squadrons had four P–47s assigned. When no more arrived in January 1945, group members thought there would be no conversion. But on February 11, the group's 392d Fighter Squadron received 13 P–47s and by the sixteenth, was flying combat missions with the new aircraft. The remaining two squadrons became operational after only four and three days, respectively. By February 26, the 367th Fighter Group operated as a fully equipped Thunderbolt outfit.[18]

The 354th Fighter Group's conversion proved equally speedy, but perhaps more interesting, in view of the problems attendant on its original conversion to P–47s. According to the group historian, when the P–51 news reached the 354th Fighter Group's headquarters on February 4, it proved to be the "signal for the beginning of a celebration unapproached in spontaneity...by any previous reveries of the Group and it lasted unabated for two days." The Mustangs began arriving on February 10, and the group celebrated its return, or reconversion, to P–51s on February 16 by downing four Bf 109s over Trier and Oberlahnstein without sustaining a loss.[19]

The group historian thought the P–51s returned because the command needed a superior, long-range fighter that could perform counterair and interdiction missions well into Germany. At the same time, however, the AAF in Europe now had received sufficient P–51Ds to make the conversion possible *and* provide needed replacements. Whether the Pioneer Mustang group performed more effectively with P–51s is unclear. Loss rates, for example, were high if not higher during comparable periods when the group flew P–47s. On the other hand, comparisons are difficult. In spite of flying close support missions on February 16, the 354th Fighter Group now assumed the more traditional fighter responsibility of fulfilling air superiority and long-range interdiction requirements. With the return of the Mustangs, the group "started right away to climb back to its own proud place in the sun."[20]

Into the Siegfried Line

At the end of the Ardennes operation in late February, the Third Army–XIX TAC team returned to the question: how best to break through the Siegfried Line. The theatrical General Patton was not at all content to end his pursuit and pin down German troops in the Eifel while the cautious Field Marshal Montgomery claimed center stage in the Allied advance. He preferred to give "active defense" the widest possible interpretation. Because General Bradley interpreted General Eisenhower's order of February 1 as authorizing Patton's army to "continue the probing attacks now in progress," General Middleton's VIII Corps could maintain its offensive at the German border (**Map 20**).[21] Patton increased Middleton's responsibilities during a meeting on February 3 with his corps commanders and General Weyland. He explained that VIII Corps would protect First Army's right flank as ordered by SHAEF, and also launch a major assault on the West Wall, or Siegfried Line, with its objective being the capture of the town of Prum. This would be coordinated with General Eddy's XII Corps, which would attack through the Echternach region, the old southern hinge of the Bulge, on February 6 or 7; cross the Sauer River; and move northeast to take the major road center of Bitburg. With both Prum and Bitburg in Third Army hands, Patton hoped to convince Bradley and Eisenhower to allow Third Army to continue attacking eastward to the Rhine. By launching the Bitburg Offensive without permission, Patton knew he would be "taking one of the longest chances of [his] chancy career." He informed his corps commanders that the offensive would end four days later, on February 10, 1945, if sufficient progress toward the two towns had not been made.[22]

Following the February 3 planning conference, General Weyland joined the other TAC commanders at Ninth Air Force headquarters to allocate the air effort for the upcoming offensives. To provide Ninth Army with sufficient tactical air support in the Aachen region, General Nugent's XXIX TAC received units from the IX and XIX TACs. As a result, on February 8 Weyland lost two of his longest serving fighter groups, the 405th Raiders and 406th Tiger Tamers, leaving him with four fighter groups—the 354th, 362d, 367th, and 368th—until February 15, when the 371st Fighter Group returned from the XII TAC to help support Third Army's increasingly "aggressive defense." Although General Weyland had requested the 358th Fighter Group, the 371st soon distinguished itself in combat operations as the most efficient in the command.[23] To support Third Army's drive through the West Wall and on to the Rhine, XIX TAC now had five fighter-bomber groups, totaling 225 aircraft, as well as the 425th Night Fighter Squadron and the 10th Reconnaissance Group. Like Third Army, Allied leaders reduced XIX TAC's forces with the northward shift in their combat priorities.

For both Third Army and XIX TAC, the February 1945 assault on the Siegfried Line by VIII and XII Corps troops brought back bittersweet memories of the Lorraine Campaign, in which bad weather, formidable terrain, swollen rivers, reduced forces, and stiff resistance thwarted the progress of the air-ground team. Both army corps forces had to cross rivers now swollen to twice their normal widths and press forward into the cliffs of the West Wall defenses. Moreover, the heavy winter snows not only contributed to the slow pace of the ground offensive, they also prohibited any air support for the opening assault. Once beyond the initial bridgeheads over the Our and Sauer rivers, Third Army forces crossed a series of creeks and streams as they attempted to advance along roads made almost impassable from German use and the winter thaw. Much to Patton's pleasure, however, during the first week in February his troops made slow but steady progress.

Air operations in early February also can be characterized by one word: weather.[24] When the 405th and 406th Fighter Groups left the command on the eighth, they had flown on only two days in February because of poor weather. Between January 30 and February 8, fog and drizzle prohibited air support every day except on the second, when the 354th Fighter Group flew four 12-plane missions for VIII Corps. Although February's flying weather proved to be better than January's, it nevertheless restricted operations on fully 22 days of the month; 4 more days were totally nonoperational and 3 were limited to fewer than 40 combat sorties each. The command, however, gave a strong account of itself by flying a total of 5,749 sorties for an average of 205 per day in February, 500 more than it achieved in January when it possessed three more fighter-bomber groups.[25]

Weather caused the command to adjust flying priorities. The bad weather in the Eifel in early February forced Weyland to modify the command's top-priority program—interdiction. The basic air plan called for fighter-bombers to interdict German units attempting to reinforce the Prum-Bitburg area from the east. The command historian asserted, however, that bad weather during the first 12 days of February compelled the fighter-bombers to fly armed reconnaissance missions farther east in the Rhine valley instead. Even so, XIX TAC airmen flew nearly half of their armed reconnaissance missions in the original Eifel target area. Characteristically, Weyland's pilots often disregarded minimum weather flying conditions to support a Third Army offensive.

Although interdiction was a key priority, the airmen did not neglect close air support. On February 8, 1945, the day Weyland was promoted to major general, weather allowed his fighter-bombers to provide close air support to hard-pressed XII Corps forces precariously holding their Echternach bridgehead across the Sauer River. That day the 362d Maulers and 368th Thunder Bums each flew seven missions to protect the corps' bridgehead and ward off German counterattacks. On the eighth, Third Army's active defense already found VIII Corps within a half mile of Prum and III Corps widening its bridgehead beyond the Our River north of Dasburg. Farther south, General Walker's overextended XX Corps attacked the heaviest defenses of the entire Siegfried Line southeast of Trier in what Americans termed the Saar-Mosel Triangle (**Map 22**).

Despite the horrid weather, stiff defenses, and additional units transferred away from his command, Patton's forces pressed forward. They measured their success in the number of pillboxes taken each day and in small unit penetrations of the West Wall. Even though bad weather prohibited close air support on February 12, 17, and 18, fighter-bombers covered Patton's divisions on every other day. The 362d Maulers, for example, flew every day in support of XII Corps units until the troops finally breached the Siegfried Line on February 25. For the other two corps attacks, the 354th and 368th Fighter Groups shared the close support missions until the seventeenth, when the 354th Fighter Group, now flying P–51s again, concentrated on armed reconnaissance and fighter sweeps. Then the 368th and 371st Fighter Groups picked up the army

Ninth Air Force fighters entrenched in snow

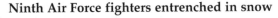

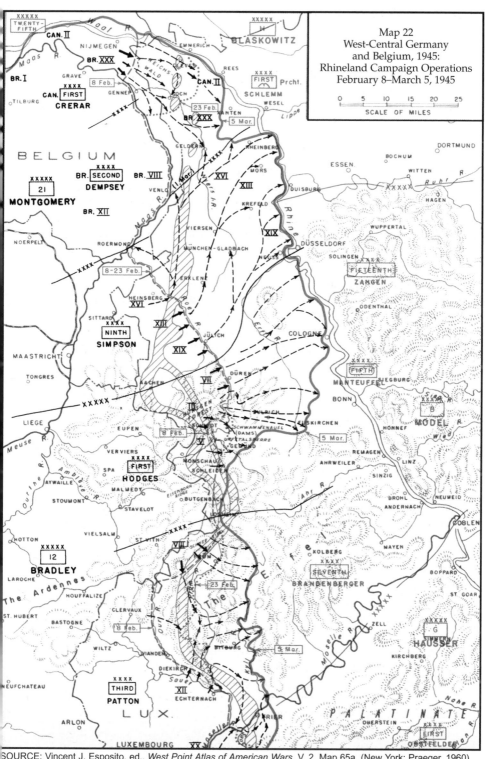

Map 22
West-Central Germany
and Belgium, 1945:
Rhineland Campaign Operations
February 8–March 5, 1945

0   5   10   15   20   25
SCALE OF MILES

SOURCE: Vincent J. Esposito, ed., *West Point Atlas of American Wars*, V. 2, Map 65a, (New York: Praeger, 1960)

"cooperation" mission, or what air leaders increasingly termed close air support.[26]

During the West Wall assault in February, the command followed its practice of assigning specific fighter-bomber groups to cover specific army corps. That permitted the aviators to become entirely familiar with the methods of particular ground controllers and with special combat conditions in a given area. In the Eifel, the 362d Fighter Group normally supported XII Corps and the 371st Fighter Group covered XX Corps. General Weyland, however, preferred to retain flexibility in mission assignments. The VIII Corps, for example, received close air support from all but the 367th Fighter Group, which generally flew armed reconnaissance missions. Moreover, individual squadrons from the same group often supported different corps on the same day, then followed their cooperation mission with armed reconnaissance or bomber escort flights. In short, the command continued to adjust its priorities and assignments as rapidly as circumstances dictated.[27]

Gradually, close air support sorties began to outnumber those for armed reconnaissance/interdiction. In fact, even during the first 12 days of February, the command flew the same number of sorties for both close air support and interdiction missions. Thereafter close air support became the command's priority program until the breakthrough to Prum on February 25. Although the statistical record does not always clearly distinguish between mission types, operational records indicate that from February 12–25, XIX TAC pilots flew 1,494 close air support and 1,315 armed reconnaissance/interdiction sorties. For the entire month of February, close support outnumbered armed reconnaissance sorties by 1,976 to 1,884. Third Army ground forces' offensive requirements meant that close air support, normally last on the doctrinal-mission priority scale, became the first and most important mission in early 1945.[28]

The high level of close support flying might suggest that Weyland's pilots flew many missions against the pillboxes that dominated Germany's West Wall defenses. The air commander always considered this type of target better suited to attack by army artillery or medium and heavy bombers in spite of earlier evaluations that suggested fighter-bombers armed with at least 1,000-lb. general-purpose bombs stood the best chance against this type of heavily defended target. How much effort did General Weyland accord West Wall pillboxes and river defenses? In this period of static warfare, did his fighter-bombers replace artillery against these difficult targets in the immediate battle zone? Records suggest that most close air support targets involved attacks on troop concentrations, convoys, rail yards, and fortified towns near or at the front line. In fact, when the 362d Fighter Group reported attacking a pillbox on February 16, it proved to be the only recorded occasion in the entire Siegfried Line offensive of February when command fighter-bombers struck such targets. Although General Weyland willingly gave close support requirements priority during ground offensives, he remained uncompromising about what he deemed proper targets for his forces and Patton invariably supported him. Pillboxes and casemented guns never appeared on General Weyland's list of approved targets—unless the ground forces faced an emergency situation. He much preferred to leave these to Third Army's artillery batteries and special assault teams. Relying on previous experience in Lorraine, the airmen concentrated on repelling enemy counterattacks and protecting bridgeheads.[29]

In February the weakened state of the *Luftwaffe* encouraged Weyland to experiment with new tactics. Indeed, the *Luftwaffe* seldom appeared during the February attack on the Siegfried Line. During the first 12 days of the month, fighters destroyed only one plane in the air and ten on the ground. From that time until February 25, even better weather did not bring out the *Luftwaffe* in force. As a result, command claims were a modest 18 aircraft destroyed in the air and four on the ground. The *Luftwaffe's* relative inactivity convinced Weyland to forego squadron-sized missions and initiate four-plane close air support flights, the command's major tactical adjustment for the spring of 1945. On February 20, the 371st Fighter Group flew four-plane sweeps over XX Corps divisions continuously from first light to sunset. Although the small flights had been flown occasionally in the past in lieu of the normal eight- or twelve-plane squadron mission, the 371st Fighter Group began what immediately became common practice for all close air support flying during the next three and a half weeks.[30]

General Weyland considered conditions especially good for using the four-plane flight. The modest *Luftwaffe* threat meant that the command could risk low-level bombing and strafing runs without the protection of a top cover flight. Flying close to the home base allowed tactical control radars to monitor the area and alert the flights should *Luftwaffe* aircraft suddenly appear. In late February, Weyland also expected the ground action to become more fluid. Under Third Army's incessant pressure, retreating enemy forces would be forced into the open, where they would become excellent targets for the airmen. In short, four-plane missions now could be flown safely and profitably. Moreover, they proved popular with airmen and field troops alike. From the air side, it meant that each flight had more time to concentrate on ground targets because they lost no time coordinating two flights working together. Then, too, the smaller formation gave new pilots practice flying as mission leaders. As for Patton's ground forces, they enjoyed what amounted to the proverbial, albeit doctrinally proscribed, air umbrella as they came and went throughout the day.

Although the airmen considered the four-plane missions more productive than the larger formations, the statistical record is not entirely clear on the issue. Indeed, the whole question of tactical air power's effectiveness as it was applied in this manner remains next to impossible to determine with precision. The ground force elements receiving this air support, however, harbored no doubts whatsoever. They judged XIX TAC aircraft as having played a crucial role in the spring offensive. Nearly every day, the flying command's intelligence reports referred to complimentary messages from ground units that received "excellent cooperation" and "splendid support" from XIX TAC fighter-bombers that blunted counterattacks or destroyed enemy positions. General Weyland, too, never entertained second doubts over his decision to supply this kind of air coverage at this point in the war. By February 20, 1945, he could look forward to mobile warfare in the near future. From previous experience in the Battle for France, he knew Patton's artillery would have difficulty advancing rapidly and providing front line coverage by itself. Command of the air permitted Weyland to take liberties with tactical air doctrine, a doctrine that favored concentrated use of air power and frowned on penny-packet combat air patrols. Use of the four-plane flight, however, demonstrated the inherent flexibility of tactical air power and the ability of the airmen to adapt to changing needs and circumstances. Although Weyland's airmen believed the small formations represented the most productive and efficient method of flying in February, a stronger enemy would have required squadron- or group-sized missions with perhaps a corresponding decline in efficiency. In short, battle conditions guided the XIX TAC commander's actions and determined the command's aerial operations.[31]

Through the Eifel to the Rhine

While the aircraft conversions took place in mid-February, operationally the command continued to support Third Army's slow movement through the Siegfried Line. On February 20, 1945, with the 371st Fighter Group providing continuous four-plane coverage, XX Corps' divisions began clearing the Saar-Mosel Triangle in earnest. In two days of stiff fighting against the *Wehrmacht's* weakened Army Group G, Third Army troops secured the area, and Patton's troops poised themselves for the final drive toward Trier. Meanwhile, the 362d Fighter Group attacked convoys, tanks, and gun positions in the VIII Corps zone, where General Middleton's forces finally cleared Dasburg and eliminated the Vianden Bulge (**Map 22**).

On February 21, the 368th Fighter Group led the command in achieving a new five-group record of 504 sorties. It divided its 25 missions between XII Corps' 5th Infantry Division and units of VIII Corps just to the north, then making the Third Army's fifth complete breakthrough of the West Wall. The group also added two armed reconnaissance missions in the Rhine valley for good measure. As for the other groups, the 362d and 367th Fighter Groups flew armed reconnaissance/interdiction missions east of the Rhine as far as Wuerzburg, while the 371st Fighter Group continued its support of XX Corps' mopping up operation southwest of Trier.

February 22 proved to be a more important flying day, even though morning fog grounded General Weyland's aircraft until midday and limited the command to 33 missions and 358 sorties. On this day the command participated in Operation Clarion, one of the greatest air shows of the war. For Clarion, SHAEF planned a massive, theaterwide air assault on Germany's key rail and water transportation network launched in conjunction with Operation Grenade, Ninth Army's two-week delayed drive to the Rhine. On the twenty-second, more than 8,000 Allied aircraft dropped 8,500 tons of bombs on more than 200 German targets. The day's claims included 15 locomotives, 404 railroad cars, 16 barges, 44 buildings, 18 marshaling yards, 78 rail cuts, and 65 *Luftwaffe* aircraft shot down.[32] In Clarion, XIX TAC escorted 25 formations of medium bombers attacking bridges and marshalling yards east and west of the Rhine in front of Third Army. At the same time, Weyland ensured Patton's

Dicing shot of Saarburg, Germany

255

front line ground units received sufficient air cover. The 368th Fighter Group flew just one squadron-sized mission for VIII Corps, while the 362d Fighter Group flew two missions for XX Corps and one for XII Corps. The fighter-bombers also flew armed reconnaissance in conjunction with the bomber escort missions, once they made sure their big brothers were safe.

Allied planners hoped that the disruption produced in one day by Operation Clarion would overwhelm German railway repair capabilities and force the enemy to rely temporarily on motor transport. Their assessment proved absolutely correct. German vehicles clogged the roadways on February 23, making themselves ideal targets for the fighter-bombers. While the 368th and 371st Fighter Groups provided what Third Army leaders termed splendid air cooperation, the other three groups flew armed reconnaissance in the Rhine region and eastward along key communications routes. A final total of 269 tanks and armored vehicles and 1,308 railroad cars represented a command record for the number of enemy vehicles claimed destroyed or damaged in a single day. The total of 527 sorties flown surpassed the month's previous high set just two days earlier.[33]

A few days later, on February 25, 1945, Third Army forces were completely through the Siegfried Line; on the twenty-sixth Bitburg fell to XII Corps' 4th Armored Division. With the West Wall defenses breached, the time had arrived for General Patton to exploit his position, provided he could convince reluctant superiors that a Third Army offensive had the best chance against the enemy. Yet Allied attention in late February still focused on the northern sector where, under Montgomery's command, General Simpson's Ninth Army had crossed the Roer River and began the drive to the Ruhr (**Map 31**). The Eifel remained a secondary front. Patton wanted to drive his army forward, seizing every opportunity that promised rapid gains. His immediate objective became the city of Trier. In Versailles, General Eisenhower remained unconvinced that a major thrust should occur in the Eifel. Then, on February 25, General Bradley arrived at Third Army's Luxembourg City headquarters and notified Patton to cease attacking and prepare to designate and hold one infantry and one armored division as SHAEF reserves. Appalled, General Patton, his corps commanders, and his air commander importuned Bradley otherwise. Weyland expressed the frustration felt by all in his diary that evening:

> If this episode could be truly written up, it would be a remarkable historical occasion. An Army commander, Tactical Air Commander, and 3 corps commanders pleading for permission to continue to fight against the German Army they had defeated![34]

Their entreaties caused Bradley to relent and, perhaps contrary to the orders he received, to allow Patton to proceed against Trier, but under severe time limits for use of the 10th Armored Division. Originally assigned to SHAEF reserve, the division was on loan to Patton only until that day, February 25. During the conference at Luxembourg City, Bradley agreed to extend the loan of the 10th Division for another 48 hours. Meanwhile, 4th Armored Division spearheads, which led the way, were gaining up to ten miles a day as pressure mounted on both Bitburg and Trier. Three days later, at the end of February, Bitburg was cleared, and elements of the 76th Infantry Division were within three miles of Trier. Direct air support for the offensive continued to come primarily from the 368th and 371st Fighter Groups, while the other groups flew armed reconnaissance along the Rhine.[35]

With Third Army returned to mobile operations at the end of February 1945, the airmen looked forward to propelling its troops on to the Rhine River. Yet bad weather and the rapidity of the ground advance eventually conspired to limit the effectiveness of the air arm. During the first three days of March, however, with good weather, the 368th and 371st Fighter Groups provided excellent cooperation to XII Corps' 76th and 5th Infantry Divisions near Bitburg and to XX Corps' 10th Armored Division, which spearheaded the drive on Trier from the southwest (**Map 22**). On each of the three days close air support accounted for over half of the missions flown, and the 368th Fighter Group established a new record for the command with 124 close air support sorties on March 3. Ground forces continued to shower XIX TAC pilots with praise.

By March 3, 1945, Trier had fallen and the XX and XII Corps joined forces at the Mosel River. General Patton now planned an VIII Corps attack across the Prüm River and a strike for the Rhine at Brohl, with the 11th Armored Division in the lead. The major thrust, however, would come from XII Corps, which would attack from its Kyll River bridgehead and send the 4th Armored Division racing along the north bank of the Mosel to intersect the Rhine at Andernach. Meanwhile, XX Corps would send one division north along the Mosel as far as Bernkassel while consolidating its positions around Trier (**Map 22**).[36]

Unfortunately for the XIX TAC, the next five days repeated those of early February. Low overcast, drizzle, snow showers, and generally poor visibility grounded the air arm almost completely and Third Army began its offensive toward the Rhine without air support. Weather for the remainder of March proved generally good and, compared with February's weather, certainly offered much better flying conditions. In fact, the command flew a total of 12,427 sorties in March, the highest monthly figure for the entire campaign.[37]

With Operation Veritable proceeding in the north, Third Army resumed its drive to the Rhine as a part of Operation Lumberjack, which involved a coordinated assault by First and Third Armies. Lumberjack called for First Army's VII Corps, which had been protecting Ninth Army's right flank in late February, to turn toward Cologne. Once there, part of its forces would wheel southeast and head for the Rhine near its junction with the Ahr River, then continue south to meet Patton's forces (**Map 23**). On March 5, 1945, VII Corps forces entered the bombed-out city of Cologne and XII Corps jumped off in force on a solid 15-mile front with 4th Armored Division in the lead. Late on March 7, it was poised on the last ridge before Andernach, while remnants of nine German divisions scrambled to escape south of the Mosel or across the Rhine. The poor roads and rugged countryside now presented a greater problem to Patton's troops than did enemy resistance. On March 8, the day after First Army troops made the first Allied crossing of the Rhine at Remagen, elements of the 4th Armored Division reached Andernach, culminating an advance of 52 miles in 58 hours![38] Sidelined by the weather, the airmen compared the swift drive through the Eifel to the Brittany Blitz of the previous summer. With the enemy disorganized and in rapid retreat, Patton's armor could advance rapidly without benefit of air cover.

On March 9, 1945, shortly after he returned from a week's rest on the French Riviera, General Weyland met with General Patton and his staff to discuss the course ahead. Although the Third Army commander did not hide his eagerness to cross the Rhine, he decided against taking undue risks. Ultra data indicated that the Germans expected him to attempt a Rhine crossing between Niederlahnstein and Ruedesheim. As a result, after first securing the West Bank, he planned to cross the Rhine 20 miles farther south, after crossing the Mosel above Trier and ensuring protection of his supply lines. He also requested that Weyland's fighter-bombers protect XII Corps' right flank, especially along the Mosel. The air commander immediately passed these instructions to his reconnaissance officer and Colonel Ferguson.[39]

Meanwhile, the 4th Armored Division continued south along the west bank of the Rhine and moved on Coblenz in conjunction with VIII Corps forces. Infantry formations from the two corps, which had been left far behind, continued to mop up and secure territory north of the Mosel. The XIX TAC now concentrated on column cover for the armored spearheads, but it provided little cover for the infantry. The rapid pace of the armored advance created a "series of pockets too small to permit employment of air power" to support infantry units. Without air liaison officers or a clear separation between Patton's troops and the enemy's, Weyland chose not to fly close air support for the infantry. Instead, the fighters focused on armed reconnaissance, while tactical reconnaissance P–51s kept a close watch on the Mosel River. Although infrequent in the XIX TAC–Third Army experience, instances like this help explain why officers serving in armored divisions generally expressed much more satisfaction with XIX TAC air support than did infantry officers.[40]

With the ground assault gathering momentum in March, Weyland prepared to test the mobility of his command once again. He considered using Trier's airfield for two fighter-bomber groups, but that required extending the runway on both ends with pierced steel planking to achieve the needed fight-

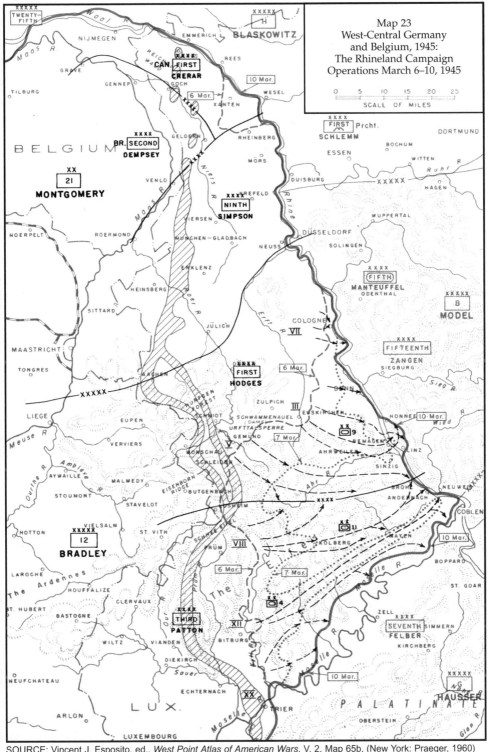

Map 23
West-Central Germany
and Belgium, 1945:
The Rhineland Campaign
Operations March 6–10, 1945

0   5   10   15   20   25
SCALE OF MILES

SOURCE: Vincent J. Esposito, ed., *West Point Atlas of American Wars*, V. 2, Map 65b, (New York: Praeger, 1960)

er-bomber length of 5,000 feet. It is unclear whether the time needed to prepare a longer runway caused the air commander to change his mind. In any event, he altered course immediately and earmarked the airfield for the 10th Photo Reconnaissance Group, whose lightly loaded aircraft did not require the longer runway. The first tactical reconnaissance squadron arrived on March 15 to provide coverage of the Mosel flank. The remainder of the group arrived on the twenty-ninth. Weyland had no immediate plans for additional airfields west of the Rhine, but he already had his sights on bases farther east in the Frankfurt area.[41] Indeed, by March 12, 1945, Third Army forces had eliminated all organized resistance along the western bank of the Rhine. They now prepared for a new operation that would create a disaster for Gen. Hans Felber's Seventh German Army, Operation Undertone, which centered on a drive by General Patch's Seventh Army from the Siegfried Line near Saarbruecken to the Rhine at Mainz.

In early March 1945, General Patton passed to General Bradley an even more audacious plan, one that gave to Third Army a larger role predicated on the position achieved in its recent gains. In this plan, the 4th Armored Division would continue south along the Rhine to sever German communications and eventually link up with U.S. Seventh Army units, while other XII Corps forces would attack southeast across the lower Mosel from Coblenz to Trier. To complete the trap, XX Corps would swing southeast of Trier and strike the German First Army troops, still in the Sigfried Line defenses, from the rear. That would ease pressure on Seventh Army troops attempting to force their way through the West Wall and destroy the bulk of the German forces remaining west of the Rhine (**Map 24**).

In deciding in favor of this plan, both Generals Bradley and Patton recognized that the greater operational commitment for the Third Army would prevent its transfer either to Field Marshal Montgomery's 21st Army Group in the north or to General Devers's 6th Army Group in the south. Moreover, it was a bold, well-designed plan. If it worked, the entire German First and Seventh Armies, then positioned west of the Rhine, would be trapped between the Saar, Mosel, and Rhine rivers. Weyland hoped the good weather would permit maximum support from his fighter-bombers.[42]

Springing the Saar-Mosel-Rhine Trap—and Across the Rhine River

On March 13, 1945, Patton launched his offensive with the 4th Armored Division attacking across the Mosel toward Mainz, while VIII Corps' divisions moved on Coblenz. From its Trier bridgehead, XX Corps assaulted West Wall defenses with three divisions. What the Allies termed the Saar-Mosel-Rhine trap began to close on the German First and Seventh Armies almost at

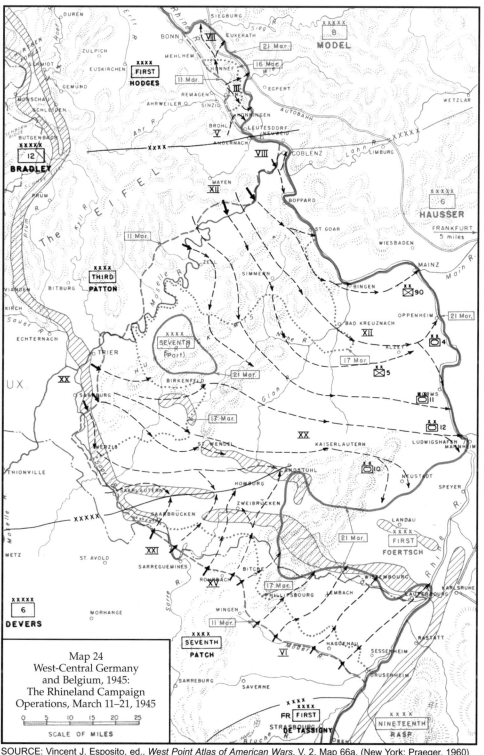

Map 24
West-Central Germany
and Belgium, 1945:
The Rhineland Campaign
Operations, March 11–21, 1945

0   5   10   15   20   25

SCALE OF MILES

SOURCE: Vincent J. Esposito, ed., *West Point Atlas of American Wars*, V. 2, Map 66a, (New York: Praeger, 1960)

once. Blessed with a series of good weather days for a change, the XIX TAC also began what became perhaps the most outstanding ten-day period in the command's history. Relying on proven fighter-bomber-tactical reconnaissance coordination, it would provide wall-to-wall air support that seemed limited only by the difficulty of keeping pace with the ground forces. At the same time it suffered exceedingly high aircraft losses.[43]

Once the morning fog cleared on March 13, the 371st Fighter Group covered the XX Corps' front near Trier throughout the day with 16, 4-plane close support missions, while the 362d Fighter Group supported both the VIII Corps and XII Corps sectors with six 8-plane and two 16-plane armed reconnaissance missions throughout the afternoon and early evening. This left the remaining three groups available to provide armed reconnaissance, to fly escort and leaflet missions, and to strike pinpoint interdiction targets. The following day, the same pattern prevailed with the 362d and 371st Fighter Groups each flying 20 close air support missions for XII and XX Corps, respectively, yet able to fly armed reconnaissance as well.

Third Army's sudden advance unhinged the entire German defensive line south of the Mosel from Trier to Coblenz. Realizing Patton's intentions, the *Wehrmacht* began a frantic mass evacuation to escape the rapidly closing trap. The resultant congestion of surface traffic reminded airmen of similar turkey shoots that had occurred in France and again late in the Ardennes Battle. In the words of one XIX TAC official, it was a "fighter-bomber's paradise." Tactical reconnaissance aircraft continued the well-established practice of spotting retreating columns and calling in fighter-bombers, then leading them to the targets. For the first time in the war, German columns, often consisting of as many as 1,000 closely packed vehicles, preferred to pull over, show the white flag, and surrender rather than risk further strafing attacks. Pilot claims of German transport destroyed were understandably high. Because the retreating columns contained little armor, the pilots normally abandoned bombs and napalm in favor of strafing and rocket attacks. Mindful of the Brittany Campaign the previous summer, they also realized that any bombs dropped would only crater the roads and slow the Allied advance. Vehicles destroyed by strafing, however, could be quickly pushed aside. The 362d and 368th Fighter Groups shared honors as "the rocket groups," and they had a "field day" against the German massed withdrawal in the XII Corps zone.[44]

On March 15, 1945, Weyland proudly announced that his forces had compiled the highest mission rate ever attained for a five-group command in a single day. Of the 101 missions (involving 643 sorties) flown, fully 58 were in direct support of the ground forces. Although the command did not surpass the 101 mission figure to the rest of the campaign, the daily sortie rate for a five-group command continued to climb and break existing records. On March 18, for example, the command achieved a record 714 sorties and claimed 1,022 vehicles destroyed in what Third Army officers called magnificent air cooperation. On that day alone, the 371st Fighter Group flew 144 close support sorties, while the 362d Fighter Group, which the 4th Armored Division requested by name, flew 178. Such high figures proved typical of operations from March 15–23, as German forces struggled to escape the trap. By March 18, VIII Corps had nearly cleared Coblenz, while rampaging columns of the 4th Armored Division neared Mainz and Worms and sliced through the Palatinate farther west.[45]

With the remaining German forces west of the Rhine facing annihilation, XIX TAC prepared to counter any effort mounted by the *Luftwaffe*. About one-third of the approximately 400 daily *Luftwaffe* sorties were directed against the Remagen bridgehead. Earlier, on March 7, elements of General Hodges's 9th Armored Division reached Remagen just south of Bonn in time to prevent German demolition teams from destroying that bridge across the Rhine. This span permitted the first Allied bridgehead on the East Bank and compelled General Eisenhower to reconsider his original plan that conceded the main thrust in northern Germany to Montgomery's forces.[46] Despite the *Luftwaffe's* focus on the Remagen bridgehead, Third Army continued to report German air activity, and General Weyland's pilots eagerly sought out encounter missions. The 354th Fighter Group's P–51s gained the lion's share of enemy aircraft destroyed, but poorly piloted *Luftwaffe* aircraft proved no match for the P–47s either. On March 16, for example, the 354th and the 362d Fighter Groups accounted for 13 enemy aircraft shot down in air combat.

The command lost only one aircraft to enemy air action from March 13–24, yet its heavy air commitment during the Third Army Rhine Offensive led to a loss of 59 for the month. Only December's toll was higher, and in that

Troops of the 90th Infantry Division crossing the Mosel River

month the Ardennes Offensive was at its height. The command lost 34 of these 59 aircraft in the effort to spring the Saar-Mosel-Rhine trap; most were downed by flak. This is not surprising because more light flak units now joined the retreating convoys. Although the command and Ninth Air Force took great care to report aircraft losses accurately, only half of the March total is identified with flak. "Unknown" is the category cited for most of the remaining half. Other losses were incurred due to crashes and a midair collision. One must presume that enemy flak claimed the majority of aircraft lost to "unknown" causes.[47]

In relating losses to particular mission types, unit records show that XIX TAC lost more than twice as many aircraft on close air support missions than it did on armed reconnaissance/interdiction missions. Air force doctrine judged Priority III Close Air Support missions to be the most dangerous and least cost-effective in terms of results and losses. Pilots on armed reconnaissance and close air support missions, however, attacked remarkably similar targets, most of them trains, marshaling yards, and road convoys. In any event, low-level strafing represented the common denominator for both missions. Here the fighter-bomber was the most effective but also the most exposed to enemy surface defenses and likely to suffer high losses.[48]

Loss figures should be used with care when measuring the success or effectiveness of particular fighter groups. The 362d Maulers provide an example. Long considered one of the command's top groups, the Maulers

A tank destroyer of the 4th Armored Division crossing a treadway bridge over the Mosel River.

were showered with praise in the last three months of the war for their outstanding work with XII Corps' 4th Armored Division. Unfortunately, the group also lost 21 airplanes in March, one of the more unhappy records of the campaign. Little in the documentary record explains the 362d Fighter Group's high losses. Operational reports cite a variety of causes, with "unknown" and "flak" recorded approximately equally. Although the group flew close air support missions for the most part, so too did the 371st Fighter Group, which lost a mere four aircraft in March. On the other hand, former 371st Fighter Group pilot Lieutenant Burns recalled that the Maulers had a reputation for aggressive, if not occasionally reckless, flying. Its commanders, he recalled, allowed 362d pilots great latitude in flying operations. Commanders of the 371st, on the other hand, demanded that pilots avoid excessive risks. Despite the Maulers' loss rate, nothing suggests that the command viewed this group with less confidence or more concern. However high its losses, the 362d Fighter Group also claimed more unit and individual records than any other.[49]

The command counted aircraft losses per 1,000 sorties as its unit of measure. During February, March, and April 1945, a XIX TAC average of 5.2 aircraft lost per 1,000 sorties was the lowest for the entire campaign. If losses appear high, the command also had a high sortie rate. Colonel Hallett's Intelligence Flak Section continued to publicize all known flak locations in special reports and the daily intelligence summaries. His section also distributed photographs of flak sites, took care to brief this information to pilots, and recommended attack headings to minimize the threat. Even so, XIX TAC command lost nearly as many aircraft in April when it targeted heavily defended *Luftwaffe* airfields for a knockout blow against the remaining German air force.[50]

By mid-March 1945, the fast-moving U.S. First and Third Armies at the Rhine River dominated Allied discussion and planning. As Third Army's advance across the Mosel and down the West Bank of the Rhine gained momentum, Allied leaders reassessed the roles first planned for the 12th and 6th Army Groups. In a meeting with General Eisenhower at Seventh Army headquarters in Luneville on March 17, General Devers, commander of the 6th Army Group, agreed that Patton's troops could cross his group's boundary line in their quest for maximum destruction of the enemy. Patton, however, remained obsessed with crossing the Rhine before either Montgomery in the north or Devers in the south. Earlier, Eisenhower authorized only Devers's 6th Army Group to establish Rhine bridgeheads in the south, a decision that rankled Patton. With his army advancing rapidly, a Rhine crossing had become a real possibility, especially when it would upstage the slow-moving, methodical preparations of Field Marshal Montgomery in the north. On March 19, Patton got the word he wanted: General Bradley ordered him to take the river on the run. Two days later the Supreme Commander confirmed Bradley's

Thunderbolt hits on trucks and railroads

injunction, authorizing both Third and Seventh Armies to cross whenever the opportunity presented itself. These directives, along with Ultra's confirmation of weak German defenses, were all that Patton needed.[51]

On March 20, 1945, while Third Army continued to harry the enemy and insured that bridging equipment would be ready for a crossing, General Weyland directed flying cooperation missions to attack German convoys frantically fleeing eastward toward Speyer, the only West Bank crossing point remaining to the enemy. That day the 362d and 371st Fighter Groups, assisted by two squadrons from the 367th Fighter Group, turned the attack on surface forces into a slaughter. Next day, on March 22, Weyland accompanied General Patton on a jeep tour that extended from Saarburg eastward well beyond Kaiserslautern. The XIX TAC commander described the enormous destruction of surface convoys from air action as "terrific," and commented on the thousands of refugees and unarmed Germans that now clogged the roads. One of the most vivid scenes occurred along the Bad Durkeim–Frankenstein road east of Kaiserslautern. Here, XX Corps headquarters reported that Allied officials witnessed the remains of an entire German division "massacred by the Air Corps." The "twisted mass of death and destruction…is so enormous that the mind cannot measure it!"[52]

Patton's mobile operations once again challenged the tactical air forces to keep pace with a swiftly advancing ground offensive, a challenge accentuated by the increasing distance from the flying fields. By the third week in March, the flying distance to Rhine valley targets required an hour's time in each direction for aircraft flying armored column cover, and longer for armed reconnaissance flights east of the Rhine. The tactical control center's radar

Generals Patton, Eisenhower, and Devers

found it increasingly difficult to keep these flights on the radar scopes, and land line communications had to be abandoned in favor of FM radio links. Even though the command believed that an emergency supply of long-range fuel tanks solved the air support problem, it is clear that shorter en route distances would have permitted significantly more loiter time in the target area. Although the fighter-bombers achieved great success interdicting a retreating enemy, if even more effort had been devoted to this mission, air power might have prevented more of the *Wehrmacht's* First and Seventh Armies from escaping across the Rhine.[53]

As Third Army forces approached the Rhine on March 21, General Weyland executed a well-prepared air plan to support a successful crossing. For several days, both reconnaissance aircraft and fighters flying armed reconnaissance missions kept the potential crossing area near Mainz under close observation to monitor any buildup or defensive construction. Beginning on the twenty-first, Weyland altered the reconnaissance plan to permit constant reconnaissance of the front lines. This included six missions along the Darmstadt-Frankfurt-Aschaffenburg route and five on either flank.[54] At the same time, armed reconnaissance/interdiction, performed primarily by the 368th and 367th Fighter Groups, focused on communications centers east of the river that might be staging sites for potential reinforcements. Although targets included important motor transportation facilities and ordnance and supply depots, the fighter-bombers targeted the railroad system in particular. The 368th and 367th Fighter Groups flew 29 squadron-sized rail-cutting missions in an arc from Limburg south to Mannheim. Claims for the two days totaled an impressive 112 rail lines severed (**Map 25**). To preclude any interference from the *Luftwaffe*, Weyland directed continuous day and night air patrols on March 22 and 23. Command P–51s flew 19 patrol missions on March 22 and 31 area cover missions on March 23, while P–61 Black Widows provided the same coverage at night. Moreover, beginning on March 21, an Allied air assault against German airfields took place all along the front, which rendered many *Luftwaffe* bases unserviceable.

Patton's forces indeed hit the river on the run, and the 5th Infantry Division crossed the Rhine near Oppenheim on the night of March 22, 1945, meeting only token opposition. The following day the *Luftwaffe* did mount a serious effort to destroy this Third Army bridgehead. Although it flew an impressive 150 fighter sorties on March 23 the Germans lost 22 aircraft in the attacks. Unlike the Rhine crossing next day, on the evening of the twenty-third, by Field Marshal Montgomery's enormous force to the north in Operation Varsity, the XIX TAC–Third Army team needed no massive air or artillery barrage preparations. Third Army's rapid offensive had destroyed any significant opposition that might have defended on the east bank of the Rhine, while fighter-bomber attacks against German forces on land and in the sky "gave General Patton confidence that no dangerous force could be brought against him."[55]

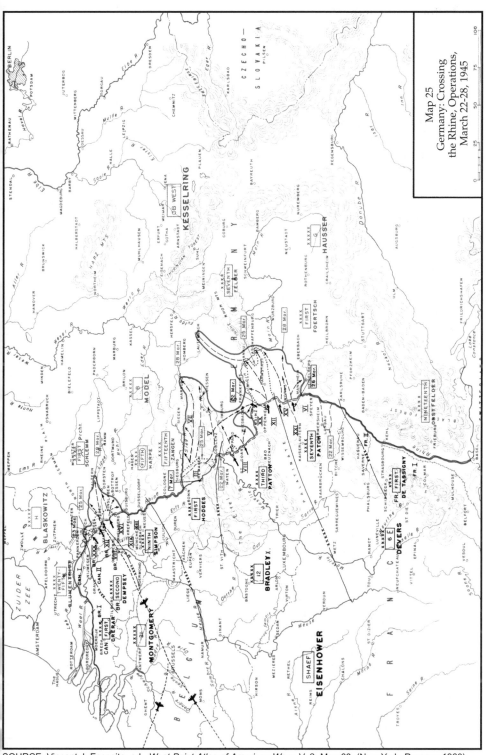

Map 25
Germany: Crossing
the Rhine, Operations,
March 22-28, 1945

SOURCE: Vincent J. Esposito, ed., *West Point Atlas of American Wars*, V. 2, Map 68, (New York: Praeger, 1960)

Once More: "Blitz Warfare U.S. Style"

On March 21, 1945, the day before the 5th Infantry Division crossed the Rhine and established a bridgehead at Oppenheim, General Patton told his air commander that the XIX TAC and the Third Army "have again been committing treason in reverse as we did so happily in August and September. By this I mean that instead of giving aid and comfort to the enemy, we have been giving him pain and discomfort, and doing it in a big way. Let us keep it up!"[56] General Weyland relayed Patton's words to his air units, adding, "XIX TAC–Third Army again is showing the world what a perfectly coordinated fighting air-ground team can do. I knew that you would be with me to a man when I assured General Patton that we would 'keep it up' with the Third Army." By the spring of 1945, the cooperative spirit established in France had spread from the leadership throughout the lower echelons of the air-ground team.[57]

Like the rapid dash across France, the planned drive into the heart of Germany promised to stretch the lines of communication and again challenge Weyland's forces to keep pace with the swift ground offensive. Armored column cover and armed reconnaissance would certainly be the primary missions against lucrative enemy targets on the roads. General Weyland knew that the speed of the advance once again would likely require air cover for Third Army's exposed flanks and greater reliance on reconnaissance. The air commander also realized, without the pernicious distraction of a Brittany, that the airmen did not have to protect an extended front expanding in opposite directions. Moreover, the Allies were better supplied to confront an enemy that, despite fighting on his homeland, seemed on the brink of collapse. Perhaps most important, air and ground forces both brought months of combat experience to the final offensive.

On the evening of March 23, 1945, while Field Marshal Montgomery initiated Operation Varsity in the north, featuring two entire airborne divisions leading the air assault portion of his highly publicized and elaborately prepared Rhine crossing, General Patton readied his forces for an advance from the Oppenheim bridgehead on the Rhine to the Main River, 30 miles to the northeast. The next day armored columns of the hard-driving 4th Armored Division bypassed Darmstadt and dashed toward Hanau and Aschaffenburg. On March 25, they seized bridgeheads at both of these sites on the Main River, while other XII Corps forces closed on Frankfurt. Further north, VIII Corps units made two additional Rhine crossings south of Coblenz on the twenty-fifth and moved toward Limburg on the Lahn River. General Walker's XX Corps troops crossed two days later, then moved north to join VIII Corps units and encircle Wiesbaden before driving toward Giessen and a planned link-up with First Army (**Map 25**).

The speed and relative ease of the ground advance now owed as much to the air support provided by General Weyland's fighter-bombers as it did to enemy collapse. Good weather prevailed until March 29, when Third Army had all three army corps across the Rhine and well on their way northeast. Following past practice, General Weyland assigned a specific air group to support each of the army corps. The 367th Fighter Group's P–47s provided armored column cover for General Eddy's XII Corps pacesetters exclusively, and drew rave reviews from the corps commander. The VIII and XX Corps crossings and breakouts received air cover from the 368th and 362d Fighter Groups, respectively.

With the 367th Fighter Group leading the way, the 371st, 362d, and 368th Fighter Groups flew armed reconnaissance in front of the advancing troops as far east as Giessen and Schweinfurt. The fighter-bombers found the roads congested with German convoys fleeing eastward as Third Army's rapidly moving armored forces allowed no time for the German Seventh Army to organize defenses. On March 27, in spite of restrictive flying weather, the airmen claimed more than 1,000 motorized vehicles destroyed or damaged. Claims for March 23–28, before bad weather set in, were impressive: 3,100 vehicles, 211 locomotives, and 2,954 railroad cars. Yet the pilots eagerly looked ahead to the following month when longer days and the weatherman's promise of better weather offered prospects of the campaign's best flying.

The command's Mustangs had an equally important role. The 354th Fighter Group's P–51s flew eight-plane area cover missions over the Rhine

Third Army crossing the Rhine River

and Main bridgeheads, readily accepting any *Luftwaffe* challenge. Although the enemy directed its primary effort against Montgomery's forces threatening the Ruhr industrial region, its 150 sorties flown against the Oppenheim bridgehead on March 23 represented an impressive effort. It could not, however, sustain that level of response. Heavy casualties restricted its attack to 60 sorties on March 24 and all *Luftwaffe* opposition along the Rhine ended when Third Army troops overran its bases in the Frankfurt area on March 25.[58]

Anticipating a wide front and extremely fluid situation in the weeks ahead, the XIX TAC's 10th Photo Reconnaissance Group introduced an important reconnaissance key system on March 28 to uncover potential enemy attacks. Group and Army intelligence personnel plotted 33 squares, each representing 20 square miles of territory. Planners gave each square a name, and the key allowed them to change the air-ground reconnaissance plan daily by combining two or more squares into the desired area. Once Third Army overran the squares, a new base line would be established and the key moved over it. Coverage could be changed merely by a telephone call. The key system eliminated the need for providing the corps new reconnaissance overlays every day and gave tactical reconnaissance planners much greater flexibility.[59]

In the air-ground arena, fighter-bomber and reconnaissance pilots achieved new levels of coordination with ground forces through their tactical air liaison officers. To respond rapidly to the changing situation, tactical reconnaissance aircraft, on March 24, received permission to talk over fighter-bomber channels directly with the division air liaison officer, rather than with his counterpart at corps headquarters. The tactical control center only monitored the VHF transmissions. This procedure enabled a division to request reconnaissance directly from the pilots and, after receiving the reports, immediately divert fighter-bombers in the vicinity to any reported targets.

In this change, which decentralized air-ground operations even further, air leaders advanced another step down the road of providing dedicated air support for ground forces. To be sure, AAF air liaison officers retained operational control of the aircraft, but the change meant that fighter-bombers could be diverted by controllers at the front rather than by those in the tactical control center where the information was often outdated. It also became common practice for fighter-bombers on armed reconnaissance missions to first check with the corps air liaison officer to learn of any immediate targets before flying his assigned route. Such were the needs of mobile warfare and the pragmatic solutions that tactical air officers adopted to meet the problems they faced. Although such procedures might have proved of value in static situations, air leaders in those circumstances preferred to rely on more traditional methods of centralized control.[60]

While Weyland, in late March 1945, considered the challenge of moving his aircraft to bases farther forward, he became aware of a Third Army operation that proved to be one of the most controversial of General Patton's career. On March 27, a security blackout affected all activities concerning the 4th Armored Division which, as Weyland recorded in his diary, had sent a combat team of more than 300 men 50 kilometers east of Aschaffenburg to a POW camp. Rather than send a large, heavily defended force, Patton elected to send a small task force far behind enemy lines to liberate a camp near Hammelburg that Allied intelligence knew contained many Americans, including, most likely, Patton's son-in-law, Col. John Waters. Unfortunately, a German observation plane spotted the American force as it approached the camp. Shortly after liberating many prisoners and setting out on the return journey, German forces cut off and decimated the rescue force. Critics ever since have charged that Patton, for personal reasons, recklessly jeopardized the main task force in a very risky operation of questionable value.[61]

Whatever the validity of these accusations, given the impressive air-ground coordination in evidence by late March 1945, one must ask why Third Army planners failed to provide for air support in this operation? Intended as a highly secret, quick-strike mission, no ground controller was assigned to the task force to call on F–6s and P–47s in case of emergency. Even the bad weather on March 29–30 would not have prevented Weyland from sending his aircraft to help. One can only speculate whether air-ground coordination would have been sufficient to save the mission. Such a contingency seems not to have been considered by Patton, who apparently planned and executed the operation without consulting his air commander.

While General Patton dealt with the abortive rescue mission, his three rampaging armored divisions pushed northeastward deeper into Germany. Typically, 4th Armored Division led the assault. By March 31, its forward elements approached the Fulda River, more than 100 miles northeast of their Rhine bridgehead. Indeed, by the end of the month, Third Army had cleared the Rhein-Main triangle and had linked up with First and Seventh Armies on its flanks. Meanwhile, after crossing the Rhine in force, Montgomery prepared to lead the Allied assault to the Elbe, then on to Berlin. To his profound displeasure, Eisenhower decided to shift the main effort in the north from Montgomery's to Bradley's group, thereby de-emphasizing the drive toward Berlin. By month's end, the unhappy field marshal would lose Simpson's Ninth Army to Bradley's 12th Army Group and occupy a supporting role guarding Bradley's northern flank (**Map 26**).[62]

As the Third Army advance continued, General Weyland acted promptly to bring his own command forward. When Third Army moved its command post on March 27, from Luxembourg City to Idar-Oberstein, 30 miles east of Trier, the air commander sent along his X-Ray liaison detachment, again directed by Weyland's chief of staff Colonel Browne. In this manner, the air arm maintained close coordination with General Patton until the XIX TAC advance headquarters arrived. This occurred shortly thereafter, when Weyland

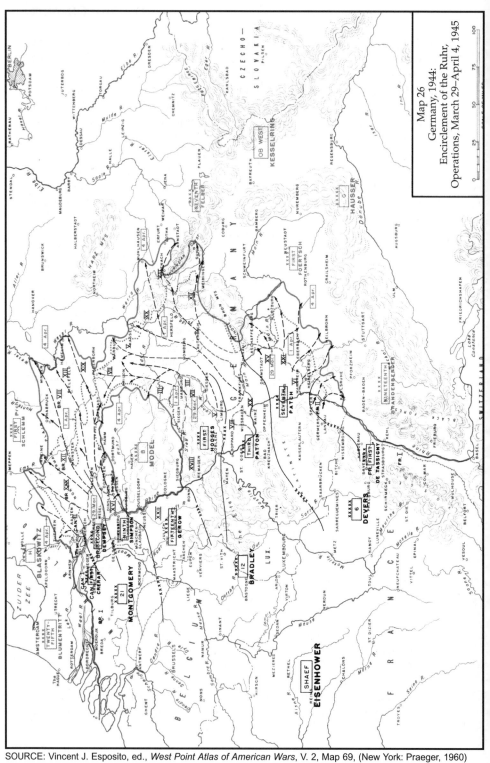

Map 26
Germany, 1944:
Encirclement of the Ruhr,
Operations, March 29–April 4, 1945

SOURCE: Vincent J. Esposito, ed., *West Point Atlas of American Wars*, V. 2, Map 69, (New York: Praeger, 1960)

sent the advance elements to Oberstein in two echelons to maintain communications and operational continuity. By the end of the month, advance headquarters operated from Oberstein, and rear headquarters personnel began moving from Chalons to Luxembourg City.[63]

Moving the flying groups forward proved more difficult. At the Third Army morning briefing on March 26, General Weyland learned that the ground forces had already liberated several airfields in the Frankfurt area. He acted promptly to claim them for XIX TAC. That same day he conferred with his chief of staff for operations, Colonel Ferguson, and his chief engineer, Colonel Smyser, who continued as commander of the IX Engineer Command's 2d Brigade. Weyland had an experienced team facing a familiar challenge.[64] Both the engineers and the operations officers wanted to base the groups in a cluster of airfields, which would maximize command and control and ease the burden of maintenance and supply. On the other hand, in view of the speed of the ground offensive, the engineers decided that they would improve existing German sod and hard-surfaced airfields rather than build new ones. General Weyland willingly accepted the use of British steel-meshed track for surfacing instead of the heavier American pierced steel-plank to accelerate the conversion of German fields.[65]

Indeed, Weyland tried to operate from fields east of the Rhine the very next day (March 27), even though the city of Frankfurt remained unsecured. He realized the futility of his effort when he visited two of the airfields and examined the condition of the runways. The Rhein-Main field south of Frankfurt had been damaged the most, and engineers optimistically estimated that at least two weeks of work would be required before flying groups could move in. General Weyland contented himself with making sure the three Frankfurt sites would go to XIX TAC. On the morning of March 27, after first clarifying the rapidly changing army group boundaries to make sure the airfields remained within Third Army's jurisdiction, he called General Vandenberg to protect his "air interests." The next day, Ninth Air Force approved the three airfields in the vicinity of Frankfurt for use by the XIX TAC, and by month's end, the mobility planners were hard at work preparing for the imminent move.[66]

Defeat of the *Luftwaffe*

Once General Eisenhower decided, on March 28, 1945, to shift the locus of the Allied thrust to General Bradley's 12th Army Group's central position, the forces of Bradley and Montgomery had encircled and overrun the Ruhr. This change meant downgrading the priority assigned to Montgomery's area, much to the dismay of the British field marshal, and it bespoke Eisenhower's commitment to a broad-front offensive all along the line. Third Army forces continued to advance at a breakneck pace, out in front of the other Allied armies: they cleared Gotha, Kassel, and Mulhausen on April 4 and Eisenach and Meiningen on the fifth. Supported by its tactical air force, Third Army's thrust into Germany in early April reminded the XIX TAC historian of the sweep through France the previous August (**Map 26**).[67] Eisenhower's broad-front strategy, however, did not mean an offensive free-for-all. Now, with his armor moving into good tank country on the Thuringian plain, Patton had to rein in his army and hold his forces in position, at least until General Hodges's First Army troops caught up. If, in the north, the British field marshal resented Eisenhower's strategy, in the south, the Third Army commander chafed under restrictions that held him in place (**Map 27**).[68]

During the drive northeast in early April, General Weyland maintained his close air support assignments. For the first eight days of the month, the 367th Fighter Group flew 87, eight-plane missions (including 513 sorties) in support of XII Corps despite bad weather on three of the days. With the exception of two missions on April 6 for VIII Corps troops clearing Eisenach, the 367th Fighter Group flew every mission for General Eddy's troops. Likewise, the 362d Maulers flew every day during the period exclusively for General Walker's XX Corps. The 362d Fighter Group played a key role in blunting the only serious German counterattack of the final weeks at Mulhausen.[69] On April 5, armored elements of XX Corps' 6th Armored Division cleared the town of Mulhausen, 20 miles north of Eisenach, freeing 4,000 British POWs in the process. Then German forces counterattacked two days later, and for two days the fighting raged fiercely.

In the emergency, General Weyland elected to maintain dedicated support for the XX Corps and armed reconnaissance in advance of the forward elements, which meant that the 362d Fighter Group alone dealt with the German counterattacking forces. During a two-day period, it flew 22 close air support missions (including 264 sorties) for the corps, achieving impressive results. On April 7, for example, corps officers on the scene credited the 362d with destroying 69 armored and 173 motorized vehicles. The best measure of its achievement, however, came from Maj. Gen. Robert W. Grow, commander of the 6th Armored Division, who claimed his division received the "finest air cooperation in its history." The Mulhausen counterattack proved to be the only significant effort the *Wehrmacht* mounted against Third Army in April.[70]

Luftwaffe remnants, too, reeled under the constant pressure of the air and ground assault. The XIX TAC set the tone for the month on April 1, when two fighter groups, the 367th and 371st, attacked two German airfields and claimed 39 enemy aircraft destroyed on the ground and another 38 damaged. Next day, two P–51s on a weather reconnaissance mission dispersed a formation they estimated at more than 90 FW 190s and Bf 109s after shooting down

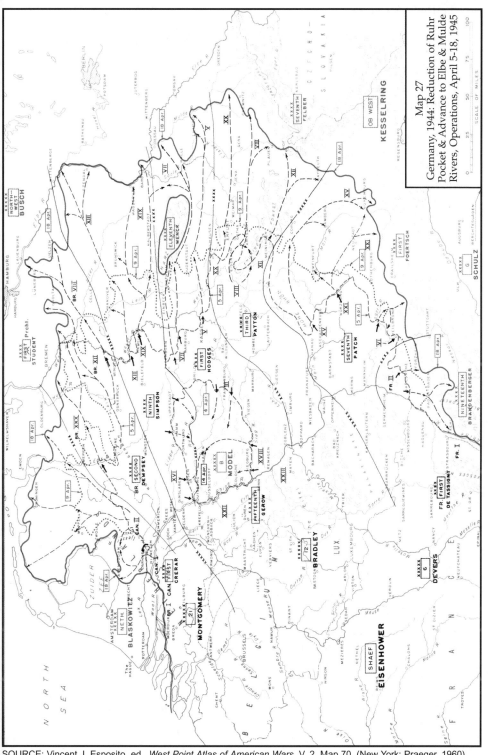

Map 27
Germany, 1944: Reduction of Ruhr
Pocket & Advance to Elbe & Mulde
Rivers, Operations, April 5-18, 1945

SOURCE: Vincent J. Esposito, ed., *West Point Atlas of American Wars*, V. 2, Map 70, (New York: Praeger, 1960)

two with no losses to themselves. Together with other air encounters the next day, XIX TAC fighters claimed a total of 17 *Luftwaffe* planes destroyed and five damaged with a loss of only one P–47.

General Weyland considered the final destruction of the *Luftwaffe* in the Third Army operational area the command's major achievement during April. During the month his fighters engaged the *Luftwaffe* every day but one, while simultaneously maintaining consistent assaults on *Luftwaffe* bases. As the month progressed, the *Luftwaffe* found itself unable to find a safe haven for its aircraft. Third Army units continued to overrun airfields at an alarming rate on the ground, and in the air Weyland's fighter-bombers left no airfield free from attack. Together with the ever-growing shortage of aviation fuel, the *Luftwaffe*, which after the first of April had declined to 400 serviceable flying machines on the western front, often could mount no more than 150 sorties daily.[71]

The command's aggressive pilots sought combat with the *Luftwaffe* in traditional aerial encounters whenever possible. Weyland, however, became unhappy with the growing number of encounters that involved reconnaissance aircraft. Despite an existing policy that directed them to avoid combat, on April 8 reconnaissance pilots claimed ten enemy planes shot down on what the command historian touted as a "banner day." General Weyland thought otherwise, responding with terse messages to the 12th and 15th Tactical Reconnaissance Squadrons directing pilots to avoid unnecessary combat. One reconnaissance pilot even came close to a court-martial for participating in a dog fight. Despite the injunction, however, reconnaissance pilots seemed unable to avoid air combat as *Luftwaffe* pilots sought, in particular, to thwart their missions. Although the high incidence of air combat is borne out by the statistical record for April, these claims should be used with caution. The 10th Photo Group claimed 41 enemy aircraft destroyed, four probably destroyed, and nine more damaged for the confirmed price of five of its own lost.[72]

As part of the Allied air plan in April, General Weyland designated the *Luftwaffe* the command's primary target, with destruction of Germany's transportation system running a close second. While the 367th and 362d Fighter Groups provided close air support to ground units, all fighter groups participated in the effort to destroy the *Luftwaffe*. The 354th, 368th, and 371st Fighter Groups specialized in daily interdiction missions against a desperate, retreating enemy. Although the April figure of 9,325 motorized vehicles destroyed fell short of the 9,869 claimed in March, the figures for locomotives and railroad cars were much higher. The command considered this especially significant because of the cumulative effect on the enemy's rapidly disintegrating transportation system.[73]

While his forces continued to lead the way for Third Army's armored spearheads at the beginning of April 1945, Weyland oversaw the move of XIX TAC aircraft to the Frankfurt bases. On April 1, following a meeting with

Third Army officials on the ground plan, he outlined his movement plan. His command met this timetable for the most part:[74]

Group	Location	Proposed Date	Actual Date
10th P/R	Ober Olm (Y-64)	ASAP	Apr 3
371st	Eschborn (Y-74)	ASAP	Apr 4
354th	Ober Olm	after Apr 15	Apr 9
362d	Rhein-Main (Y-73)	Apr 8	Apr 16
368th	Rhein-Main	Apr 15	Apr 16
367th	Eschborn	Apr 10	Apr 10

Rhein-Main airfield proved to be the only problem. Its concrete runway, severely damaged in a campaign to decimate bases housing turbojet aircraft, required constant maintenance to remain operational. The air commanders soon preferred the sod strips for their efficient drainage and consistent operation, but only after they acquired a layer of square-mesh track.

On April 3, Weyland reviewed logistic requirements for the move with Colonel Thompson, commander of the rear headquarters. They decided to request maximum airlift, which they calculated to be 100 C–47 transports for a ten-day period. That same day Weyland chaired a conference with his communications and operations officers concerning the best locations for the

Winners and losers: P-51 of the Pioneer Mustang Group, the first plane to be serviced east of the Rhine, at a field in the Frankfurt area, in the background, destroyed FW 190 in the foreground.

ground radars. They decided to position the forward director post radars to ensure coverage of the airfields as well as Third Army's exposed left flank. In this regard, they chose to locate the tactical control group and the MEW radar in the vicinity of Hersfeld, over 125 miles northeast of the Frankfurt area. The distance, however, did not prove to be a problem and the command maintained good communications links throughout April.[75]

On April 4, 1945, General Weyland flew to Luxembourg City for another meeting on the status of the airfields. Ninth Air Force officials assured him first priority on movement and stocking the new fields. Yet, General Weyland received only five C–47s for each group for three days. Once again airfield movement required ground transport. The IX Service Command chief arranged for 60 trucks to supplement the command's vehicles. Unfortunately, during the move 27 broke down and replacements could not be found. As the 368th Fighter Group historian recounted, unit personnel used whatever transportation could be requisitioned, including captured German vehicles.[76]

Although this movement occurred with far less difficulty than similar moves the previous summer, supply bottlenecks and front line shortages on April 12 convinced Ninth Air Force to prohibit further movement of aerial units to the Frankfurt airfields until it gave formal approval. By then, howev-

Generals Patton; Spaatz, Commanding General, USSTAF; Lt. Gen. James Doolittle, Commanding General, Eighth Air Force; Lt. Gen. Hoyt S. Vandenberg, commander, Ninth Air Force (behind Doolittle); and Weyland.

er, only the Rhein-Main airfield remained unoccupied.[77] With arrangements for the move to new airfields in hand, General Weyland stayed over in Luxembourg City on the fourth and the next day flew—not to Oberstein but to Frankfurt—to join the initial A party of his advance headquarters. This became the first of three headquarters moves in April. By April 10, General Weyland had his forces positioned to provide Third Army effective support when it altered its line of advance from the northeast to a more easterly direction, and headed for a bridgehead on the Elbe River and a rendezvous with Soviet forces. With his groups now operating from the Frankfurt area, Weyland already had his sights set farther east, on Nuremberg, as the next basing area for his command.[78]

Advance to the Mulde River

Despite the impressive gains for Third Army and the XIX TAC during the first 10 days of April, both commanders chafed under the restraints placed on their offensive. On April 10, Patton's Third Army attacked east on a broad front with all three Corps in line (**Map 27**). In the center, VIII Corps headed toward Plauen and Chemnitz. On the left, XX Corps drove toward Jena and Dresden, while XII Corps on the right flank moved southeast in the direction of Hof and Bayreuth. Taking advantage of good flying weather, fighter-bombers supported the offensive from first to last light, and the armored forces made sweeping gains all along the front. By the thirteenth, Weyland's pilots reported the 4th Armored Division to be on the outskirts of Chemnitz, while the 6th Armored approached Altenburg and the 11th neared Bayreuth.

On April 11, 1945, Generals Eisenhower and Bradley arrived at Third Army headquarters to view captured gold reserves and visit Ohrdruf, the first concentration camp overrun by Patton's troops. Conditions at the camp shocked and disgusted Weyland and the army officers. A XIX TAC officer declared afterward that the obvious evidence of Nazi atrocities gave the airmen added incentive to redouble their efforts. At a meeting the following day Eisenhower explained to a bewildered Patton that the Third Army drive would not continue to Berlin. Berlin, Eisenhower observed, had no tactical or strategic value, and its capture would burden American troops with responsibility to care for overwhelming numbers of people. Patton objected, but he would obey. Later that evening he heard a radio broadcast that reported President Franklin Roosevelt's death. At the morning briefing on April 13, Patton told his staff that the SHAEF commander had ordered Third Army to change course and move south after securing its present objectives.[79]

The halt line described by General Eisenhower extended generally along the Mulde River from Leipzig to Chemnitz (**Map 27**). This had been the boundary line established for reconnaissance flights on April 10 by SHAEF at the start of the eastward drive. On that day, Ninth Air Force told General Weyland that tactical air would be restricted to a line running along the Mulde River from Leipzig through Chemnitz to Prague, because of "possible conflict with Russian air." Weyland, too, objected. His tactical reconnaissance aircraft had been patrolling east of the front lines every day in early April to observe possible German moves to reinforce their troops with forces drawn from the eastern front. He called General Vandenberg immediately to recommend that the area be extended eastward to the Torgau-Dresden-Prague axis, which he considered absolutely essential for reconnaissance. In this instance, the XIX TAC commander was successful in his quest.[80]

Operationally, good weather on the first three days of the drive east found the first fighter-bombers taking off into darkness before the last night fighter had landed. Continuing the same basic air support assignment pattern, the 371st and 362d Fighter Groups provided the majority of column cover missions for the armored forces, while the three remaining groups concentrated on interdiction targets. On April 10, the command claimed 1,075 railroad cars and 455 motor vehicles destroyed, and figures for the next two days were nearly as impressive. Even three days of restricted weather, from April 13–15, failed to halt the wholesale destruction of German transportation facilities and equipment.

The aerial assault also continued against the *Luftwaffe*. During the three-day period from April 15–17, the command targeted 18 remaining airfields in central Germany and Czechoslovakia and broke the back of the remaining *Luftwaffe*. The best results occurred on April 16, when the 367th and 368th Fighter Groups claimed 107, setting a new command record with 84 enemy aircraft destroyed and 74 damaged on the ground. The *Luftwaffe* also lost an estimated 21 that were destroyed in air combat, mostly to the 354th Pioneer Mustangs. April 16 was a big day against the *Luftwaffe* all along the front as Allied claims totaled 50 destroyed and 9 damaged in air combat and 1,000 destroyed and 581 damaged on the ground. The command also had one of its best missions involving coordination between fighter and reconnaissance aircraft. On April 16, a reconnaissance pilot led P–47s from the 371st Fighter Group to eight different targets: six trains and two marshaling yards.[81]

By mid-April, fighter-bombers flying close air support were normally armed only with .50-caliber ammunition for strafing. Although the low stocks of 500-lb. general-purpose bombs doubtless contributed to this choice, the shortage of bombs in April proved less severe than it did in March. In any case, just half of the fighter-bombers on close support missions carried one 500-lb. bomb, while aircraft flying armed reconnaissance received two 260-lb. fragmentation bombs. The central problem became ensuring that sufficient .50-caliber armor-piercing incendiary ammunition remain available. Once again emergency resupply, this time by rail to Frankfurt, alleviated the potential shortfall.[82]

By April 16, 1945, with his last two fighter-bomber groups consisting of 90 aircraft in place at Frankfurt's Rhein-Main airfield, General Weyland began preparations to secure airfield sites in the vicinity of Nuremberg. He asked General Patton, who left for a meeting at SHAEF that day, to protect "our interest" in the Nuremberg airfields. In what now was routine procedure, he met with key staff members and his group commanders to work out the details of the next move as well as the next ground offensive. On April 17, Weyland attended an important conference at Third Army headquarters. He and Patton discussed the new army–air plan that called for an attack south in the direction of the so-called German National Redoubt, with the objective of isolating German resistance and linking up with Soviet forces advancing from Vienna, Austria (**Map 28**).[83]

The new axis of attack required conference attendees to discuss boundaries and force realignments. Third Army relinquished VIII Corps to First Army; in return it received III Corps, commanded by the aggressive Maj. Gen. James A. Van Fleet. This redeployment also involved the air command, because a portion of the command's 39 tactical air liaison officers needed to be shifted, as well. Moreover, General Weyland requested Ninth Air Force send him two additional fighter-bomber groups and another tactical reconnaissance squadron, to be based closer to the expected route of advance on Nuremberg. Although the XIX TAC commander received the units he requested, the fighter groups did not arrive until near the end of the campaign, after General Quesada could be confident he no longer needed them in the north. Their late acquisition had little impact on XIX TAC operations. The 162d Tactical Reconnaissance Squadron, on the other hand, arrived from XII TAC on April 24, and helped considerably in meeting reconnaissance requirements during the drive down the Danube valley (**Map 28**).

Down the Danube Valley to Austria

The last phase of the XIX TAC's operations against an all but defeated enemy involved effective, if routine, cover for the fast-moving ground forces and superb coordination between reconnaissance and fighter-bomber aircraft. At last, on April 17, Third Army received top priority from SHAEF for its offensive. While its newly acquired III Corps regrouped southeast of Nuremberg, XII and XX Corps, positioned between Hof and Nuremberg, jumped off toward the southeast on April 19 (**Map 28**). Aided by good air cover, the 11th Armored Division led the dash down the Naab River Valley toward Regensburg, 40 miles to the southeast. In three days' time, XII Corps, now commanded by Maj. Gen. S. Leroy Irwin, was across the Czech border

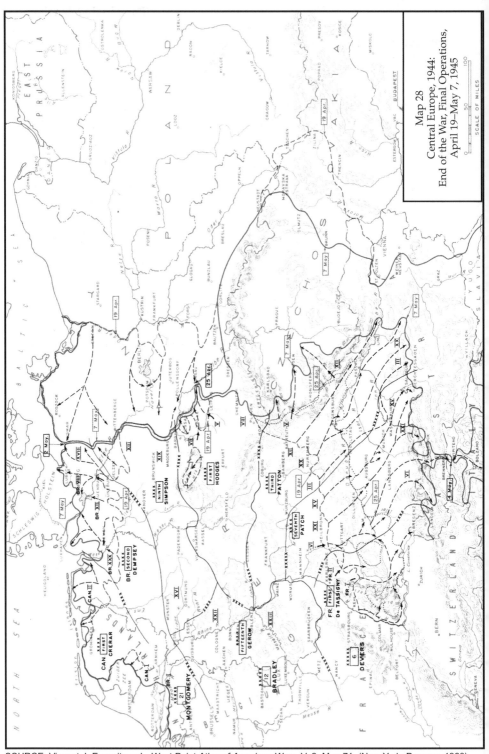

Map 28
Central Europe, 1944:
End of the War, Final Operations,
April 19–May 7, 1945

SOURCE: Vincent J. Esposito, ed., *West Point Atlas of American Wars*, V. 2, Map 71, (New York: Praeger, 1960)

and had captured Asch. The XII Corps received support throughout this drive from its own 362d Fighter Group, while on its right, the 367th Fighter Group covered XX Corps' advance to the Danube at Regensburg. Patton's offensive proceeded rapidly against a disorganized and dispirited enemy, by now able to do little more than mount roadblocks and ambush rear echelons.[84] At the same time, General Weyland's fighter-bombers continued their merciless assault on German transport and especially, airfields. They bombed seven airfields on April 19 and ten the next day—their offering on Hitler's 56th birthday. Afterward the command's intelligence section estimated that the Allies had the *Luftwaffe* remnants confined largely to the Regensburg, Munich, and Prague areas, which now became key targets.[85]

On April 21, Patton announced that the following day the Third Army would begin a new phase of the offensive, with all three corps attacking southeast and south. Given the state of enemy defenses, he was unconcerned that only two armored divisions would lead the advance. Third Army's command post would move to Erlangen on April 22, to be closer to the action.[86] At the same briefing General Weyland explained his air plan to support the ground offensive, calling for armored column cover and protection of XII Corps' exposed left flank in Czechoslovakia. As it did in the watch on the Loire during the Battle of France, the command's 10th Reconnaissance Group provided the flank-cover mission. To handle the wide front and fluid situation, the group revised the key system it had introduced the previous month. Now, smooth coordination between reconnaissance aircraft, fighter-bombers, and air liaison officers was routine. In effect, the improved flexibility of the reconnaissance program enabled the 10th to provide rapid and accurate coverage 50 miles deep within Czechoslovakia along a 120-mile front.[87]

The 10th Reconnaissance Group's mission became easier when it relocated to Fuerth, near Nuremberg. Officially, the XIX TAC declared it operational at the new base on April 28, but its tactical reconnaissance flight echelons had begun flying with the newly arrived 162d Tactical Reconnaissance Squadron four days earlier. From Fuerth, reconnaissance aircraft could fly 50 rather than 36 missions daily nearly 100 miles closer to the front lines. In addition, during the drive down the Danube valley, the 31st Photo Squadron's F–5s (P–38s) using a new nose-mounted oblique camera mapped all of the Bavarian Redoubt region in addition to filling normal pinpoint requests and providing river reconnaissance missions.[88]

Only once did a possible threat emerge on Third Army's left flank, and reconnaissance pilots reacted quickly. At 8:00 a.m. on April 29, while rain and sleet limited most operations, they spotted and radioed the position of a convoy estimated at 1,000 vehicles and 30 tanks located approximately 40 miles southwest of Prague. At the Third Army briefing that morning, General Weyland declared this convoy to be the top fighter-bomber priority and promised to "attack with all forces as long as weather permits." Three groups answered the call and flew more than 200 sorties in the Pilsen area against the convoy, the remnants of which sought cover, and against other targets in the region. At the end of the day, they claimed nearly 500 vehicles destroyed and reported that no more moving vehicles could be found. General Weyland recorded cryptically, "threat to Army flank considered wiped-out."[89] The very next day, in an underground Berlin bunker, with Red Army artillery shells raining down on the city in a fitting *Goetterdaemmerung*, Reich's Chancellor Adolf Hitler put the barrel of a pistol in his mouth and pulled the trigger. Germany's thousand-year Third Reich had ended in little more than one one hundredth of the allotted time promised by its demented Führer.

By the end of April, German opposition was essentially nonexistent. It soon became apparent that the National Redoubt was no more than emotional propaganda. Now Third Army numbered 540,000 men—its largest force in the European campaign—and continued to move south at will. Its forces drove across the Danube and Isar rivers on April 30. Ninety miles from Third Army's front lines XIX TAC reconnaissance pilots now reported Russian columns moving in their direction from Vienna (**Map 28**). The mobile offensive continued into May, while the XIX TAC put the destructive finishing touches on the German transport system in its zone of operations. Between April 18–30, the command claimed as destroyed or damaged a total of 3,308 motorized vehicles, 633 locomotives, and 3,730 railroad cars. Most of the attacks occurred along the Straubing-Linz and Pilsen-Prague armed reconnaissance routes, where pilots routinely reported good scores against little opposition.

The *Luftwaffe* was impotent, unable to mount more than 150–200 sorties daily throughout the entire European theater. Most occurred in Third Army's southern area as the other Allied armies gradually ended offensive operations. The command's best results occurred on April 25 and 26. On the twenty-fifth, the 371st Fighter Group attacked several remaining German-controlled airdromes clogged with aircraft. When the fighter-bombers finished, command claims totaled 55 aircraft destroyed on the ground and 65 more damaged. The next day the *Luftwaffe* mounted its last significant attack in the west against Third Army forces. Pilots of XIX TAC reported they lost 18 aircraft in air combat and an additional 9 damaged, at a cost of 52 German aircraft claimed destroyed on the ground and a further 39 damaged. Ground claims for the entire Allied front were only 61 destroyed and 61 damaged. By this time, surviving *Luftwaffe* pilots seemed less intent on combat than on flying their planes to American bases in the west to escape the approaching Russians. In April, XIX TAC as a whole claimed 214 enemy aircraft vanquished in air combat, 722 destroyed on the ground, and 767 more probably damaged, against 59 losses of their own, for a total of 1,703 enemy aircraft destroyed or damaged—a number eight times greater than the March figure, previously the command's highest.[90]

Yet the command bled in the process. On April 25, for example, XIX TAC lost 8 aircraft, and during Third Army's drive south, between April 18–31, its losses numbered 21 aircraft. Why so high a loss rate flying against a foe that was all but beaten? The command attributed this to an increasing concentration of flak batteries at the few remaining German airfields. The record does reflect more aircraft lost on airfield target missions as the enemy moved to reinforce its existing defenses. For the month, at least 16 XIX TAC losses can be directly associated with attacks on airfields. On the other hand, many occurred during armed reconnaissance missions against road and rail transportation targets. In such situations, it seems likely that light flak weapons became a part of the retreating convoys and, together with the traditional menace of flak rail cars, continued to pose a significant threat to the fighter-bombers. Indeed, the command's loss total for April reached 59, only 2 fewer than the previous month's total.

By late April, General Weyland's groups were operating 200 miles from their Frankfurt bases and once again facing the challenge of providing sufficient support in the target areas. Ninth Air Force solved part of the problem by assigning to Weyland's command an additional group. The 405th Fighter Group rejoined the command on April 28 and flew armed reconnaissance missions from its base at Kitzingen. A second group, the 48th Fighter Group, joined on May 1. Like the 405th, it operated from the Nuremberg area, closer to the front lines. The command continued its preference for using auxiliary fuel tanks on long missions rather than resorting to disruptive staging operations at the Nuremberg bases.

Despite the additional support, Weyland planned to bring his fighter groups forward to the Nuremberg area as quickly as possible. His advance headquarters had followed Third Army's forward command post from Hersfeld to Erlangen, 12 miles north of Nuremberg, on April 24. Three days earlier, Weyland and his operations chief, Colonel Ferguson, had visited eight airfields in the vicinity of Nuremberg to decide on suitable sites. During the remainder of April, the XIX TAC followed the same planning that had worked so well in the Frankfurt move. With the exception of the 10th Photo Reconnaissance Group, however, the command could not schedule a move of the Frankfurt-area fighter groups until early May. With the war clearly at an end, one can ask why the air commander remained intent on deploying forward once again when he could provide sufficient support in spite of the long flying distance? The available evidence suggests that SHAEF and Ninth Air Force looked ahead to securing the best deployment for a postwar occupational air force, and decided in favor of American bases located farther east

Besides overseeing operations and redeployment of his command, as the senior airman General Weyland interviewed all captured high-ranking *Luftwaffe* officers and Allied airmen who had reached Third Army lines after escaping from POW camps. Although the German officers provided interesting impressions of the effectiveness of Allied air power, they did not offer intelligence of value for current operations. The American airmen proved different. Weyland viewed his discussions with former POWs as important both for the morale of the individuals concerned and for the information they provided on current POW locations. Many Allied prisoners had been moved farther east, and the air commander made it a point to have his tactical reconnaissance crews track down every rumor. He wanted all his pilots to be on the lookout for POW camps. He especially enjoyed sending fighters to buzz known locations, such as the Moosburg camp located near Munich. On April 18, the command had sent a P–38 escorted by P–51s from the 354th Fighter Group on a photo mission of the camp and it became a primary objective for the advancing ground forces. On April 28, Weyland dispatched four P–51s purposely to perform slow rolls over the camp, which Third Army liberated the following day. This camp contained some 27,000 American airmen, including many XIX TAC pilots.[91]

The end of April found both Patton and Weyland in euphoric moods— Patton because of Third Army's record-setting campaign, and Weyland because of the smooth functioning of the air-ground team. On only one occasion in the final stages of the conflict did the two commanders differ over the use of air power. On April 28, Patton asked his air commander to cut major bridges over the Danube at Passau to help isolate enemy forces and prevent possible reinforcements from crossing. General Weyland objected to a mission he considered impractical for fighter-bombers. In his opinion the four large bridges and the adverse terrain made them too difficult to destroy. General Patton deferred to his air commander, who, in turn, promised to have his reconnaissance pilots closely monitor the Passau area for potential trouble.[92]

The personal and professional relationship between these two commanders remained excellent. As the campaign neared completion, General Patton pondered the future with Weyland and liked nothing better than to praise the XIX TAC–Third Army team before distinguished visitors. On April 28, for instance, AAF Generals Spaatz, Doolittle, and Vandenberg visited Patton's headquarters and "received [the] full Third Army treatment." This included not only a review of the team's battlefield prowess, but also a briefing on the importance of keeping the air-ground team together for transfer to the China-Burma-India theater once the Germans surrendered.[93] Although General Patton often spoke to his air commander about taking on the Japanese, General Weyland recalled that, in a moment of candor, Patton confided privately, both he and General MacArthur were showmen, and the Far East had room for only one.[94]

Victory

The final eight days of the European war proved to be little more than a victory parade for both air and ground forces. After Hitler's suicide on April 30, 1945, and despite his orders to German commanders to continue the war, Nazi forces simply were in no position to resist much longer. The month of May opened with Third Army units driving rapidly southeast through Austria and east toward Prague, Czechoslovakia. On May 4, when other Allied armies stood down, Patton's forces accepted the surrender of the entire 11th Panzer Division and at their commander's direction continued pressing southeast along a front that now extended more than 290 miles. White flags announcing the surrender of German forces appeared on every hand, every day. On May 8, V–E Day, ground operations ended with Third Army spearheads seven miles from Prague and 30 miles southeast of Hitler's birthplace, Linz, Austria, where appropriately, they met the Soviet Third Ukranian Army.

For XIX TAC the final days in May proved anticlimactic. Bad weather curtailed flying. On May 2 the 386th Thunder Bums got only 16 sorties near Straubing while all sorties had to be canceled on May 5 and 6. For the remaining five days the command averaged well below 200 sorties per day. Moreover, few enemy armored vehicles and gun positions remained to attack and most missions involved strikes against routine targets such as motor transport and marshaling yards. At least the reconnaissance pilots could cover activity in the Brenner Pass, monitor the Russian advance, and search for POW camps.

On May 4, the command's fighter-bombers responded to reconnaissance reports of several thousand enemy vehicles heading eastward, away from the battle area near Linz in northern Austria. Subsequent attacks resulted in claims of 425 motorized transport and 42 horse-drawn vehicles destroyed or damaged. Action continued even after the surrender document was signed on May 8. In separate dogfights over Regensburg and near Pilsen that day, tactical reconnaissance pilots reported downing five enemy aircraft in what amounted to the last aerial combat of the war.

During the final week of the war, General Weyland continued to supervise the movement of his groups from the advance headquarters at Erlangen to the Nuremberg area. Although General Patton's command post had moved to Regensburg, Weyland remained at Erlangen and sent Colonel Browne's X-Ray detachment instead. The XIX TAC commander considered the course ahead too uncertain to warrant moving the advance headquarters again. On May 8, General Weyland flew to Wiesbaden for a conference among senior airmen to discuss redeployment, disarmament, and the occupational air force. At this meeting, he learned that he would assume command of the Ninth Air Force when General Vandenberg left for Washington later in the month.[95] The next day, May 9, he joined General Patton in signing victory messages to the officers and men. Each recounted the exploits of the Third Army–XIX TAC team. Patton complimented the airmen, "our comrades…by whose side or under whose wings we have had the honor to fight." General Weyland paid tribute to the "aggressiveness of our great comrade-at-arms." Each commander gave special thanks to the men of his command. If Patton's words were the more inspiring, the air commander's were equally appropriate. Weyland concluded with an expression of appreciation to his airmen for "all that each of you has done to make possible this victory. Your prowess and devotion are a credit to our country—and there is no higher praise."[96]

Throughout the final offensive, Weyland's aerial forces demonstrated unusual ingenuity and flexibility in support of Third Army's record-setting offensive. Although Weyland would acknowledge official AAF doctrine that decreed priorities, his priorities met Patton's needs of the day. With air superiority in hand, interdiction and close air support requirements clearly prevailed at this stage of the war. The air plan worked. During the final offensive, Weyland and his airmen introduced four-plane flights after the Siegfried Line breakthrough, and in March they introduced the reconnaissance key system, examples of the innovation that continued to characterize air-ground operations. Most importantly, General Weyland willingly stretched doctrinal pronouncements in terms of command and control. When the air-ground team faced more fluid conditions after the Rhine crossing, air controllers and their army counterparts devised new means to decentralize control of armed reconnaissance and close air support missions in the field.

The final offensive of mobile armored warfare demanded increasingly decentralized aerial operations, unlike static positional warfare which favored more centralized command and control of air assets. It also underscored the fundamental importance of air superiority to success in military operations of this nature. The sheer size of the Allied air forces allowed Weyland to take liberties with air force doctrine to support Patton's ground forces better, liberties that included assigning specific fighter groups to cover specific army units. Indeed, the decentralized close air support orchestrated by the XIX TAC in the spring of 1945 went far toward providing Third Army corps and divisions with their own air arm. That kind of close air support far exceeded the prescriptions laid down by the aerial authors of FM 100–20 (1943).

Weyland's new procedures provided ground commanders with a very rapid response from the air arm. Weyland unquestionably considered the benefits in improved air-ground operations well worth the doctrinal compromise. Moreover, by this stage of the war he could rely on the experience, trust, and confidence of the air-ground team from the leaders at the top to the lowest echelons of command. As did most other commanders of tactical air forces in the Second World War, General Weyland remained ever the pragmatist. The XIX TAC's performance in the final offensive demonstrated the soundness of his approach to providing air power for Patton's Army.

Chapter Seven

An After Action Assessment

At the close of hostilities in Europe, General Weyland could look back on the preceding nine months and eight days with great satisfaction. In the euphoria of victory, he told his officers and men that the XIX TAC–Third Army team had brought "air-ground cooperation to new heights of combat efficiency and beaten the enemy at every turn."[1] The air commander was right. Through four challenging campaigns, Weyland's tactical air forces demonstrated the soundness of their organization and operations, as well as their ability to minimize the limitations of air power.

During the first campaign in France, the command proved tactical air forces both operationally mobile and capable of employing new and effective tactics such as responsive cover to armored forces. At the same time, the pace of the ground advance and competing priorities prompted Weyland to conduct extremely decentralized operations on widely separated fronts. Attacking every challenge, his forces found it difficult to concentrate with sufficient force against the enemy in eastern France because of commitments 300 miles away in Brittany, where a large fighter-bomber force confronted heavily fortified port facilities, targets long considered unsuitable for fighter-bombers in close air support operations.

The battle in France provided Third Army and the XIX TAC the opportunity to mold a first class fighting team. After besting the enemy, the air-ground team entered the inhospitable region of Lorraine to confront a very different situation. Here, static warfare characterized by stiff defenses, bad weather, and serious materiel shortages hobbled tactical air power's key advantage: the ability to swiftly concentrate forces against targets. Although proximity to the front eliminated many problems presented earlier in France, Weyland's forces, under conditions similar to those of World War I, proved unable to blast a path for Patton's army through the Siegfried Line. If Weyland appeared overly optimistic about the capabilities of his air arm at the outset of the Lorraine Campaign, he soon realized that his light tactical aerial force required help from medium and heavy bombers to crack the Siegfried Line.

Inexorably, the challenge of operating in Lorraine compelled closer joint planning between air and ground force officers to use their limited resources to maximum advantage. This proved to be one of the central developments in air-ground cooperation. Responding to Lorraine's challenges, Weyland and his

P–47s with occupation stripes during the postwar period

fellow officers adopted a flexible approach in solving problems associated with the three tactical mission elements—air superiority, interdiction, and close air support—prescribed by AAF doctrine. Weyland, however, neither abandoned doctrine nor operated with absolute control of his forces outside the framework of established Army structure. His treatment of doctrine as a guide rather than as dogma merits praise. Flexibility rather than rigid priorities became the major ingredient of successful tactical air operations in Lorraine and would come to characterize the entire campaign in Northwest Europe.

In the Ardennes Campaign, the third major operation for the XIX TAC, tactical air power came closest to affecting enemy movement by itself. Assigned a counterattack role, General Weyland showed that, with sufficient forces, tactical air power could rapidly concentrate to first blunt and then help repel a powerful enemy assault. His forces achieved this in spite of weather delays, a small night fighter force, and heavy enemy flak defenses. At the same time, Ninth Air Force units slowly, but effectively, isolated the Ardennes battlefield from the German supply base.

The final offensive, which carried the Third Army–XIX TAC team through the Siegfried Line and into Germany, combined elements from earlier mobile and static operations. Here, Weyland's experienced forces continued to improve procedures for better reconnaissance and air-ground coordination, relying more extensively on decentralized command and control arrangements. Strongly supported by ground logistics elements, XIX TAC pilots showed that air power had become an effective and important ingredient in propelling and maintaining the Third Army's offensive momentum.

Considering XIX TAC's achievements in four major campaigns, it remains difficult to measure the effectiveness of tactical air power with precision. Postwar evaluators concluded that air power successfully achieved and maintained general air superiority and isolated the battlefield effectively from enemy aircraft, but without sufficient night fighters, it was somewhat less effective if measured in terms of preventing resupply. They also declared—perhaps over enthusiastically—that close air support operations were "individually and collectively, both deadly and decisive in their effectiveness."[2]

Beyond these general assertions, the basic question remains one of determining how to accurately judge the contribution of tactical air power in specific campaigns or battles. In the Ardennes, for example, air power certainly played a key if not decisive role in blunting the German drive in the Bulge area and later in isolating the battlefield through intensive interdiction operations. It is also possible to point to air power's support in specific bridgehead operations, such as XX Corps' desperate fight to hold its Saarlautern bridgehead in the Lorraine Campaign. During mobile operations, tactical air power also helped generate momentum and permit greater tactical mobility. Yet a more precise attempt to measure performance in these operations invariably raises the problem of using statistical or equivocal evidence and argument.

As with other commands in the European theater, XIX TAC had a statistical control section that kept a running account of aircrew and aircraft performance. Although its records provide useful data about the command's operations, when applied to performance or effectiveness such data must be interpreted with caution. Further obscuring the issue, little or no distinction is drawn between operational effectiveness and operational efficiency. Efficiency can be measured precisely in terms of sortie rates, accident statistics, quantity of bombs dropped, and other operational categories. Efficient operations, however, may not necessarily be effective operations. Effectiveness should be evaluated from the standpoint of air power's impact on the enemy, which is usually subjective and unquantifiable, thus beyond the pale of assured statistical analysis.

Did the XIX TAC become more efficient over the course of the campaign? One might assume so, but the record is unclear. For example, during the three months from February–April 1945, the command averaged an aircraft abort rate of 2.8 percent of all aircraft dispatched. Although this represented the lowest figure for any three-month period, much of the difference resulted from the relatively few flight cancellations in the spring because of improving weather. On the other hand, a comparison of August 1944 and March 1945, the two months of mobile warfare with the most sorties flown, shows the command with a one-third lower aircraft abort rate in March. In this case, the command cited mechanical problems nearly 70 percent more often in August, only 60 days after D-Day, than it did in March 1945. Although improved logistics and aircraft maintenance practices likely made the command more efficient by March, this cannot be determined from command maintenance reports or available statistical evidence.[3]

Not surprisingly, the issue of aircraft accidents also turns on weather conditions. During March and April 1945, the command averaged the low figure of one operational accident per 100 flying hours. While the two-month average suggests efficient operations, the low number represents the result of better flying weather in the spring, not the culmination of a steady trend. In fact, during comparably good weather in August and September 1944, the statistics show a lower accident rate. As expected, the accident rate remained consistently higher during the winter months.

Similarly, statistics for aircraft losses point to February, March, and April 1945, as the XIX TAC's best months. Their average of 5.2 aircraft lost per 1,000 sorties was significantly lower than comparable figures for the previous summer. Weather proved much less of a factor in this instance. Although the winter months show a higher loss per sortie ratio, the low figure also reflects the more intense flying associated with the Ardennes Operation. Cautiously, one might conclude that pilots proved themselves more efficient under mobile warfare conditions in the spring of 1945, than they did in similar circumstances the previous summer. Nevertheless, comparisons are difficult given the many variables, and the statistical evidence can only be suggestive.

Measuring operational effectiveness in terms of target destruction is much more challenging because this data is difficult to correlate with specific enemy action, especially when the data itself is not always verifiable. Indeed, most of what the command termed battle or bomb damage assessment information came from pilot reports that normally could not be substantiated. Even the clearest examples are difficult to interpret with precision. In March 1945, for example, XIX TAC claimed 267 enemy planes destroyed which, up to that point, had been exceeded only by the August 1944 figure of 293. Then, in April 1945, the command's claims skyrocketed to 1,703! Likewise, in April it reached an all-time high of 24,634 ground targets claimed as destroyed, damaged, or probably destroyed. What do the figures mean? Even though the numbers cannot be confirmed, they do not seem wholly unrealistic in view of the enemy's condition late in the spring. However, it remains difficult, if not impossible, to determine the specific impact of these losses on the German forces. They demonstrate only that command pilots operated efficiently and attacked an all-but-defeated enemy at will.

General Weyland confronted the issue of pilot reporting accuracy early in the campaign, but it remained a controversial subject throughout the nine months of operations. From his standpoint, critics questioned the integrity of his pilots on the basis of unreasonable reporting expectations. The issue became a subject of major concern throughout Ninth Air Force in the winter of 1945. In early February, SHAEF planners expressed concern about the accuracy of fighter-bomber claims of armored vehicles destroyed during the Ardennes Campaign. Understandably, the planners found it difficult to design operations against an enemy whose strength in armor either had been eliminated or could not be verified. Despite the fact that General Vandenberg responded immediately by affirming the "almost impossible task of obtaining accurate confirmation of our claims by actual count in captured or overrun territory," he asked his tactical air commanders to report on their approach to the problem.[4]

In his response, General Weyland reviewed current reporting directives and the measures his pilots and intelligence officers took to encourage the greatest possible accuracy. In fact, he argued, his command's emphasis on objective reporting resulted not only in the most accurate claims possible in light of "inherent difficulties," but in conservative figures as well. For example, because of the earlier practice of claiming half-tracks along with armored vehicles, he directed his pilots to claim "no results observed" when they bombed concealed armor concentrations in woods, even when they observed smoke rising from the target area afterward.[5]

Weyland identified the inherent difficulties of all claims reporting. Investigation on the ground, he reminded SHAEF, had been unable to distinguish between armor destroyed by air or ground action or by enemy demolition. Moreover, the enemy worked an impressive salvage system that would distort claims. Finally, information gleaned from POWs seldom proved credible. Weyland argued that:

> [t]he credibility of P/W [prisoner of war] statements is doubtful and, although a thorough study has been made of all available P/W reports of the effect of air action on tanks and armored vehicles so many discrepancies have existed that again neither conclusive proof nor disproof of claims has been forthcoming.[6]

Weyland concluded by referring to ground forces that "take credit for...vehicles that were actually knocked out by air attack." In this instance, he told his staff that General Patton "stated informally that as 3rd [*sic*] Army advances, they also claim the tanks and vehicles destroyed by [fighter-bombers]." If this had no bearing on the veracity of air claims, he said, it nevertheless made it difficult for SHAEF planners to maintain accurate estimates for enemy armored forces. In the end, authorities must accept the integrity of the claims or conclude that his pilots were "deliberately falsifying" them. For Weyland, the latter was unthinkable.[7]

General Quesada agreed. His command analyzed various factors that would influence an accounting, including smoke and fire in the target area, aircraft performance, and the diversity of weapons used. It determined that pilot claims were "not excessive, but if anything...underestimates of the actual damage inflicted." Significantly, Quesada's report argued that the major problem involved the reporting system itself, which required accurate numbers under all circumstances. The IX TAC recommended that the planners forego their insistence on numbers and be willing to accept estimates and agree to a pilot confidence factor for accuracy. This did not happen.[8] The problem of aircrew reporting accuracy serves as a useful reminder about the tyranny of numbers. The predilection for specific numbers as the standard for combat effectiveness proved as fallible in the Second World War as it did a generation later in the Vietnam conflict. Even then, bomb strike cameras did not end the difficulty of verifying aircrew claims.

In the final analysis, ground forces are often the best judge of tactical air power's effectiveness. In response to an AAF Evaluation Board questionnaire, army officers agreed that fighter-bombers consistently assisted ground operations, even when bad weather forced them to fly interdiction missions beyond the army's front line positions.[9] General Walker, XX Corps commander, wrote General Weyland in mid-April 1945, that "without your efficient and well planned operations we would have suffered far greater casualties and taken a much longer time to reach our objectives."[10] He did not need statistical evidence for his conclusion; with the assistance of General Weyland's aircraft he was there and had seen his ground forces achieve their objectives.

If it is fair to conclude that tactical air power proved effective in Northwest Europe, the question of its decisiveness remains to be considered. Might air power have achieved more decisive results if it had been employed differently in that locale? General Quesada, for one, thought that a massive, long-range fighter-bomber assault on key strategic targets in the German homeland during the winter of 1944–1945 would have brought Germany to her knees. Others have suggested more conventional proposals, such as more efforts devoted to interdiction or close air support.[11]

The question of air power's decisiveness relates to the army's effectiveness. One authority has argued that military leaders created an "army of mobility at the expense of power." Materiel superiority, for example, did not translate into heavy firepower and better equipment to confront the *Wehrmacht's* lumbering Tiger tanks and 88-mm flak/antitank guns. Paradoxically, while leaders committed the U.S. Army in Northwest Europe to "a power-drive strategy of head-on assault," they did not use its mobility to create offensive concentrations rapidly, preferring instead the broad-front approach in its advance on Germany. Consequently, the war may have been prolonged.[12]

Might tactical air power have been used differently and concentrated at crucial points like the Seine and Rhine rivers to prevent sizeable German forces from escaping? General Weyland certainly did not oppose the idea. After all, doctrine prescribed this application and he relished the opportunity to show off air power's ability to concentrate forces to secure an objective. At the same time, his command could seldom expect decisive aerial results in major battles because of competing air priorities and various operational restrictions, such as foul weather. Tactical air power, like air power in general, was first and last a supporting or, as air leaders increasingly referred to during the last years of the war, a cooperating arm of the airground team.

There is every indication that the U.S. Army relied on tactical air power to provide extra firepower and to shield ground forces. General Bradley said as much in his postwar report on air power. In a letter to General Spaatz, he asserted:

> I know that I do not need to tell you the tremendous importance which I have attached to tactical air co-operation for my armies. In this campaign, the recurring process of massing our divisions, forcing a breakthru [sic], and the subsequent exploitation of our mobility to encircle and defeat the enemy demanded almost complete air superiority to overcome our sensitiveness in supply, reserves, and the necessity for full use of road and rail communications.[13]

He might also have added that the U.S. Army had been structured in this way precisely to allow for tactical air power's additional firepower. Similarly, air superiority may have produced an overdependence by the army on air power at the expense of ground action. During the North African Campaign, General Eisenhower warned against the negative effects of an air umbrella on ground forces. Although air leaders pointed out that tactical air forces represented a limited asset, the division commander, blessed with close air support on most good-weather days, might not agree. As the campaign progressed, it is fair to question whether the ground forces depended on unnatural levels of air superiority. A few years later, more limited wars in Korea and Vietnam would also be characterized by Allied air superiority—and perhaps an overreliance on air power as a substitute for ground firepower.

General Patton, hailed as a proponent of mobile rather than positional warfare, emerged in World War II as the Allied commander most likely to produce swift, decisive military results. The Ardennes Operation to relieve Bastogne represents one demonstration. Yet, for the most part, until late in the war the Third Army moved on a secondary front in the theater. It is tempting to speculate whether the XIX TAC–Third Army team, if given higher priority in forces and supplies, might have carried out the concentrated offensive and bold exploitation of position as urged by Patton, with a resultant shortening of the European war. In any event, tactical air power was, as always, intimately connected with the Army's objectives and plan of advance. Tactical air forces appeared, in that sense, only as capable as their ground counterparts.

The success of tactical air power well-employed in the European campaign was made possible by the timely convergence of four important developments: (1) the maturation of tactical aviation doctrine; (2) effective organization and procedures; (3) a technical revolution in equipment, and above all; (4) the presence of pragmatic men of goodwill who made the system work. General Weyland typified the practical leader who came to dominate tactical air operations in the European theater. At no time in his day-to-day operations during the campaign in Europe did Weyland adhere formally to FM 100–20 or any other War Department declaration regarding tactical air power doctrine. This did not mean that the XIX TAC commander ignored aerial mission priorities. Rather, he relied on a practical approach to the employment of tactical air power and a solid relationship with army officers. Using doctrine as a loose guide and not an inflexible dogma, Weyland addressed each situation in terms of its demands. A pragmatist by nature, he would not need to wave an AAF flag or FM 100–20. Mutual trust, respect, and a close relationship with General Patton and other Third Army leaders meant that Weyland never had to resort to formal doctrinal pronouncements to support his position on questions of employing tactical air assets. Moreover, because the Allies possessed general air superiority—their number-one air objective at the start of land combat on the continent—attention could be devoted to conducting armed reconnaissance/interdiction and close air support operations in much the way Weyland and his XIX TAC planners intended.

In view of Weyland's conduct of air operations throughout the campaign, it appears surprising at first to find him in the immediate aftermath of the war reaffirming the importance and doctrinal validity of *Command and Employment of Air Power* (FM 100–20 of 1943). The experience of his command through nine months of intensive air operations in collaboration with General Patton's army, he said, showed the manual's concepts "to be basically sound." He declared that XIX TAC followed the order of priority prescribed by the manual when planning and flying combat missions. First in importance was the achievement of air superiority and measures taken to maintain it. Next came interdiction or isolation of the battlefield. "Close air cooperation with ground units in combat" completed the triumvirate. Mindful of his audience, senior airmen, Weyland carefully used the words "cooperation with" in place of the earlier phrase, "support of" Third Army. Looking ahead to institutional independence, AAF leaders had become especially sensitive over any connotations that might reflect subordinate status, and Weyland well understood the need to validate FM 100–20, especially in terms of command arrangements. Postwar politics seemed to be a driving force for many airmen involved with evaluating their wartime experiences. Nevertheless, whatever Weyland felt about the manual, in practice he, like many others, proved anything but a servant of rigid doctrine or its prescribed order of mission priorities.[14]

In response to a request from the AAF Evaluation Board assigned to the European theater in the summer of 1944 to study the role of air power, General Weyland compiled a report on combat operations of the XIX TAC. In early 1945, the War Department directed the AAF Evaluation Board to focus on the effectiveness of close-in air cooperation, what the board termed Phase III operations. In March 1945, the board solicited responses from Ninth Air Force, the First Tactical Air Force, and from the ground units to a 39-point questionnaire.

Although many individual units replied well before the end of hostilities, Generals Bradley and Devers submitted their views together in mid-May. The board issued its Phase III report in August 1945. Meanwhile, during the previous month General Bradley and his 12th Army Group Air Effects Committee used much of the information from the questionnaire to prepare their own report, *The Effect of Air Power on Military Operations*. Along with the reports from General Weyland's command, these two major studies provide a comprehensive analysis of tactical air doctrine and operations in the European theater during World War II.[15]

These postwar evaluation reports show that army commanders in the theater understood and appreciated the importance of air superiority. If the questions asked of them seemed weighted toward a validation of FM 100–20, they nevertheless provided candid answers that reflected most ground element leaders' views on the important issues surrounding the use of tactical air power. Although officers at Headquarters Army Ground Forces in Washington in late 1945 might challenge the assertion that supremacy in the air must be a prerequisite for successful ground operations, officers leaving the field in Northwest Europe had no such doubts. In the words of the AAF Phase III report, "too much emphasis cannot be laid on the advantage to the Allied cause of having virtually unchallenged supremacy in the skies above the European continent throughout the campaign."[16]

Army leaders knew that air superiority provided their forces nearly unrestricted movement and unhindered resupply on the battlefield. Free from significant enemy air attack, ground forces could, among other activities, regroup rapidly, maintain uninterrupted supply channels, and devote less attention to camouflage and air defenses. Moreover, Army leaders did not have to worry about the morale of their troops who surely would have suffered as did their German counterparts under heavy, consistent aerial assault. Indeed, the ground forces overwhelmingly concluded "air superiority can and must be the first priority task, not only of the air forces but of all military and economic forces which are directing their efforts to final victory."[17]

General Weyland agreed completely that air superiority was essential for success on the ground. As the tactical air commander, he ensured local air superiority on Third Army's front, and he worked diligently in all four campaigns to carry out this function. Like his fellow pilots, he enjoyed nothing more than to report his command's success against the *Luftwaffe*. During the campaign, his forces devoted approximately 18 percent of their sorties to priority one, or air superiority requirements. This was slightly below the figures for his sister tactical air commands in Ninth Air Force.[18] It also fell well below the effort accorded interdiction and close air support, which amounted to 40 and 42 percent of all missions flown, respectively.

Even so, on several occasions General Weyland—and Ninth Air Force planners—seemed overly focused on the threat from a struggling *Luftwaffe*, given the intelligence data available to them on the state of the enemy's air arm. This happened in the Lorraine Campaign and also in the Ardennes, during the last phase of the counteroffensive in January 1945. Although his Pioneer P–51 Mustang group flew the bulk of these counterair missions, his P–47 groups also flew bomber and transport escort and area cover missions. A good portion of these missions proved uneventful and might well have been more profitably flown as armed reconnaissance along known, highly-traveled, surface traffic routes. Weyland's actions are more defensible for the period before January 1, 1945, when Ultra and his reconnaissance pilots reported extensive *Luftwaffe* redeployment. After the New Year's Day raid, Ultra provided data on *Luftwaffe* movements away from the Third Army front along with relative inactivity for units that remained. As it transpired, the campaign showed that air superiority could be assured with Weyland's fighter-bombers and reconnaissance aircraft flying assigned interdiction and close air support missions.

The *Luftwaffe*, in fact, posed a consistent, albeit minor, threat only at night. Neither General Weyland nor any other air commander could entirely prevent enemy air attacks on friendly ground forces—or the isolated bombing of a friendly base. Once the XIX TAC command began its assault on remaining German airfields in April 1945, the nighttime threat became insignificant. Had it been otherwise, the Allies would not have dared reorient much of their night fighter force from defensive patrol to intruder interdiction missions. Allied air superiority allowed airmen to focus their attention on interdiction and close air support missions.

Army commanders also understood the value of interdiction, the isolation of the battlefield. Without referring specifically to air force doctrine, General Bradley concluded that interdiction did rank second to control of the air in terms of tactical air achievement. "The outstanding contribution of the fighter-bombers," he declared, "aside from helping to attain and maintain air superiority, was their continuous armed reconnaissance missions to isolate the battlefield to the front and flanks of the ground forces."[19]

Once again, General Weyland would concur, although he might quibble, with the word continuous. The main problem he and his colleagues faced throughout the campaign was maintenance of a consistent interdiction program in the face of other demands. As the Lorraine experience showed, tactical planners, like their strategic forces counterparts at that time, at first had difficulty deciding on the right targets. Only well into the fall buildup facing the Siegfried Line did Ninth Air Force planners conclude that primary bridges represented absolutely the best targets to attack to disrupt all German surface transport, therefore rendering enemy resupply and defensive efforts chaotic. Bridges, however, proved extraordinarily difficult targets for fighter-bombers not only to hit, but also to bring down. Even when employed against targets judged proper for their use, bad weather could intervene to negate their effectiveness. After the Normandy invasion, daylight armed reconnaissance missions forced the *Wehrmacht* to move supplies and personnel largely at night. During the long nights from late fall to early spring, a small tactical night fighter and reconnaissance force proved unable to detect and seriously disrupt enemy nighttime operations.[20]

Factors other than bad weather, darkness, and a small night fighter force hampered General Weyland's flyers. Competing priorities made it next to impossible to concentrate his force sufficiently on armed reconnaissance targets to execute a continuous, fully successful interdiction plan in the short run. Even during the Ardennes Campaign when he commanded an eight-group force, interdiction sorties amounted to less than 40 percent of the command's effort. Nevertheless, General Bradley and the airmen were certainly correct in declaring that air forces eventually isolated the Ardennes battlefield. It is tempting to speculate whether reallocating aerial assets from priority one to armed reconnaissance missions—ad hoc interdiction—might have hastened Allied success. It seems unlikely. Given the problems that prevented airmen from mounting consistent interdiction programs, it is doubtful that additional interdiction sorties would have significantly altered the outcome. Allied experience with interdiction demonstrated that tactical air power represented neither an unlimited resource nor a decisive force in and of itself. Little has changed since the Second World War to suggest altering this basic assessment of the interdiction mission.[21]

The doctrine of the tactical air force's third mission, close air support, underwent the greatest change during the campaign. Air Force theorists considered aerial attacks on enemy ground forces in the contact zone to be the most difficult to mount because of the danger of striking friendly troops and the most expensive in terms of operational efficiency and in losses to enemy defenses. They also could be the least effective if employed against inappropriate targets, such as hardened defenses or dispersed troops. Traditional airmen wanted these targets reserved for army artillery. The test of a proper aerial target usually began with the criterion, beyond artillery range. Indeed, tactical air forces seemed destined to fight primarily beyond the immediate surface battle zone except in rare emergency conditions.[22] All this had changed by the end of the campaign, largely because Allied air superiority provided the environment for pragmatic commanders like Weyland to adjust their techniques as circumstances warranted. Although the number of sorties do not represent priorities in all cases, clearly air superiority in the Northwest Europe campaign and improved communications and air control practice resulted in an unforeseen emphasis on close air support missions, missions that often operated in close proximity to Patton's troops.

The prominence of close air support missions flown in Europe during World War II, however, cannot be discerned in the AAF Evaluation Board's classic description of the air planning process, that is, the process that allocated air effort at the level of the army–tactical air command combined-operations center. Board members decided that tactical air-ground planners had actually allocated missions in the following sequence:[23]

1. Special targets or escort missions directed by Air Force headquarters.
2. Requirements to maintain air superiority.
3. Armed reconnaissance to prevent movement of enemy supplies and troops into the battle area.
4. Armored column cover missions.
5. Army requests or close air support missions.

This idealized scheme, which purported to describe the actual planning of wartime air missions, doubtless confirmed long-standing army suspicions about what third-priority air support meant for its troops in future combat.

In practice in the field, General Weyland followed neither this nor any other established sequence. Indeed, he affirmed that XIX TAC covered armored columns first. The record suggests, however, that except in highly unusual circumstances, such as the fluid conditions in the Eifel, he also invariably provided air support for infantry divisions in combat. Weyland's experience suggests that perhaps the AAF's aerial allocation sequence was suspect from its conception. The determining factor for close support allocation became the rate of advance. For relatively stable situations, as occurred during much of the Lorraine fighting, Patton's artillery could and did handle most front line targets. That allowed Weyland's fighter-bombers to focus on armed reconnaissance. For mobile operations, on the other hand, close support requirements received top priority in the form of armored column cover and attacks on defended towns and strong points, with remaining aerial forces assigned armed reconnaissance routes after minimum air superiority requirements had been met. Again, Weyland's air planners adjusted the aerial effort to meet the requirements of Patton's ground offensive, not to satisfy doctrinal pronouncements or some other formal planning arrangement.[24]

If the AAF Evaluation Board's description of the World War II air allocation process strains the credibility of army and air liaison officers fresh from the field, the board's claim that close air support of the army normally did not exceed *15 percent* of the tactical air forces available can be legitimately disputed.[25] This board figure is often cited as at least indicative of, if not the last word on, overall World War II close air support commitments. This is patently incorrect. One must look beyond the broad percentage of forces allocated and consider the actual number and percentage of sorties flown on close air support missions.

On these points, General Bradley's own report is much more revealing because it is based on operational summaries describing actual targets attacked. Significantly, among Ninth Air Force tactical air commands, only the XIX

TAC flew more close air support sorties than it did interdiction sorties during the campaign. It devoted 42 percent of its sorties to close air support and 40 percent to interdiction. The close air support and interdiction figures for General Quesada's IX TAC totaled 27 and 46 percent, respectively, and for General Nugent's XXIX TAC, they were 33 and 47 percent, respectively. In fact, armed reconnaissance outnumbered close support sorties for Weyland's forces only during the spring offensive following the Ardennes Campaign. Then, in the final drive through Germany, when the enemy facing Patton's armored columns became progressively weaker, Weyland felt free to shift priorities to armed reconnaissance targets and airfields. Is it any wonder that Patton considered Weyland his favorite airman? Or that ground force officers considered the Patton–Weyland relationship as something special?[26] If Third Army could claim 42 percent of XIX TAC aerial sorties at the front, close air support sorties for all three American armies together averaged 33 percent of the total sorties flown during the Northwest European campaigns. Although this figure is more than twice as high as the 15 percent allocation figure offered by Air Force advocates, it is far more realistic.

The most controversial aspect of close air support operations during the campaign concerned what airmen deemed proper targets for fighter-bombers. As a general rule, Army officers did not believe that tactical aircraft should avoid attacking targets within the range of artillery. Weyland agreed that targets within artillery range remained suitable for his aircraft in mobile operations, because artillery normally moved up slowly. Yet, army evaluators also believed close air support bombing necessary and effective in static operations, too. As General Bradley's analysis noted, aircraft with 500-lb. general-purpose bombs and 250-lb. fragmentation bombs often proved more destructive than any artillery preparation using much less destructive warheads.[27] General Bradley also cautioned against rules of thumb that early in the campaign had excluded defended villages, for example. In winter, many villages were filled with troops and made excellent targets for fighter-bombers attacking, first with general-purpose bombs and napalm, and then strafing exposed personnel. He argued that targets should be examined from both ground and air points of view. This, in fact, is what occurred in the combined operations system, and by the spring of 1945 fighter-bombers attacked most front line targets routinely.

One target, however, seldom appeared on the airmen's target list. As General Weyland repeatedly stated, he did not consider fixed, well-defended fortifications appropriate targets for fighter-bombers. Was he wrong? Some Army officers thought so. As one explained:

> [P]ill boxes under attack are always surrounded by troops in strong points who do not fall back in the pill box until the Infantry actually assaults. Air attack causes considerable

> casualties amongst troops manning strong points outside pill
> boxes and materially reduces their will to fight. We under-
> stand that ordinary bombing will not destroy pill boxes, but
> we do consider pill boxes excellent targets.[28]

Some AAF officers also might have rejected Weyland's argument, noting that
analysis showed fighter-bombers loaded with 1,000-lb. bombs could have a better chance of causing major damage. Others pointed to the indirect effect
achieved by attacking pillboxes and casemented guns in which fighter-bombers
served to neutralize these emplaced weapons until advancing ground forces
could overwhelm them. General Weyland remained unconvinced, granting
exceptions only in emergencies. Bespeaking his opposition, XIX TAC aircraft
reported only one pillbox attacked during the entire assault on the Siegfried Line
from the end of January to February 25, 1945. In this case, Weyland's stub-
bornness might very well have interfered with useful air support. On the other
hand, his aversion to this type of target did not prevent his fighter-bombers from
striking nearly everything else German within the artillery zone.[29]

In short, by the spring of 1945, close air support had devolved far beyond
the stilted, theoretical confines of FM 100–20. Although the manual claimed
Phase III operations to be the most expensive, most difficult to control, and
least effective of all missions, in many instances operations in Northwest
Europe proved otherwise. One is reminded that 1943's FM 100–20 emerged
from the North African experience, where much of the time the Allies did not
enjoy air superiority and often possessed few aerial resources. These conditions had changed markedly by 1944 and 1945. Moreover, improved technology in the form of radio communications and radar normally made possible
effective control and coordination between ground controllers and fighter and
reconnaissance pilots. As for cost, XIX TAC's experience suggested that
armed reconnaissance and cooperation missions were equally expensive in
terms of planes and pilots lost. Finally, the relatively high percentage of close
air support missions flown for Patton's forces and other armies in the 12th
Army Group suggests that air support of army forces within the artillery zone
achieved good results—and not just in emergency situations. As an 11th
Armored Division spokesman explained for the AAF Board:

> From our point of view, these [cooperation] missions are
> easy to control, are inexpensive in so far as loss of friendly
> aircraft is concerned, and usually show profitable results.
> Losses to friendly troops as a result of this type mission
> when controlled by experienced air corps personnel are nil.[30]

The record bears him out and suggests once again the fundamental importance
of Allied air superiority.

Like other tactical air commanders, General Weyland took liberties with formal tactical air mission priorities when the situation warranted, which underscored his pragmatic approach to doctrine that characterized air-ground operations during the combat in Northwest Europe. In Weyland's hands, doctrine served the forces, rather than the reverse, and with air superiority, he could adjust priorities according to need rather than theory. Weyland and his fellow airmen, however, never compromised on one issue. Besides designating mission priorities, FM 100–20 dealt with authority and control of air resources. Control of air assets, it stated, should be centralized and their command vested in an Air Force commander. If aircraft were separated and attached to ground units, air forces would be used improperly, nor would it be possible to recombine and concentrate the force when necessary. The XIX TAC commander reacted swiftly and strongly to any perceived infringement of his control. Such incidents were few and quickly settled by General Weyland within local channels—with solid support from General Patton and his staff, if necessary.

If Weyland exercised the control he wanted during the last few months of the campaign, decentralized operations became the order of the day. In late February 1945, XIX TAC supplied a second VHF radio to corps tactical air liaison officers and authorized them a separate channel for more direct and efficient communication between reconnaissance aircraft, other liaison officers, and (by extension) the army corps fire-direction center. Now liaison officers could request and receive information directly from the reconnaissance aircraft overhead without first communicating with the tactical control center.[31] This decentralization of control at the combat front preserved ultimate air force authority while providing the army corps its organic reconnaissance. Technology made possible this more efficient use of resources and General Weyland embraced it as long as his prerogatives remained unaffected. He always believed that the tactical air doctrine dealing with command and control, if applied effectively, would assure the army the support it needed. Air officers during a campaign might decentralize operations or massage mission priorities according to need, but they remained uncompromising in adhering to the principle that the ultimate control of air forces rested with air commanders. In postwar analyses, army officers also recognized and accepted the need for centralized control of air power, even if this point was appreciated more at the corps and army level than at the division level.

Tactical air doctrine also prescribed the organization and procedures for conducting air-ground operations. On assessment and on balance, these organizational prescriptions proved sound. In a letter to General Spaatz in May 1945, General Bradley praised the effectiveness of joint air-ground operations. Essential "joint planning at the appropriate command levels," he said, was obtained first by "the close physical association of headquarters and second by the operational linking up of ground and staff personnel in your various air headquarters. The latter [innovation] is original within this theater and has thoroughly justified itself."[32] One might differ with the 12th Army Group commander's claim to originality. The much maligned FM 31–35 (April 1942), *Aviation in Support of Ground Forces*, established the procedures and practices for air-ground operations that airmen first introduced in North Africa, and then further developed in the Italian theater. Yet no one could doubt the effectiveness of joint operations in the European theater, which stressed the collocation of air and ground headquarters, establishment of combined operations centers, and exchange of air and ground liaison officers within air and surface units.

Despite an almost obsessive concern for centralized control of air forces, Weyland and his colleagues permitted far more initiative and latitude for action at lower echelons than anyone could have foreseen. As he and his command demonstrated, operational decentralization became key to successful joint operations during the campaign. His separate headquarters elements were a case in point. So, too, was the coordination that evolved among forces in the field. The airmen realized, for example, that accurate and *timely* field intelligence required tactical reconnaissance pilots to communicate directly with the air liaison officers at corps and, sometimes, at division level without first communicating with the higher headquarters tactical control center. By the spring of 1945, Weyland's fighter-bomber pilots routinely monitored reconnaissance radio channels and reacted promptly to attack targets of opportunity. In such instances, the tactical control center often performed only a monitoring function.[33]

During the final three months of the European war, fighter-bombers flying armed reconnaissance increasingly contacted corps or division headquarters to learn of any immediate targets before flying their assigned routes. Responses to the AAF Evaluation Board's questionnaire, however, indicated that not all air-ground teams followed this procedure; some followed it only occasionally. Third Army's XX Corps, for example, declared, regretfully, that this did not happen on their front, but General Walker's XX Corps staff might have responded to the board's questionnaire in March rather than in May, when the practice appeared to be more common throughout the XIX TAC–Third Army team.[34] Also, as the 6th Armored Division's response indicated, although armed reconnaissance flights might not check in with the corps or division, the daily reconnaissance program, whereby tactical reconnaissance pilots flew assigned routes for the different Army corps, made it possible for the pilots to obtain immediate air cooperation for the ground units. If the demands of mobile warfare predictably required flexible operational procedures at lower echelons, the commanders also resorted to these practices during static warfare in the fall and winter months.[35]

By 1945, decentralized air-ground operations and procedures often provided local army units with what amounted to an air umbrella, one that air force doctrine abhorred as a misuse of air power. Although air force representatives retained control of the air assets, army commanders often had essentially their own aircraft supporting their units in all but name. In such cases, the Allies' overwhelming air superiority and the growing weakness of German defenders made it increasingly possible to take liberties with doctrine in the name of better and more effective operations. The XIX TAC experience shows that this kind of air support provided to ground forces was directly proportional to the air resources available for that particular function. Unlike in North Africa, where relatively few resources translated into limited to modest air support, an abundance of resources in Northwest Europe at the end of 1944 enabled Allied air forces to provide formidable, if sometimes inconsistent, air support.

Two key technical developments during the war also contributed mightily to the success of tactical air operations. One was the appearance of the well-armored, long-range fighter-bomber as the primary aircraft for close air support. The other involved a revolution in communications that made efficient coordination, command, and control at all echelons possible. Effective air-ground procedures would hardly have been as successful without the timely arrival of the turbo-supercharged, air-cooled, radial engine, P–47 Thunderbolt fighter-bomber as the premier ground support aircraft in the European theater. Taking advantage of Allied air superiority in 1944, the P–47 made close air support far more effective than the authors of air force doctrine had imagined possible a year earlier. Without Allied air superiority in North Africa, not the P–39 Airacobra, the P–40 Warhawk, nor the A–20 Havoc light bomber proved capable of accurate, low-level bombing in Phase III operations without unacceptable losses.

By the time General Weyland arrived in England in early 1944, the AAF had three new candidates for the fighter-bomber role. The Thunderbolt was joined by the P–38 Lightning and the P–51 Mustang that mounted liquid-cooled, in-line engines. All three models were initially developed as pursuit, or fighter, aircraft for air combat at altitude against opposing fighters. When airmen added racks to carry bombs and rockets, however, all three proved highly adaptable to the tactical bombing mission. Likewise, they usually bested enemy fighters even against considerable odds. Fortunately for Ninth Air Force, Eighth Air Force selected the more agile P–51, rather than the P–47 as its main fighter aircraft for bomber escort work. Despite the latter's good speed, range, bomb-carrying capacity, and firepower, authorities preferred the P–51 for Priority I fighter missions, and withdrew the P–38 from fighter-bomber operations entirely. Both proved more vulnerable to flak at low altitudes because of the extensive radiator plumbing that served their liquid-cooled engines. On the other hand, they performed superbly as reconnaissance planes and served as such throughout the campaign.[36]

General Weyland's command preferred the rugged Thunderbolt unequivocally for fighter-bomber operations. Its sturdy frame, ease of maintenance, and capacity to carry a large bomb or rocket load, combined with an air-cooled, radial engine that could take a licking and still keep on running, made the P–47 the natural choice for close air support operations. Moreover, with or without bombs and rockets, eight wing-mounted .50-caliber machine guns gave to this flying engine of war enormous fire power in support of ground forces. In its report to the AAF Evaluation Board, the XIX TAC submitted a list of characteristics for the ideal fighter-bomber, which the board accepted without change. Confining itself to its experience in the European theater, the XIX TAC preferred the armament of the P–47, but it favored the more efficient performance capabilities of the P–51. Although not commenting on engine characteristics, the command no doubt favored the radial-type air-cooled engine that helped make the P–47 better able to withstand hits from enemy flak and continue flying. In light of German turbojet aircraft that had appeared in combat, however, it is surprising that the American airmen did not project beyond familiar, propeller-driven airplanes to include jet aircraft as they identified characteristics of their ideal fighter-bomber.[37]

With the arrival of the P–47 and improved communications, close air support or Phase III missions could no longer be considered the most expensive, least effective, and most difficult to control. Equipped with external fuel tanks, fighter-bombers could also meet the range challenges of mobile warfare. Even so, General Weyland was quick to remind General Patton and his staff of the limitations of modern fighter-bombers. Despite the impressive technical performance, their pilots could not operate them effectively in bad weather or darkness. Army planners understood these problems. Nevertheless, if Patton's ground commanders always included air support in joint operational plans, they seldom postponed an offensive because weather conditions prohibited the fighter-bombers from flying. General Weyland frequently permitted pilots to violate weather minimums in declared emergencies, but not for sustained offensive drives. Third Army's XX and XII Corps assaults on the Siegfried Line in February 1945, for example, began without air cover in spite of strong enemy defenses and rugged terrain. Normally, Third Army offensives would not be rescheduled unless they required medium or heavy bombers. Even then, individual circumstances might convince the commander to move forward without air support since medium bombers required two days to schedule, or to reschedule. Army commanders widely criticized the Army Air Force's inability to provide medium bomber support on short notice.[38]

Bad weather and darkness probably had a greater effect on fighter-bomber efforts to isolate the battlefield than they did on close air support operations. German troops invariably moved the bulk of their troops and supplies to and from the front lines during bad weather or after sundown, when Allied aircraft harassed them the least. Similarly, German transports could move at night almost at will because of the small Allied night fighter force. Although initially designed for night interception operations, the P–61 Black Widow became a more effective fighter-bomber after acquiring napalm ordnance and rockets to complement its four 20-mm cannons in early 1945. Despite the limitations associated with the Black Widow's armed reconnaissance missions, however, the XIX TAC valued the twin-engine, humpbacked P–61, which presented a frightening presence at night, more for its effect on enemy morale and less for its bombing statistics. The command simply had too few P–61s. Except for the Ardennes emergency, Weyland's night fighter force never amounted to more than a single squadron of 12–15 Black Widows.[39]

In its evaluation of air operations, the AAF Evaluation Board highlighted the weakness of Allied night flying efforts. In truth, that weakness had been painfully obvious to all from the beginning of the drive across France. "The absence of adequate night fighters and fighter-bombers," the report stated, "was found to be probably the most serious handicap to the air forces throughout the war."[40] When taken together, bad weather and darkness gave the Germans a degree of freedom for movement and clearly enabled them to prolong the war.

A second major development involving technology offered the promise of overcoming the fighter-bomber's fundamental visibility problem when flying in poor weather and at night. Radio communications and the use of radar as an offensive weapon had progressed a long way in this direction by 1944. Together, they provided command and control of fighter-bombers and were basic in the first attempts to develop a capability to bomb accurately in close air support operations. General Weyland, for example, communicated directly with General Vandenberg at Ninth Air Force headquarters and other key officers over the Redline communications system. Four communications networks and five methods of communicating tied XIX TAC units together, even under conditions of extreme mobility. Good VHF radio equipment met the challenge of creating air-ground coordination. Also during the winter months, ground-based radar became increasingly important for accurate navigation and bombing of targets beyond the bomb safety line. Indeed, any useful flying at night and during winter would have been impossible without these developments.

In this area, too, limitations affected the impressive capabilities of new technology. Allied forces turned to the scientists and engineers of the operational research offices at the various command levels for solutions to overcome technical constraints. By early 1945, the XIX TAC had become deeply involved in this research, which included methods to improve aircraft control procedures and determine optimum bomb size and fuze types, in addition to the study of bridge destruction by aircraft. The most attention, however, focused on producing an effective bomb strike camera and the accurate blind bombing radar system, SCR–584.

Despite major efforts throughout the spring of 1945, improvements in both systems fell short of hopes. The SCR–584 blind bombing system and bomb strike camera projects serve as valuable reminders that, wherever new technology is involved, initial expectations often go unfulfilled. Such overestimation of technical potentials would become commonplace in a later age. Altogether, Allied scientists did far better than their Axis counterparts in recognizing the potential of such systems and working to make them fulfill their promise. Moreover, though the war proved to be a catalyst for advances in technology, radar and radio communications were still in their infancy. Solutions for blind bombing and bomb damage assessment would have to await more sophisticated technical developments that lay farther in the future than most supposed.

Cooperation was the final ingredient that contributed to the success of tactical air-ground operations. Cooperation, not confrontation, characterized army and air force relations in Northwest Europe far more than anyone could have imagined during the difficult days in North Africa in late 1942. Ninth Air Force analysts at war's end correctly assessed the effectiveness of the air-ground team at the army–tactical air command level. "The principle of establishing a separate, autonomous tactical air command to operate in an indissoluble operational partnership with each army proved sound and successful in combat."[41] Although no one would deny the importance of doctrine, in large part the personal element proved crucial. In his letter to General Spaatz, General Bradley concluded by emphasizing this most important factor. "I think that one of the most effective measures to insure good cooperation," he said, "has been the excellent personal relationship between air and ground commanders which we have enjoyed during this campaign and which has been highly gratifying to me."[42] He certainly had in mind the excellent personal rapport he developed with air colleagues in joint headquarters, first with General Quesada, then with General Vandenberg. Cooperation and trust, together with an abundance of airplanes, served to diminish the importance of organizational principles and mission priorities.

The air-ground partnership reflected both personal and professional considerations. The team of Patton and Weyland, perhaps more than any other, illustrated the professional respect and understanding that proved absolutely vital for good air-ground relations. It would be difficult to imagine two such different personalities: the flamboyant, theatrical, implacable "man of destiny" from California, and the soft-spoken but determined Texan. Colonel Ferguson, XIX TAC operations officer, recounted later that General Weyland made sure well before the Normandy invasion that the two commanders understood each other and the capabilities and limitations of their forces. "There was such good rapport established early on about what one could and could not do that there were no serious difficulties."[43] As a one-star, Weyland remained the responsible subordinate rather than a coequal commander envisioned in FM 100–20. Regardless, he had the three-star army commander's confidence from the beginning. He could always call on Patton to help convince higher headquarters to provide additional air units or change target priorities, and Patton would do so, vigorously. Furthermore, Patton was never known to override General Weyland when, on occasion, his air commander declined to have fighter-bombers attack targets he judged unsuitable.

Above all, Patton knew that he could count on the XIX TAC commander to support Third Army efforts to the maximum. Apparently, for others, that kind of aerial support could be considered excessive at times. Looking back on the air-ground experience of World War II from another perch, Ninth Air Force officials warned future tactical airmen:

> [It] was demonstrated repeatedly that the commander of a tactical air command, deeply engrossed in and intimately associated with the ground campaign, is subject to many strong influences to insure the maximum amount of close air cooperation in his area of responsibility at the possible expense of the proper employment of the air force as a whole in the combined air and ground battle.[44]

Although the evaluators did not name General Weyland's XIX TAC in this instance, they doubtless knew that Third Army received more close air support sorties than had been provided to the First and Ninth Armies by the other two tactical air commands in Ninth Air Force. Moreover, General Patton's reputation as a strong leader might have suggested to them that he had ridden roughshod over his air commander to extract so much close air support for his forces.

This was not the case. General Weyland always spoke for air interests whenever he thought necessary. General Patton, on his part, did not interfere in the overall air plan, and he let the air commander run the air side of operations. He backstopped Weyland and supported his requests at higher headquarters, knowing full well that in return he would receive all possible aerial support, given the vagaries of weather and other priorities. Throughout the campaign Patton publicized the air-ground team's performance at every opportunity. Although comparatively obscure, one reference in particular captures the confidence he had in his air commander's determination to support the Third Army. On January 15, 1945, with the Germans in full retreat from the Bulge, he wrote to his wife, "we have had three nice clear days and hope that our air has done half as much as it says. However, they do try, especially Weyland and his fighter-bombers."[45]

Following the campaign, the two former comrades-in-arms corresponded several times before Patton's death in December 1945. In September, Patton sent the first three chapters of his manuscript, *War As I Knew It*, to a dispirited Weyland, who after his European exploits, instead of receiving an operational assignment, had been named Assistant Commandant of the Army's Command and General Staff School. In reply to Weyland's letter of thanks,

Patton told him that the students would benefit enormously from his experience "because I am sure that now everyone realizes that the phenomenal success of the combined operations of the XIX TAC and Third Army was due primarily to your forethought and breadth of understanding." Offering further encouragement and perhaps the greatest possible compliment, Patton wrote, "As you know, I told General Eisenhower during the campaign that I would be perfectly happy to have you as a Corps Commander, at any time."[46]

At the end of the war Allied leaders did seek to preserve the lessons learned in the cooperative air-ground effort. Yet they faced the formidable challenge of somehow institutionalizing the unusual personal and professional relationships that often proved so successful. In later years, once the experience levels declined and professional relationships forged in combat disappeared, it would prove difficult to rely only on a shared wartime background. Eisenhower, SHAEF Commander and a strong proponent of air-ground cooperation and centralized control of air power, took the first steps in May 1945, when he convened a meeting among commanders of the key air-ground teams in the European theater at General Bradley's headquarters. General Weyland recalled that the group unanimously reaffirmed centralized control of air power as prescribed by FM 100–20 (1943), but not before General Hodges, U.S. First Army commander, proposed that the individual army headquarters be authorized direct control of all reconnaissance aircraft.[47]

The reports from army field units made it clear that General Hodges's suggestion would be welcome in some Army circles. Weyland found this expression of sentiment familiar. Both he and General Vandenberg spoke out forcefully against Hodges's plan, and they were supported strongly by General Weyland's "collaborator," General Patton. As Weyland remembered the incident, the Third Army commander explained to those assembled that although his intelligence officer had first favored Third Army control of reconnaissance, he realized that reconnaissance had other responsibilities, in addition to those for his army. Weyland recalled, "Old Patton was a believer."[48]

Eisenhower and his colleagues had good reason for concern about preserving the lessons of tactical air power. In the European theater, individual army commanders had long expressed reservations about command and control arrangements for tactical air forces. Many remained convinced that the U.S. Army needed its own air force and would in the future continue to advocate a strong army air arm. Normally, these officers held command positions below corps level, where they would be less likely to appreciate air power's larger responsibilities. Moreover, while Eisenhower and his commanders met at Luxembourg City, Army Ground Forces headquarters published a preliminary report compiled by its Equipment Review Board under the chairmanship of Maj. Gen. Gilbert R. Cook. Army Air Forces leaders became alarmed as soon as they learned that its conclusions entirely opposed the precepts of FM 100–20 and the air-ground experience in Europe.[49] The so-called Cook Board report recommended that the army have "ground support aviation organic to and operated by ground forces…," and that the aircraft procured for this purpose be of the "flying artillery and flying tank type" for exclusive support of ground forces.

Characteristically, air leaders mobilized to refute the findings of the Cook Board. In response to their expressions of concern, the War Department established a committee, with air force representation, to gather information pertaining to the Cook Board's findings. After the committee completed its investigation in the fall, the War Department convened an Equipment Board in December 1945, under the chairmanship of Gen. Joseph W. Stilwell, to hear testimony from key air and ground forces officers. General Weyland was among those airmen called to testify in December. Like his colleagues, he had access to the records at AAF headquarters in Washington and at the AAF Tactical Center's library at Orlando, Florida, before appearing for a "coordinating rehearsal" of all air force testimony. Weyland's views reflected his own experience and partnership in the most successful air-ground team of the war. In response to the report's view that there must be one team with one commander, Weyland affirmed the AAF's view that the theater commander is the single commander. Moreover, "all offensive combat aircraft must be under unified air control to permit flexibility of employment." He referred to his own interview with German Field Marshal von Rundstedt, who had agreed that aircraft dispersed to corps and divisions could never be concentrated to support one corps or an army at the expense of another. As for the army's "flying tank," he argued that this represented nothing more than the kind of dive-bomber that had been shot out of the sky and abandoned in Europe. The fighter-bomber had been developed to meet Army needs, he declared, and it was "found by actual experience to be better than the slow planes especially designed for army support." Any aircraft designed for a single purpose loses flexibility that is essential for successful air operations. He also cited the experience of the Third Army–XIX TAC team as an example of how army support could be attained and maintained. Moreover, on the sensitive issue of air force interest in flying close air support, he asserted that U.S. Army ground forces had "misinterpreted" the meaning of "third priority." Despite the implications of formal tactical air doctrine, close air support should not be considered third in importance, but must follow air superiority and interdiction missions so that ground forces "enter [the] battle with hope of success without disproportionate losses."[50]

The War Department's own Equipment Review Board eventually decided against the Cook Board's recommendations. Instrumental in its decision, General Eisenhower and key army and corps commanders supported AAF's views. They agreed that air-ground support in Europe had been more than sufficient to defeat the Germans without a "duplicate air organization for ground cooperation."[51] While the War Department considered the merits of views presented by the army ground forces, its evaluation boards completed their studies of air power's impact in the various theaters. These studies also confirmed the essential importance of joint operations and cooperation between air and ground forces, and they recommended that the doctrine and procedures that had proved so successful be updated accordingly.

General Arnold directed the AAF Evaluation Board to revise FM 31–35 to incorporate the lessons of World War II. The new manual updated sections of the 1942 version, *Aviation in Support of Ground Forces*, and incorporated

Field Marshal von Rundstedt (right) reviews his troops.

portions of FM 100–20, *Command and Employment of Air Power*, which the War Department chose not to rescind. The new manual, however, did not have FM 100–20's stridency; in fact, the authors gave to the revised manual a new, more neutral title, *Air-Ground Operations*. Headquarters Army Ground Forces now was commanded by General Devers, an experienced veteran of the European theater and sympathetic supporter of air-ground cooperation. Indeed, the new manual received swift approval from the War Department and both headquarters, and it was published in August 1946.[52]

Yet would a revised manual and sound doctrine be sufficient to preserve the lessons of air-ground cooperation of World War II in the absence of good-will? To be sure, in the postwar period of rapid and massive demobilization goodwill did not prevail in the competition for declining budgets, lobbying for an independent Air Force, and a growing emphasis on the strategic nuclear mission to confront the Soviet Union in the Cold War. In later years interservice rivalry among military leaders would lead to precisely the kind of aerial duplication that other leaders in the euphoria of victory after the Second World War argued against. The future would see separate tactical aviation organizations grow and evolve in the U.S. Army, Navy, and Marine Corps, in addition to the Air Force.[53]

General Bradley called the victory in Europe a victory for combined arms and joint operations. Though correct, command of the air proved the key to the campaign. In a sense, everything else flowed from the fundamental fact that the Allies achieved and maintained air superiority and their enemy had not. General Weyland realized this as much as any airman. A few years later, when he assumed command of Far Eastern Air Forces and directed air operations in Korea, few could match his level of tactical air experience and competence. Yet even Allied air superiority and his impressive background in tactical aviation did not guarantee effective air-ground operations. In fact, Weyland faced enormous problems in coordinating air-ground operations and centralizing control of the Air Force, Navy, and Marine air. At the same time, he struggled to convince the U.S. Army to abandon a traditional view that it should control its own air forces. As Weyland's official report on the war observed, "an astounding facet of the Korean War was the number of old lessons that had to be relearned."[54] That same refrain would be repeated during the Vietnam War.

The lesson, of course, is that air superiority by itself does not ensure either centralized control of air assets by airmen or a proper balance between interdiction and close air support efforts. Although doctrine may serve well in principle, no air-ground program can succeed without the cooperation and goodwill of air and ground commanders and their staffs. Given sufficient resources, people who will work together toward a commonly shared goal can turn theory into effective practice. Assessing a later war, General Quesada put it succinctly: "You can have all the doctrine you want, but unless you have people, commanders, to implement those doctrines, you might as well throw your doctrines away."[55] Generals Weyland and Patton knew this. Theirs was a partnership founded on mutual trust, respect, and a common mission-directed interest. That is *the* basic lesson from the Second World War for tactical air power. It is a lesson worth remembering.

Notes

Chapter 1

1. On general doctrinal development during the interwar period, see Robert F. Futrell, *Ideas, Concepts, Doctrine: Basic Thinking in the United States Air Force,* vol 1, 1907–1964 (Maxwell AFB: Air University, reprint 1989), pp 1–110; Thomas H. Greer, *The Development of Air Doctrine in the Army Air Arm, 1917–1941,* USAF Historical Studies No. 89 (Maxwell AFB: 1955; Washington, D.C.: Office of Air Force History, reprint, 1985), *passim*; Richard G. Davis, *Carl A. Spaatz and the Air War in Europe* (Washington, D.C.: Center for Air Force History, 1993), pp 180–193; Daniel R. Mortensen, "A Pattern for Joint Operations: World War II Close Air Support in North Africa," Historical Analysis Series (Washington, D.C.: Office of Air Force History, 1994), pp 6–13; Wesley Frank Craven and James Lea Cate, eds., *The Army Air Forces in World War II,* vol 1, *Plans and Early Operations, January 1939 to August 1942* (Chicago: University of Chicago Press, 1948; reprint, Washington, D.C.: Office of Air Force History 1984), pp 17–74; John F. Shiner, *Foulois and the US Army Air Corps, 1931–1935* (Washington, D.C.: Office of Air Force History, 1983), pp 43–75, 212–235; William A. Jacobs, "Tactical Air Doctrine and AAF Close Air Support in the European Theater, 1944–45," *Aerospace Historian* (Mar 1980), pp 35–49.

2. The Army normally delineated the contact zone by what it called the bombline, a line close to its own forces beyond which aircraft could attack enemy targets *without* coordinating with ground commanders. Despite the confusion that subsequently would occur in the use of statistical measurements to determine tactical air power's effec-tiveness during the World War II, officials found the bombline a good means to distinguish between air interdiction and close air support targets. Only much later, during the Vietnam era, would planners introduce the concept of battlefield air interdiction, which became accepted as a subset of air interdiction. When first introduced, the term battlefield air interdiction referred to the component of the air interdiction mission that supported army ground forces beyond the range of their own artillery. See the discussion in Robert F. Futrell, *Ideas, Concepts, Doctrine: Basic Thinking in the United States Air Force,* vol 2, 1961–1984 (Maxwell AFB: Air University, reprint 1989), pp 551–555.

3. For the best revisionist interpretation that legitimately downplays Air Corps antipathy for close air support operations, see Daniel R. Mortensen, "Tactical Aviation Technology Tested in World War II: Keeping Doctrine Abreast of Equipment," chap. 3 in "The Low Road to Independence: From Origins to the Codification of Modern Tactical Aviation in World War II," unpublished manuscript, Air Force History and Museums Program, Washington, D.C. See also Wesley Frank Craven and James Lea Cate, eds., *The Army Air Forces in World War II,* vol 6, *Men and Planes* (Chicago: University of Chicago Press, 1948; reprint, Washington, D.C.: Office of Air Force History 1984), pp 212–214; Greer, *Development of Air Doctrine,* pp 52–57.

4. Greer, *Development of Air Doctrine,* pp 49–52; Mortensen, *Pattern for Joint Operations,* pp 6–7.

5. Davis, *Spaatz,* pp 180–181; Greer, *Development of Air Doctrine,* pp 40–43; Mortensen, *Pattern for Joint Operations,* p 7.

6. Mortensen, *Pattern for Joint Operations,* pp 11–13; Jacobs, "Tactical Air Doctrine," pp 182–184.

7. A later manual, FM 100–5, "Operations," dated May 22, 1941, established mission priorities and stressed the basic importance of air superiority as a prerequisite for effective ground operations. Kent Roberts Greenfield, *Army Ground Forces and the Air-Ground Battle Team, Including Organic Light Aviation,* U.S. Army Study No. 35 (Washington, D.C.: Historical Div, Department of the Army, 1948), pp 1–5; Mortensen, *Pattern for Joint Operations,* pp 11–13; Jacobs, "Tactical Air Doctrine," pp 182–184.

8. Riley Sunderland, *Evolution of Command and Control Doctrine for Close Air Support* (Washington, D.C.: Office of Air Force History, 1973), pp 7–9; Davis, *Spaatz,* pp 185–186; Greenfield, *Army Ground Forces,* pp 5–12. Organizationally, Air Force Combat Command replaced GHQ Air Force in June 1941.

9. Interwar air board reports had shown that air support commands should support field armies because the range of their fighter-bombers could be expected to cover the frontage of a field army. See War Department, FM 31–35, "Aviation in Support of Ground Forces," 9 Apr 1942, paras. 5–9; see also Greenfield, *Army Ground Forces,* pp 3–5; Jacobs, "Tactical Air Doctrine," pp 38–39; Davis, *Spaatz,* pp 186–189; Mortensen, *Pattern for Joint Operations,* pp 20–24.

10. FM 31–35, para. 26(b).

11. *Ibid.,* para. 6.

12. *Ibid.,* para. 31; David Syrett, "Northwest Africa, 1942–1943," in B. Franklin Cooling, ed., *Case Studies in the Achievement of Air Superiority* (Washington, D.C.: Center for Air Force History, 1993), p 6.

13. FM 31–35, para. 10.

14. Davis, *Spaatz,* p 189.

15. Mortensen, *Pattern for Joint Operations,* pp 47–56; Syrett, "Northwest Africa," p 10.

16. Mortensen, *Pattern for Joint Operations,* pp 47–56; Wesley Frank Craven and James Lea Cate, eds., *The Army Air Forces in World War II,* vol 2, *Europe: Torch to Pointblank, Aug 1942 to Dec 1943* (Chicago: University of Chicago Press, 1949; reprinted, Washington, D.C.: Office of Air Force History, 1984), pp 50–66.

17. Craven and Cate, eds., vol 2, *Europe: Torch to Pointblank,* pp 56–62. For the ground campaign, see George F. Howe, *Northwest Africa: Seizing the Initiative in the West,* [U.S. Army in World War II, Mediterranean Theater of Operations] (Washington, D.C.: Office of Chief of Military History, 1957).

18. Howe, *Northwest Africa,* pp 62–69. The British Western Desert Air Force, with headquarters in Egypt, was not a component of the Allied Air Force headquartered in Algeria.

19. Craven and Cate, eds., vol 2, *Europe: Torch to Pointblank,* pp 136–145. The *Luftwaffe* maintained a close air support strength of 300–330 aircraft from early January to mid-April 1943. See Air Ministry (Great Britain), *The Rise and Fall of the German Air Force, 1933–1945* (Old Greenwich, Conn.: WE Inc., 1969), p 250.

20. Mortensen, *Pattern for Joint Operations,* p 69.

21. Germany's Field Marshal Erwin Rommel, the "Desert Fox," mounted a surprise attack in central Tunisia against II Corps positions first in Faid Pass on February 14, 1943 and then at Kasserine four days later. Although the Allies rallied and pushed back the German advance on February 23, the Axis offensive wrecked Allied plans to divide German forces by thrusting eastward into Tunisia. Inexperienced American troops suffered more than 6,000 casualties compared with 989 German and 535 Italian casualties. See Howe, *Northwest Africa,* pp 438–481; Mortensen, *Pattern for Joint Operations,* pp 153–161; Sunderland, *Evolution,* pp 11–12.

22. Vincent Orange, *Coningham: A Biography of Air Marshal Sir Arthur Coningham* (Washington, D.C.: Center for Air Force History, 1992 reprint), chap. 10;

Mortensen, *Pattern for Joint Operations,* pp 72–73. Kuter continued to serve in the command as Coningham's deputy.

23. The incident provoked a crisis in Allied and joint relations. Apparently the theater commander, General Eisenhower, threatened to resign over the issue. For additional discussion of this affair, see George S. Patton, Diary Entries, Apr 1–4, 1943, Patton Collection, Box 3, Manuscript Division (MD), Library of Congress (LC). The diary account in the collection includes the official messages. See also Martin Blumenson, ed., *The Patton Papers*, vol 2 (Boston: Houghton Mifflin, 1974), pp 203–208; Orange, *Coningham*, pp 146–147; Laurence S. Kuter, "Goddamit Georgie: North Africa, 1943: The Birth of TAC Doctrine," *Air Force Magazine* vol 56 (Feb 1973), p 55; Craven and Cate, eds., vol 2, *Europe: Torch to Pointblank*, pp 174–175; Mortensen, *Pattern for Joint Operations,* pp 84–85.

24. A.F. Hurley and R.C. Ehrhart, eds., "The Perceptions of Three Makers of Air Power History," *Air Power and Warfare*, proceedings of the 8th Military History Symposium, United States Air Force Academy, 18–20 October 1973 (Washington, D.C.: Office of Air Force History and the United States Air Force Academy, 1979), p 109; Syrett, "Northwest Africa, 1942–1943," pp 153–192; Mortensen, *Pattern for Joint Operations,* pp 4–5.

25. Craven and Cate, eds., vol 2, *Europe: Torch to Pointblank*, pp 113–115, 161–165.

26. "Some Notes on the Use of Air Power in Support of Land Operations, Introduced by B.L. Montgomery, Dec 1944," USAFHRA, 168.6006–137; see also Air Marshal Sir Arthur Coningham, "The Development of Tactical Air Forces," *Journal of the Royal United Service Institution* vol 91 (May 1946), p 215; Davis, *Spaatz*, p 311.

27. Mortensen, *Pattern for Joint Operations,* p 85; Davis, *Spaatz*, p 321.

28. Mortensen, *Pattern for Joint Operations,* p 86; Craven and Cate, eds., *Europe: Torch to Pointblank*, vol 2, pp 166–206.

29. Memo, Brig Gen L.S. Kuter, Dep Comdr, Northwest African Tactical Air Force, to H.H. Arnold, CG AAF, Subject: "Organization of American Air Forces," May 12, 1943, USAFHRA, 614.201–1; for events, see Craven and Cate, eds., *Europe: Torch to Pointblank*, vol 2, pp 47–56.

30. Mortensen, *Pattern for Joint Operations,* pp 47–56.

31. Memo, Kuter, "Organization of American Air Forces."

32. Davis, *Spaatz*, pp 312–315.

33. War Department, FM 100–20, "Command and Employment of Air Power," July 21, 1943, paras. 3, 9(e); Jacobs, "Tactical Air Doctrine," pp 39–40.

34. FM 100–20, paras. 1, 2, and 3. The manual at no time used the word "support" to characterize the AAF's role in air-ground operations. Instead, it termed the air element "coordinate" forces that must not be distributed among or subordinated to ground elements. Although the manual permitted one exception, a theater situation in which "GROUND FORCE UNITS ARE OPERATING INDEPENDENTLY OR ARE ISOLATED BY DISTANCE OR LACK OF COMMUNICATION," tactical air operations in Northwest Europe required far more decentralized command and control arrangements than the manual's authors envisioned.

35. *Ibid.*, para 2.

36. *Ibid.*, para 16.

37. *Ibid.*

38. Davis, *Spaatz*, p 322.

39. *Ibid.*, pp 312–314; Greenfield, *Army Ground Forces*, pp 47–50.

40. For example, Memo, Kuter, "Organization of American Air Forces."

Chapter 2

1. The description of Patton's career that follows is based for the most part on Claude S. Erbsen, "Old Blood and Guts," *Weekly Philatelic Gossip* (Nov 21, 1953), pp 366–368; and "Biographical Notes on Gen George S. Patton, Jr.," in the Patton Collection, Box 5, Chronological File, MD, LC. See also Martin Blumenson, *Patton: The Man Behind the Legend, 1885–1945* (New York: William Morrow, 1985); and Blumenson, ed., *Patton Papers*.

2. U.S. Third Army (hereafter cited as US3A), "After Action Report, Aug 1, 1944–May 9, 1945," vol 2: Staff Section Reports, Part 4: "G–3 Section Report"; Blumenson, ed., *Patton Papers*, p 407. On Operation Fortitude, see Alfred D. Chandler, ed., *The Papers of Dwight David Eisenhower: The War Years*, vol 3 (Baltimore: Johns Hopkins University Press, 1970), pp 1789, 1978–1979, 2035; and Chester Wilmot, *The Struggle for Europe* (New York: Harper & Row, 1952), pp 199–201, 332–333. See also Charles Cruickshank, *Deception in World War II* (New York: Oxford University Press, 1979), pp 170–189, 235–236.

3. "84th Fighter Wing" lineage and honors history in Maurer Maurer, ed., *Air Force Combat Units of World War II* (Washington, D.C.: Office of Air Force History, 1983), pp 407–408. On Weyland's career, see Intvw, Gen O.P. Weyland by James C. Hasdorff, Nov 19, 1974, USAFHRA, K239.0512–813; Ninth AF (hereafter cited as 9AF), "Biographies," 1944, USAFHRA, 533.293, 1944–45; "Biographical Sketch," n.d., USAFHRA, 168.7104–103; XIX TAC, "History of XIX Tactical Air Command," Dec 4, 1943–Jun 30, 1944, USAF-HRA, 537.01, 1943–44.

4. Blumenson, *Patton: Man Behind Legend,* especially the preface and chaps. 1 and 10.

5. Blumenson, ed., *Patton Papers,* pp, 354–355; Blumenson, *Patton: Man Behind Legend,* p 216.

6. Thomas J. Mayock, "Notes on the Development of AAF Tactical Air Doctrine," *Military Affairs* vol 14 (Winter 1950), p 187.

7. Intvw, Weyland, Nov 19, 1974, p 140.

8. Intvw, Gen James Ferguson by Lyn R. Officer and James C. Hasdorff, May 8–9, 1973, USAFHRA, K239.0512–672, p 129.

9. George S. Patton, Jr., *War As I Knew It* (Boston: Houghton Mifflin, 1947), p 99.

10. William C. Stancik and R. Cargill Hall, "Air Force ROTC: Its Origins and Early Years," *Air University Review* vol 35 No. 5 (Jul–Aug 1984), p 42.

11. For the background of Operation Overlord, see Gordon A. Harrison, *Cross-Channel Attack,* [U.S. Army in World War II: Mediterranean Theater of Operations] (Washington, D.C.: Office of the Chief of Military History, 1951); John Keegan, *Six Armies in Normandy* (New York: Viking Press, 1982); Carlo D'Este, *Decision in Normandy* (New York: E. P. Dutton, 1983); Thomas E. Griess, ed., vol 1, *The Second World War: Europe and the Mediterranean* (Wayne, N.J.: Avery Publishing Group, 1984), pp 253–281; Charles B. MacDonald and Martin Blumenson, "Recovery of France," in Vincent J. Esposito, ed., *A Concise History of World War II* (New York: Praeger, 1964), pp 70–85; and Charles B. MacDonald, *The Mighty Endeavor: The American War in Europe* (New York: Quill, 1986), pp 269–284.

12. HQ AAF, *Condensed Analysis of Ninth Air Force in the European Theater of Operations* (Washington, D.C.: Office of Air Force History, 1984), pp 49–55; Wesley Frank Craven and James Lea Cate, eds., *The Army Air Forces in World War II,* vol 3, *Europe: Argument to V–E Day, January 1944–May 1945* (Chicago: University of Chicago Press, 1951; reprint, Washington, D.C.: Office of Air Force History, 1983), pp 107–121; Rpt, Col H.J. Knerr, Dep, Air Support Command (ASC) to CG, AAF, "Report on Manpower and Shipping Requirements,"

prepared by Bradley Committee, Jun 23, 1943, USAFHRA, 612–201A.

13. Rpt, Col Philip Cole *et al.*, VIII ASC to HQ, 8AF, "Observers Report: Air Operations in Support of Ground Forces in North West Africa, March 15–April 5, 1943," Jul 1, 1943, USAFHRA, 650.03–2 [hereafter cited as Rpt, 8AF, "Observers Report" (1943)]. I am indebted to Edgar Raines for pointing out that the range of aircraft provided the air-ground organization with the logic for pairing tactical air commands with field armies, numbered air forces with army groups, and strategic air forces under the theater commander. The interwar Air Board reports made this clear, and air and ground leaders established this standard for World War II. Accordingly, evaluators deemed the range of a tactical air command's fighter-bombers sufficient to cover a field army's frontage, and they tested this concept in the 1941 air-ground maneuvers. Memo, Edgar R. Raines, Historian, Army Center of Military History, May 20, 1991. See also HQ AAF, *Condensed Analysis of Ninth AF*, p 50; John F. Ramsey, *Ninth Air Force in the ETO, Oct 16, 1943 to Apr 16, 1944*, USAF Historical Studies No. 32 (Washington, D.C.: AAF Historical Office, 1945), pp 1–29, 49–65, and appendix 1, pp 198–208.

On doctrinal and organizational analyses during the interwar period, see Futrell, *Ideas, Concepts, Doctrine,* vol 1, *1907–1960*, pp 1–110; Greer, *Development of Air Doctrine, passim*; Davis, *Spaatz*, pp 180–193; Mortensen, *Pattern for Joint Operations,* pp 6–13; Craven and Cate, eds., vol 1, *Plans and Early Operations*, pp 17–74; Shiner, *Foulois*, pp 43–75, 212–235.

14. Rpt, 8AF, "Observers Report" (1943), p 37.

15. *Ibid.*, p 40.

16. *Ibid.*, p 4.

17. *Ibid.*, pp 20, 40. In organizing the crucial air-ground support effort and in establishing the procedures for its practice in that theater, the experience already acquired in combat proved far more significant in shaping action than did the doctrinal pronouncements from army headquarters in Washington, D.C., important as the latter might be. Despite the publication of FM 100–20 (1943), army air and ground leaders in the field relied on what worked, on common sense, and on the more practical FM 31–35 (1942) when ordering their cooperative air-ground operations. For air operations in Sicily and Italy, see Alan F. Wilt, "Allied Cooperation in Sicily and Italy, 1943–45," in B. Franklin Cooling, ed., *Case Studies in the Development of Close Air Support* (Washington, D.C.: Office of Air Force History, 1990), pp 193–236; Harry L. Coles, *Participation of the Ninth and Twelfth Air Forces in the Sicilian Campaign*, USAF Historical Studies No. 37 (Washington, D.C.: AAF Historical Office, 1945); Carlo D'Este, *Bitter Victory: The Battle for Sicily, 1943* (New York: E. P. Dutton, 1988); and Craven and Cate, eds., vol 2, *Europe: Torch to Pointblank*, pp 415–596. For Patton's comments, see Memo, Lt Gen Carl Spaatz, CG, NAAF to Maj Gen Barney Giles, C/S, AAF, Sep 12, 1943, Arnold Collection, File 1938–46, 370.2 (Africa) (34), Box 104, MD, LC. Although Ninth Air Force pilots preparing for the invasion of France benefited from observing air operations in Italy, they considered most innovations like the Rover Joe land-based air force controller system less applicable for the mobile operations they expected in Northwest Europe. Intvw, Weyland, Nov 19, 1974; Ltr, Maj Gen Robert L. Delashaw, 405th FG Comdr, to author, Aug 21, 1989.

18. HQ AAF, *Condensed Analysis of Ninth AF*, p 50; Ramsey, *Ninth Air Force*, pp 1–29, 49–65; and appendix 1, pp 198–208.

19. W. A. Jacobs, "Air Command in the United Kingdom, 1933–44," *Journal of Strategic Studies*, vol 11 (Mar 88), pp 51–78; D'Este, *Decision in Normandy*, p 213.

20. Jacobs, "Air Command," pp 62–64; Lewis H. Brereton, *The Brereton Diaries* (New York: William Morrow, 1946), pp 213–276.

21. HQ 12th Army Group, "Brief of Joint Operations Plan—U.S. Forces for Operation Overlord (revised May 8, 1944)," in RG 331, Records of Allied Operational and Occupation Headquarters, WWII, File 1943–45, 370.2, Box 85, NA.

22. For the often bewildering array of organizational changes from December 1943 to May 1944, see XIX TAC, "History," Dec 4, 1943–Jun 30, 1944; Ramsey, *Ninth Air Force*, appendix 1, pp 198–208; and John Schlight, "Elwood R. Quesada: TAC Air Comes of Age," in John L. Frisbee, ed., *Makers of the Modern Air Force* (Washington, D.C.: Office of Air Force History, 1987), pp 177–198.

23. Schlight, "Elwood R. Quesada," pp 177–198.

24. XIX TAC, "History," Dec 4, 1943–Jun 30, 1944; War Department: The Adjutant General's Office, *Official Army Register*, Jan 1, 1945 (Washington, D.C.: U.S. Government Printing Office, 1945).

25. Eugene M. Greenberg, XIX TAC Signal Office, "Signals: The Story of Communications in the XIX Tactical Air Command up to V–E Day," Jun 15, 1945, USAFHRA 537.901; XIX TAC, "A Report on the Combat Operations of the XIX Tactical Air Command," May 30, 1945, pp 18–23, USAFHRA, 537.02, 1945; George R. Thompson and Dixie R. Harris, *The Signal Corps: The Outcome, Mid-1943 through 1945* [U.S. Army in World War II] (Washington, D.C.: Office of the Chief of Military History, 1966), chap. 4.

26. XIX TAC, "Tactical Air Operations in Europe: A Report on Employment of Fighter-Bombers, Reconnaissance and Night Fighter Aircraft by XIX Tactical Air Command, Ninth Air Force, in Connection with the Third US Army Campaign from 1 August 1944 to VE Day 9 May 1945," May 19, 1945, pp 39–41, USAFHRA, 537.04A, 1945; Blanche D. Coll, Jean E. Keith, and Herbert H. Rosenthal, *The Corps of Engineers: Troops and Equipment*, [U.S. Army in World War II] (Washington, D.C.: Center of Military History, 1958), chap. 14, pp 25, 56, 60.

27. XIX TAC, "History," Dec 4, 1943–Jun 30, 1944; 9AF, "Annual Statistical Summary, 1944," USAFHRA, 533.3083, 1944.

28. XIX TAC, "History," Dec 4, 1943–Jun 30, 1944. See also the monthly histories of the individual flying groups for precise manning and aircraft statistics.

29. Rpt, AAF Evaluation Board, ETO, "Effectiveness of Third-Phase Tactical Air Operations in the ETO, 4 May 1944 to 8 May 1945," pp 305–308, USAFHRA, 138.4–36, Aug 1945 (hereafter cited as AAF Eval Bd, "Third Phase Tactical Air Ops"); U.S. Forces, European Theater, Battle Studies, vol 2: Air Operations, No. 14: "Fighter-Bomber Cooperation" (USFET, n.d.), US Army Military History Institute (MHI).

30. Ninth Air Force's procurement problem worsened initially when General Quesada, among others, agreed to have projected P–51s sent to the Eighth Air Force where they could be better used as fighter escorts for the heavy bombers in the struggle for air supremacy. Until late spring, the Ninth had to make do with the Eighth's cast-off P–47 "clinkers." By D-Day, however, the Ninth began receiving the D25 and D27 Thunderbolts, which had paddle-blade propellers, bubble canopies, and larger fuel tanks. These Thunderbolt models became famous in the battle for France. Likewise, new P–51Ds arrived in late spring, and this model, with its teardrop plexiglass canopy and extra gun in each wing, proved more than a match for the German FW 190 and Bf 109 aircraft. Supply procedures in Britain called for common user items to be sent to units through Army supply channels, while specialized air forces' items were supplied through air forces channels but under USSTAF auspices. In practice, both channels broke down and supply officials often resorted to informal cooperation. See XIX TAC, "History," Dec 4, 1943–Jun 30, 1944; Craven and Cate, eds., vol 3, *Europe: Argument to V–E Day*, pp 631–664; Rpt, IX Fighter

Command, A–4, n.d., Quesada Collection, Box 3, MD, LC; Memo, 9AF, Jan 29, 1944, USAFHRA, 168.6005–1033; Intvw, Lt Gen Elwood R. Quesada by Steve Long and Ralph Stephenson, May 1975, USAFHRA, K239.0512–838.

31. XIX TAC, "History," Dec 4, 1943–Jun 30, 1944.

32. *Ibid.*

33. Ramsey, *Ninth Air Force*, pp 91–94, 101–107; XIX TAC, "History," Dec 4, 1943–Jun 30, 1944; IX TAC, "Unit History," Apr 1944, USAFHRA, 536.02, Apr 1944, May 1944; Intvw, Lt Gen John J. Burns, USAF (Ret) by the author, Jan 7, 1992. General Quesada's range program set the stage for extensive collaboration with civilian technicians on the continent. Ultimately, each tactical air command possessed an Operational Research Section that applied scientific and engineering expertise to tactical air power problems.

34. 9AF, "Weekly Intelligence Summaries" (hereafter cited as "Weekly Intsum"), Nov 3, 1943–Jun 1, 1944, USAFHRA, 533.607, 1944–45; 9AF, "Operational Statistics," Jan 1, 1944–Jun 1, 1944, USAFHRA, 533.3082, 1944.

35. Craven and Cate, eds., vol 3, *Europe: Argument to V–E Day*, chap. 2; Air Ministry (Great Britain), *German Air Force*, chap. 13; MacDonald, *Mighty Endeavor*, pp 266–268.

36. 9AF, "Weekly Intsum"; 9AF, "Operational Statistics"; IX TAC, "Unit History," Apr 1944, p 4; XIX TAC, "History," Dec 4, 1943–Jun 30, 1944. Ninth Air Force leaders successfully promoted a vigorous program to upgrade the status of fighter-bomber achievements in the Northwest European campaign. After the invasion, combat experience found the fighter-bomber employed far more often as a bomber than as a fighter, significantly altering the fighter-bomber pilot's image.

37. Robert H. George, *Ninth Air Force, Apr to Nov 1944*, USAF Historical Studies No. 36 (Washington, D.C.: AAF Historical Office, 1945), pp 30–49.

38. George, *Ninth AF,* pp 52–60; AAF Eval Bd, "Third Phase Tactical Air Ops," pp 48–49; Craven and Cate, eds., vol 3, *Europe: Argument to V–E Day*, pp 139–140.

39. XIX TAC, "History," Dec 4, 1943–Jun 30, 1944. By mid-April, XIX TAC was deployed at the following airstrips in Kent:

Unit	Location
100th Ftr Wing	Lashenden ALG
354th Ftr Gp	Lashenden ALG
358th Ftr Gp	High Halden ALG
362d Ftr Gp	Headcorn ALG
363d Ftr Gp	Staplehurst ALG
303d Ftr Wing	Ashford ALG
36th Ftr Gp	Kingsnorth ALG
373d Ftr Gp	Woodchurch ALG
406th Ftr Gp	Ashford ALG

40. *Ibid.*

41. Schlight, "Elwood R. Quesada," p 189.

42. HQ AAF, AAF Ltr 80–3, "Air Employment Terminology," Nov 16, 1944, Arnold Collection, File 1938–46, Box 104, MD, LC.

43. See for example, XIX TAC, "Combat Operations," May 30, 1945, introduction.

44. IX TAC, "Unit History," Apr 1944, p 4.

45. Cooperative efforts between the First Army and IX TAC fell short of collocating their headquarters. For details on the lecture program, see Ramsey, *Ninth Air Force*, p 104; Rpt, IX Fighter Command, A–3, n.d., Quesada Collection, Box 3, MD, LC; IX ASC, "Reference Guide on Tactical Employment of Air Power Organization and Control Channels of Tactical Units, Prepared Oct 29, 1943, revised Feb 24, 1944," USAFHRA, 168.6005–103A, Feb 25, 1944.

46. US3A, "After Action Report, Aug 1, 1944–May 9, 1945," vol 2: Staff Section Reports, part 3: "G–2 Section Report," pp 4–5; XIX TAC, "History," Dec 4, 1943–Jun 30, 1944.

47. US3A, "After Action Rpt," vol 2, part 3: "G–2 Section Rpt," pp 5–7.

48. Rpt, IX Fighter Command, A–3.

49. Intvw, Weyland, Nov 19, 1974, pp 64–76; XIX TAC, "History," Dec 4, 1943–Jun 30, 1944.

50. Patton, Diary Entries, May 26, 27, 1944.

51. Blumenson, ed., *Patton Papers*, p 30.

52. Rpt, HQ Seventh Army, "Notes on the Sicilian Campaign," Oct 30, 1943.

53. *Ibid.*, p 6.

54. *Ibid.*, p 12.

55. *Ibid.*, Annex, p 2.

56. Intvw, Weyland, Nov 19, 1974, pp 67, 76.

57. Memo, Raines, May 20, 1991.

58. Ltr, Gen Sir B.L. Montgomery to Lt Gen George S. Patton, Jr., May 4, 1944, Patton Collection, Box 14, MD, LC.

59. Ltr, Lt Gen George S. Patton, Jr., to Gen Sir B.L. Montgomery, May 7, 1944, Patton Collection, Box 14, MD, LC.

60. Omar N. Bradley, *A Soldier's Story* (New York: Henry Holt, 1951), p 249. Despite Bradley's understandable irritation, Brereton did not refuse joint training because he preferred other missions before close air support. His background in tactical operations, his experience with the British in the Middle East, and his offer to conduct such training in May argue to the contrary. Moreover, he assigned Major General Ralph Royce, his deputy commander, to serve as Ninth Air Force liaison officer with General Bradley on board the USS *Augusta* command ship during the invasion. Later, Royce would accompany Bradley ashore when the First Army commander established his Normandy command post. See Rpt, Col Philip Cole, "Air Planning for Overlord," Aug 8, 1944, USAFHRA, 248.411–16, 1944.

61. For narrative and analysis of the landing and Normandy campaign, see Harrison, *Cross-Channel Attack*; Martin Blumenson, *Breakout and Pursuit*, [U.S. Army in World War II: European Theater of Operaions] (Washington, D.C.: Office of the Chief of Military History, 1965); D'Este, *Decision in Normandy*; Griess, ed., vol 1, *Second World War*, pp 253–281; MacDonald, *Mighty Endeavor*, pp 241–319.

62. AAF Eval Bd, "Third Phase Tactical Air Ops," pp 65–75; Craven and Cate, eds., vol 3, *Europe: Argument to V–E Day*, pp 185–199; George, *Ninth AF*, pp 76–81.

63. HQ 12th Army Group, "Joint Operations Plan"; AAF Eval Bd, "Third Phase Tactical Air Ops," pp 62–63; 9AF, "Weekly Intsum"; 9AF, "Operational Statistics." See also W. A. Jacobs, "The Battle for France," in Cooling, ed., *Close Air Support*, pp 237–293; Col E.L. Johnson, G–3 (Air), FUSA to AGF (Army Ground Forces) Board, HQ ETOUSA, "Information Regarding Air-Ground Joint Operations," Jul 16, 1944, RG 337, Entry 29, Box 51, NA.

64. IX TAC, "Unit History," June 1944, p 2, USAFHRA, 536.02, Jun 1944; AAF Eval Bd, "Third Phase Tactical Air Ops," pp 65–75; Craven and Cate, eds., vol 3, *Europe: Argument to V–E Day*, pp 185–199; George, *Ninth AF*, pp 76–81.

65. IX TAC, "Unit History," Jun 1944; XIX TAC, "History of the XIX Tactical Air Command," Jul 1, 1944–Feb 28, 1945, part 2, Operations Narrative, USAFHRA, 537.01, 1944–45; George, *Ninth AF*, pp 97–98.

66. For the Cherbourg campaign, see George, *Ninth AF*, pp 101–108; AAF Eval Bd, "Third Phase Tactical Air Ops," pp 75–76; Craven and Cate, eds., vol 3, *Europe: Argument to V–E Day*, pp 199–204; and Memo, Brig Gen D. M. Schlatter, Dep C/S-Opns, 9AF, to CG, USSTAF, "Report on Cherbourg Attack, Jul 21, 1944," Spaatz Collection, Box 164, MD, LC.

67. Memo, Brig Gen Schlatter, to USSTAF, "Report on Cherbourg Attack."

68. This analysis is based on Rpt, Col E. L. Johnson, G–3 (Air), FUSA to AGF Board, HQ ETOUSA, "Information Regarding Air-Ground Joint Operations," Jul 16, 1944, RG 337, Entry 29, Box 51, NA (hereafter cited as "Johnson Report,"). See also First Army (hereafter cited as US1A) G–3 (Air), "Air

Support Report, 6 Aug 1944," USAFHRA, 533.4501–3, May–Aug 1944. Military designations for Army air specialists were G–2 (Air), Army air intelligence, and G–3 (Air), Army air operations. For the airmen, intelligence was termed A–2 and operations A–3, except at the squadron level, which used S–2 and S–3, respectively.

69. "SCR" designated a Signal Corps Radio. For air support party liaison communications, Weyland's command relied primarily on the long-range SCR–399, a 400-watt mobile HF set paired with a SCR–624 VHF set operating on 110 volts. Half-tracks transported the equipment with armored divisions, while 2½-ton trucks operated with the infantry. The SCR–399 100-mile range radio replaced the less durable SCR–299 early in the campaign, while the SCR–624, an adaptation of the SCR–522 for ground use, provided a 130-mile line-of-sight range from ground to plane. The command used ground force land lines with the HF radio for standby during static situations, but it relied on HF sets for mobile operations for requesting air missions, passing bomblines, field orders, weather reports, and operations results. The VHF radio remained the mainstay for contacting aircraft, adjusting artillery fire, and receiving immediate "flash" reconnaissance reports. See also Greenberg, "Signals"; XIX TAC, "Combat Operations," May 30, 1945, pp 18–23; Thompson and Harris, *Signal Corps*, chap. 4.

70. IX TAC, "Unit History," Jul 1–31, 1944, pp 12–13, USAFHRA, 536.02, July 1944.

71. *Ibid.*; 9AF, "Reconnaissance in the Ninth Air Force: A Report on Reconnaissance Operations During the European Campaign," pp 21–27, n.d. [May 9, 1945], MHI; AAF Eval Bd, "Third Phase Tactical Ops," pp 346–350.

72. See FM 100–20, para 16. See also FM 31–35, para 10.

73. Johnson Report.

74. IX TAC, "Unit History," July 1944, p 14; Rpt, IX TAC, A–3, n.d., Quesada Collection, Box 3, MD, LC.

75. IX Engineer Command completed six airfields in June. See George, *Ninth AF*, pp 99–101; AAF Eval Bd, "Third Phase Tactical Ops," p 67; 9AF, "Progress Report, Airfield Construction," July 24, 1944, USAFHRA, 168.7104–83.

76. IX TAC, "Unit History," July 1944, p 7; Thompson and Harris, *Signal Corps*, pp 102–104, 433–435. See also Thompson and Harris chap. 4, pp 174–176, for a discussion of the modified SCR–584 introduced by Weyland's command in the fall of 1944.

77. IX TAC, "Unit History," July 1944, pp 7–8.

78. *Ibid.*, p 8; 513th Fighter Sqdn, "Unit History Report for Period Ending Jul 31, 1944," USAFHRA, GP–406–HI.

79. George, *Ninth AF*, chaps. 3, 4; XIX TAC, "History," July 1, 1944–Feb 28, 1945, pt. 2.

80. In June 1944 planners reshuffled reconnaissance units to support the larger visual and photographic requests. The newly designated 10th Photo Reconnaissance Group sent two of its four photo squadrons to the 67th Tactical Reconnaissance Group in return for the 12th and 15th Tactical Reconnaissance Squadrons. Each group now had two photo and two reconnaissance squadrons. On June 16, the 10th joined the XIX TAC, but remained under IX TAC control until after XIX TAC became operational with Third Army. See IX TAC, "Unit History," June 1944. See also Thomas G. Ivie, *Aerial Reconnaissance: The 10th Photo Recon Group in World War II* (Fallbrook, Calif.: Aero Publishers, 1981), pp 37–38; Ltr, Brig Gen Russell A. Berg, USAF (Ret) to author, Sep 6, 1989.

81. George, *Ninth AF*, p 91.

82. AAF Eval Bd, "Third Phase Tactical Ops," p 1. See also chapter 1 in "Third Phase Tactical Ops" for a discussion of the

more contemporary concept of Battlefield Air Interdiction.

83. Rpt, 8AF, "Observers Report" (1943).

84. George, *Ninth AF*, p 149.

85. 9AF, "Report on Activities of the Ninth Air Force, period Jun 6–Aug 28, 1944," p 9, USAFHRA, 533.306–2, 1944.

86. For Weyland's awareness of the problem, see XIX TAC, "Twelve-Thousand Fighter-Bomber Sorties: XIX Tactical Air Command's First Month of Operations in Support of Third US Army in France," Sep 30, 1944, "Recapitulation," USAFHRA, 168.7104–69.

87. Memo, Brig Gen Schlatter to USSTAF, "Rpt on Cherbourg Attack," p 5.

88. George, *Ninth AF*, p 118.

89. XIX TAC, "History," Jul 1, 1944–Feb 28, 1945, pt 2; US3A, "After Action Rpt," vol 2, part 3: "G–2 Section Rpt," pp 8–9; Cmd, p 2; G–3, p 11.

90. US3A, "After Action Rpt," vol 2, part 3: "G–2 Section Rpt," p 8.

91. *Ibid.*, p 9; II, Cmd, p 2; II, G–3, p 9; Rpt, IX TAC, G–3 (Air), n.d., Quesada Collection, Box 5, MD, LC.

92. On Operation Cobra, see D'Este, *Decision in Normandy*, part 3; Blumenson, *Breakout and Pursuit*, part 3; Russell F. Weigley, *Eisenhower's Lieutenants: The Campaigns of France and Germany, 1944–45* (Bloomington: Indiana University Press, 1981), chap. 8; Bradley, *Soldier's Story*, chap. 17.

93. AAF Eval Bd, "Third Phase Tactical Air Ops," pp 85–94; Craven and Cate, eds., vol 3, *Europe: Argument to V–E Day*, pp 228–238; IX TAC, "Unit History," July 1944, pp 2–5; Rpt, 12th Army Group, Air Effects Committee, "Effect of Air Power on Military Operations, Western Europe," 15 July 1945, pp 102–105, MHI (hereafter cited as Rpt, Air Effects Committee, "Effect of Air Power").

94. Intvw, Quesada, May 12, 1975; IX TAC, "Unit History," July 1944, pp 2–5; Craven and Cate, eds., vol 3, *Europe: Argument to V–E Day*, pp 238–243; Schlight, "Elwood R. Quesada," pp 177–198.

95. US1A "Air Support Report," Aug 6, 1944, pp 10–11; 9AF, "Weekly Intelligence Summary," Jul 24–31, 1944; 9AF, "Operational Statistics," Jul 24–31, 1944.

96. XIX TAC, "History," Jul 1, 1944–Feb 28, 1945, pt. 2; Blumenson, ed., *Patton Papers*, pp 489–493.

Chapter 3

1. Weyland began a daily diary on July 29, 1944, which is indispensable to an understanding of XIX TAC operations. See Otto P. Weyland, "Diary, Jul 29, 1944–May 18, 1945," USAFHRA, 168.7104–1, 1944–45. For an overview of the campaign in France, see Weigley, *Eisenhower's Lieutenants*; Blumenson, *Breakout and Pursuit*; D'Este, *Decision in Normandy*; Craven and Cate, eds., vol 3, *Europe: Argument to V–E Day*, chap. 8.

2. This discussion of the drive across France is based in large part on the Weyland diary and the following: US3A, "After Action Rpt," vol 1, Aug and Sep Ops; XIX TAC, "12,000 FB Sorties" Sep 30, 1944; XIX TAC, "History," Jul 1, 1944–Feb 28, 1945, part 2; Blumenson, ed., *Patton Papers*, pp 494–560; US3A, "After Action Rpt," vol 1, Aug 1, 1944; and Weyland, "Diary," Aug 1, 1944. The fighter groups seem to have been assigned on the basis of their location and current operational commitment.

3. US3A, "After Action Rpt," vol 1, Aug 1, 1944; Weyland, "Diary," Aug 1, 1944.

4. For a discussion of XIX TAC's communication systems, see XIX TAC, "Combat Operations," pp 18–22; Greenberg, "Signals"; XIX TAC, "Combat Operations,"

May 30, 1945, pp 18–23; and Thompson and Harris, *Signal Corps*, chap. 4.

5. Weyland, "Diary," Aug 1, 1944; XIX TAC, "12,000 FB Sorties," Aug 1, 1944. The first week was a transitional period marked by a gradual buildup of forces. See XIX TAC, "Morning Summaries," Aug 8–Sep 30, 1944, USAFHRA, 537.306A, Aug–Sep 1944.

6. XIX TAC, "History," Jul 1, 1944–Feb 28, 1945, part 2; XIX TAC, "12,000 FB Sorties," pp 1–6. Normally, the fighter control center (later renamed the tactical control center), or the ground controller, would provide new bombline information to pilots.

7. Intvw, Weyland, Nov 19, 1974, p 143. Air liaison officers assigned to ground units were initially called Air Support Party Officers, and later Tactical Air Party Officers.

8. Criticism of Patton's generalship is found in Weigley, *Eisenhower's Lieutenants*, pp 243–245.

9. For Weyland's views, see XIX TAC, "Combat Operations," p 43; On the air umbrella concept, see FM 100–20, sec 3 para 16a (3)b.(1), p 11.

10. The phrase is the XIX TAC historian's.

11. 9AF, "Schedule of Operations, Aug 2, 1944," USAFHRA, 533.3082, Aug 1944.

12. XIX TAC, "12,000 FB Sorties," pp 1–6. Lt John J. Burns, a 371st Fighter Group pilot, recalled that pilots served as air liaison officers with the ground units, but only exclusively after the drive east. In Brittany, his main air control officer was a former armor officer. Lieutenant Burns considered the air control officer, who eventually was killed at Brest, an outstanding air-ground liaison officer. See Intvw, Lt Gen John J. Burns by Hugh N. Ahmann, Jun 5–8, 1984, and Jan 1986, reel no. 41509, USAFHRA, K239.0512–1587, pp 21–27; Intvw, Burns, Jan 7, 1992.

13. XIX TAC, "12,000 FB Sorties," pp 1–6; Intvw, Burns, Jun 5–8, 1984, p 14; Intvw, Burns, Jan 7, 1992.

14. XIX TAC, "Combat Operations," pp 27–31, 38–40; XIX TAC, "Tactical Air Operations in Europe, pp 39–41; AAF Evaluation Board, ETO, "HQ Ninth AF, Report on Tactical Air Cooperation, Organization, Methods and Procedures with Special Emphasis on Phase III Operations," Jul 31, 1945, pp 327–361, USAFHRA, 138.4–34, 1945.

15. "Prepared Hessian surfacing" is the British term for prefabricated bituminized surfacing, the ready-made, tarred canvas, or Hessian-type material, used for aircraft runways, taxiways, and storage areas in World War II.

16. XIX TAC, "History," Jul 1, 1944–Feb 28, 1945, part 1, pp 114–126; Craven and Cate, eds., vol 3, *Europe: Argument to V–E Day*, p 132; *Roulement* is a French term meaning "rolling" (forward).

17. In this regard, Patton agreed with Bradley, who told him privately that Brest had to be taken to uphold the view that the U.S. Army could not be beaten. Blumenson, ed., *Patton Papers*, p 532.

18. 36th FG, "Unit History," Jul–Sep 1944, USAFHRA, GP–36–HI.

19. For Weyland's early views on statistical problems, see XIX TAC, "12,000 FB Sorties," p 1.

20. Keegan, *Six Armies*; D'Este, *Decision in Normandy;* Griess, ed., vol 1, *Second World War*, chaps. 14, 15; MacDonald and Blumenson, "Recovery of France," in Esposito, *Concise History*, pp 91–103; MacDonald, *Mighty Endeavor*, pp 331–376.

21. Von Kluge replaced von Rundstedt on July 5, after the latter advised Hitler to abandon Caen's defense. Later, von Kluge assumed direct command of Army Group B after British fighter-bombers severely wounded its commander, Rommel, on July 17. Although von Kluge and other senior *Wehrmacht* officers questioned Hitler's strategy, they dared not oppose the *Fuehrer*, especially after the abortive plot of July 20, 1944.

22. HQ 9AF, "Operations Journal," Aug 6, 1944, USAFHRA, 533.305, Apr–Dec 1944. For most of the campaign in France, the 100th Wing controlled the 354th, 358th, 371st, and 405th Fighter Groups, and the 10th Photo Reconnaissance Group; the

303d Wing controlled the 36th, 373d, and 406th Fighter Groups.

23. US3A, "After Action Rpt," vol 2, part 3: "G–2 Section Rpt," pp 11–12; Ivie, *Aerial Reconnaissance*, pp 54–56; Patton, Diary Entry, Aug 6, 20, 1944.

24. XIX TAC, "12,000 FB Sorties," Aug 7, 1944; XIX TAC, "Tactical Air Operations in Europe," pp 16–17.

25. Weyland, "Diary," Aug 16, 1944; Thompson and Harris, *Signal Corps,* chap. 4; Rpt, Ninth Air Force, "Tactical Air Operations, Jun 6–Aug 28, 1944," p 16, USAF-HRA, 533.306–2, 1944.

26. Ltr, Dr. David Griggs, Member, Advisor Specialist Group, USSTAF, to E. L. Bowles, Expert Consultant to Secy War, Oct 17, 1944, Quesada Collection, Box 5, MD, LC. In late September the command renamed the fighter control center the tactical control center (TCC) and decided to locate it near the advance headquarters rather than in the rear, between the wing and the operational groups. In this instance, the civilians seemed most concerned with fixed interdiction targets, while Weyland's chief worry centered on the *Luftwaffe* threat.

27. XIX TAC, "12,000 FB Sorties," Aug 7–8, 1944; XIX TAC, "Morning Summary," Aug 8, 1944.

28. Weyland, "Diary," Aug 6, 1944.

29. *Ibid.*, Aug 6, 9, 1944. On direct orders from General Arnold on January 25, 1945, Brigadier General Grandison Gardner, Eglin Field commander, conducted extensive tests under strict security against simulated Crossbow targets using a variety of weapons and attack methods. After completing their report on March 1, General Gardner and his team briefed their findings to commanders at every major headquarters in England. Craven and Cate, eds., vol 3, *Europe: Argument to V–E Day*, pp 97–99.

30. XIX TAC, "Morning Summary," Aug 10–11, 1944.

31. D'Este, *Decision in Normandy*, pp 418–460; Blumenson, *Breakout and Pursuit*, pp 479–589; Griess, ed., vol 1, *Second World War,* pp 336–338.

32. Craven and Cate, eds., vol 3, *Europe: Argument to V–E Day*, chap. 2; Air Ministry (Great Britain), *German Air Force*, pp 333–339, 354, 365–367; XIX TAC, "History," Jul 1, 1944–Feb 28, 1945, part 2, August Operations.

33. XIX TAC, "12,000 FB Sorties," Aug 17, 1944. On German losses see D'Este, *Decision in Normandy*, pp 431–432, 437–438; and AAF Eval Bd, "Third Phase Tactical Air Ops," p 121.

34. Weyland, "Diary," Aug 13, 1944; XIX TAC, "Tactical Air Operations in Europe," p 17. The name "X-Ray" appears to have been given to the liaison detachment after the summer campaign.

35. US3A, "After Action Rpt," vol 2, part 4: "G–3 Section Rpt," p 12.

36. Weyland, "Diary," Aug 16, 1944.

37. *Ibid.*, Aug 14, 1944. In France the command's forward directional post radars consisted of British Type 15 and 11 radars. Thompson and Harris, *Signal Corps*, pp 151, 639. In an intriguing incident at this August 14 meeting, General Vandenberg proposed in the event First and Third Armies reversed their areas of operations, that Quesada and Weyland should exchange fighter-bomber groups as well. Weyland did not concur. Although such a move might also demonstrate tactical air power's flexibility and mobility, Weyland clearly believed that his units should remain under his control to maintain the integrity of the command.

38. Ivie, *Aerial Reconnaissance*, pp 54–61.

39. XIX TAC comments on the Y-service focus on its importance in the Ardennes Campaign rather than in the battle of France. XIX TAC, "Tactical Air Operations in Europe," p 31; Weyland, "Diary"; Rpt, 9AF, "Tactical Air Operations, Jun 6–Aug 28, 1944," p 16, USAFHRA, 533.306–2, 1944.

40. XIX TAC, "Morning Summary," Aug 10, 11, 13, 1944.

41. XIX TAC, "Morning Summary," Aug 15, 16, 17, 1944; XIX TAC, "12,000 FB Sorties," Aug 17, 1944.

42. Geoffrey Perret, *There's a War to Be Won: The United States Army in World War II* (New York: Random House, 1991), chap. 6; Weigley, *Eisenhower's Lieutenants*, chaps. 1 and 2.

43. MacDonald, *Mighty Endeavor*, pp 320–327; Weigley, *Eisenhower's Lieutenants*, pp 218–237; Griess, ed., vol 1, *Second World War*, pp 347–350.

44. XIX TAC, "12,000 FB Sorties," Aug 20, 1944.

45. Weigley, *Eisenhower's Lieutenants*, pp 243–245; US3A, "After Action Rpt," vol 1, Aug 23–24, 1944; Blumenson, ed., *Patton Papers*, pp 526–528.

46. AAF Eval Bd, "Third Phase Tactical Air Ops," p 118.

47. XIX TAC, "12,000 FB Sorties," pp 1–6; AAF Eval Bd, "Third Phase Tactical Air Ops," pp 305–309.

48. XIX TAC, "Morning Summary," Aug 20–24, 1944; XIX TAC, "12,000 FB Sorties," Aug 20–24, 1944. The command favored the small, high-velocity rockets before bombs because of their flexibility of use in combat and because they added little to an airplane's weight and did not appreciably effect an airplane's speed.

49. XIX TAC, "12,000 FB Sorties," Aug 24, 1944; 371st FG, "Unit History," Aug 1944, USAFHRA, GP–371–HI, Aug 1944.

50. US3A, "After Action Rpt," vol 1, Aug 26, 1944; Blumenson, ed., *Patton Papers*, p 547; Blumenson, *Breakout and Pursuit*, pp 664–670.

51. XIX TAC, "Morning Summary," Aug 25, 1944; XIX TAC, "12,000 FB Sorties," Aug 25, 1944; 354th FG, "Unit History," Aug–Sep 1944, USAFHRA GP–354–HI(FI).

52. Memo, Lt Col Charles H. Hallet, AC/S, to CG, XIX TAC, "Air Support of Third Army's Drive to the East," Aug 23, 1944, USAFHRA, 168.7104–85; Weyland, "Diary." Weyland also discussed the urgent need for air base defenses because of Third Army's departure from the Le Mans area.

53. XIX TAC, "12,000 FB Sorties," Aug 30, 1944.

54. US3A, "After Action Rpt," vol 1, Aug 30, 1944. See Memo, untitled, undated, on IX Troop Carrier supply flights to Third Army, USAFHRA, K110.7006–2. For a concise analysis of Third Army's supply dilemma, see Martin L. Van Creveld, *Supplying War: Logistics from Wallerstein to Patton* (Cambridge and New York: Cambridge University Press, 1977), chap. 7. Third Army's low supply priorities even extended to communications equipment. Early in the campaign, its radios consisted of one set each for the entire army of the following short-range (less than 25 miles) sets: SCR–300, the celebrated FM walkie-talkie, SCR–508 portable radio, and SCR–510 (like the 508, but vehicle-mounted), and eight SCR–511 portable cavalry guidon sets. See Thompson and Harris, *Signal Corps*, pp 151, 638–639.

55. Craven and Cate, eds., vol 3, *Europe: Argument to V–E Day*, pp 583–585; Intvw, Burns, Jan 7, 1992.

56. US3A, "After Action Rpt," vol 1, Aug 30, 1944. See Memo, on IX Troop Carrier supply flights; Van Creveld, *Supplying War*, chap. 7.

57. US3A, "After Action Rpt," vol 2, part 3: "G–2 Section Rpt," p 52.

58. XIX TAC, "12,000 FB Sorties." See also, HQ AAF, "Air-Ground Teamwork on the Western Front: The Role of the XIX Tactical Air Command during August 1944," Wings at War Series, No. 5, USAFHRA, 537.04C, Aug 1944; XIX TAC, "Planes Over Patton: XIX Tactical Air Command's Support of Third Army in Its Swift End-Run Through France," Sep 30, 1944, USAFHRA, 168.7104–86, Sep 30, 1944. The command's exploits are also highlighted in "U.S. Tactical Airpower in Europe," in *Impact*, vol 3, No. 5 (May 1945), USAFHRA, 168.7104–92, May 1945.

59. XIX TAC, "History," Jul 1, 1944–Feb 28, 1945, part 1, Sep 1944, p 4.

60. US3A, "After Action Rpt," vol 1, p 52; XIX TAC, "Morning Summary," Sep 1–16, 1944. Memo, National Security Agency (hereafter cited as NSA), "Ultra

and Its Use by XIX TAC," May 30, 1945, in "Reports by U.S. Army Ultra Representatives with Army Field Commands in the European Theater of Operations," part 2, XIX TAC, pp 104–109, NSA, Special Research, History–023. For a discussion of Ultra's role with Third Army and the XIX TAC, see chap. 4, p 186.

61. 36th FG, "Unit History," Sep 1944; XIX TAC, "12,000 FB Sorties," Aug 24, 1944; 371st FG, "Unit History," Aug 1944.

62. General Weyland needed the A–20 Havoc (F–3) for daytime reconnaissance, and Ninth Air Force agreed to its use until the night program got underway. As Colonel Berg later recalled, however, the squadron became available for daylight operations, not because of modest requirements for night photography during mobile operations, but because it lacked night navigation aids at the time. In any event, it proved to be a valuable if vulnerable reconnaissance asset. Ltr, Brig Gen Berg to author, Sep 8, 1989; Ivie, *Aerial Reconnaissance*, p 68.

63. XIX TAC, "History," Jul 1, 1944–Feb 28, 1945; 406th FG, "Unit History," Jun 1, 1944–May 1, 1945, USAFHRA, GP–406–HI, 1944–45.

64. Weyland, "Diary," Sep 9–11, 1944.

65. Air Force chief, General Arnold, sent his congratulations, adding he thought it "most appropriate that the Air Force Tactical Commander was present with the Army Commander at the surrender ceremony." XIX TAC, "12,000 FB Sorties," p 5; 9AF, "Rpt on Activities, Jun 6–Aug 28, 1944"; Craven and Cate, eds., vol 3, *Europe: Argument to V–E Day*, pp 265–266.

66. XIX TAC, "Tactical Air Operations in Europe," p 1.

67. *Ibid.*

68. Blumenson, *Breakout and Pursuit*, chap. 30.

69. Weyland, "Diary," Aug 22, 1944, Sep 2, 1944.

70. For operational information on the command's role in the Brittany assault in September, see XIX TAC, "Morning Summaries," Sep 3–18, 1944. Although a single

mission normally involved three 12-plane squadrons, variations to match needs occurred frequently.

71. On the Third Army buildup for the Mosel Offensive, see US3A, "After Action Rpt," vol 1, Sep 1–5, 1944. Characteristically, Weyland met personally with Third Army leaders on the proposed offensive. Although this meeting took place on the eve of the attack, both his command's proven flexibility and the X-Ray detachment's liaison work offset potential problems that might otherwise have arisen on such short notice.

72. US3A, "After Action Rpt," vol 1, Sep 4–5, 1944. For the Third Army's offensive, see Weigley, *Eisenhower's Lieutenants*, pp 327–344; Blumenson, *Breakout and Pursuit*, chap. 32.

73. B.H. Liddell Hart, *History of the Second World War* (New York: G. P. Putnam's Sons, 1970), p 557.

74. AAF Eval Bd, "Third Phase Tactical Air Ops," pp 113–114.

75. For the air role, see AAF Eval Bd, "Third Phase Tactical Air Ops," pp 113–118; Craven and Cate, eds., vol 3, *Europe: Argument to V–E Day*, pp 262–265; XIX TAC, "Combat Operations," pp 55–57; XIX TAC, "History," Sep 1944."

76. Blumenson, *Breakout and Pursuit*, chap. 30.

77. Weyland, "Diary," Aug 22, 1944, Sep 2, 1944; AAF Eval Bd, "Third Phase Tactical Air Ops," pp 113–114.

78. XIX TAC, "History," Jul 1, 1944–Feb 28, 1945, Sep 1944; AAF Eval Bd, "Third Phase Tactical Air Ops," pp 113–118; XIX TAC, "History," Jul 1, 1944–Feb 28, 1945, part 2, pp 172–173; XIX TAC, "Combat Operations," pp 9–10; XIX TAC, "Tactical Air Operations in Europe," pp 5–8.

79. XIX TAC, "Combat Operations," p 56. See also Third Army's similar assessment in US3A, "After Action Rpt," vol 1, Aug Ops, p 52, and vol 2, part 4: "G–3 Section Rpt," p 16.

80. Weyland, "Diary," Sep 8, 1944; US3A, "After Action Rpt," vol 1, Sep 8, 1944.

81. This analysis of tactical air support at Brest is based primarily on XIX TAC, "Morning Summaries," Sep 3–16, 1944; 9AF, "Weekly Intsum," Sep 3–16, 1944; and XIX TAC, "History," Jul 1, 1944–Feb 28, 1945, pp 7–25. See also 358th FG, "Unit History," Aug–Sep 1944, USAFHRA, GP–358–HI; 358th FG, "Operational Reports," Aug–Sep 1944, USAFHRA, GP–358–SU–OP–S, Aug–Sep 1944; 362d FG, "Unit History," Aug–Sep 1944, USAF-HRA, GP–362–HI; 362d FG, "Operational Reports," Aug–Sep 1944, USAFHRA, GP–362–SU–OP–S, Aug–Sep 1944.

82. Appropriately, the 362d Fighter Group appeared for the finale at Brest. With the 358th, it had flown in support of VIII Corps in Brittany nearly every day since August 1, 1944. Their efforts intensified from August 25, and after September 10, these two groups normally flew against Brest targets daily. After the fortress surrendered on September 18, both groups immediately began flying armed reconnaissance missions in Germany from their new bases in eastern France. See 358th FG, "Unit History," Aug–Sep 1944; 358th FG, "Operational Rpts," Aug–Sep 1944; 362d FG, "Unit History," Aug–Sep 1944; 362d FG, "Operational Rpts," Aug–Sep 1944.

83. Weyland, "Diary," Sep 6, 1944.

84. Ibid. For airfield construction programs, see XIX TAC, "12,000 FB Sorties," pp 1–6; Intvw, Burns, Jun 5–8, 1984, p 14; Intvw, Burns, Jan 7, 1992; XIX TAC, "History," Jul 1, 1944–Feb 28, 1945, pp 77–82.

85. XXIX TAC received the 36th and 373d Fighter Groups on October 1, 1944, and September 29, 1944, respectively. The 371st Fighter Group was transferred to the XII TAC. Weyland, "Diary," Sep 7–8, 1944; XIX TAC, "History," Jul 1, 1944–Feb 28, 1945, pp 77–82.

86. Weyland, "Diary," Sep 10, 1944; US3A, "After Action Rpt," vol 1, Sep 21, 1944.

87. The worsening supply situation is recorded in the daily ops analyses and summaries. See also US3A, "After Action Rpt," vol 1, Aug–Sep 1944.

88. XIX TAC, "History," Jul 1, 1944–Feb 28, 1945, pp 121–124. Unit movements are also described in the group histories for August and September 1944. For unit movements, the command used its own trucks, but it always needed assistance from Ninth Air Force and Third Army for necessary additional transportation.

89. 36th FG, "Unit History," Aug–Sep 1944; 354th FG, "Unit History," Aug–Sep 1944.

90. Bad weather in September forced the aviation engineers to lay heavier pierced-steel planking, also known as Marston Mat, for its runways. See chap. 4, pp 188–189, and 36th FG, "Unit History," Aug–Sep 1944; 354th FG, "Unit History," Aug–Sep 1944.

91. Weyland, "Diary," Sep 17, 1944.

92. XIX TAC, "Morning Summaries," Sep 19–25, 1944; 9AF, "Weekly Intsum," Sep 19–25, 1944; XIX TAC, "History," Jul 1, 1944–Feb 28, 1945; 9AF, "Operational Statistics," Sep 19–25, 1944.

93. Weyland, "Diary," Sep 20–21, 1944. Weyland, to his credit, rarely imposed with requests for this kind of assistance, and then only on command matters he judged critical. General Wood did not appear especially preoccupied with bureaucratic minutia at this time, although Patton would relieve him during the Lorraine Campaign because of combat stress.

94. Weyland, "Diary," Sep 24–25, 1944; XIX TAC, "Morning Summary," Sep 24–25, 1944; 405th FG, "Unit History," Sep 1944, USAFHRA, GP–405–HI(FTR), Sep 1944. Regarding weather conditions, the command normally required a 3,000-foot ceiling with broken clouds and at least three miles of visibility. Takeoff minimums were a 1,000-foot ceiling and three miles of visibility. However, as Weyland readily admitted, "in cases of great urgency," like the 4th Armored Division crisis, he sent his crews out when the target areas had weather down to 1,500 or 1,000 feet. XIX TAC, "Combat Operations," p 37.

95. Ltr, Lt Gen George S. Patton, Jr., CG, Third Army, to Corps Commanders and CG,

XIX TAC, "Letter of Instruction Nr 4," Sep 25, 1944, in XIX TAC, "History," Jul 1, 1944–Feb 28, 1945, appendix 8, USAF-HRA, 537.01, 1944–45. See also US3A, "After Action Rpt," vol 1, Sep 25, 1944.

96. XIX TAC, "12,000 FB Sorties," pp 5–6. By the end of August, as Weyland noted, his command operated on fronts 350 miles apart. By mid-September 1944, however, the distance separating operations in Brittany and Patton's forward elements in eastern France totaled nearly 500 miles.

97. XIX TAC, "Combat Operations," p 53.

98. XIX TAC, "12,000 FB Sorties," pp 3–5. The command possessed an average of 439 and 429 operational aircraft during August and September 1944, respectively.

99. XIX TAC, "History," Jul 1, 1944–Feb 28, 1945, appendix 10: Statistical Summary; XIX TAC, "History," Jul 1, 1944–Feb 28, 1945, part 1, pp 99–126, 193–194; XIX TAC, "Combat Operations," pp 4–5. Ninth Air Force had no official policy on fighter pilot combat tour length. The XIX TAC normally rotated pilots to the continental United States after 200 combat hours; however, to maintain fitness, the command found that pilots required frequent leave and rest periods before accumulating 200 combat hours.

100. XIX TAC, "History," Jul 1, 1944–Feb 28, 1945, part 1, pp 99–126; XIX TAC, "Combat Operations," pp 4–5.

101. Intvw, Weyland, Nov 19, 1974," p 140.

102. Weyland, "Diary," Sep 23, 1944.

Chapter 4

1. For land and air action during the campaign, see H.M. Cole, *The Lorraine Campaign* [U.S. Army in World War II: European Theater of Operations] (Washington, D.C.: Office of the Chief of Military History, 1950); Weigley, *Eisenhower's Lieutenants*, pp 327–346, 385–401; Blumenson, ed., *Patton Papers* pp 536–591; Craven and Cate, eds., vol 3, *Europe: Argument to V–E Day*, pp 595–635; HQ AAF, *Condensed Analysis of Ninth AF*, pp 31–39; Griess, ed., vol 1, *Second World War*, chap. 15; Charles B. MacDonald and Martin Blumenson, "Defeat of Germany," in Brig Gen Vincent J. Esposito, USA (Ret), ed., *A Concise History of World War II* (New York: Praeger, 1964), pp 97–105; MacDonald, *Mighty Endeavor*, pp 366–387; and Christopher R. Gabel, "The Lorraine Campaign: An Overview, September–December 1944" (Ft Leavenworth: US Army CGSC, 1985).

2. Almost a half-century afterward, the Combat Studies Institute at the United States Army's Command and General Staff College and the Army War College made the Third Army's Lorraine Cam-paign the centerpiece of its military courses. From the perspective of Army educators, this campaign represented a well-documented, modern, complex military operation that permitted officers to evaluate a wide variety of arms and branch activities at different organizational levels, from company to corps. Ltr, Col Donald P. Shaw, USAMHI, to Lt Gen DeWitt C. Smith, Jr., USA (Ret.), "Study of the Lorraine Campaign at USMAWC," Feb 11, 1982; Ltr, Jerold E. Brown, USACGSC, Combat Studies Institute, to author, Mar 8, 1990; Gabel, "Lorraine Campaign."

Unfortunately the Lorraine Campaign has been mostly ignored by airmen. The aerial phase of this campaign generally has been viewed as an unhappy experience in which bad weather, hardened targets, and limited achievements offered few lessons for tactical air power. Most students of air power have instead fixed on the glorious days of armored column cover in August 1944, the exciting December counterattack in the Ardennes, or the strategic bombing campaign and struggle for aerial supremacy high over Fortress Europe. For them, the Lorraine Campaign has offered little drama or instruction. In the official Army Air Forces account of air action in Northern Europe during World War II, for example, tactical operations are submerged entirely in the coverage of the strategic bombing campaign and special operations. See Craven and Cate, eds., vol 3, *Europe: Argument to V–E Day*, pp 595–635.

3. Gabel, "Lorraine Campaign," pp 1–10; Weigley, *Eisenhower's Lieutenants*, pp 327–328; Cole, *Lorraine Campaign*, chap. 1. This analysis of land operations is based on the works listed in note 1, *supra*. Allied forces in the north faced similar, if larger, river obstacles in their path leading to the Ruhr industrial region of Germany.

4. XIX TAC, "Combat Ops," pp 57–64; XIX TAC, "History," Jul 1, 1944–Feb 18, 1945, part 2: Sep, Oct 1944.

5. Air Ministry (Great Britain), *German Air Force,* pp 336–341, 365–381; Ralph Bennett, *Ultra in the West: The Normandy Campaign 1944–1945* (New York: Charles Scribner's Sons, 1979), pp 175–185.

6. XIX TAC, "History," Jul 1, 1944–Feb 18, 1945, part 5: Statistical Summary.

7. Blumenson, ed., *Patton Papers*, pp 552–553. Patton called September 23 "one of the bad days of my military career. Bradley called me to say that higher authority had decided that I would have to give up the 6th Armored and also assume a defensive attitude, owing to lack of supplies." Patton, *War as I Knew It*, p 130.

8. XIX TAC, "History," Jul 1, 1944–Feb 28, 1945, part 1, pp 82–88; XIX TAC, "Combat Ops," pp 57–64; XIX TAC, "History," Jul 1, 1944–Feb 28, 1945, part 2: Sep, Oct 1944. Although XIX TAC officers complained about their smaller force, if pressed they also admitted that their ground support responsibility lessened because of Third Army's reduction to two corps along a narrow front. For a description of XII TAC, see HQ AAF, *Condensed Analysis of Ninth AF*, p 72.

9. The analysis of communication operations that follows is based on Rpt, J.E.

Faulkner, "Operational Employment of Radar in the XIX Tactical Air Command," Advanced Science Base Laboratory, British Branch Radiation Laboratory, MIT, n.d. [ca 1945], USAFHRA, 537.906, 1945, and on 9AF, "MEW Operations in XIX Tactical Air Command," ORS Report No. 65, Nov 20, 1944; XIX TAC, "Combat Ops," pp 19–23; XIX TAC, "Tactical Air Ops in Europe," pp 16–29; and Rpt, AAF Evaluation Board, ETO, "Tactics and Techniques Developed by the United States Tactical Air Commands in the European Theater of Operations," Mar 11, 1945, USAFHRA 138.4–33, 1945, pp 39–48.

10. XIX TAC, "12,000 FB Sorties," p 2.

11. Thompson and Harris, *Signal Corps*, chap. 4 and appendix: "Signal Corps Equipment, World War II"; XIX TAC, "Tactical Air Ops in Europe," pp 16–31; AAF Eval Bd, "Third Phase Tactical Air Ops," pp 370–373; XIX TAC, "Signals: The Story of Communications in the XIX Tactical Air Command Up to V–E Day," Jun 15, 1945, USAFHRA 537.901.

12. See Rpt, Faulkner, "Operational Employment of Radar"; Thompson and Harris, *Signal Corps*.

13. Weyland, "Diary," Sep 27, 1944; XIX TAC, "Combat Ops," pp 25–26; XIX TAC, "History," Jul 1, 1944–Feb 28, 1945, Sep–Oct 1944; AAF Eval Bd, "Third Phase Tactical Air Ops," pp 384–385.

14. Ltr, David Griggs, Member, Advisor Specialist Group, USSTAF, to Brig Gen O.P. Weyland, Oct 3, 1944, USAFHRA 537.l01, 1944.

15. *Ibid.* The staff correspondence consists of various routing sheets, dated October 10 and 17, 1944, and filed under XIX TAC, "History," Jul 1, 1944–Feb 28, 1945, appendix 8, USAFHRA 537.01, 1944.

16. Cole, *Lorraine Campaign*, pp 1–255; Weigley, *Eisenhower's Lieutenants*, pp 253–319; Griess, ed., vol 1, *Second World War*, pp 360–365.

17. Charles B. MacDonald, *The Siegfried Line Campaign,* [U.S. Army in World War II: European Theater of Operations] (Wash-

ington, D.C.: Office of the Chief of Military History, 1963), pp 119–206.

18. Bernard Montgomery received his fifth star and Field Marshal's baton effective September 1, 1944, just before the debacle of Market Garden. With the additional star he outranked the Supreme Allied Commander, General Eisenhower. To be sure, American authorities were not far behind and promoted Eisenhower to General of the Army on December 20, 1944.

19. Weigley, *Eisenhower's Lieutenants*, pp 350–355; Richard Lamb, *Montgomery in Europe, 1943–1945: Success or Failure?* (New York: Franklin Watts, 1984), pp 252–262. Eisenhower realized, certainly by September 23, 1944, when at his direction Bradley instructed Patton's Third Army to assume a defensive posture, that the Allies could not continue major offensive operations without supplies unloaded at the Belgian port of Antwerp.

20. Ltr, Lt Gen Patton to Corps Commanders and CG, XIX TAC, "Letter of Instruction," Sep 25, 1944, in XIX TAC, "History," Jul 1, 1944–Feb 28, 1945, appendix 8, USAFHRA, 537.01, 1944–45; see also US3A, "After Action Rpt," vol 1, Sep 25, 1944.

21. See Mary H. Williams, *Chronology, 1941–1945,* United States Army in World War II: Special Studies (Washington, D.C.: Office of the Chief of Military History, 1960).

22. The framework for this discussion of the Lorraine Campaign is based in large part on the Weyland diary and on US3A, "After Action Rpt," vol 1: Sep, Oct, Nov, Dec Ops; XIX TAC, "Morning Summaries," Sep 25–Dec 16, 1944; 9AF, "Summary of Operations," Sep 25–Dec 16, 1944, USAFHRA, 533.3082, 1944 (hereafter cited as "Ops Summary"); XIX TAC, "Daily Intsum," Sep 25–Dec 16, 1944, USAFHRA, 537.606, 1944 (hereafter cited as "Daily Intsum"); Kit C. Carter and Robert Mueller, compilers, *The Army Air Forces in World War II: Combat Chronology, 1941–1945* (Washington, D.C.: Office of Air Force History, 1973); XIX TAC,

"History," Jul 1, 1944–Feb 28, 1945, part 2: Sep, Oct, Nov, Dec 1944.

23. Rpt, Lt Col Charles H. Hallet, AC/S, to CG, 9AF, "Use of Napalm Bombs," Oct 3, 1944, USAFHRA, 537.453, Oct–Nov 1944.

24. See also XIX TAC, "Report on Bombing of Metz Forts," Sep–Nov 1944, USAFHRA, 537.453, 1944; Rpt, "Use of Napalm Bombs," Oct 3, 1944; Rpt, AAF Eval Bd, ETO, "The Effect of Air Power in the Battle of Metz," Jan 19, 1945, USAFHRA, 138.4–30.

25. Cole, *Lorraine Campaign*, p 241. Army Air Forces records indicate that the attacks Cole refers to on September 28 actually occurred on September 29, 1944.

26. On the Ninth Air Force's autumn rail interdiction program, see Craven and Cate, eds., vol 3, *Europe: Argument to V–E Day*, pp 613–623.

27. Weyland, "Diary," Oct 3, 1944; XIX TAC, "History," Jul 1, 1944–Feb 28, 1945, part 2: Oct 1944.

28. Americans fighting in the Lorraine Campaign would readily concede that the French military engineers deserved their high reputation for building effective fortifications.

29. Weyland, "Diary," Oct 2, 1944.

30. US3A, "After Action Rpt," vol 1: Sep, Oct, Nov, Dec Ops; XIX TAC, "Morning Summaries," Sep 25–Dec 16, 1944; 9AF, "Ops Summary," Sep 25–Dec 16, 1944; XIX TAC, "Daily Intsum," Sep 25–Dec 16, 1944; Carter and Mueller, *Army Air Forces in World War II*; XIX TAC, "History," Jul 1, 1944–Feb 28, 1945, part 2: Sep, Oct, Nov, Dec 1944.

31. XIX TAC, "History," Jul 1, 1944–Feb 28, 1945, part 2: Oct 1944.

32. Weyland, "Diary"; Hallet appears to have understood the importance of Ultra data much sooner, or have felt less threatened by its special access channel through a lower ranking officer, than did Koch. Irving mistakenly asserts that Patton did not have access to Ultra. David Irving, *The War Between the Generals* (New York: Congdon & Lattes, 1981). See Thomas Parrish, *The*

Ultra Americans: The U.S. Role in Breaking the Nazi Codes (New York: Stein and Day, 1986), pp 189–228, and the two National Security Agency Reports: Memo, NSA, "Ultra and the Third Army," May 28, 1945 in NSA, Special Research, History–023, "Reports by U.S. Army Ultra Representatives with Army Field Commands in the European Theatre of Operations," part 1: Third Army, pp 22–26; and Memo, NSA, "Ultra," in *Ibid.* part 2: XIX TAC, pp 104–109. Along with Patton and Colonel Koch, the following Third Army officers received Ultra briefings: Maj Gen Hobart R. Gay, Chief of Staff, Col Paul D. Harkins, Dep Chief of Staff, Brig Gen Halley G. Maddox, G–3 (Operations), Col Robert S. Allen, Asst G–2. In the XIX TAC, Weyland's executive officer, Lieutenant Col Walter E. Bligh was the only other officer authorized to receive Ultra intelligence. Apart from the German counterattack in early August 1944 and one in the spring of 1945, the National Security Agency reports do not elaborate on Ultra's impact on specific air or ground events.

33. Richard H. Kohn and Joseph P. Harahan, eds., *Air Superiority in World War II and Korea* (Washington, D.C.: Office of Air Force History, 1983), p 57; Air Ministry (Great Britain), *German Air Force*, pp 336–341, 365–381; Bennett, *Ultra in the West*, pp 175–185.

34. Although Ultra information confirmed a sizeable *Luftwaffe* recovery and buildup in October and November 1944, the Ultra intercepts did not indicate the purpose of the *Luftwaffe* actions. Memo, Lt Col Charles H. Hallet, AC/S, to A–3, XIX TAC, Oct 6, 1944, USAFHRA, 537.306A, Oct 1–15, 1944.

35. Weyland, "Diary,"; XIX TAC, "History," Jul 1, 1944–Feb 28, 1945, part 1, 124–133; XIX TAC, "Tactical Air Ops in Europe," pp 39–41; Richard K. Smith, "Marston Mat," in *Air Force Magazine* (Apr 1989), pp 84–88.

36. Weyland, "Diary"; XIX TAC, "History," Jul 1, 1944–Feb 28, 1945, part 1,

124–133; XIX TAC, "Tactical Air Ops in Europe," pp 39–41; Smith, "Marston Mat," pp 84–88.

37. Weyland, "Diary,"; XIX TAC, "History," Jul 1, 1944–Feb 28, 1945, part 1, 124–133; XIX TAC, "Tactical Air Ops in Europe," pp 39–41.

38. Weyland, "Diary,"; XIX TAC, "History," Jul 1, 1944–Feb 28, 1945, part 1, 124–133; XIX TAC, "Tactical Air Ops in Europe," pp 39–41.

39. XIX TAC, "History," Jul 1, 1944–Feb 29, 1945, part 2: Oct, Nov 1944; Weyland, "Diary," Dec 10, 1944; XIX TAC, "History," Jul 1, 1944–Feb 28, 1945, part 1, 124–133.

40. US3A, "After Action Rpt," vol 1, Oct Ops.

41. XIX TAC's attack against the dam was the first attempt by P–47s against such a target. Weyland, "Diary," Oct 18, 1944; US3A, "After Action Rpt," vol 1, Oct 18, 1944.

42. Intvw, Burns, Jan 7, 1992.

43. 362d FG, "Unit History," Oct 1944; XIX TAC, "History," Jul 1, 1944–Feb 28, 1945, part 2, pp 11–14.

44. XIX TAC, "History," Jul 1, 1944–Feb 28, 1945, part 2, pp 11–14.

45. US3A, "After Action Rpt," vol 1, Oct 18, 1944.

46. Weyland, "Diary," Oct 1944; Rpt, XIX TAC, A–3, "Operation Madison: Air Plan in Support of Third U.S. Army," Nov 3, 1944.

47. US3A, "After Action Rpt," vol 1, Oct Ops. See also Cole, *Lorraine Campaign*, pp 296–310; Weigley, *Eisenhower's Lieutenants*, pp 383–431; Bradley, *Soldier's Story*, pp 430–450.

48. Weyland, "Diary," Oct 27, 1944.

49. Memo, Brig Gen O.P. Weyland, CG, XIX TAC, to Lt Gen G.S. Patton, CG, US3A, Oct 28, 1944, USAFHRA, 537.01, 1944; XIX TAC, "History," Jul 1, 1944–Feb 28, 1945, appendix 8.

50. Weyland, "Diary," Oct 29, 1944; Patton, Diary Entry, Oct 29, 1944.

51. XIX TAC, "History," Jul 1, 1944–Feb 28, 1945, part 2: Oct 1944. See

also AAF Eval Bd, "Third Phase Tactical Air Ops," part 2 for analysis of equipment effectiveness.

52. US3A, "After Action Rpt," vol 1, Oct 30, 1944.

53. Weyland, "Diary," Nov 1–2, 1944; Blumenson, ed., *Patton Papers*, p 567.

54. Weyland, "Diary," Nov 2, 1944; Van Creveld, *Supplying War*, chap. 7.

55. Weyland, "Diary," Oct 1944; Rpt, "Operation Madison," Nov 3, 1944.

56. Weyland, "Diary," Oct 1944; Rpt, "Operation Madison," Nov 3, 1944.

57. US3A, "After Action Rpt," vol 2, part 3: "G–2 Section Rpt," pp 19–20; Ivie, *Aerial Reconnaissance*, pp 80, 92.

58. XIX TAC "Combat Ops," p 32. General Weyland believed that two tactical reconnaissance squadrons and one photo squadron adequately met the needs of his command and Third Army's two corps, but only without including requirements from higher headquarters. This had become an issue in October because Ninth Air Force requests took priority over those of Third Army until October 25. Not until that date did XIX TAC and Third Army convince the requesters that the urgency of Operation Madison required moving Army requests to the top of the priority list. Like its photo squadron, Colonel Russell Berg's 10th Photo Group played an increasingly important role in the fall. Despite the fact that the weather deteriorated considerably in November, the group flew 831 sorties, or 138 more than it did in October. Much of the increase can be attributed to the ground offensive early in the month and reconnaissance requirements for the major assault planned for early December. Ltr, Brig Gen Russell A. Berg, USAF (Ret), to author, Oct 24, 1989.

59. Weyland, "Diary," Oct 31, 1944.

60. Weyland, "Diary," Nov 5, 1944; Craven and Cate, eds., vol 3, *Europe: Argument to V–E Day*, p 597. The new air force would support the operations of Lieutenant General Jacob Devers' 6th Army Group.

61. Weyland, "Diary," Nov 1, 1944; XIX TAC, "Combat Ops," pp 27–30; XIX TAC, "Tactical Air Ops in Europe," pp 24–29. Although Weyland would continue to have problems coordinating air defense in Third Army's area of operations, he and his army colleagues avoided the sometimes bitter dispute between ground and air authorities over command and control of air defense components. The AAF argued for air force control. See HQ AAF, *Condensed Analysis of Ninth AF*, pp 100–101.

62. Blumenson, ed., *Patton Papers*, p 570; 405th FG, "Unit History," Nov 1944; XIX TAC, "History," Jul 1, 1944–Feb 28, 1945, part 2: Nov Ops, p 6. See appendix 3 for pilot claims for November 8, 1944.

63. Weyland, "Diary," Nov 8, 1944; XIX TAC, "Combat Ops," p 37; 362d FG, "Unit History," Nov 1944.

64. Weyland, "Diary," Nov 9, 1944; AAF Eval Bd, "Third Phase Tactical Air Ops," pp 156–165. Although good reasons beyond Patton's friendship with Spaatz and Doolittle dating from North Africa existed for employing heavy bombers in tactical operations, using them in a tactical role violated established Army Air Forces doctrine. Yet the record shows that Weyland and his fellow tactical airmen did not concern themselves with this issue. If the heavy bombers might help the army move, they argued for employing them and welcomed their support.

65. XIX TAC, "Rpt on Bombing Metz Forts," Sep–Nov 1944; Rpt, "Use of Na-palm Bombs," Oct 3, 1944; Rpt, AAF Eval Bd, "Air Power in Battle of Metz," Jan 19, 1945.

66. AAF Eval Bd, "Third Phase Tactical Air Ops," p 165.

67. *Ibid.*, pp 166–175. Cobra, with its short bombing, continued to haunt Allied planners until the spring campaign and the return to mobile warfare.

68. Gabel, "Lorraine Campaign," pp 24–25.

69. XIX TAC, "Combat Ops," pp 60–62. According to Richard K. Smith, napalm's effectiveness in World War II did not match later, more deadly versions because the earlier variety did not have a barometric proximity fuze which detonated the container

approximately 100 feet above ground. Because this type of fuzing was unavailable in 1944–1945, the weapon did not produce the lethal 360-degree spread of fire. Richard K. Smith, "Manuscript Comments" to the author, Apr 21, 1992. For a discussion of the ethical concerns of airmen, see Conrad C. Crane, *Bombs, Cities, and Civilians: American Airpower Strategy in World War II*, (Lawrence, Kan.: University of Kansas Press, 1993).

70. Air Ministry (Great Britain), *German Air Force*, pp 336–341, 365–381; Bennett, *Ultra in the West*, pp 175–185.

71. Weyland, "Diary," Nov 8–15, 1944.

72. XIX TAC, "Operational Statistics," 1944–1945; XIX TAC, "Morning Summaries," Sep 25–Dec 16, 1944; 9AF, "Ops Summary," Sep 25–Dec 16, 1944; XIX TAC, "Daily Intsum," Sep 25–Dec 16, 1944; XIX TAC, "History," Jul 1, 1944–Feb 28, 1945, part 2: Nov, 1944.

73. XIX TAC, "History," Jul 1, 1944–Feb 28, 1945, part 2: Nov, Dec 1944; Rpt, Faulkner, "Operational Employment of Radar"; 9AF, "MEW Ops in XIX TAC," Nov 20, 1944; XIX TAC, "Combat Ops," pp 19–23; XIX TAC, "Tactical Air Ops in Europe," pp 16–29; Rpt, AAF Eval Bd, "Tactics and Techniques," pp 39–48.

74. 354th FG, "Unit History," Nov 1944.

75. Weyland, "Diary," Nov 1944; XIX TAC, "History," Jul 1, 1944–Feb 28, 1945, part 1, 133–147.

76. Weyland, "Diary," Nov 1944; XIX TAC, "History," Jul 1, 1944–Feb 28, 1945, part 1, 133–147.

77. Ltr, CG, XIX TAC, to CG, 9AF, "Authorized Aircraft in Fighter Groups," Nov 14, 1944, USAFHRA, 537.01, appendix 8, 1944–45; Weyland, "Diary," Nov 1944; XIX TAC, "History," Jul 1, 1944–Feb 28, 1945, part 1, 133–147.

78. Ltr, HQ 9AF to CG, XIX TAC, Nov 25, 1944, in USAFHRA, 537.01, appendix 8, 1944–45.

79. Weyland, "Diary," Nov 14, 1944.

80. 362d FG, "Unit History," Nov 1944. The 362d's air echelon moved by surface transportation from Prosnes near Reims to Rouvres near Verdun on November 5, 1944. The ground echelon followed later over a three-day period, November 19–21, while the flight echelon arrived on November 19.

81. 405th FG, "Unit History," Nov 1944.

82. Weyland, "Diary," Nov 15, 1944.

83. Weyland, "Diary," Nov 17, 1944; Blumenson, ed., *Patton Papers*, pp 575, 586. See comments from U.S. ground force officers in AAF Eval Bd, "Third Phase Tactical Air Ops," part 1, sec D.

84. XIX TAC, "History," Jul 1, 1944–Feb 28, 1945, part 2: Nov 1944, pp 12–14, appendix.

85. XIX TAC, "History," Jul 1, 1944–Feb 28, 1945, appendix 10: Statistical Summary; XIX TAC, "Combat Ops," p 41; XIX TAC, "History," Jul 1, 1944–Feb 28, 1945, part 1, pp 28–33; Rpt, "Conference between General Patton, General Weyland and Third Army Correspondents," Dec 9, 1944, USAFHRA, 168.7104–101, 1944; Cole, *Lorraine Campaign*, p 415.

86. XIX TAC, "Combat Ops," pp 25–61; XIX TAC, "Tactical Air Ops in Europe," pp 3–4. Like so many European theater firsts, this counter-flak measure was used first in the North African campaign, and then the Allies subsequently employed it in the Italian theater, well before its rediscovery and adoption in Northwest Europe.

87. XIX TAC, "Combat Ops," p 61; US3A, "After Action Rpt," vol 2, part 3: "G–2 Section Rpt," p 23.

88. Gabel, "Lorraine Campaign," pp 32–37; Cole, *Lorraine Campaign*, pp 417–519; Weigley, *Eisenhower's Lieutenants*, pp 383–401.

89. US3A, "After Action Rpt," vol 1, pp 144–145.

90. Patton, Diary Entry, Nov 21, 1944.

91. US3A, "After Action Rpt," vol 1, pp 144–145.

92. Weyland, "Diary," Nov 19, 1944; XIX TAC, "Combat Ops," p 62. Although the Merzig bombing was second among the four joint operations in Lorraine, both XIX

TAC and Third Army considered it less significant than the other three, the abortive Operation Tink.

93. XIX TAC, "Combat Ops," pp 62–63.

94. Weyland, "Diary," Nov 29, 1944; US3A, "After Action Rpt," vol 1, Nov 29, 1944.

95. Weyland, "Diary," Nov 30, 1944; 9AF, "Operational History of the Ninth Air Force, Bk I, Battle of the Ardennes: Dec 1, 1944–Jan 1945," sec 1: pp 11–21, USAF-HRA, 533.01–2; Patton, Diary Entry, Nov 30, 1944.

96. Weigley, *Eisenhower's Lieutenants*, pp 402–431; Griess, ed., vol 1, *Second World War*, pp 362–365.

97. Weyland, "Diary," Dec 1, 1944. See also Weigley, *Eisenhower's Lieutenants*, pp 397–401, 437–441.

98. Weyland, "Diary," Dec 2, 1944.

99. 9AF, "Op History of Ninth AF," pp 11–21.

100. XIX TAC, "Combat Ops," pp 62–63; XIX TAC, "History," Jul 1, 1944–Feb 28, 1945, part 2: Dec Ops, pp 2–4; XIX TAC, "Operational Summary," Dec 2, 1944; 9AF, "Op History of Ninth AF," pp 11–21.

101. The fighter-bombers seemed unable to suppress the enemy defenses using regular bombs.

102. US3A, "After Action Rpt," vol 2, part 3: "G–2 Section Rpt," pp 23, 26–27.

103. XIX TAC, "Morning Summaries," Sep 25–Dec 16, 1944; 9AF, "Ops Summary," Sep 25–Dec 16, 1944; XIX TAC, "Daily Intsum," Sep 25–Dec 16, 1944; XIX TAC, "History," Jul 1, 1944–Feb 28, 1945, part 2: Nov, 1944.

104. Weyland, "Diary," Dec 5, 1944.

105. Weyland, "Diary," Dec 6, 1944; XIX TAC, AC/S, A–3, "Operation Tink: Air Plan in Support of Third US Army," Dec 17, 1944, USAFHRA, 537.205A, 1944; XIX TAC, "Combat Ops," p 63.

106. Weyland, "Diary," Dec 7–8, 1944. The inner artillery zone represented a defined airspace under army control in which all aircraft, hostile or friendly, would be fired on by antiaircraft artillery. See chap. 5.

107. XIX TAC, "History," Jul 1, 1944–Feb 28, 1945, part 2: Dec 1945; US3A, "After Action Rpt," vol 1, Dec 1944.

108. XIX TAC, "History," Jul 1, 1944–Feb 28, 1945, part 2: Dec 1945.

109. The hectic activity is recorded in Weyland's diary for this period. See also Patton, Diary Entry, Dec 10, 1944.

110. Weyland, "Diary," Dec 1944; Patton, Diary Entry, Dec 10, 1944.

111. Weyland, "Diary," Dec 16, 1944. The only problem that surfaced was whether XV Corps would receive air support at the expense of XII Corps. General Eddy apparently had reversed an earlier agreement that provided XV Corps the air support in question. Weyland wisely sidestepped the matter, explaining that Third Army should notify XV Corps because it was not an air force matter. In any event, Operation Tink, his plan to break through the Siegfried Line, was to proceed as originally designed.

112. XIX TAC, "History," Jul 1, 1944–Feb 28, 1945, part 2: Dec 1944, pp 11–12.

113. XIX TAC, "Operation Tink," Dec 17, 1944.

114. Weyland, "Diary," Dec 18–19, 1944.

115. Weyland, "Diary," Dec 19–20, 1944.

116. Blumenson, ed., *Patton Papers*, pp 588–589. Lorraine has been valued for its ore deposits for centuries, and with these words Patton masked his own displeasure in the outcome of the Lorraine Campaign.

117. Although the weather and the size of his force limited the XIX TAC the most, the situation would have been far worse had the Allies not benefited from a shortening of the logistic tail that, before the port of Antwerp became available, led all the way back to Brittany.

118. Cole, *Lorraine Campaign*, p 598.

119. Rpt, "Conference Between Gen Patton, Gen Weyland and Third Army Correspondents," Dec 9, 1944.

120. *Ibid.*

Chapter 5

1. On the land campaign, see Hugh M. Cole, *The Ardennes: Battle of the Bulge* [U.S. Army in World War II: European Theater of Operations] (Washington,D.C.: Office of the Chief of Military History: 1965); John S.D. Eisenhower, *The Bitter Woods* (New York, Putnam: 1969); Charles B. MacDonald, *A Time for Trumpets: The Untold Story of the Battle of the Bulge* (New York, William Morrow: 1985); and Weigley, *Eisenhower's Lieutenants*, pp 445–566. This account of the ground campaign is based on the works cited above, on Griess, ed., vol 1, *Second World War*, chap. 16; and on 9AF, "Op History of Ninth AF."

2. Eisenhower had the benefit of available Ultra information on the Germans' logistics situation when he chaired the December 19 meeting. See Bennett, *Ultra in the West*, pp 210–211.

3. For the air contribution, see 9AF, "Op History of Ninth AF"; Col William R. Carter, "Air Power in the Battle of the Bulge: A Theater Campaign Perspective," in *Airpower Journal* (Winter 1989), pp 10–33; Craven and Cate, eds., vol 3, *Europe: Argument to V–E Day,* pp 672–711.

4. Weigley, *Eisenhower's Lieutenants*, pp 445–566; Griess, ed., vol 1, *Second World War*, chap. 16; 9AF, "Op History of Ninth AF"; Cole, *The Ardennes*, pp 1–74; Eisenhower, *Bitter Woods*, pp 105–161.

5. Craven and Cate, eds., vol 3, *Europe: Argument to V–E Day*, p 673. On *Luftwaffe* and air doctrine, see 9AF "Op History of Ninth AF," sec 4, pp 38–39; and Carter, "Air Power in Battle of the Bulge."

6. Griess, ed., vol 1, *Second World War*, pp 375–377; Craven and Cate, eds., vol 3, *Europe: Argument to V–E Day*, pp 673–682; Weigley, *Eisenhower's Lieutenants*, pp 456–464. Hitler actually intended to begin the German assault in late November, but weather and supply mobilization delays forced postponement to mid-December. See Bennett, *Ultra in the West*, pp 188–227.

7. Craven and Cate, eds., vol 3, *Europe: Argument to V–E Day*, pp 673–682; XIX TAC, "History," Jul 1, 1944–Feb 28, 1945, part 1: Dec Ops 1944; US3A, "After Action Rpt," vol 2, part 3: "G–2 Section Rpt", pp 23, 26–27. German communications security helped prevent Ultra from providing sufficient information of enemy intentions if not his preparations, while Allied planners assumed the *Wehrmacht* would *not* follow the same Ardennes attack route it did when it invaded France in 1940.

8. Blumenson, ed. *Patton Papers*, p 582; Bennett, *Ultra in the West*, pp 188–204.

9. Cole, *The Ardennes*, p 63.

10. Weigley, *Eisenhower's Lieutenants*, pp 445–566; Griess, ed., vol 1, *Second World War*, chap. 16; Cole, *The Ardennes*, pp 33–74; Eisenhower, *Bitter Woods*, pp 217–257.

11. AAF Eval Bd, "Third Phase Tactical Air Ops," pp 175–191.

12. 9AF, "Op History of Ninth AF," sec 2, pp 5–6.

13. Carter, "Air Power in Battle of the Bulge," p 28. The author discusses the reversal of second- and third-priority missions as prescribed in FM 100–20.

14. 9AF, "Op History of Ninth AF," sec 2, pp 5–6.

15. See XIX TAC, "History," Jul 1, 1944–Feb 28, 1945, part 2: Dec Ops 1944, pp 11–12, appendix.

16. 9AF, "Op History of Ninth AF," sec 2, pp 32–34; XIX TAC, "History," Jul 1, 1944–Feb 28, 1945, part 2: Dec Ops 1944, pp 11–12, appendix.

17. XIX TAC, "Daily Intsum," Dec 17, 1944. One of the aircraft was lost when it collided with a P–38.

18. Weyland, "Diary," Dec 19, 1944; 9AF, "Ops Summary," Dec 17–22, 1944.

19. Weigley, *Eisenhower's Lieutenants*, pp 445–566; Griess, ed., vol 1, *Second World War*, chap. 16; Cole, *The Ardennes*,

pp 75–106; Eisenhower, *Bitter Woods*, pp 261–304.

20. Weyland, "Diary," Dec 18, 1944; US3A, "After Action Rpt," vol 1, Dec 18, 1944.

21. See especially, Weigley, *Eisenhower's Lieutenants*, pp 496–501; and Griess, ed., vol 1, *Second World War*, pp 381–383.

22. Blumenson, ed., *Patton Papers*, pp 599–600.

23. Weyland, "Diary," Dec 19, 1944.

24. 9AF, "Op History of Ninth AF," sec 2, pp 8–16.

25. Weyland, "Diary," Dec 20, 1944; US3A, "After Action Rpt," vol 1, Dec 20, 1944.

26. Weyland, "Diary," Dec 20, 1944.

27. *Ibid.*; Rpt, Faulkner, "Operational Employment of Radar."

28. For accounts of Field Marshal Montgomery's troubles with his American colleagues, see Weyland, "Diary," Dec 20, 1944; Rpt, Joseph A. Wyant, 9AF Historian to Brig Gen. R.C. Candee, "Material in Response to Telephone Request of Sept 28, 1945 Concerning Allied Air Effort During the Battle of the Bulge," n.d. [1945], part 1, Dec 1, 1944–Jan 26, 1945, USAFHRA, 533.4501–5; Weigley, *Eisenhower's Lieutenants*, pp 445–566; Griess, ed., vol 1, *Second World War*, chap. 16; and Cole, *The Ardennes*, pp 48–74, 423–444.

29. Weyland, "Diary," Dec 21, 1944.

30. *Ibid.*, Dec 22, 1944. Although it certainly was in Patton's best interest to support Weyland's proposal, the Third Army commander never refused Weyland's requests to intervene with higher authorities. "Spitfire" and "Lucky" were the XIX TAC and Third Army call signs, respectively.

31. *Ibid.*; XIX TAC, "History," Jul 1, 1944–Feb 28, 1945, part 1, pp 88–91.

32. Weyland, "Diary," Dec 23, 1944. The transfer of the Eighth Air Force fighter group proved the exception to the general rule of speedy transfers. The delay in preparing the Metz airfield seems to have been the main reason for this exception.

33. *Ibid.*, Dec 20–23, 1944; US3A, "After Action Rpt," vol 2, part 3: "G–2 Section Rpt," appendix, pp 26–27.

34. US3A, "After Action Rpt," vol 1, Dec 22, 1944.

35. Weigley, *Eisenhower's Lieutenants*, pp 445–566; Griess, ed., vol 1, *Second World War*, chap. 16; Cole, *The Ardennes*, pp 423–444; Eisenhower, *Bitter Woods*, pp 261–346.

36. 406th FG, "The 406th Occupier," Sep 28, 1945, p 16, USAFHRA, GP–406–SU–NE, Sep 45.

37. US3A, "After Action Rpt," vol 1, Dec 23, 1944. This Third Army report dryly recorded that "the Army Commander's prayer for fair weather was followed in a few days by a break in the lowering skies that had prevented full air support by XIX Tactical Air Command."

38. See XIX TAC, "History," Jul 1, 1944–Feb 28, 1945, part 2: Dec Ops, pp 14–15. The framework for discussion of the Ardennes Campaign is based in large part on the Weyland diary and the following sources: US3A, "After Action Rpt," vol 1, Dec, Jan Ops; XIX TAC, "Morning Summaries," Dec 16, 1944–Jan 31, 1945; 9AF, "Ops Summary," Dec 16, 1944–Jan 31, 1945; XIX TAC, "Daily Intsum," Dec 16, 1944–Jan 31, 1945; Carter and Mueller, *Army Air Forces in World War II*; and XIX TAC, "History," Jul 1, 1944–Feb 28, 1945, vol 2: Dec 1944, Jan 1945 Ops, and appendix 10: Statistical Summary.

39. See the preceding note for the statistical record, and Ivie, *Aerial Reconnaissance*, p 108.

40. US3A, "After Action Rpt," vol 2, part 3: "G–2 Section Rpt," p 27; Cole, *The Ardennes*, p 468. For good measure, the 354th also scrambled two planes on December 23 to intercept "bogies" in the XX Corps zone. None were found.

41. See US3A, "After Action Rpt," vol 1, Dec, Jan Ops; XIX TAC, "Morning Summaries," Dec 16, 1944–Jan 31, 1945; 9AF, "Ops Summary ," Dec 16, 1944–Jan 31, 1945; XIX TAC, "Daily Intsum," Dec

16, 1944–Jan 31, 1945; Carter and Mueller, *Army Air Forces in World War II*; XIX TAC, "History," Jul 1, 1944–Feb 28, 1945, vol 2: Dec 1944, Jan 1945 Ops, and appendix 10: Statistical Summary.

42. Memo, A.C. McLean, XIX TAC/ORS to A–3, "Analysis of Attacks on Targets of Opportunity, Dec 15, 1944 to Jan 31, 1945," Feb 16, 1945, USAFHRA, 537.01; XIX TAC, "History," Jul 1, 1944–Feb 28, 1945, appendix 7: 1944–45.

43. 9AF, "Op History of Ninth AF," sec 3, pp 16–17; Carter and Mueller, *Army Air Forces in World War II*.

44. See XIX TAC, "History," Jul 1, 1944–Feb 28, 1945, part 2: Dec Ops; US3A, "After Action Rpt," vol 1, Dec, Jan Ops; XIX TAC, "Morning Summaries," Dec 16, 1944–Jan 31, 1945; 9AF, "Ops Summary," Dec 16, 1944–Jan 31, 1945; XIX TAC, "Daily Intsum," Dec 16, 1944–Jan 31, 1945; Carter and Mueller, *Army Air Forces in World War II*; XIX TAC, "History," Jul 1, 1944–Feb 28, 1945, vol 2: Dec 1944, Jan 1945 Ops and appendix 10: Statistical Summary.

45. Air Ministry (Great Britain), *German Air Force*, pp 374–381; Bennett, *Ultra in the West*, p 216.

46. Air Ministry (Great Britain), *German Air Force*, pp 374–381; 9AF, "Op History of Ninth AF," sec 3, pp 8–16, 57–61. The author of a recent article suggested that the *Luftwaffe* committed the classic mistake of failing to make air superiority the first priority for the assault, and instead divided its attention between support for its ground assault force and attacking the medium and heavy bombers that were striking key airfields and communications targets. Perhaps this resulted from the inappropriate nature of the air forces assembled for the operation, when Hitler and his advisors thought that interceptor pilots would have little trouble flying ground attack missions. German leaders realized they stood little chance of wresting control of the air from the Allies and, apart from doctrinal reasons, decided they had a better chance of supporting the ground

assault in the Ardennes directly rather than attempting to render Allied air forces ineffective. On the other hand, the Germans' one chance may have been their planned massive air assault on Allied bases in the forward area that bad weather prevented them from carrying out on the eve of the battle. Indeed, the *Luftwaffe*'s later raid on Allied airfields on January 1, 1945, would suggest the success such a gamble might have produced at the start of the Ardennes assault. In any event, the *Luftwaffe* would remain a major focus of interest for Weyland and his fellow airmen. See Carter, "Air Power in Battle of the Bulge," pp 27–29.

47. XIX TAC, "History," Jul 1, 1944–Feb 28, 1945, part 2: Dec Ops, appendix 10: Statistical Summary; Air Ministry (Great Britain), *German Air Force*, pp 378–379. During the period December 23–27 the *Luftwaffe* fought well. After the Bastogne period, pilot inexperience and poor maintenance began to take their toll.

48. XIX TAC, "History," Jul 1, 1944–Feb 28, 1945, part 2: Dec, Jan Ops, pp 2–3.

49. XIX TAC, "Op Statistics," 1944–45, USAFHRA, 537.391, 1944–45; XIX TAC, "History," Jul 1, 1944–Feb 28, 1945, part 2: Dec Ops; US3A, "After Action Rpt," vol 1, Dec, Jan Ops; XIX TAC, "Morning Summaries," Dec 16, 1944–Jan 31, 1945; 9AF, "Ops Summary," Dec 16, 1944–Jan 31, 1945; XIX TAC, "Daily Intsum," Dec 16, 1944–Jan 31, 1945; Carter and Mueller, *Army Air Forces in World War II*; XIX TAC, "History," Jul 1, 1944–Feb 28, 1945, vol 2, Dec 1944, Jan 1945 Ops.

50. XIX TAC, "Daily Intsum," Dec 23, 1944; Intvw, Burns, Jan 7, 1992.

51. XIX TAC, "Rpt on Combat Ops," pp 38–39; Smith, "Marston Mat," pp 84–88.

52. Weyland, "Diary," Dec 24, 1944; XIX TAC, "History," Jul 1, 1944–Feb 28, 1945, part 1, 88–91.

53. Weyland, "Diary," Dec 24, 1944; XIX TAC, "History," Jul 1, 1944–Feb 28, 1945, part 1, pp 88–91.

54. See XIX TAC, "History," Jul 1, 1944–Feb 28, 1945, part 2: Dec Ops;

US3A, "After Action Rpt," vol 1, Dec, Jan Ops; XIX TAC, "Morning Summaries," Dec 16, 1944–Jan 31, 1945; 9AF, "Ops Summary," Dec 16, 1944–Jan 31, 1945; XIX TAC, "Daily Intsum," Dec 16, 1944–Jan 31, 1945; Carter and Mueller, *Army Air Forces in World War II*; XIX TAC, "History," Jul 1, 1944–Feb 18, 1945, vol 2: Dec 1944, Jan 1945 Ops, appendix 10: Statistical Summary.

55. 9AF, "Op History of Ninth AF," sec 3, p 35; MacDonald, *Time for Trumpets*, p 522; U.S. Forces, European Theater, Battle Studies, vol 2: Air Operations, ca 1945, No. 21: "Air Resupply, Ardennes Counter-Offensive (Dec 16, 1944–Feb 21, 1945)," USMHI. Although the loss rate of 2 percent might appear high, especially when compared with Eighth Air Force statistics for the same period, much of the *Luftwaffe* force normally assigned to defend against the heavy bombers had been operating in the Ardennes region.

56. Weyland, "Diary," Dec 26, 1944.

57. XIX TAC, "Tactical Air Ops in Europe," p 31.

58. XIX TAC, "Rpt on Combat Ops," pp 31–34; Ivie, *Aerial Reconnaissance*, p 115; Rpt, 10th Photo Group, to HQ 9AF, "Employment of Reconnaissance Aircraft, Tactics and Techniques," Feb 10, 1945, USAFHRA, 537.628, 1945.

59. Rpt, Air Effects Committee, "Effect of Air Power," p 151.

60. Weyland, "Diary," Dec 26–27, 1944; US3A, "After Action Rpt," vol 1, Dec 26–27, 1944.

61. Weigley, *Eisenhower's Lieutenants*, pp 445–566; Griess, ed., vol 1, *Second World War*, chap. 16; 9AF, "Op History of Ninth AF"; Cole, *The Ardennes*, pp 606–648; MacDonald, *Time for Trumpets*, Book 6.

62. See XIX TAC, "History," Jul 1, 1944–Feb 28, 1945, part 2: Dec Ops; US3A, "After Action Rpt," vol 1, Dec, Jan Ops; XIX TAC, "Morning Summaries," Dec 16, 1944–Jan 31, 1945; 9AF, "Ops Summary," Dec 16, 1944–Jan 31, 1945; XIX TAC, "Daily Intsum," Dec 16, 1944–Jan 31,

1945; XIX TAC, "History," Jul 1, 1944–Feb 28, 1945, vol 2, Dec 1944, Jan 1945 Ops, appendix 10: Statistical Summary.

63. 9AF, "Op History of Ninth AF," sec 4, pp 6–9, 31–45; Craven and Cate, eds., vol 3, *Europe: Argument to V–E Day*, pp 701–711; Bennett, *Ultra in the West*, p 216.

64. See XIX TAC, "History," Jul 1, 1944–Feb 28, 1945, part 2: Dec Ops; US3A, "After Action Rpt," vol 1, Dec, Jan Ops; XIX TAC, "Morning Summaries," Dec 16, 1944–Jan 31, 1945; 9AF, "Ops Summary," Dec 16, 1944–Jan 31, 1945; XIX TAC, "Daily Intsum," Dec 16, 1944–Jan 31, 1945; XIX TAC, "History," Jul 1, 1944–Feb 28, 1945, vol 2, Dec 1944, Jan 1945 Ops, appendix 10: Statistical Summary.

65. US3A, "After Action Rpt," vol 1, Dec 23–31, 1944.

66. Craven and Cate, eds., vol 3, *Europe: Argument to V–E Day*, p 699; XIX TAC, "Rpt on Combat Ops," pp 25–26; AAF Evaluation Board, ETO, "Tactics and Techniques Developed by the United States Tactical Air Commands in the European Theater of Operations," Mar 1, 1945, pp 21–23, USAFHRA, 138.4–33, 1945; Rpt, Faulkner, "Operational Employment of Radar."

67. XIX TAC, "History," Jul 1, 1944–Feb 28, 1945, part 1: pp 88–91. One must remember that not only did the night fighters do a good job with the resources available, their avionics technology was more complex than most military aircraft of the day and hence prone to reliability problems.

68. XIX TAC, "Tactical Air Ops in Europe," pp 26–29; XIX TAC, "Rpt on Combat Ops," pp 27–30.

69. XIX TAC, "Tactical Air Ops in Europe," pp 26–29; XIX TAC, "Rpt on Combat Ops," pp 27–30.

70. See the file entitled XIX TAC, "Reports of Attacks by Friendly-Type Aircraft," Dec 1944–Jan 1945, USAFHRA, 537.599. Most incidents were attributed to pilots flying with other commands, such as Eighth Air Force, who were less familiar with terrain and flying conditions in Third Army's area of operations.

71. Weyland, "Diary," Dec 30–31, 1944; Intvw, Gen Robert M. Lee, USAF (Ret) by author, Sep 22, 1989.

72. Weyland, "Diary," Dec 30–31, 1944; Intvw, Lee, Sep 22, 1989.

73. Patton, Diary Entry, Dec 31, 1944.

74. See the file entitled, XIX TAC, "Attacks by Friendly-Type Aircraft"; Davis, *Spaatz*, p 535.

75. Air Ministry (Great Britain), *German Air Force*, pp 379–381; Bennett, *Ultra in the West*, pp 218–219; Weyland, "Diary," Jan 1, 1945; US3A, "After Action Rpt," vol 1, Jan 1, 1945; XIX TAC, "History," Jul 1, 1944–Feb 28, 1945, part 2: Jan Ops; 9AF, "Op History of Ninth AF," sec 4, pp 20–21, 38–41; Patton, Diary Entry, Jan 1, 1945.

76. Air Ministry (Great Britain), *German Air Force*, pp 379–381; Bennett, *Ultra in the West*, pp 218–219; Weyland, "Diary," Jan 1, 1945; US3A, "After Action Rpt," vol 1, Jan 1, 1945; XIX TAC, "History," Jul 1, 1944–Feb 28, 1945, part 2: Jan Ops; 9AF, "Op History of Ninth AF," sec 4, pp 20–21, 38–41; Patton, Diary Entry, Jan 1, 1945.

77. Weyland, "Diary," Jan 1, 1945. On reaction by command personnel, see for example, 362d FG, "Unit History," Jan 1945.

78. Weyland, "Diary," Jan 1–2, 1945.

79. Rpt, Faulkner, "Operational Employment of Radar."

80. XIX TAC, "Tactical Air Ops in Europe," pp 26–29; XIX TAC, "Rpt on Combat Ops," pp 27–30. Coordination improved greatly when XIX TAC supplied Third Army controllers better FM radio (FM 1498) sets. The TCC also began continuous broadcasts via SCR–399 radio, and controllers became more proficient. See HQ AAF, *Condensed Analysis of Ninth AF*, pp 100–101.

81. Weyland, "Diary," Jan 1–2, 1945; see also XIX TAC, "History," Jul 1, 1944–Feb 28, 1945, part 2: Dec Ops; US3A, "After Action Rpt," vol 1, Dec, Jan Ops; XIX TAC, "Morning Summaries," Dec 16, 1944–Jan 31, 1945; 9AF, "Ops Summary," Dec 16, 1944–Jan 31, 1945; XIX TAC, "Daily Intsum," Dec 16, 1944–Jan 31,

1945; XIX TAC, "History," Jul 1, 1944–Feb 28, 1945, vol 2: Dec 1944, Jan 1945 Ops, appendix 10: Statistical Summary.

82. XIX TAC, "History," Jul 1, 1944–Feb 28, 1945, part 1, pp 88–91; 361st FG, "Unit History," Dec 1944–Jan 1945, USAF-HRA, GP–361–HI–FI, 1945; 367th FG, "Unit History," Dec 1944–Jan 1945, USAF-HRA, GP–367–HI, 1944–45.

83. FM 100–20, para 9.

84. US3A, "After Action Rpt," vol 1: Jan Ops; 9AF, "Op History of Ninth AF," sec 4, pp 30, 46–48; Bennett, *Ultra in the West*, p 219.

85. See XIX TAC, "History," Jul 1, 1944–Feb 28, 1945, part 2: Dec Ops; US3A, "After Action Rpt," vol 1, Dec, Jan Ops; XIX TAC, "Morning Summaries," Dec 16, 1944–Jan 31, 1945; 9AF, "Ops Summary," Dec 16, 1944–Jan 31, 1945; XIX TAC, "Daily Intsum," Dec 16, 1944–Jan 31, 1945; XIX TAC, "History," Jul 1, 1944–Feb 28, 1945, vol 2, Dec 1944, Jan 1945 Ops, appendix 10: Statistical Summary.

86. Bennett, *Ultra in the West*, p 221.

87. 9AF, "Op History of Ninth AF," sec 10, p 7. Although the command attempted to use its more battle-weary aircraft for combat air patrols, these aircraft also could have seen better action if used against interdiction targets.

88. Weigley, *Eisenhower's Lieutenants*, pp 445–566; Griess, ed., vol 1, *Second World War*, chap. 16; 9AF, "Op History of Ninth AF"; Cole, *The Ardennes*, pp 606–648.

89. See especially, Griess, ed., vol 1, *Second World War*, pp 386–388; Weigley, *Eisenhower's Lieutenants*, pp 550–556.

90. 9AF, "Op History of Ninth AF," sec 5, p 7; Weyland, "Diary," Jan 2, 1945. This kind of flexibility in aerial assignment had become routine by this stage of the war.

91. XIX TAC, "History," Jul 1, 1944–Feb 28, 1945, vol 2, Jan Ops.

92. US3A, "After Action Rpt," vol 2, part 3: "G–2 Section Rpt," pp 31–32.

93. XIX TAC, "History," Jul 1, 1944–Feb 28, 1945, part 2: Jan Ops, pp 6–7; Ivie, *Aerial Reconnaissance*, pp 121–122.

94. Weyland, "Diary," Jan 9–10, 1945; XIX TAC, "History," Jul 1, 1944–Feb 28, 1945, part 2: Jan Ops, pp 6–7.

95. Weyland, "Diary," Jan 8–10, 1945.

96. *Ibid.*, Jan 10, 1945; Rpt, Faulkner, "Operational Employment of Radar." The GCA radar was unidirectional unlike the MEW, whose omnidirectional capability also enabled it to provide good navigational assistance. David R. Mets, "Manuscript Comments," May 15, 1992.

97. Weyland, "Diary," Jan 10, 1945; Rpt, Faulkner, "Operational Employment of Radar."

98. *Ibid.*

99. Weyland, "Diary," Jan 12, 1945. The command also encouraged its pilots to visit Third Army units and meet their personnel whenever flying commitments permitted.

100. 9AF, "Op History of Ninth AF," sec 4, pp 1–5, sec 5, pp 1–7.

101. Bennett, *Ultra in the West*, pp 219–220.

102. Weyland, "Diary," Jan 14, 1945.

103. XIX TAC, "History," Jul 1, 1944–Feb 28, 1945, part 2: Jan Ops, p 10; XIX TAC, "Rpt on Combat Ops," p 64.

104. XIX TAC, "Rpt on Combat Ops," pp 6–12; XIX TAC, "Tactical Air Ops in Europe," pp 5–13. The command was most critical about the absence of a good marker bomb in the inventory.

105. XIX TAC, "History," Jul 1, 1944–Feb 28, 1945, part 2: Jan Ops, p 11; US3A, "After Action Rpt," vol 2, part 3: "G–2 Section Rpt," p 31; XIX TAC, "History," Jul 1, 1944–Feb 28, 1945, part 1: pp 22–28.

106. XIX TAC, "History," Jul 1, 1944–Feb 28, 1945, vol 2: Jan Ops, p 2; XIX TAC, "Rpt on Combat Ops," p 47.

107. XIX TAC, "History," Jul 1, 1944–Feb 28, 1945, part 2: Jan Ops, p 12. The evening of January 17 General Patton appeared as guest of honor at a special XIX TAC senior officers' dinner in Luxembourg City to help the airmen celebrate their recent successes and consider the path ahead. Weyland, "Diary," Jan 17, 1945.

108. US3A, "After Action Rpt," vol 1, pp 15–22.

109. Weyland, "Diary," Jan 21, 1945; XIX TAC, "History," Jul 1, 1944–Feb 28, 1945, part 1: pp 88–91.

110. 9 AF "Op History of Ninth AF," sec 5, pp 17–19.

111. Weyland, "Diary," Jan 22, 1945; XIX TAC, "History," Jul 1, 1944–Feb 28, 1945, part 2: Jan Ops, pp 14–16.

112. 368th FG, "Unit History," Jan 1945, USAFHRA, GP–368–HI, 1944–45.

113. XIX TAC, "History," Jul 1, 1944–Feb 28, 1945, part 2: Jan Ops, pp 14–16; Weyland, "Diary," Jan 22–23, 1945.

114. XIX TAC, "History," Jul 1, 1944–Feb 28, 1945, part 2: Jan Ops, p 16.

115. See XIX TAC, "History," Jul 1, 1944–Feb 28, 1945, part 2: Dec Ops; US3A, "After Action Rpt," vol 1, Dec, Jan Ops; XIX TAC, "Morning Summaries," Dec 16, 1944–Jan 31, 1945; 9AF, "Ops Summary," Dec 16, 1944–Jan 31, 1945; XIX TAC, "Daily Intsum," Dec 16, 1944–Jan 31, 1945; XIX TAC, "History," Jul 1, 1944–Feb 28, 1945, part 2: Dec 1944, Jan 1945 Ops, appendix 10: Statistical Summary.

116. Weyland, "Diary," Jan 22–23, 1945; Ivie, *Aerial Reconnaissance*, p 126.

117. AAF Eval Bd, "Third Phase Tactical Air Ops," p 373.

118. See XIX TAC, "History," Jul 1, 1944–Feb 28, 1945, part 2: Dec Ops; US3A, "After Action Rpt," vol 1: Dec, Jan Ops; XIX TAC, "Morning Summaries," Dec 16, 1944–Jan 31, 1945; 9AF, "Ops Summary," Dec 16, 1944–Jan 31, 1945; XIX TAC, "Daily Intsum," Dec 16, 1944–Jan 31, 1945; XIX TAC, "History," Jul 1, 1944–Feb 28, 1945, part 2: Dec 1944, Jan 1945 Ops and appendix 10: Statistical Summary.

119. Weyland, "Diary," Jan 24, 28, 1945.

120. Rpt, "Allied Air Effort During Battle of the Bulge."

121. Rpt, Air Effects Committee, "Effect of Air Power," p 63.

122. 9AF "Op History of Ninth AF," sec 5, p 18.

Chapter 6

1. XIX TAC, "Daily Intsum," Feb 2, 1945; Air Ministry (Great Britain), *German Air Force*, pp 389–392.

2. US3A, "After Action Rpt," vol 2, part 3: "G–2 Section Rpt," p 34. German troop strength in the Eifel was uncertain, complicated by a *Wehrmacht* policy of constantly shifting troops out of the line. By the end of the Eifel Campaign in late March 1945, Third Army analysts estimated German forces had dwindled to about the size of one American division, approximately 16,000 troops. See Charles B. MacDonald, *The Last Offensive* [U.S. Army in World War II: European Theater of Operations] (Washington, D.C.: Office of the Chief of Military History, 1973), p 16.

3. For the land campaign, see MacDonald, *Last Offensive*; Bradley, *Soldier's Story*, pp 490–554; Weigley, *Eisenhower's Lieutenants*, pp 567–730; Williams, *Chronology*, pp 365–534; MacDonald, *Mighty Endeavor*, pp 455–569; and Griess, ed., vol 1, *Second World War*, pp 393–410.

4. On U.S. Army weaknesses, see Weigley, *Eisenhower's Lieutenants*, pp 567–574. Allied military leaders chose Malta for their discussions because it had been selected as the site for a meeting between Churchill, Roosevelt, and their advisors, on their way to the Yalta conference.

5. MacDonald, *Last Offensive*, pp 55–69; Bradley, *Soldier's Story*, pp 490–554; Weigley, *Eisenhower's Lieutenants*, pp 567–730; MacDonald, *Mighty Endeavor*, pp 455–569; Griess, ed., vol 1, *Second World War*, pp 393–395.

6. 368th FG, "Unit History," Feb 1945; XIX TAC, "History," Feb 1945, pp 16–17. For the air war, see Craven and Cate, eds., vol 3, *Europe: Argument to V–E Day,* pp 756–808; HQ AAF, *Condensed Analysis of Ninth Air Force*, pp 43–48. The discussion and chronological format for this discussion of the campaign is based in large part on the Weyland Diary and the following

sources: XIX TAC, "History," Feb, Mar, Apr, May, 1945; XIX TAC, "Morning Summaries," Jan 28–May 8, 1945; XIX TAC, "Daily Intsum," Jan 28–May 8, 1945; 9AF, "Ops Summary," Jan 28–May 8, 1945; and Carter and Mueller, *Army Air Forces in World War II*.

7. XIX TAC, "History," Jan–May 1945, appendix 8: Operational Research Data. Ninth Air Force established the Operational Research Section at XIX TAC on January 13, 1945, although General Weyland's interest in the project dated from early October 1944. See XIX TAC, "History," Jul 1, 1944–Feb 28, 1945, part 1, p 205.

8. XIX TAC, "History," Jan–May 1945, appendix 8: Operational Research Data.

9. Carter, "Air Power in Battle of the Bulge," pp 26–27.

10. XIX TAC, ORS, Rpt No. 91, "Operational Testing of SCR 584 Blind Bombing Procedure," Apr 7, 1945; XIX TAC, ORS, Memo No. 79, "SCR 584 Blind Bombing in XIX TAC Command," Apr 20, 1945, USAFHRA, XIX TAC, "History," May 1945, sec 2: Annexes.

11. AAF Eval Bd, "Third Phase Tactical Air Ops," p 33.

12. XIX TAC, "Operational Testing of SCR 584 Blind Bombing Procedure," Apr 7, 1945; see also XIX TAC, "SCR 584 Blind Bombing," Apr 20, 1945.

13. *Ibid.*; 9AF, ORS, Rpt No. 85, "Operational Accuracy of the Modified SCR 584 in Controlling Tactical Air Coordination Missions," May 8, 1945, USAFHRA, XIX TAC, "History," May 1945, sec 2: Annexes.

14. XIX TAC, "SCR 584 Blind Bombing," Apr 20, 1945.

15. XIX TAC, "History" Feb 1945, pp 4–5; XIX TAC "History" Mar 1945, pp 105–108; XIX TAC, "Ordnance-Armament Handbook for Tactical Air Liaison Officers," Mar 1945, USAFHRA, XIX

TAC, "History," May 1945, sec 2: Annexes. More powerful than TNT, the British RDX could be considered the "original plastic" explosive.

16. Craven and Cate, eds., vol 3, *Europe: Argument to V–E Day*, pp 756–808; HQ AAF, *Condensed Analysis of Ninth AF*, pp 43–48; Weyland, "Diary," Mar, 1945; XIX TAC, "History," Mar 1945; XIX TAC, "Morning Summaries," Jan 28–May 8, 1945; XIX TAC, "Daily Intsum," Jan 28–May 8, 1945; 9AF, "Ops Summary," Jan 28–May 8, 1945; Carter and Mueller, *Army Air Forces in World War II*.

17. Weyland "Diary," Feb 4, 1945. On February 4, the day after General Weyland discussed reinforcing General Nugent's command, he announced to his staff that the 354th would convert back to P–51s, while the 367th would replace its P–38 Lightnings with Thunderbolts.

18. 362d FG, "Unit History," Feb 1945.

19. 354th FG, "Unit History," Feb 1945.

20. *Ibid.*

21. For Patton's operations in the Eifel, see especially MacDonald, *Last Offensive*, pp 55–69, 84–115.

22. *Ibid.*

23. The 371st Fighter Group transferred to XII TAC on September 29, 1944. In the spring of 1945 it boasted the fewest number of pilots and aircraft lost, and the lowest aircraft abort rate in the command.

24. Craven and Cate, eds., vol 3, *Europe: Argument to V–E Day*, pp 756–808; HQ AAF, *Condensed Analysis of Ninth AF*, pp 43–48; Weyland, "Diary," Feb, Mar, Apr, May, 1945; XIX TAC, "History," Feb, Mar, Apr, May, 1945; XIX TAC, "Morning Summaries," Jan 28–May 8, 1945; XIX TAC, "Daily Intsum," Jan 28–May 8, 1945; 9AF, "Ops Summary," Jan 28–May 8, 1945; Carter and Mueller, *Army Air Forces in World War II*.

25. XIX TAC, "History," appendix 10: Statistical Summary (see appendix 4).

26. Patton lost an infantry division and his III Corps headquarters to General Simpson's Ninth Army.

27. Squadrons seem to have supported different corps on the same day, less from proximity to the target area than to needs of the particular ground element. Siegfried Line fighting often saw artillery assume primary responsibility for close support.

28. 9AF, "Ops Summary," Feb 1–25, 1945. Tactical air power's flexibility also applied to priorities, which in this case found close air support becoming most important.

29. *Ibid.* The special assault teams are described in MacDonald, *Last Offensive*, p 111. Weyland never mentioned earlier AAF tests that suggested fighter-bombers might have the best chance against pillbox-type targets. On the other hand, Third Army leaders seem to have preferred their assault team tactics rather than face the coordination problems required for fighter-bomber attacks against potential flak traps close to friendly troops in bad weather.

30. For discussion of four-plane flight operations, see XIX TAC, "Tactical Air Ops in Europe," p 3, and 362d FG, "Unit History," Mar 1945. Four-plane missions had been flown in North Africa, but the tactic received criticism from airmen, albeit under very different circumstances.

31. To be sure, in mid-March 1945, when the front moved far to the east and the *Luftwaffe* began to contest the Allied advance to the Rhine River more seriously, Weyland returned to the larger eight-plane close support formation.

32. Craven and Cate, eds., vol 3, *Europe: Argument to V–E Day*, pp 732–735; AAF Eval Bd, "Third Phase Tactical Air Ops," pp 195–196; Rpt, Air Effects Committee, "Effect of Air Power," pp 64–65. Allied losses included only seven of 1,411 heavy bombers, which bombed at exceptionally low altitudes. The XIX TAC lost two P–51s in this operation.

33. General Bradley's report downplays Clarion's impact because his evaluators considered it too isolated an operation.

34. Weyland, "Diary," Feb 25, 1945.

35. *Ibid.*, Feb 28–Mar 7, 1945; XIX TAC, "Tactical Air Ops in Europe," p 35.

General Weyland, who was promoted to major general on February 6, 1945, decided to spend a week in Cannes on the Riviera at the Hotel Martinez, popularly known as Flak House. In his absence, chief of staff Colonel Roger Browne assumed command. Opened in early 1945 for Ninth Air Force personnel, the Hotel Martinez had 50 beds reserved weekly for XIX TAC personnel. The command invariably filled its quota and viewed the rest-area policy as a major factor in reducing combat fatigue and preserving high morale. As for General Weyland, the vacation was his first of the campaign and gave him a chance to celebrate his recent promotion in pleasant surroundings.

36. MacDonald, *Last Offensive*, pp 196–197.

37. XIX TAC, "History," appendix 10: Statistical Summary.

38. MacDonald, *Last Offensive*, pp 185–207; Weigley, *Eisenhower's Lieutenants*, pp 619–622.

39. Weyland, "Diary," Mar 9, 1945; Bennett, *Ultra in the West*, p 242.

40. XIX TAC, "Rpt on Combat Ops," p 68. See also the "Statements from Allied Ground Forces" in AAF, "Third Phase Tac Air Ops," pp 215–254, and the report compiled under General Bradley's direction, Rpt, Air Effects Committee, "Effect of Air Power," Annex 1.

41. Weyland, "Diary," Mar 9, 1945; XIX TAC, "History," Mar 1945.

42. See especially, Weigley, *Eisenhower's Lieutenants*, pp 633–639.

43. On the Saar-Mosel-Rhine Trap, see *Ibid.*, pp 633–639; XIX TAC, "Rpt on Combat Ops," pp 68–70; and MacDonald, *Last Offensive*, pp 185–207.

44. XIX TAC, "Rpt on Combat Ops," pp 68–70.

45. Mission rates varied considerably with the combat conditions. With smaller, four-plane missions, the rate was relatively high. Sortie rates, by contrast, refer to the number of individual airplane flights during a given amount of time.

46. MacDonald, *Last Offensive*, chap. 11; Air Ministry (Great Britain), *German Air Force*, p 389.

47. XIX TAC, "Casualties, Mar 1944–May 1945," USAFHRA, 537.391, 1944–45.

48. Many close air support targets appear to have been what might be termed battlefield air interdiction targets. Such aircraft were normally assigned to a corps for cooperation missions, then released for armed reconnaissance-interdiction flying. XIX TAC, "Casualties, Mar 1944–May 1945."

49. 362d FG, "Unit History," Mar 1945; Intvw, Burns, Jan 7, 1992.

50. XIX TAC, "History," Mar, Apr, 1945, appendix 10: Statistical Summary.

51. Eisenhower, it must be said, was unwilling to cater any longer to Bernard Montgomery's crushing ego. Indeed, his public carping a few weeks earlier during the Battle of the Bulge nearly cost the Field Marshal his job. When he learned he was about to be sacked, only an obsequious letter to Eisenhower, wherein he pledged to the Supreme Commander his future support as a subordinate in all matters, saved him his European command in World War II. For this episode, see Bradley, *Soldier's Story*, pp 509–522; Weigley, *Eisenhower's Lieutenants*, pp 641–644; and Bennett, *Ultra in the West*, p 242.

52. Weyland, "Diary," Mar 20–22, 1945; XIX TAC, "Rpt on Combat Ops," pp 69–70.

53. Without a better means of forestalling German movement at night, tactical air power could not prevent some degree of German escape. See XIX TAC, "History," Mar 1945; Griess, ed., vol 1, *Second World War*, pp 399–400.

54. US3A, "After Action Rpt," vol 2, part 3: "G–2 Section Rpt," p 39.

55. XIX TAC, "Rpt on Combat Ops," p 70; Air Ministry (Great Britain), *German Air Force*, p 390.

56. XIX TAC, "History," Mar 1945, sec 2, Annexes.

57. XIX TAC, "History," Mar 1945; Air Ministry (Great Britain), *German Air Force*, p 390.

58. US3A, "After Action Rpt," vol 2, part 3: "G–2 Section Rpt," p 39.

59. *Ibid.*, p 45.

60. Weyland, "Diary," Mar 27, 1945. For details on the Hammelburg incident, see Blumenson, ed., *Patton Papers*, pp 664–676; Weigley, *Eisenhower's Lieutenants*, pp 654–657; and MacDonald, *Last Offensive*, pp 280–284.

61. Griess, ed., vol 1, *Second World War*, pp 404–405.

62. Weyland, "Diary," Mar 23–31, 1945.

63. *Ibid*, Mar 26, 1945.

64. 9AF, "Report on Tactical Air Cooperation, Organization, Methods and Procedures with Special Emphasis on Phase III Operations," Jul 31, 1945, USAFHRA, N138.4–34, 1945, pp 37–43. Although easier to transport, the British mesh track could prove troublesome on site and, once broken, would require considerable time and effort to repair. Smith, "Marston Mat," pp 84–88.

65. Weyland, "Diary," Mar 27–31, 1945; XIX TAC, "History," Mar 1945.

66. XIX TAC, "History," Apr 1945.

67. Blumenson, ed., *Patton Papers*, pp 680–681; Weigley, *Eisenhower's Lieutenants*, pp 681–687.

68. XIX TAC, "History," Apr 1945; 362d FG, "Unit History," Apr 1945.

69. *Ibid.*

70. Air Ministry (Great Britain), *German Air Force*, pp 391–392.

71. Weyland, "Diary," Apr 8, 1945; XIX TAC, "History," appendix 10: Statistical Summary; Ivie, *Aerial Reconnaissance*, pp 151–157.

72. XIX TAC, "History," Apr 1945.

73. Weyland, "Diary," Apr 1, 1945; XIX TAC, "History," Apr 1945; XIX TAC, "Tentative Moving Schedule," Apr 5, 1945, USAFHRA, 537.391, Aug 1944–Mar 1945.

74. Weyland, "Diary," Apr 3, 1945.

75. 368th FG, "Unit History," Apr 1945.

76. Weyland, "Diary," Apr 12, 1945.

77. *Ibid*, Apr 4–10, 1945.

78. Weyland, "Diary," Apr 11–13, 1945; Blumenson, ed., *Patton Papers*, pp 683–685; and MacDonald, *Last Offensive*, pp 379–384.

79. Weyland, "Diary," Apr 10, 1945.

80. See Air Ministry (Great Britain), *German Air Force*, pp 391–392.

81. XIX TAC, "History," Apr 1945, pp 101–103.

82. Weyland, "Diary," Apr 16–17, 1945; Patton, Diary Entry, Apr 17, 1945.

83. XIX TAC, "History," Apr 1945.

84. XIX TAC, "Daily Intsum," Apr 19–20, 1945.

85. Weyland, "Diary," Apr 21, 1945.

86. US3A, "After Action Rpt," vol 2, part 3: "G–2 Section Rpt," pp 39, 45.

87. *Ibid.*

88. Weyland, "Diary," Apr 29, 1945.

89. XIX TAC, "History," appendix 10: Statistical Summary; Ivie, *Aerial Reconnaissance*, pp 151–157.

90. Weyland, "Diary," Apr 18–30, 1945; XIX TAC, "History," Apr 1945.

91. Weyland, "Diary," Apr 28, 1945.

92. *Ibid.*

93. Intvw, Weyland, Nov 19, 1974, p 157.

94. Weyland, "Diary," May 1–8, 1945.

95. US3A, "Gen Order No. 98," and XIX TAC, "Gen Order No. 34," both May 9, 1945, in XIX TAC, "History," May 1945, sec 2: Annexes, USAFHRA, 537.01.

Chapter 7

1. US3A, "GO 98," and XIX TAC, "GO 34," both May 9, 1945.

2. AAF Eval Bd, "Third Phase Tactical Air Ops," Aug 1945, p 38.

3. XIX TAC, "History," appendix 10: Statistical Summary; XIX TAC, "Op Statistics," 1944–45. An aborted sortie refers to a combat sortie in which the airborne aircraft returns to its base or flies toward another friendly base before completing the scheduled mission for reasons other than enemy action (e.g., engine trouble).

4. Ltr, Brig Gen Robert M. Lee, Dep CG for Ops, 9AF, to Maj Gen O.P. Weyland, CG, XIX TAC, Mar 5, 1945, USAFHRA 537.01, 1945, appendix 8.

5. Rpt, Maj Gen Weyland to CG, 9AF, "Tank and Armored Vehicle Claims," Mar 17, 1945.

6. *Ibid.*

7. *Ibid.* Authorities also allowed for reporting constraints based on a pilot's abbreviated view while operating a 300-mph airplane.

8. Rpt, IX TAC, "Assessment of Fighter-Bomber Claims," Apr 15, 1945, Quesada Collection, Box 5, MD, LC.

9. The questionnaire, responses, and correspondence among key commanders are found as an untitled Board report, AAF Evaluation Board, ETO, 1945, USAF-HRA, 138.36A, 1945. This information was used to prepare the Board's report on Phase III operations (USAFHRA, 138.4–36, 1945), which included extracts entitled "Statements from Allied Ground Forces on the Effectiveness of Air Cooperation." The Board's report resulted from the initiative of Lieutenant General Barney Giles, AAF Deputy Commander, in late January 1945, who wanted an assessment of close air support procedures, operations, and effectiveness from both ground and air viewpoints. Army Major General Jacob E. Fickel served as president of the board, whose members included three air officers and one ground officer, supported by a staff of one ground and four air officers. Board members visited 18 major air and ground headquarters in the European theater, including those of Third Army and the XIX TAC. After its European survey, the board convened at Orlando Army Air Base, Florida, assigned to the AAF's Tactical Center. The report was issued on August 20, 1945.

10. Ltr, Maj Gen Walton H. Walker, CG, XX Corps, US3A to Maj Gen O.P. Weyland, CG, XIX TAC, Apr 16, 1945, USAF-HRA 537.01, 1945, sec 2: Annexes. Like most of his fellow airmen in tactical aviation during World War II, Weyland did not discuss his views on air power at great length. Quesada, who did speak out, left the Air Force. Later, when Weyland served as a four-star general and commander of the Tactical Air Command, he often expressed himself on the nature of tactical air power. His theme remained that of FM 100–20, centralized control of air assets at the theater level with air and ground elements directing their own forces.

11. Gen Quesada's winter assault plan is discussed in Ltr, Dr. David Griggs to E.L. Bowles, Oct 17, 1944.

12. Weigley, *Eisenhower's Lieutenants*, pp 727–730. Whatever difficulty one might have with the logic of Weigley's argument, Patton always argued that mobility and superior numbers and tactics prevailed against the heavier-gun German weapons. See for example, "Transcript of Conference between Lt Gen G.S. Patton, Jr, and Third Army Correspondents," Sep 7, 1944, in Patton Collection, Box 15, Chronological File, MD, LC.

13. Ltr, Gen O.N. Bradley, CG, 12th Army Group, to Gen Carl Spaatz, CG, USSTAF, May 17, 1945, USAFHRA, 138.4–36A, 1945.

14. XIX TAC, "Rpt on Combat Ops," Introduction.

15. AAF Eval Bd, "Third Phase Tactical Air Ops," p 38; Rpt, Air Effects Committee, "Effect of Air Power," pp 151.

16. AAF Eval Bd, "Third Phase Tactical Air Ops," p 1. On the relations between U.S. Army Ground Forces and U.S. Army Air Forces headquarters and on postwar tactical air power developments, see Caroline F. Ziemke, "In the Shadow of the Giant: USAF Tactical Air Command in the Era of Strategic Bombing, 1945–1955" (PhD diss, Ohio State University, 1989), pp 1–75. In late 1945 General Devers, then commanding general of Army Ground Forces, could be expected to support the AAF view on air superiority as prerequisite for ground action.

17. AAF Eval Bd, "Third Phase Tactical Air Ops," p 25.

18. See the statistics and charts in Rpt, Air Effects Committee, "Effect of Air Power," plates 1, 2.

19. *Ibid.*, p 193.

20. Despite Ninth Air Force's outstanding record flying against the Seine and Loire bridges prior to D-Day, planners initially focused on destroying enemy road and rail convoys in the fall of 1944, before deciding to concentrate air power against bridge targets.

21. On the subject of air interdiction, see Richard H. Kohn and Joseph P. Harahan, eds., *Air Interdiction in World War II, Korea, and Vietnam* (Washington, D.C.: Office of Air Force History, 1986).

22. FM 100–20, Introduction and para 16 b.(3); Jacobs, "Tactical Air Doctrine," pp 35–49.

23. AAF Eval Bd, "Third Phase Tactical Air Ops," p 342.

24. *Ibid.*, pp 341–343; XIX TAC, "Tactical Air Ops in Europe," p 1.

25. AAF Eval Bd, "Third Phase Tactical Air Ops," p 1.

26. Memo, Raines, May 20, 1991.

27. Rpt, Air Effects Committee, "Effect of Air Power," p 43. The 105- and 155-mm howitzers, the most widely used American artillery pieces, fired projectiles weighing approximately 30 and 100 pounds, respectively. See MacDonald, *Last Offensive*, p 12; and Roland G. Ruppenthal, *Logistical Support of the Armies*, vol 2 [U.S. Army in World War II: European Theater of Operations] (Washington, D.C.: Office of the Chief of Military History, 1989), pp 524–543; also, Department of the Army, *The Army Almanac* (Washington, D.C.: U.S. Government Printing Office, 1950), pp 123–126.

28. Rpt, AAF Evaluation Board, ETO, "Questionnaire for Army Officers, 1945," USAFHRA, 138.36A, 1945, response to question #2.

29. The fact remains that P–47s with standard 500-lb bombs normally could do little damage to pillbox-type targets. As H. M. Cole described a three-squadron air attack during the Lorraine Campaign, "the planes hit their targets, but the 500-pound bombs carried by the P–47's had little effect on reinforced concrete." Cole, *Lorraine Campaign*, p 154.

30. Rpt, AAF Eval Bd, "Questionnaire for Army Officers," response to question #14.

31. US3A, "After Action Rpt," vol 2, part 3: "G–2 Section Rpt," p 39, 45.

32. Ltr, Gen Bradley to Gen Spaatz, May 17, 1945.

33. Despite the laudatory emphasis on individual initiative in air-ground operations in western Europe, clearly future technology would enable commanders of Weyland's generation to centralize control more effectively and by so doing constrain junior officer initiative. Advanced technology for command and control eventually would give to less-disciplined leaders far from the scene the ability to micro-manage events on the battlefield, and along with that, a corresponding decrease in the delegation of authority to leaders on the scene (though responsibility for the outcome remained securely tied to the field commanders). By the time of the Vietnam War in the 1960s, this trend had captured the President of the United States in the Oval Office! How might General Eisenhower, Supreme Com-

mander of Allied Expeditionary Forces, have responded at the eleventh hour to imprecations from President Franklin Roosevelt for a delay of D-Day?

34. Rpt, AAF Eval Bd, "Questionnaire for Army Officers," response to questions #23 and #36.

35. *Ibid.*, response to question #23.

36. AAF Eval Bd, "Third Phase Tactical Air Ops," pp 305–309. To be sure, the effectiveness of Allied fighters against the *Luftwaffe*'s Bf 109 and FW 190 aircraft depended on more than technology alone. Piloting skills and experience, among other considerations, also proved crucial.

37. XIX TAC, "Rpt on Combat Ops," p 5.

38. Rpt, AAF Eval Bd, "Questionnaire for Army Officers," response to questions #20 and #21.

39. AAF Eval Bd, "Third Phase Tactical Air Ops," pp 384–385; XIX TAC, "Rpt on Combat Ops," pp 25–26.

40. AAF Eval Bd, "Third Phase Tactical Air Ops," p 33.

41. HQ AAF, *Condensed Analysis of Ninth Air Force*, p 105.

42. Ltr, Gen Bradley to Gen Spaatz, May 17, 1945.

43. Intvw, Gen James Ferguson, USAF, Jun 14, 1988, videotape on file at Air University television studio, Maxwell AFB, Alabama.

44. HQ AAF, *Condensed Analysis of Ninth AF*, p 121.

45. Blumenson, ed., *Patton Papers*, p 624.

46. Ltr, Patton to Weyland, Sep 21, 1945, Box 32, Personal and Professional Correspondence, Patton Collection, MD, LC.

47. Gen O.P. Weyland, "Interview," Nov 19, 1974, pp 151–152, USAFHRA, K239.0512–813; see also Kohn and Harahan, eds., *Air Superiority*, pp 68–69.

48. Weyland, "Interview," Nov 19, 1974, pp 151–152.

49. AGF, "Report of the Army Ground Forces Equipment Review Board," Jun 20, 1945, and subsequent correspondence and reports, including Weyland's notes, in Weyland Papers, USAFHRA, 168.7104–89, 1945. Cook had been XII Corps commander briefly under General Patton during the first half of August 1944, before blood and circulatory problems forced his reassignment and return to the United States. Had he served a longer tour with the air-ground team, perhaps his views on air support would have been more in accord with his former commander's.

50. *Ibid.*

51. *Ibid.*

52. See Kohn and Harahan, eds., *Air Superiority*, p 68; Futrell, *Ideas, Concepts, Doctrine*, pp 74–75, 165; Ziemke, "In the Shadow of the Giant," pp 1–30; War Department FM 31–75, "Air Ground Operations" (Aug 1946).

53. For postwar developments, see Futrell, *Ideas, Concepts, Doctrine*; Ziemke, "In the Shadow of the Giant."

54. The official report in two volumes is in the Weyland Papers, USAFHRA, 168.7104–53, 1954. On tactical air problems in Korea, see especially, Allan R. Millett, "Korea, 1950–1953," in Cooling, ed., *Close Air Support*, pp 345–405.

55. Kohn and Harahan, eds., *Air Superiority*, p 72.

Sources

The study of close air support for Lt. Gen. George S. Patton, Jr.'s, army is based mainly on primary materials located in two superb government repositories. The United States Military History Institute at Carlisle Barracks, Pennsylvania, maintains an important World War II collection of air-ground records and invaluable after action reports prepared by the U.S. Third Army. The comprehensive archival collection of the United States Air Force Historical Research Agency at Maxwell Air Force Base, Alabama, provided the bulk of the primary sources on tactical aviation's role in general and of the XIX Tactical Air Command's support of Third Army operations in particular. Among these records, the XIX Tactical Air Command file, General O. P. Weyland's personal papers, and the XIX Tactical Air Command's unit histories proved especially rewarding. The materials at both repositories can be examined in their original hard copy forms. Specific archival listings cited below also identify other valuable records examined for this history.

United States Government

Archives

USAF Historical Research Agency, Maxwell AFB, Alabama

Class 138: AAF Evaluation Board

Rpt, AAF Evaluation Board, ETO, "The Effect of Air Power in the Battle of Metz," Jan 19, 1945 (K138.4–30).

Rpt, AAF Evaluation Board, ETO, "Tactics and Techniques Developed by the United States Tactical Air Commands in the European Theater of Operations," Mar 11, 1945 (138.4–33, 1945).

Rpt, AAF Evaluation Board, ETO, "HQ Ninth AF, Report on Tactical Air Cooperation, Organization, Methods and Procedures with Special Emphasis on Phase III Operations," Jul 31, 1945 (138.4–34, 1945).

Rpt, Ninth AF, "Report on Tactical Air Cooperation, Organization, Methods and Procedures with Special Emphasis on Phase III Operations," Jul 31, 1945 (138.4–34, 1945).

Rpt, AAF Evaluation Board, ETO, "Effectiveness of Third Phase Tactical Air Operations in the ETO, May 4, 44 to May 8, 45" (138.4–36, May 19, 45).

Rpt, AAF Evaluation Board, ETO, "Questionnaire for Army Officers, 1945" (138.36A, 1945).

Ltr, Gen. O. N. Bradley, CG, 12th Army Group to Gen. Carl Spaatz, CG, USSTAF, May 17, 1945 (K138.4–36A, 1945).

Class 168: Papers of Retired Officers
Weyland Papers

Weyland, Maj. Gen. Otto P. "Diary, Jul 29, 44–May 18, 45" (K168.7104–1, 1944–1945).
Lecture, "Air Power and Its Application," Sep 21, 1955 (168.7104–46, 1954).
Diary, "Korea, Dec 1, 1951–May 31, 1952" (168.7104–52, 1951–52).
FEAF, "Report on the Korean War" 2 Vols, 1954 (K168.7104-53, 1954).
"Twelve-Thousand Fighter-Bomber Sorties: XIX Tactical Air Command's First Month of Operations in Support of Third US Army in France," Sep 30, 1944 (168.7104–69).
"Progress Report, Airfield Construction," Jul 24, 1944 (168.7104–83).
"Planes Over Patton: XIX Tactical Air Command's Support of Third Army in its Swift End-Run Through France," Sep 30, 1944 (168.7104–86, Sep 30, 44).
"Ziegenburg Hq Attack," Mar 19, 1945 (168.7104–87, 1945).
Cook Board Correspondence, 1945 (K168.7104-89, 1945).
HQ AAF, "Impact: U.S. Tactical Airpower." Vol 3, No. 5 (May 1945) (168.7104–92, May 45).
Intvw, Rundstedt, Field Marshal Gerd von, with Maj. Gen. O. P. Weyland, Jul 2, 1945 (168.7104–95).
"Conference between General Patton, General Weyland and Third Army Correspondents," Dec 9, 1944 (168.7104–101, 1944).
Weyland/XIX TAC Photo Album (168.7104–114, 1944–45).

Miscellaneous Reports

IX Air Support Command, "Reference Guide on Tactical Employment of Air Power Organization and Control Channels of Tactical Units," Prepared Oct 29, 1943, revised Feb 24, 1944 (168.6005–103A), Feb 25, 1944).
"Some Notes on the Use of Air Power in Support of Land Operations, Introduction by B. L. Montgomery," Dec 1944" (168.6006–137)

Class 520: Eighth Air Force

Rpt, "Report on Manpower and Shipping Requirements Prepared by Bradley Committee," Jun 23, 1943 (K520.122–1, 1943).
"Statistical Summary of Eighth Air Force Operations, Aug 17, 42–May 8, 45" (520.308–11, 1942–45).

Class 533: Ninth Air Force
Studies and Statistics

Ninth AF, "Annual Statistical Summary, 1944" (K533.3083, 1944).
"Operational History of the Ninth Air Force, Bk I, Battle of the Ardennes: Dec
    1, 1944–Jan 26, 1945" (K533.01–2).
"Operational Statistics, Jan 1, 44–Jun 1, 44" (K533.3082, 1944).
"Operations Journal, Aug 6, 1944" (K533.305, Apr–Dec 1944).
"Schedule of Operations, Aug 2, 1944" (K533.3082, Aug 1944).
"Weekly Intelligence Summaries, Nov 3, 43–Jun 1, 44" (K533.607, 1944–45).

Reports

First Army G–3 (Air), "Air Support Report, Aug 6, 44" (K533.4501–3, May–
    Aug 1944).
"Report on the Activities of the Ninth Air Force, period 6 Jun–20 Aug 1944"
    Sep 27, 1944 (533.306–2, 1944).
"Fighter-bomber Control: A Compilation of Procedures Used by the Ninth Air
    Force during Operations on the European Continent" (Brig. Gen. Robert
    M. Lee, Chief of Staff) (533.503–1, 1945).
"ORS Report No. 65, MEW Operations in XIX Tactical Air Command," Nov
    20, 1944.
"Reconnaissance in the Ninth Air Force: A Report on Reconnaissance Opera-
    tions During the European Campaign," n.d. (May 9, 1945).
Joseph A. Wyant, Ninth AF Historian to Brig. Gen. R. C. Candee, "Material
    in Response to Telephone Request of Sep 28, 1945 Concerning Allied
    Air Effort During the Battle of the Bulge," n.d. [1945] (533.4501–5).
ORS Rpt No. 85, "Operational Accuracy of the Modified SCR 584 in Con-
    trolling Tactical Air Coordination Missions," May 8, 1945 (XIX TAC
    Hist/May/Annexes).
"Air Force Operations in Support of Attack on Cherbourg, Jun 22 thru Jun 30,
    1944," File 536: IX Tactical Air Command.
"IX TAC in Review: Organization, Personnel, Equipment, Maintenance, Oper-
    ations, Costs," Nov 43–May 45 (536.01, 1945).
IX TAC, "Unit History, Apr, May, Jun, Jul 1944" (536.02)

Class 537: XIX Tactical Air Command
Studies and Histories

XIX TAC, "History of XIX Tactical Air Command," Dec 4, 1943–Jun 30,
    1944 (537.01, 1943–44).
XIX TAC, "History of the XIX Tactical Air Command," Jul 1, 1944–Feb 28,
    1945, Part 1: "Administrative Narrative, Aug 44–May 45" (537.01).

XIX TAC, "History of the XIX Tactical Air Command," Jul 1, 1944–Feb 28, 1945, Part 2: "Operations Narrative, Aug 44–May 45" (537.01).

XIX TAC, "History of the XIX Tactical Air Command," Jul 1, 1944–Feb 28, 1945, App 1: "General Orders, Aug 44–May 45" (537.01).

XIX TAC, "History of the XIX Tactical Air Command," Jul 1, 1944–Feb 28, 1945, App 2: "Special Orders, Aug 44–May 45" (537.01).

XIX TAC, "History of the XIX Tactical Air Command," Jul 1, 1944–Feb 28, 1945, App 3: "Memoranda, Aug 44–May 45" (537.01).

XIX TAC, "History of the XIX Tactical Air Command," Jul 1, 1944–Feb 28, 1945, App 4: "Movement of Troops Orders, Aug 44–May 45" (537.01).

XIX TAC, "History of the XIX Tactical Air Command," Jul 1, 1944–Feb 28, 1945, App 5: "Assignment/Attachment Orders, Aug 44–May 45" (537.01).

XIX TAC, "History of the XIX Tactical Air Command," Jul 1, 1944–Feb 28, 1945, App 6: "Twelve-Thousand Fighter-Bomber Sorties, Aug 44–May 45" (537.01).

XIX TAC, "History of the XIX Tactical Air Command," Jul 1, 1944–Feb 28, 1945, App 7: "Operational Research Data, Aug 44–May 45" (537.01).

XIX TAC, "History of the XIX Tactical Air Command," Jul 1, 1944–Feb 28, 1945, App 8: "Correspondence, Aug 44–May 45" (537.01).

XIX TAC, "History of the XIX Tactical Air Command," Jul 1, 1944–Feb 28, 1945, App 9: "Periodic Staff Reports, Aug 44–May 45" (537.01).

XIX TAC, "History of the XIX Tactical Air Command," Jul 1, 1944–Feb 28, 1945, App 10: "Statistical Summary of the XIX Tactical Air Command, Aug 44–May 45" (537.01).

XIX TAC, "Signals: The Story of Communications in the XIX Tactical Air Command up to V–E Day," Jun 15, 1945 (537.901).

Reports

"Reports of Attacks by Friendly-Type Aircraft," Dec 1944–Jan 1945. (537.599).

"Report on Bombing of Metz Forts," Sep–Nov 1944.

"A Report on the Combat Operations of the XIX Tactical Air Command," May 30, 1945 (537.02).

10th Photo Gp, to HQ Ninth AF, "Employment of Reconnaissance Aircraft, Tactics and Techniques," Feb 10, 1945 (537.628, 1945).

Faulkner, J. E., Advanced Science Base Laboratory, British Branch Radiation Laboratory, MIT, "Operational Employment of Radar in the XIX Tactical Air Command," n.d. [1945] (537.906, 1945).

ORS Rpt No. 91, "Operational Testing of SCR 584 Blind Bombing Procedure," Apr 7, 1945.

ORS Memo [Rpt] No. 79, "SCR 584 Blind Bombing in XIX Tac Command,"

Apr 29, 1945 (Hist/May/Sec 2: Annexes).

A–3, "Operation Madison: Air Plan in Support of Third U.S. Army," Nov 3, 1944 (537.4501, 1944).

A–3, "Operation Tink: Air Plan in Support of Third U.S. Army," Dec 17, 1944 (537.205A, 1944).

Weyland, Maj. Gen. to CG, Ninth AF, "Tank and Armored Vehicle Claims," Mar 17, 1945 (XIX Hist, App 8).

"Immediate Report No. 41 (Combat Observations)," ca 1945 (537.01, 1945).

Hallett, Lt. Col. Charles H., AC/S to CG, Ninth AF, "Use of Napalm Bombs," Oct 3, 1944 (537.453, Oct–Nov 44).

"Tactical Air Operations in Europe: A Report on Employment of Fighter-Bomber, Reconnaissance and Night Fighter Aircraft by XIX Tactical Air Command, Ninth Air Force, in Connection with the Third U.S. Army Campaign from Aug 1, 1944 to V–E Day, May 9, 1945." (537.04A, 1944–45).

HQ AAF, "Air–Ground Teamwork on the Western Front: The Role of the XIX Tactical Air Command during Aug 1944 [Wings at War Series, No. 5] (537.04C, Aug 44).

Correspondence

Ltr, Dr. David Griggs, Member, Advisor Specialist Group, USSTAF, to Brig. Gen. O. P. Weyland, Oct 3, 1944 (K537.101, 1944).

Ltr, CG, XIX TAC to CG, Ninth AF, "Authorized Aircraft in Fighter Groups," Nov 14, 1944 (537.01, App 8, 1944–45).

Ltr, Maj. Gen. Walton H. Walker, CG, XX Corps, U.S. Third Army to Maj. Gen. O. P. Weyland, CG, XIX TAC, Apr 16, 1945 (537.01, Apr, 1945, Sec 2: Annexes).

Ltr, "Tentative Moving Schedule," Apr 5, 1945 (537.391).

Ltr, Brig. Gen. Robert M. Lee, Dep CG for Ops, Ninth AF to Maj. Gen. O. P. Weyland, CG, XIX TAC, Mar 5, 1945 (537.01, 1945, App 8).

Memo, Brig. Gen. O. P. Weyland, CG, XIX TAC to Lt. Gen. G. S. Patton, CG, U.S. Third Army, Oct 28, 1944 (537.01, 1944).

Memo, Lt. Col. Charles H. Hallet, AC/S, to CG, XIX TAC, "Air Support of Third Army's Drive to the East," Aug 23, 1944 (168.7104–85).

Memo, Lt. Col. Charles H. Hallet, AC/S to A–3, XIX TAC, Oct 6, 1944 (537.306A, Oct 1–15, 1944).

Memo, A. C. McLean, XIX TAC/ORS to A–3, "Analysis of Attacks on Targets of Opportunity, Dec 15, 1944 to Jan 31, 1945," Feb 16, 1945 (537.01, App 7).

Memo, No. 100–25B, "SOP, Tactical Air Communications," Apr 29, 1945.

"Ordnance-Armament Handbook for Tactical Air Liaison Officers," Mar 1945 (537.01, Mar 1945, Sec 2: Annexes).

Statistics

"Daily Intelligence Summaries (Intsum)," Aug 9–May 8, 1945 (537.606, 1944–45).

"Morning Summaries," Aug 8, 1944–May 8, 1945 (537.306A).

"Operational Statistics," Aug 8, 1944–May 9, 1945 (537.3800–3900, 1944–45).

Class 612: Northwest African Air Forces

Rpt, Col. H. J. Knerr, Dep, ASC to CG, AAF, "Report on Manpower and Shipping Requirements Prepared by Bradley Committee," Jun 23, 1943 (K612.201A).

Class 614: Northwest African Tactical Air Force

Memo, Brig. Gen. L. S. Kuter, Dep Comdr/Allied Air AF to CG, AAF, subj: Organization of American Air Forces, May 12, 1943 (614.201–1).

Class 626: Mediterranean Allied Tactical Air Force

Rpt, HQ, MASAAF, "XXII Tactical Air Command's Close Support of the Fifth Army" (K626.4501–1, 1944).

Class 651: XII Air Support Command

Rpt, AEAF, "Notes on Air Power Taken During a Visit to Fifth Army Front Between the 5th to 20th of Feb 1944." (K651.152, Feb 5, 1944).

Unit Histories

36th Fighter Group (GP–36–HI/Apr–Sep 44).
354th Fighter Group (GP–354–HI/Nov 43–May 45).
358th Fighter Group (GP–358–HI/Feb–Nov 44).
361st Fighter Group (GP–361–HI/Dec 44–Jan 45).
362d Fighter Group (GP–362–HI/Jan 44–May 45).
367th Fighter Group (GP–367–HI/Dec 44–Feb 45).
368th Fighter Group (GP–368–HI/Dec 44–Feb 45).
371st Fighter Group (GP–371–HI/Mar–Sep 44; Feb–May 45).
405th Fighter Group (GP–405–HI/Apr 44–Feb 45).
406th Fighter Group (GP–406–HI/Feb 44–Feb 45).
"The 406th Occupier: Special Historical Issue," (GP–406–SU–NE/Sep 45)

Miscellaneous Reports

Rpt, Philip Cole, et al., VIII Air Support Command to HQ, Eighth AF, "Observers Report. Air Operations in Support of Ground Forces in North West Africa Mar 15–Apr 5, 1943," Jul 1943 (K650.03–2).

Rpt, George S. Patton, HQ, Seventh Army, "Notes on the Sicilian Campaign,"
Oct 30, 1943.

U.S. Army Military History Institute, Carlisle Barracks, Pennsylvania

U.S. Third Army, "After Action Report," Aug 1, 1944–May 9, 1945, Vol 1:
Operations; Annex No. 3: "XIX Tactical Air Command," Regensburg,
1945.

———, "After Action Report," Aug 1, 1944–May 9, 1945, Vol 2: Staff Section Reports, Part 1: "Command Section Report." Regensburg, 1945.

———, "After Action Report," Aug 1, 1944–May 9, 1945, Vol 2: Staff Section Reports, Part 3: "G–2 Section Report," Regensburg, 1945.

———, "After Action Report," Aug 1, 1944–May 9, 1945, Vol 2: Staff Section Reports, Part 4: "G–3 Section Report" Regensburg, 1945.

12th Army Group, Air Effects Committee, "Effect of Air Power on Military
Operations, Western Europe," Jul 15, 1945.

———, "Answers to Questionnaire for Key Commanders on the Effects of
Strategic and Tactical Air Power on Military Operations, ETO," 1945.

———, "Answers to AAF Evaluation Board Guide Questions on Air–Ground
Cooperation." May 11, 1945.

———, "Destruction of the German Armies in Western Europe, Jun 6, 1944–
May 9, 1945." ca 1945.

U.S. Army Ground Forces, Observer Board, European Theater, "Reports of
Observers," 3 Vols, Bad Nauheim, Germany, 1944–46.

U.S. Forces, European Theater. Battle Studies, Vol 2: Air Operations, ca 1945:
No. 2: "Army Air Forces Logistical Summary (During WWII in ETO)."
No. 5: "Tactical Development of Fighters in the European Theater."
No. 14: "Fighter-Bomber Cooperation."
No. 15: "AAF Tactical Reconnaissance in the European Theater."
No. 19: "The Battle for Metz and the Surrounding Forts, 1500 Years–15
Days."
No. 21: "Air Resupply: Ardennes Counter-Offensive (Dec 16, 1944–Feb
21, 1945)."
No. 22: "Air Force Participation in the Battle of the Ardennes (Dec 16,
1944–Jan 16, 1945)."
No. 29: "Employment of the Air Forces in the European Theater During
WW II and the Role of Fighter Aviation."

U.S. Forces, European Theater, General Board, "The Utilization of Tac Air
Recce Units of the Army Air Forces to Secure Information for Ground
Forces in the European Theater." Study No. 19, ca 1945–46.

General Board. "Liaison Aircraft with Ground Force Units." Study No. 20, ca
1945–46.

————, General Board, "Organization, Operations and Equipment of Air–Ground Liaison in All Echelons from Divisions Upwards." Study No. 21, ca 1945–46.

————, General Board, "Air Power in the European Theater of Operations." Study No. 54, ca 1945–46.

————, General Board, "The Control of Tactical Aircraft in the European Theater of Operations." Study No. 55, ca 1945–46.

————, General Board, "The Tactical Air Force in the European Theater of Operations." Study No. 56, ca 1945–46.

Ninth Air Force. "Reconnaissance in the Ninth Air Force: A Report on Reconnaissance Operations During the European Campaign," May 9, 1945.

Library of Congress (LC), Washington, D.C.

Henry H. Arnold Collection

HQ, AAF, AAF Ltr 80–3, "Air Employment Terminology," Nov 16, 1944, File 1938–46, Box 104, MD, LC.

Memo, Lt. Gen. Carl Spaatz, CG, NAAF to Maj. Gen. Barney Giles, C/S, AAF, Sep 12, 1943. Arnold Collection, File 3 1938–46, (370.2/Africa/34), Box 104, MD, LC.

George S. Patton, Jr., Collection

Chronological File: Miscellaneous Correspondence, 1944–1945, Boxes 14–16, MD, LC.

Diaries and Correspondence, 1942–1945, Boxes 2–4, MD, LC.

Photo Albums, 1944–1945, Boxes 111–113, MD, LC.

Elwood R. Quesada Collection

Ltr, Dr. David Griggs, Advisory Specialist Group, USSTAF, to Dr. E. L. Bowles, Expert Consultant to the Secretary of War, Mar 17, 1944, Box 5, MD, LC.

Rpt, IX Fighter Command, A–3, n.d., Box 3, MD, LC.

Rpt, IX Fighter Command, A–4, n.d., Box 3, MD, LC.

Rpt, IX TAC, G–3 (Air), n.d., Box 5, MD, LC.

Carl A. Spaatz Collection

Rpt, IX TAC, "Assessment of Fighter-Bomber Claims." Apr 45, Box 5, MD, LC.

Memo, Brig. Gen. D. L. M. Schlatter, Dep C/S-Opns, Ninth AF, to CG, USSTAF, "Report on Cherbourg Attack, Jul 21, 44," Box 164, MD, LC.

National Archives, Washington, D.C.

RG 331: Records of Allied Operational and Occupation Headquarters, WWII

HQ, Twelfth Army Group, "Brief of Joint Operations Plan—U.S. Forces for Operation Overlord" (revised May 8, 1944), File 1943–45 (370.2), Box 85, NA

RG 337: Records of the Army Ground Forces

Rpt, Col. E. L. Johnson, G–3 (Air), U.S. First Army to AGF Board, HQ ETOUSA, "Information Regarding Air–Ground Joint Operations," Jul 16, 1944, RG 337, Entry 29, Box 51, NA

National Security Agency Reports

Memo, NSA, "Ultra and the Third Army," May 28, 1945, in NSA, Special Research, History–023.

Rpt, NSA, "Reports by U.S. Army Ultra Representatives with Army Field Commands in the European Theater of Operations," parts 1 and 2, in NSA, Special Research, History–023

Books and Studies

Department of the Army. *The Army Almanac*. Washington: U.S. Government Printing Office, 1950.

HQ AAF, *Condensed Analysis of the Ninth Air Force in the European Theater of Operations*. Washington, 1946. repr, Washington, 1984.

Air Ministry (Great Britain). *The Rise and Fall of the German Air Force, 1933–1945*. Old Greenwich, Conn: WE Inc., 1969.

Beck, Alfred M., Abe Bortz, Charles W. Lynch, Lida Mayo, and Ralph F. Weled. *The Corps of Engineers: The War Against Germany* [United States Army in World War II: The Technical Services]. Washington: Center of Military History, 1985.

Blumenson, Martin. *Breakout and Pursuit* [United States Army in World War II: The European Theater of Operations]. Washington: Office of the Chief of Military History, 1965.

Boog, Horst. *Die Deutsche Luftwaffenfuehrung, 1935–1945*. Stuttgart: Deutsche Verlags-Anstalt, 1982.

Bykofsky, Joseph and Harold Larson. *The Transportation Corps: Operations Overseas* [United States Army in World War II: The Technical Services]. Washington, D.C.: Center of Military History, 1985.

Carter, Kit and Robert Mueller, compilers. *The Army Air Forces in World War II: Combat Chronology, 1941–1945*. Washington: Office of Air Force

History, 1973.

Cole, Hugh M. *The Ardennes: Battle of the Bulge* [United States Army in World War II: The European Theater of Operations]. Washington: Office of the Chief of Military History, 1965.

Cole, H. M. *The Lorraine Campaign* [United States Army in World War II: The European Theater of Operations]. Washington: Office of the Chief of Military History, 1950.

Coles, Harry L. *Participation of the Ninth and Twelfth Air Forces in the Sicilian Campaign* [USAF Historical Studies No. 37]. Washington: AAF Historical Office, 1945.

Coll, Blanche D., Jean E. Keith, and Herbert H. Rosenthal. *The Corps of Engineers: Troops and Equipment* [United States Army in World War II: The Technical Services]. Washington: Center of Military History, 1985.

Cooling, Benjamin Franklin, ed. *Case Studies in the Development of Close Air Support*. Washington: Office of Air Force History, 1990.

Craven, Wesley F., and James L. Cate, eds. *The Army Air Forces in World War II*. 7 Vols. Chicago: University of Chicago Press, 1948–59; reprint ed. Washington: Office of Air Force History, 1984.

Craven, Wesley Frank and James L. Cate, eds. *The Army Air Forces in World War II*. Vol 1: *Plans and Early Operations, Jan 1939 to Aug 1942*. Chicago: University of Chicago Press, 1948; repr, 1984.

———, eds. *The Army Air Forces in World War II*. Vol 2: *Europe: Torch to Pointblank, Aug 1942 to Dec 1943*. Chicago: University of Chicago Press, 1949; repr, 1984.

———, eds. *The Army Air Forces in World War II*. Vol 3: *Europe: Argument to V–E Day, Jan 1944–May 1945*. Chicago: University of Chicago Press, 1951; repr, 1983.

———, eds. *The Army Air Forces in World War II*. Vol 6: *Men and Planes*. Chicago: University of Chicago Press, 1955; repr, 1984.

Davis, Richard G. *Carl A. Spaatz and the Air War in Europe, 1942–1945*. Washington: Office of Air Force History, 1994.

Ellis, Major L. F. *Victory in the West: The Battle of Normandy* [History of the Second World War: United Kingdom Military Series]. London: Her Majesty's Stationery Office, 1962.

Futrell, Robert F. *Ideas, Concepts, Doctrine: A History of Basic Thinking in the United States Air Force, 1907–1964*. Maxwell AFB, Ala.: Air University Press, 1971.

———, *Ideas, Concepts, Doctrine: A History of Basic Thinking in the United States Air Force*. Vol 2: 1961–1984. Maxwell AFB, Ala.: Air University Press, 1989.

Gabel, Christopher R. "The Lorraine Campaign: An Overview, Sep–Dec 1944." Ft. Leavenworth, Kan.: U.S. Army CGSC, 1985.

George, Robert H. *Ninth Air Force, Apr to Nov 1944* [USAF Historical Studies No. 36]. Washington: AAF Historical Office, 1945.

Greenfield, Kent Roberts. *Army Ground Forces and the Air–Ground Battle Team, Including Organic Light Aviation* [U.S. Army Study No. 35] Washington: Army Ground Forces, 1948.

Greenfield, Kent Roberts, Robert R. Palmer, and Bell I. Wiley. *The Organization of Ground Combat Troops* [United States Army in World War II. The Army Ground Forces]. Washington: Historical Division. Department of the Army, 1947.

Greer, Thomas H. *The Development of Air Doctrine in the Army Air Arm, 1917–1941* [USAF Historical Studies No. 89]. Maxwell AFB, Ala.: USAF Historical Division, 1955; repr., 1985.

Howe, George F. *Northwest Africa: Seizing the Initiative in the West* [United States Army in World War II: The Mediterranean Theater of Operations]. Washington: Office of the Chief of Military History, 1957; repr, 1970.

Jacobs, William A. "The Battle for France," in *Case Studies in the Development of Close Air Support*. B. Franklin Cooling, ed. Washington: Office of Air Force History, 1990, pp. 237–293.

Kohn, Richard H., and Joseph P. Harahan, eds. *Air Superiority in World War II and Korea*. Washington: Office of Air Force History, 1983.

———, eds. *Condensed Analysis of the Ninth Air Force in the European Theater of Operations*. USAF Warrior Studies. New imprint. Washington: Office of Air Force History, 1984.

———, eds. *Air Interdiction in World II, Korea, and Vietnam*. Washington: Office of Air Force History, 1986.

LeMay, Gen. Curtis E., Gen. O. P. Weyland, and Vice Adm. William I. Martin, "The Perceptions of Three Makers of Air Power History," in *Air Power and Warfare: Proceedings of the 8th Military History Symposium*, United States Air Force Academy, Oct 18–29, 1973. A. F. Hurley and R. C. Ehrhart, eds. Washington: Office of Air Force History, 1979, pp. 186–196.

MacDonald, Charles B. *The Last Offensive* [United States Army in World War II: European Theater of Operations]. Washington: Office of the Chief of Military History, 1973.

———, *The Siegfried Line Campaign* [United States Army in World War II: European Theater of Operations]. Washington: Office of the Chief of Military History, 1963.

Millett, Allan R. "Korea, 1950–1953," in *Case Studies in the Development of Close Air Support*. B. Franklin Cooling, ed. Washington: Office of Air Force History, 1990, pp. 345–410.

Momyer, Gen. William W., USAF, Ret. *Air Power in Three Wars (WWII, Korea, Vietnam)*. Washington: Government Printing Office, 1978.

Mortensen, Daniel R. "A Pattern for Joint Operations: World War II Close Air

Support in North Africa" [Historical Analysis Series] Washington: Office of Air Force History and U.S. Army Center of Military History, 1987.

——, "Tactical Aviation in World War II." Draft manuscript.

Pogue, Forrest. *The Supreme Command* [United States Army in World War II. The European Theater of Operations]. Washington: Center of Military History, United States Army, 1989.

Ramsey, John F. *Ninth Air Force in the ETO, 16 Oct 1943 to 16 Apr 1944* [USAF Historical Studies No. 32]. Washington: AAF Historical Office, 1945.

Ross, William F. and Charles F. Romanus. *The Quartermaster Corps: Operations in the War Against Germany* [United States Army in World War II. The Technical Services]. Washington: Office of the Chief of Military History, 1965.

Ruppenthal, Roland G. *Logistical Support of the Armies*. 2 vols [United States Army in World War II. The European Theater of Operations]. Washington: Office of the Chief of Military History, 1953, 1959.

Schlight, John. "Elwood R. Quesada: Tac Air Comes of Age," in *Makers of the Modern Air Force*. John L. Frisbee, ed. Washington: Office of Air Force History, 1987, pp. 177–204.

Shiner, John F. *Foulois and the US Army Air Corps, 1931–1935*. Washington: Office of Air Force History, 1983.

Sunderland, Riley. *Evolution of Command and Control Doctrine for Close Air Support*. Washington: Office of Air Force History, 1973.

Syrett, David "Northwest Africa, 1942–1943," in *Case Studies in the Achievement of Air Superiority*. B. Franklin Cooling, ed. Washington: Office of Air Force History, 1994.

Thompson, George R., and Dixie R. Harris. *The Signal Corps: The Outcome* [United States Army in World War II. The Technical Services]. Washington: Office of the Chief of Military History, 1966.

War Department: The Adjutant General's Office. *Official Army Register*. Jan 1, 1945. Washington: U.S. Government Printing Office, 1945.

Williams, Mary H. *Chronology, 1941–1945* [United States Army in World War II: Special Studies]. Washington: Office of the Chief of Military History, 1960.

Wilt, Alan F. "Allied Cooperation in Sicily and Italy, 1943–45," in *Case Studies in the Development of Close Air Support*. B. Franklin Cooling, ed. Washington: Office of Air Force History, 1990, pp. 193–236.

Wolfert, Michael L. "From Acts to Cobra: Evolution of Close Air Support Doctrine in World War Two." Student Report, USAF Air Command and Staff College, 1988.

Wolk, Herman S. *Planning and Organizing the Postwar Air Force, 1943–1947*. Washington: Office of Air Force History, 1984.

Symposia

Air Power and Warfare: Proceedings of the 8th Military History Symposium, United States Air Force Academy, Oct 18–20, 1978. Washington: Office of Air Force History and the United States Air Force Academy, 1979.

Interviews

Burns, Lt. Gen. John J., USAF (Ret), with author, Jan 7, 1991.

Burns, Lt. Gen. John J., USAF (Ret), with Hugh N. Ahmann, Jun 5–8, 1984 (USAF/HRA, K239.0512–1587)

Ferguson, Gen. James, USAF (Ret), with James C. Hasdorff, May 8–9, 1973 (USAF/HRA, K239.0512–672)

Ferguson, Gen. James, USAF (Ret), with Col. William R. Carter, Jun 14, 1988, on file at Air University television studio, Maxwell AFB, Ala.

Harkins, Gen. Paul D., USAF (Ret), with James C. Hasdorff, Feb 23, 1972 (USAF/HRA, K239.0512–522).

Lee, Gen. Robert M., USAF (Ret), with author, Aug 1989, Sep 1990.

Quesada, Lt. Gen. Elwood R., USAF (Ret), with Lt. Cols. Stephen Long and Ralph Stephenson, USA, May 12, 1975 (USAF/HRA, K239.0512–838).

Weyland, Gen. Otto P., USAF (Ret), with Brig. Gen. George W. Goddard, Sep 17, 1967 (USAF/HRA K239.0512–1032).

Weyland, Gen. Otto P., USAF (Ret), with James D. Hasdorff, Nov 19, 1974 (USAF/HRA K239.0512–813).

Regulations

War Department Field Manual 100–5, "Operations." May 22, 1941.

War Department Field Manual 31–35, "Aviation in Support of Ground Forces." Apr 9, 1942.

War Department Field Manual 100–20, "Command and Employment of Air Power." Jul 21, 1943.

War Department Field Manual 31–35, "Air–Ground Operations." Aug 1946.

Correspondence

Berg, Brig. Gen. Russell A., USAF (Ret), to author, Sep 6, Oct 24, 1989.

Brown, Jerold E., USACGSC, Combat Studies Institute, to author, Mar 8, 1990.

Delashaw, Maj. Gen. Robert L., USAF (Ret), to author, Aug 21, 1989.

Ferguson, Gen. James, USAF (Ret), to author, Aug 23 1989, Nov 15, 1989, Apr 11, 1990.

Miscellaneous Draft Manuscript Comments

Jamieson, Perry L. "Manuscript Comments." May 15, 1991.

Mark, Eduard. "Observations." Mar 1, 1991.

Mets, David R., "General Comments." May 15, 1991.

Mortensen, Daniel R. "Manuscript Comments." n.d. [spring 1991].

Raines, Edgar R. Memo for the Record May 20, 1991.

Schlight, John. "Manuscript Comments." n.d. [spring 1991].

Smith, Richard K. "Manuscript Comments." n.d. [spring 1991].

Wolk, Herman S. "Manuscript Comments." n.d. [1991].

NonGovernment Sources

Books

Allen, Robert S. *Lucky Forward.* New York: Vangard Press, 1947.

Ambrose, Stephen E. *The Supreme Commander: The War Years of Dwight David Eisenhower.* New York: Doubleday, 1970.

Bennett, Ralph. *Ultra in the West: The Normandy Campaign, 1944–45.* New York: Charles Scribner's Sons, 1979.

Blumenson, Martin, ed. *The Patton Papers.* 2 vols. Boston: Houghton Mifflin, 1972–74.

———, *Patton: The Man Behind the Legend, 1885–1945.* New York: William Morrow, 1985.

———, *The Battle of the Generals: The Untold Story of the Falaise Pocket-The Campaign that Should Have Won World War II.* New York: William Morrow, 1993.

———, *Patton: The Man Behind the Legend, 1885–1945.* New York: William Morrow, 1985.

Bradley, Omar N. *A Soldier's Story.* New York: Henry Holt, 1951.

Brereton, Lewis H. *The Brereton Diaries.* New York: William Morrow, 1946.

Butcher, Captain Harry C., USNR. *My Three Years with Eisenhower.* New York: Simon & Schuster, 1946.

Chandler, Alfred D., ed. *The Papers of Dwight David Eisenhower: The War Years.* Vol 3. Baltimore: The Johns Hopkins University Press, 1970.

Colgan, Bill. *World War II Fighter-bomber Pilot.* Blue Ridge Summit, Pa: TAB Books, Inc., 1985.

Crane, Conrad C. *Bombs, Cities, and Civilians: American Airpower Strategy in World War II.* Lawrence, Kan.: University Press of Kansas, 1993.

Cruickshank, Charles. *Deception in World War II.* New York: Oxford University Press, 1979.

D'Este, Carlo. *Bitter Victory: The Battle for Sicily, 1943.* New York: E. P. Dutton, 1988.

———, *Decision in Normandy.* New York: E. P. Dutton, 1983.

Eisenhower, Dwight D. *Crusade in Europe*. Garden City, New York: Doubleday, 1948.

Esposito, Vincent J., ed. *A Concise History of World War II*. New York: Praeger, 1964.

———, *The West Point Atlas of American Wars,* V. II, 1900-1953. New York: Frederick A. Praeger, 1959.

Farago, Ladislas. *Ordeal and Triumph*. New York: Astor-Honor, 1964.

Graham, Dominick and Shelford Bidwell. *Tug of War: The Battle for Italy, 1943–1945*. New York: St. Martin's Press, 1986.

Griess, Thomas E., series ed. *The Second World War: Europe and the Mediterranean*. West Point Military History Series, Wayne, N.J.: Avery Publishing Group, 1984.

———, *Atlas of the Second World War: Europe and the Mediterranean*. West Point Military History Series, Wayne, N.J.: Avery Publishing Group, 1984.

Hallion, Richard P. *Strike from the Sky: The History of Battlefield Air Attack, 1911–1945*. Washington: Smithsonian Institution Press, 1989.

Hastings, Max. *Overlord: D-Day and the Battle for Normandy*. New York: Simon & Schuster, 1984.

Hughes, Thomas Alexander. *Overlord: General Pete Quesada and the Triumph of Tactical Air Power in World War II*. New York: The Free Press, 1995.

Irving, David. *The War Between the Generals*. New York: Congdon & Lattes, 1981.

Ivie, Thomas G. *Aerial Reconnaissance: The 10th Photo Recon Group in WWII*. Fallbrook, Calif: Aero Publishers, 1981.

Keegan, John. *Six Armies in Normandy*. New York: The Viking Press, 1982.

Kelsey, Benjamin S. *The Dragon's Teeth: The Creation of United States Air Power for World War II*. Washington: Smithsonian Institution Press, 1982.

Lamb, Richard. *Montgomery in Europe, 1943–1945: Success or Failure?* New York: Franklin Watts, 1984.

Liddell Hart, B. H. *History of the Second World War*. New York: G. P. Putnam's Sons, 1970.

MacDonald, Charles B. *The Mighty Endeavor: The American War in Europe*. New York: Quill, 1986.

———, *A Time for Trumpets: The Untold Story of the Battle of the Bulge*. New York: William Morrow, 1985.

Mets, David R. *A Master of Airpower: General Carl A. Spaatz*. Presidio, Calif: Air Force Historical Foundation/Aerospace Education Foundation, 1988.

Murray, Williamson. *Strategy for Defeat: The Luftwaffe, 1933–1945*. Maxwell Air Force Base, Ala: Air University Press, 1983.

Overy, R. J. *The Air War, 1939–1945*. New York: Stein & Day, 1980.

Patton, George S., Jr. *War As I Knew It*. Boston: Houghton Mifflin, 1947.

Perret, Geoffrey. *There's A War To Be Won: The United States Army in World War II.* New York: Random House, 1991.

———, *Winged Victory: The Army Air Forces in World War II.* New York: Random House, 1993.

Rostow, W. W. *Pre-Invasion Bombing Strategy: General Eisenhower's Decision of Mar 25, 1944.* Austin: University of Texas Press, 1981.

Rust, Kenn C. *The 9th Air Force in World War II.* Fallbrook, Calif.: Aero Publishers, 1967.

Schaffer, Ronald. *Wings of Judgement: American Bombing in World War II.* New York: Oxford University Press, 1985.

Shulman, Milton. *Defeat in the West.* New York: E. P. Dutton, 1948.

Smith, Peter C. *Vengeance! The Vultee Vengeance Dive Bomber.* Washington: Smithsonian Institution Press, 1986.

Tedder, Lord. *With Prejudice: The War Memoirs of Marshal of the Royal Air Force Lord Tedder G. C. B.* Boston: Little, Brown, 1966.

Van Creveld, Martin. *Supplying War.* Cambridge, U.K.: Cambridge University Press, 1977.

Weigley, Russell F. *Eisenhower's Lieutenants: The Campaigns of France and Germany, 1944–45.* Bloomington, Ind: Indiana University Press, 1981.

Wilmot, Chester. *The Struggle for Europe.* New York: Harper & Row, 1952.

Ziemke, Caroline F. "In the Shadow of the Giant: USAF Tactical Air Command in the Era of Strategic Bombing, 1945–1955." PhD diss, Ohio State University, Columbus, 1989.

Articles

Balkoski, Joseph. "Patton's Third Army: The Lorraine Campaign, Nov 8–Dec 1, 44." *Strategy and Tactics* 78 (1980): 4–15.

Carter, Col. William R. "Air Power in the Battle of the Bulge: A Theater Campaign Perspective." *Airpower Journal* III No. 4 (Winter 1989): 10–33.

Coningham, Air Marshal Sir Arthur. "The Development of Tactical Air Forces." *Journal of the Royal United Service Institution* 91 (May 1946): 211–227.

Deutsch, Harold. "Commanding Generals and the Uses of Intelligence." *Intelligence and National Security* 3, No. 3 (Jul 1988): 194–260.

Huston, James A. "Tactical Use of Air Power in World War II: The Army Experience." *Military Affairs* XIV (Winter 1950): 166–185.

Jacobs, William C. "Air Command in the United Kingdom, 1933–44." *The Journal of Strategic Studies* 11 (Mar 1988): 51–78.

———, "Tactical Air Doctrine and AAF Close Air Support in the European Theater, 1944–45." *Aerospace Historian* (Mar 1980): 35–49.

Kuter, Laurence S. "Goddamit Georgie: North Africa, 1943: The Birth of TAC Doctrine." *Air Force Magazine* 56 (Feb 1973): 51–56.

Mayock, Thomas J. "Notes on the Development of AAF Tactical Air Doctrine." *Military Affairs* XIV (Winter 1950): 186–191.

Murray, Williamson. "Attrition and the Luftwaffe." *Air University Review* 34 (Mar–Apr 1983): 66–77.

————, "A Tale of Two Doctrines: The Luftwaffe's 'Conduct of the Air War' and the USAF's Manual 1–1." *Journal of Strategic Studies* 6 (Dec 1983): 84–93.

Quesada, Lt. Gen. E. R. "Tactical Air Power." *Air University Quarterly Review* (Spring 1948): 37–45.

Smith, Richard K. "Marston Mat." *Air Force Magazine* (Apr 1989): 84–88.

Stevenson, Frank E. "Third Army's Planning for the Crossing of the Rhine River." *Military Review* XXX (Mar 1951): 33–42.

Wilt, Alan F. "Coming of Age: XIX TAC's Roles During the 1944 Dash Across France." *Air University Review* XXXVI (Mar–Apr 1985): 71–87.

Index